MW00815296

School Counselors as Practitioners

Versatilely designed for both school counseling course work and as a reference for school district personnel, this text demystifies the roles and responsibilities of the school counselor and teaches students and practitioners how to perform, conduct, follow through, and carry out various roles and responsibilities required on the job. *School Counselors as Practitioners* conveys strategic, step-by-step processes and best practice recommendations, with emphasis on ethical and multicultural considerations. The 14 chapters in this textbook maintain, and are consistent with, the basis of school counselors' work in the school counseling core curriculum, responsive services, individual planning, and system support, and special attention is paid to ASCA and CACREP standards. An eResource provides students with templates and handouts for on-the-job responsibilities, as well as quiz questions for every chapter.

Lisa A. Wines, PhD, LPC, CSC, is an associate professor in the Department of Counseling at Lamar University. She holds a license as a professional counselor and a certification in school counseling in Texas. She has a private practice in the Cypress area and holds memberships to the Texas Counseling Association and American Counseling Association.

Judy A. Nelson, PhD, LPC, CSC, is a retired associate professor from Sam Houston State University with over 30 years of experience in the field of counseling. She is a licensed professional counselor in Arizona and practiced as a marriage and family therapist and certified school counselor in Texas. Dr. Nelson was the president of the Texas Counseling Association from 2009 to 2010. Currently, she conducts program evaluations, presents workshops, and offers trainings on a variety of topics.

School Counselors as Practitioners

Building on Theory, Standards, and Experience for Optimal Performance

Edited by

Lisa A. Wines
Judy A. Nelson

NEW YORK AND LONDON

First published 2019
by Routledge
711 Third Avenue, New York, NY 10017

and by Routledge
2 Park Square, Milton Park, Abingdon, Oxon, OX14 4RN

Routledge is an imprint of the Taylor & Francis Group, an informa business

Library of Congress Cataloging-in-Publication Data
A catalog record for this book has been requested

ISBN: 978-1-138-03977-3 (hbk)
ISBN: 978-1-138-03978-0 (pbk)
ISBN: 978-1-315-17564-5 (ebk)

Typeset in Palatino
by Apex CoVantage, LLC

eResources available: www.routledge.com/9781138039780

The authors' dedication serves as our way of paying homage to those experiences incurred during the course of writing this textbook. Because life carries onward, in spite of any responsibility or commitment, the dichotomy of these truths exists, cannot be changed, or rationalized away. This book is dedicated:

For those who experienced the excitement of new love or the tragedy of losing a loved one . . .

For those who responded to or were a victim of Hurricane Harvey . . .

For those who found freedom in or numbness of a medical diagnosis . . .

For those who discovered, grappled with, and/or accepted the truths of their circumstance . . .

For those who amended and severed broken relationships . . .

Editors' Dedication

In light of our authors' dedication, we recognize that there are children who have been tangentially or directly affected by the aforementioned occurrences. These people, who are students in our schools, have school counselors to intercede on their behalf.

Contents

Acknowledgments

Lisa A. Wines

I would like to thank GOD for instilling this vision within me in 2014, where I immediately returned home and drafted the outline for each chapter of this book. GOD is amazing in this way, and it was my choice to respond with obedience by acting upon this internal prompting. To GOD be the glory in all things, working together for his good.

I will always acknowledge my son through it all. As an early teen at the age of 14, he demonstrates discernment, humor, balance, fairness, compassion, and will. I love you son, with all that is in me. Last, but never least, I acknowledge my mother. She is my best friend, my advocate, and my strength. My mother is everything one could hope for–loving, funny, supportive, resolution-driven, and constructive. Saying I love you is not enough, so I hope to be in position, always, to show you how valuable you are to me. GOD, my son, and my mother are the true and utmost constants in my life.

Judy A. Nelson

I would like to acknowledge my husband, Tom Nelson, who tolerated this project even as I proclaimed that I was retired. For the sake of my work, he postponed trips and spent many mornings and late nights listening to the tapping of fingers on the computer rather than hiking or watching a good film with me. That is the beauty of a long-term commitment!

The editors of the textbook would like to acknowledge the graduate students in the counseling program at the University of Houston in the Department of Psychological, Health, and Learning Sciences for their contributions to the chapter PowerPoints. They are Anusha Atmakuri, Gerranda Poole, Alexandra Price, and Melanie Singleton. Ms. Singleton also served in an editorial role for all PowerPoints contributed by her cohort members.

About the Contributors

Sharon D. Bey holds two Masters of Arts degree in Education, one in guidance and counseling from the University of Northern Iowa and one in Educational Administration from Prairie View A&M University. Currently, she serves as the Counseling Coordinator in Waller Independent School District, with 32 years as a school counselor across all levels. She holds both a certification in school counseling and administration and memberships to Texas School Counseling Association, a division of Texas Counseling Association, where she has been the president, director, board member, and a recipient of the Counselor of the Year Award in 2005.

Dr. Carleton H. Brown is currently an Assistant Professor at the University of Texas at El Paso in the Educational Psychology and Special Services department. Dr. Brown has worked in school districts as a secondary education teacher, school counselor, as well as workshop leader and advisor to school leaders. He studies issues related to the role of the school counselor in areas of leadership, advocacy, and supervision.

Dr. Rebecca M. Bustamante is a professor of Educational Leadership at Sam Houston State University. Her research interests include organizational and leadership development for culturally responsive and equitable education, faculty development, and educational opportunities for traditionally marginalized groups. She has held leadership positions in schools in South America, has written extensively about culturally responsive educational practices, and has presented at national and international conferences.

Dr. Ernest Cox Jr. is an Assistant Professor in School Counseling at Texas A&M University San Antonio. Previously he served as the Director of Guidance and Counseling for Judson Independent School District in San Antonio, Texas. He holds a B.S. in Psychology from Queens University of Charlotte, North Carolina, a Master's degree in Clinical and School Counseling from Our Lady of the Lake University, and his doctoral studies were completed in Counselor Education and Supervision at the University of Texas at San Antonio. Mr. Cox is the president for the Texas School Counseling Association, a member of the Texas Counseling Association (TCA), and the Director of Guidance and Counseling member-at-large for the Texas Association of Counseling Educators and Supervisors (TACES), Texas School Counselors Association (TSCA), Texas College Counselors Association (TCCA), and the

American School Counselor Association (ASCA). In addition, Mr. Cox has represented the counseling profession as a member of committees including: Texas Counseling Association (Director of Programs—Professional Growth Conference), Bexar County Directors of Guidance and Counseling, and the Military Child Education Committee.

Dr. Lia D. Falco is assistant professor of Counseling in the Department of Disability & Psychoeducational Studies at the University of Arizona. Career counseling and development are her areas of expertise, although she also teaches Professional Orientation to School Counseling and Multicultural Counseling as well as supervising school counseling practicum and internship. Her research examines motivation frameworks associated with occupational choice in early adolescence, with specific interest in gender differences in STEM participation. The focus of her research for the past several years has been on developing and implementing school-counselor-led interventions designed to increase participating students' self-efficacy for STEM education and career decision-making. She is a certified school counselor in the state of Arizona and worked as a middle school counselor for four years.

Dr. Carol Hightower-Parker is a clinical associate professor in the Department of Counseling at Texas Southern University. She received a bachelor of arts in teaching degree from Sam Houston State University. She went on to receive an MA and Ed.D. in counselor education from Texas Southern University in Houston, Texas. Dr. Parker has served in various positions in public school and higher education over the past 30 years, including counselor, building administrator in secondary education, dean, and vice president for enrollment management. She is a licensed professional counselor-supervisor and certified school counselor. Her primary research interests are in the areas of school counselor reform, diversity, spirituality, supervision, leadership, and policy in counseling and public education.

Dr. Glenda S. Johnson is an assistant professor in the professional school counseling program at Appalachian State University. She has worked as an assistant professor for three years, a professional school counselor for 17 years, a teacher of students who are deaf or hard-of-hearing for seven years, and a part-time licensed professional counselor for three and a half years. Her scholarly focus includes school counselors delivering a comprehensive guidance and counseling program, students who are at-risk of dropping out of high school, and mentoring new counseling professionals.

Benny Malone has a Master of Social Work from the University of Houston and more than 100 hours of post-graduate work in professional counseling, special education, and educational leadership. She served as the Director of Guidance, Counseling, and Special Programs for the third largest school district in Texas, where she supervised more than 200 professional staff. In her 2014 publication, *Psychotic Rage! A True Story of Mental Illness, Murder, and Reconciliation*, Benny tells the story of her family's long and difficult journey with her younger son's severe mental illness. Benny is a respected and sought-out keynote speaker and staff development presenter for conferences, professional organizations, mental health advocacy groups, community groups, and churches. She volunteers in her community, church, and mental health organizations, and is a trained volunteer educator for the National Alliance on Mental Illness. Benny's current professional interest is in early identification of First Episode Psychosis. Benny is the co-founder of The Broken Wings Project, whose mission is helping other families like hers create a legacy of the unfinished talent and promise of a loved one struggling with or lost to mental illness.

Dr. Kathy McDonald is passionate about the field of school counseling, particularly in the areas of childhood trauma, crisis intervention, and animal-assisted therapy. Her therapy dogs, Winston and Milo, provided comfort and encouragement to public school students and to the clients in her private practice. Dr. McDonald earned her Ph.D. in Counselor Education from Sam Houston State University in Huntsville, Texas. She is currently an Assistant Professor at Southeastern Oklahoma State University in Durant, Oklahoma.

Dr. Kimberly McGough is an assistant professor at Lamar University. Before working at Lamar, Dr. McGough worked as a school counselor for 13 years at the secondary level. Her counseling specialty includes working with adolescents and their families within the school system and in private practice. Her research interests include phenomenon surrounding at-risk adolescent behavior, the development of grit among various populations, and entitlement beliefs and behaviors in today's society.

Dr. Jana McLain is a licensed professional counselor supervisor, professional school counselor serving at-risk students, and an adjunct professor for Our Lady of the Lake University. Dr. McLain was the first counselor in her district to win a CREST award, along with many district awards. In addition to her service to students in the educational system, Dr. McLain has worked with children and adolescents in a private practice setting. Dr. McLain presents at local, state, and national conferences on topics relating to both school counseling and professional counseling. In her role as an at-risk counselor, Dr. McLain developed and facilitated the mentors' program and community outreach program. She earned her doctorate in counselor education from Sam Houston State University in May 2014.

Dr. Robika Modak Mylroie is a distance clinical professor in the Department of Counseling and Special Populations at Lamar University and the school counselor at St. Anthony's Catholic School. She received her bachelor's degree in psychology from Millsaps College and her Master's and Ph.D. in counseling from Mississippi State University. Dr. Mylroie was a school counselor in the middle school setting for several years as well as a licensed professional counselor in Mississippi. Her current research interests include childhood obesity's impact on personal, social, and academic growth in children and adolescents and yoga in therapy.

Dr. Judy A. Nelson is a retired associate professor from Sam Houston State University and co-editor of this book. She worked in the field of counseling for more than 30 years and continues to contribute to the profession through her teaching as an adjunct and her research and writing. Her research and subsequent publications have won numerous awards. She was a licensed professional counselor, marriage and family therapist, and certified school counselor in Texas and is now a licensed professional counselor in Arizona. Dr. Nelson was the president of the Texas Counseling Association from 2009 to 2010. Her research interests continue to be professional school counseling, at-risk students, families with school-aged children, and organizational cultural competence. Dr. Nelson currently conducts program evaluations, presents workshops, and offers trainings on a variety of topics.

Letitia Powell has her Bachelor of Arts in Psychology from Texas A&M University, and her Master of Arts in Counseling from Prairie View A&M University. She is currently working on her Ph.D. in Counselor Education and Supervision from Capella University. She has more than 18 years in secondary education experience as a certified English teacher and school counselor. She has been instrumental in moving her current district forward by creating counseling handbooks and developing school counseling programs that have made a system-wide impact. Letitia is often sought out to provide mentorship, consultation, and educational workshops to new counselors as well as district leaders. She is currently a lead counselor at Carl Wunsche Senior High School in Spring, Texas, therapist and owner of Restorative Counseling Service, and an adjunct professor at Our Lady of the Lake University in San Antonio, Texas.

Dr. Lia Rosales began her career in 1987 as an elementary teacher in Corpus Christi Independent School District (CCISD). After teaching in the classroom for seven years, she decided to become a school counselor. She earned her

Master's Degree in Guidance and Counseling in 1994 from Texas A&M–Corpus Christi. Working in the counseling field has always been her lifelong dream. After 10 years as an elementary counselor, she decided to try middle school counseling and loved it. In 2008, she earned a doctorate degree in Counselor Education from Texas A&M–Corpus Christi. Soon after that, she became the Coordinator for Guidance and Counseling and Section 504 Coordinator for CCISD. After six years of working as Coordinator, she became a high school counselor. She has also served as an adjunct professor at Texas A&M–Corpus Christi, where she taught future school counselors. She has enjoyed her 31 years as an educator and 24 years in the field of school counseling. Working with students, parents, teachers, the community, and serving others is her passion.

Franklin D. Sampson earned a Bachelor of Science in Criminal Justice, and a Master of Arts in Counseling. He has been an instructor and an advisor at Prairie View A&M University in Texas. He holds additional certifications from the Texas Education Board in the fields of Special Education, Counseling, and Administration (Principal). He is also currently the Director of Guidance and Counseling in the third largest school district in the state of Texas, Cypress Fairbanks Independent School District. He is charged with the responsibility of directing 270 counselors in a district with 115,000 students.

Dr. Tiffany Simon, a Sam Houston State University graduate, has been a counselor educator since 2014 and a professional school counselor since 2006. During her years as a school counselor, she had the opportunity to work with students from various demographics (ranging from at-risk students to very high-achieving students). She has been an integral member of counseling teams working towards the development of comprehensive school counseling programs and provided support to school staff and community members. Dr. Simon has helped to train school counselors by presenting at the local, state, and national levels on topics including teen dating violence, career awareness, social media trends, and school counselor/administrator partnerships. In 2015, Dr. Simon was awarded the Sam Houston State University Distinguished Support Professional Award for her work as a school counselor in public schools.

Dr. Joydel Snook is an Assistant Professor in the Department of Counseling at Lamar University. Additionally, she is a board-certified counselor who specializes in clinical mental health counseling and supervising counselors in training. Dr. Snook is also an advocate and mentor for members of the LGBTQIA population as well as individuals with disabilities. Her research interests include but are not limited to perceptions of wellness from adults with mobility impairments, wellness and wellness models, advocacy for disabled populations, advocacy for LGBTQ populations, application of person-centered, feminist theory, and solution-focused techniques in supervision. In the summer of 2017, Dr. Snook was awarded the National Wellness Institute's Excellence Award for her research surrounding wellness and advocacy for adults with mobility impairments.

Dr. Le'Ann Solmonson is a Professor at Stephen F. Austin State University in Nacogdoches, Texas. She is a Licensed Professional Counselor and Certified School Counselor with both clinical and school experience. Dr. Solmonson is an active advocate for counseling-related issues and has served in multiple leadership roles in Texas, including the president of the Texas Counseling Association. Her research interests include professional identity and school counseling-related topics.

Dr. Sam Steen is an Associate Professor of Disabilities and Psychoeducational Studies in the College of Education at the University of Arizona. He is a counselor educator and a practitioner-researcher. He served as a professional school counselor for 10 years prior to entering academia and has spent approximately eight years consulting, collaborating, and conducting school-based research within public schools in Washington, D.C. His experience as a practitioner heavily shapes his research agenda, approach to teaching, and choices for service.

Dr. Helena Stevens is an assistant professor of counselor education at Minnesota State University. Her background is in school counseling and addictions counseling. Her professional experience has revolved around implementing comprehensive programs for wellness development in adolescents. Her research focuses on the role of the school counselor in implementing comprehensive developmental guidance programs and integrating new theoretical foundations for curriculum and program development.

Dr. Rachael Whitaker received her Bachelor of Science in Audiology and Speech Pathology from Delta State University in 2006. She completed her Masters of Education in Clinical Mental Health with a focus on Special Education from Delta State University in 2009. She completed her Ph.D. in Counselor Education with an emphasis on School Counseling from Mississippi State University in 2015. Dr. Whitaker has worked as a behavioral interventionist, clinical supervisor, professional school counselor, field experience coordinator, residency program leader, and assistant professor. Dr. Whitaker is the program director for the counseling program at the University of Houston in the Department of Psychological, Health, and

Learning Sciences. Her research interests include school counselor development, childhood health/nutrition, technology integration in counselor education, and program development.

Dr. Lisa A. Wines has a doctorate degree in Counselor Education from Sam Houston State University, a master's degree in counseling from Prairie View A&M University, and a bachelor's degree in English from Grambling State University. She is an associate professor in the Department of Counseling and Special Populations at Lamar University. She holds a license as a professional counselor and a certification in school counseling in Texas. She has a private practice in the Houston-Memorial area and holds memberships to the Texas Counseling Association and the American Counseling Association.

Dr. Kathy Ybañez-Llorente is an associate professor at Texas State University. She has worked clinically with children, adolescents, and families in community agencies, private practice, and inpatient psychiatric settings. Her scholarly interests include clinical and multicultural supervision, ethics, advocacy, professional identity, and licensure. She provides post-graduate clinical supervision, is a past president of the Texas Association for Counselor Education and Supervision (TACES), and a past liaison to the state's professional counselor licensing board. She also currently serves as a Co-chair of the American Counseling Association Ethics Committee.

A Note From the Editors

The purpose of this text, titled *School Counselors as Practitioners: Building on Theory, Standards, and Experience for Optimal Performance*, is to highlight and operationalize the role and work of the school counselor. Often, stakeholders may question this role and wonder if funding should be allocated elsewhere. It is no secret that school counselors struggle to establish a consistent school counselor identity and may not be in optimal workplaces that allow for the innovation and design of comprehensive school counseling programs.

Counselor educators, who teach in graduate programs, often utilize school counseling resources that are theoretically based and standard-driven. Although these resources have proven to have relevance, a resource such as ours fills the educational gap that is sometimes evident in school counseling graduate students' learning. At the state level, this text is ideal to assist with the development of proposed rules, state law, and statues that outline and govern the role of professional school counselors.

In an effort to lessen the inherent ambiguity of what school counselors actually should be doing, we decided to provide a textbook, or what we refer to as a tool used for training. This tool is a guide for all school counselors, guidance counseling directors, counselor educators, and state lawmakers to help these individuals better understand the intricacies of that particular job role or function. Our work is grounded in the authentic work-related experiences of contributing authors across the nation—experts in their own rights who are passionate about the field.

We invite you to utilize this book in the training and development of graduate students who wish to become school counselors, school counselors currently employed in school districts, counselor educators who are on the front lines of developing competent school counselors, and district and guidance counseling directors who are able to utilize this information for professional development or workshops.

Dr. Lisa A. Wines
Dr. Judy A. Nelson

Foreword

Roles of the School Counselor and System Support

Historically, system support was the *other duties as assigned* clause that promoted the wearing of so many hats that school counselors lost sight of the roles that are truly appropriate for the benefit of all students. Fortunately for the success of students and for the professional integrity of school counselors, the meaning of system support has evolved to a more palatable and very important list of duties according to the American School Counselor Association (2012a) [ASCA]. This does not mean, however, that all school districts, schools, principals, and even all school counselors have embraced the concept of system support as an integral part of the school counselor's role in providing a comprehensive program for all students. Thus, it is important to include a discussion of the role of school counselors in system support as it should be defined and also as it could be defined that would interrupt the implementation and management of the Comprehensive School Counseling Program (CSCP).

What Is System Support?

An important starting place should be the recommendation of the American School Counselor Association, which clearly states in the *ASCA National Model: A Framework for School Counseling Programs* (ASCA, 2012b) that school counselors should spend 80% of their time providing direct and indirect services to students, including both prevention and intervention. Direct services include school counseling core curriculum, individual and group counseling, crisis management, and individual planning for academic success. Indirect services consist primarily of managing the CSCP and might include consulting with teachers, parents, and administrators; collaborating with various stakeholders in the school and the community such as other support personnel and volunteers; creating an advisory board for the CSCP; creating a calendar and managing the CSCP in ways that allow for services to be provided to all students on whatever level they need; and collecting and analyzing the data that supports the CSCP. These roles would comprise the system support services as defined in recent school counseling literature

(ASCA, 2012b; Gysbers & Henderson, 2012), and each of these roles will be described in detail in our textbook.

Many principals and superintendents are probably scratching their heads now and wondering about bus duty, recess duty, lunch duty, arrival and dismissal duties, state testing mandates, teacher absences with no substitutes available, chairing Admission, Review, and Dismissal (ARD) or Individual Education Plan (IEP) committees, and so on. These are commonly referred to as fair share duties. These duties so often are the very ones that overwhelm the school counselor and ultimately interrupt the effective management of the CSCP. So, what's a school counselor to do?

What School Counselors Actually Do and What They Prefer to Do

In a research study conducted by Goodman-Scott (2015), in which frequent job roles of school counselors (n = 1,052) who graduated between 2002 and 2012 were assessed using *The School Counselor Activity Rating Scale* (SCARS; Scarborough, 2005). The instrument was designed to measure the relationship between what school counselors *actually* do compared to what they *prefer* to do. Goodman-Scott found that the five highest items on the actual job activities list included consult with school staff concerning student behavior, counsel students regarding academic issues, participate on committees within the school, counsel with students regarding school behavior, and counsel with students regarding personal/family concerns. Apart from participation on committees, the other four activities include meeting with individual teachers or students regarding academic, behavioral, or personal problems.

These activities would not reach all students in the school and could take up a great deal of the counselor's time, thereby eliminating services for many other students. School counselors can often be a safe haven for the misbehaving student, which works two ways: the teacher gets a breather for a slice of time while the student is in the counselor's office, and the student escapes the wrath of the teacher for a short time. These students can take a great deal of time away from the CSCP, and the student, teacher, and counselor can be triangulated into a symbiotic relationship that benefits the wrong behaviors in all three. In the end, this symbiotic relationship takes away from the systematic nature of the CSCP, where all students and staff benefit from the prevention programs and interventions.

In the same study (Goodman-Scott, 2015), the following were reported as the lowest activities provided by the participants: conduct or coordinate teacher in-service programs, conduct classroom lessons regarding substance abuse, handle discipline of students, substitute teach and/or cover classes for teachers at school, conduct small group counseling for students regarding substance abuse issues (own use or family/friend use). Three of these activities would be very effective ways of providing services to more students and would be consistent with the management of the CSCP. Conducting or coordinating teacher professional development programs can impact the entire student body depending on the topic. For example, all teachers should be aware of how to detect child abuse and how to report it to the proper authorities based on state law. Also, teachers who are provided with information regarding culturally responsive teaching practices can be instrumental in creating a welcoming environment for all students. Opportunities for school counselors to impact many students through teacher in-service programs are abundant. Likewise, conducting school counseling core curriculum lessons and small group counseling on relevant topics for the school counselor's specific demographics can address both prevention and intervention with more than one student, as in individual counseling. The other two activities might come under the fair share duties mentioned previously, but both would be inappropriate for the school counselor to conduct. Placing the school counselor in either the role of disciplinarian or substitute teacher diminishes the relationship that school counselors have with students, and furthermore, does not allow these professionals to work utilizing the skills and training necessary to being an effective counselor. The relationship of counselors to students should never be evaluative in terms of grades or punitive in terms of disciplinary actions.

According to The Texas Model for Comprehensive School Counseling Programs (Texas Education Agency, 2018), system support includes two areas: management of the school counseling program and indirect services integral to student success. Gysbers and Henderson (2012) posited that system support is an aspect of the CSCP that counselors often overlook and may not be aware of the importance of it to the overall program. Counselors incorporate outreach to administrators, teachers, other school staff, the community-at-large, and outside mental health practitioners and agencies. As counselors create their yearly calendars, they want to include not only the needs of these other entities but also the wealth of information and support that they can bring to the CSCP.

Managing Your Comprehensive School Counseling Program

Both ASCA (2012b) and other state models (Missouri Comprehensive Counseling and Guidance Program, 2011; Texas Education Agency, 2018) stress the importance of the intentional management of the CSCP. This management is the global vision of the program based on grade levels, demographics, and students' needs informed by assessment. Tools that drive the effective management of the school counseling program include the program agreement with the principal, assessment instruments or data trackers, the yearly calendar, accountability resources, and school staff, parents, and community member outreach, including professional development and educational workshops. Each of these tools allows for a wide variety of approaches for different state mandates, school district policies and practices, grade levels in elementary and secondary schools, and individual schools and their specific needs.

Program Agreement

The ASCA National Model (2012b) includes information regarding a letter of agreement with the principal in which the appropriate roles of the school counselor are described in detail. In the case of a team of counselors at one campus, each counselor should have an agreement letter detailing the specific job roles of that person and gain clarity on whether or not what was outlined will be used as a basis for the end-of-year evaluation. Principals do not always know what school counselors are trained to do, and the program agreement is an excellent resource for helping administrators understand the training, skills, and knowledge that counselors bring to the students, families, and faculty in the school community. For principals who have used the school counselor for many non-counseling duties, the program agreement can begin to train the principal on how to use the counselor's skills in a more effective and efficient way. The ASCA letter of agreement information can be found on page 46 of the ASCA National Model (2012b).

Assessment Instruments

Assessment should occur regularly and often to make well-thought-out decisions regarding the CSCP and to ensure that the school counselor is meeting the needs of all students. These assessments, also described as tools to collect data, can be in the form of surveys, interviews, or focus groups. For example, school counselors might assess student needs at the beginning and at the end of each school year to determine if those needs are the same or if there are new needs. These assessments can include students, teachers, and/or parents depending on the age and grade levels of the students involved. In addition to driving the CSCP, assessment can also show the counselor immediately if students, teachers, and/or parents are satisfied with specific interventions. Take, for example, a series of school counseling core curriculum lessons with high school sophomores on dating violence. Once the lessons have been completed, the assessment process can determine if the intervention was effective. In addition, the counselor can make note of students who sought counseling after these sessions because they were struggling with dating violence. See Chapter 11 for information on assessments.

Use of Standards, Competencies, CACREP1 Requirements, and Professional Ethics

While we encourage school counselors to provide the appropriate services to students, faculty, and community, administrative duties and *other duties as assigned* are most likely the reality for most school counselors. Therefore, the need for efficient organizing and managing the school counseling program is essential. We have addressed the appropriate school counseling functions and provided resources to help the new or seasoned school counselor provide the services that all students deserve. Our guidelines, activities, and step-by-step examples are designed to help you maximize time; create programs that are relevant to the demographics and special needs of each campus; and lead and advocate using the unique counseling skills that you possess, which builds professional identity—both locally and nationally. Working smart is the best way to accomplish these lofty goals! We believe the chapters in our text will provide you with abundant tools to create, implement, and manage the best CSCP possible.

We also highly recommend using the standards, competencies, and principles of our profession that are outlined at the beginning of each chapter. You should share these professional guidelines with administrators and teachers and outline them in the school newspaper or handbook. Promoting the profession is really promoting the school counselor and the CSCP by providing the most current thinking in the school counseling profession to all stakeholders in the school and community. As you initiate prevention programs and interventions, it is critical that information regarding the professional standards and expectations be shared with everyone involved. The competencies related to managing the CSCP are enumerated in the next section.

ASCA National Model School Counselor Professional Competencies

The professional school counselor:

I-B-2e. *Creates a plan to challenge the non-counseling tasks that are assigned to school counselors.* Make certain that your principal has a copy of the ASCA National Model (2012b) as well as your state model (if there is one) on his or her bookshelf. Refer to these documents in emails, written memos, and in verbal discussions often with your principal.

The chart on appropriate and inappropriate counseling duties in the ASCA Model is a great visual to point to when you feel that your time, energy, and training are not being used to truly assist students. This orientation or conversation should be conducted prior to the school year beginning and often throughout the year. You will find a copy of this Figure on page xxxi of this introductory section.

III-B-4. *Assesses use of time in direct and indirect student services and program management and school support.* Know when, where, and how to access campus data (e.g. discipline or at-risk reports) to coalesce with survey data to use as a basis for time allocation. Keep a log of your activities and track where you are spending your time to assess if you are working smart. You can do this in a variety of ways: track your daily activities one week out of every month, one day out of each week, and so forth. Provide your principal and advisory board or committee with this information, so it is clear how serious you are about using your time in the most efficient way possible and evident how students are being impacted as a result of your CSCP.

III-B-4a. *Organizes and manages time to effectively implement a comprehensive school counseling program.* When you feel that you are not organizing and managing your time effectively, revisit your CSCP and yearly calendar. Are you following it? Are you in alignment with your mission and goals? Is it the first consideration when you plan each day? What changes need to be made, and how can you make those changes with the help of your principal? Have you published your CSCP in the school newsletter and on the school counseling website of your school? Have you provided copies to parents, teachers, and administrators?

III-B-4b. *Identifies appropriate distribution of school counselor's time based on the school data and program goals.* Data collection and analysis help you meet your goals and help you revise them when the data shows that goals are met or are not realistic. Collect and share data often! Revisit the chapter on data and assessment (Chapter 11) frequently to review the importance of collecting and analyzing data and how to do it.

III-B-4c. *Creates a rationale for school counselor's use of time in the delivery component to focus on the goals of the comprehensive school counseling program.* Help your principal understand your work by providing a rationale for your interventions and prevention programs. If your needs assessment shows that your school needs a bullying prevention program, share that data with your principal, other administrators, and teachers. Visual presentations can be emailed or presented in person to stakeholders.

III-B-4d. *Identifies and evaluates fair-share responsibilities, which articulate appropriate and inappropriate counseling and non-counseling activities.* Of course, school counselors must pitch in and do their fair share of the duties that keep schools running. With the help of your principal and armed with your chart (see page xxxi) showing appropriate and inappropriate activities, choose the duties that do not interfere with your counseling obligations and that do not compromise your relationship with your students.

III-B-7. *Implements program management and school support activities for the comprehensive school counseling program.* Be an effective manager by enlisting others to help with the CSCP and by providing the appropriate support activities for your program. Ask for volunteers and enlist the help of your advisory council (see Chapter 7) whenever possible.

III-B-7a. *Creates a program management and school support planning document addressing school counselor's responsibilities for program management and professional development.* Providing your principal with a chart outlining your responsibilities for the CSCP is another way to enlist his or her understanding and support. Be willing to provide teachers with professional development that helps them understand the developmental needs of their students and make sure that you advocate for your own professional development by informing your principal early regarding times when you will be off campus.

III-B-7b. *Coordinates activities that establish, maintain, and enhance the school counseling program as well as other educational programs.* Creating your calendar and your program are important, but implementing it is critical, and maintaining it through ongoing assessment and improvement is what gives your program credibility. Showing your principal how the CSCP fits into the mission, vision, and goals of the campus plan will help win his or her support for your program.

III-C-1. *A school counseling program/department must be managed like other programs and departments in a school.* Many principals may not realize that your chief responsibility is to create and implement the CSCP. Have protocols (or policies as described in the leadership chapter) in place such as how to access students, what time of day you conduct certain activities, how paraprofessionals are used in the counseling department, and so forth. Share your budgetary needs, projected expenses, and how money is spent in your department.

III-C-2. *Planning, organizing, implementing, and evaluating a school counseling program are critical responsibilities for a school counselor.* As you plan your program, write down its components and share these with your principal, so he or she knows what a counseling program looks like and what it can accomplish. Gysbers and Henderson (2012) explained how to effectively use their model of planning, designing, implementing, evaluating, and enhancing a counseling program. Help your principal understand the importance of this type of a cycle in the management of the CSCP.

III-C-3. *Management of a school counseling program must be done in collaboration with administrators.* Ask your principal for input, feedback, and ideas for improvement. When the CSCP goals and activities add to the total school improvement plan, find ways to collaborate with administrators, teachers, and school support staff.

V-B-2. *Understands and advocates for appropriate school counselor performance appraisal process based on school counselor competencies and implementation of the comprehensive school counseling program.* Many school counselors are evaluated based on a teacher's job role. Ask your principal to use a performance appraisal process that is relevant to your competencies and the implementation of the CSCP. Make sure that your principal has the competencies listed in the ASCA Model (2012b). When you receive your principal's appraisal, if there are areas of improvement needed, write down how you plan to address these and share them with your principal.

V-B-2a. *Analyzes self-assessment related to school counseling skills and performance.* When it is time for your principal's evaluation of your performance, conduct an honest appraisal of yourself and share that information with your principal along with your plans for improvement. Remember to include both qualitative and quantitative information to best describe your abilities, attributes, and successes.

V-B-2b. *Identifies how school counseling activities fit within categories of a performance appraisal instrument.* Be able to explain to your principal the activities that you conduct in your CSCP and how and where they fit in the appraisal instrument. This might be worthwhile doing before the actual appraisal.

V-B-2c. *Encourages administrators to use a performance appraisal instrument reflecting appropriate responsibilities for school counselors.* If your district does not have an appropriate appraisal instrument for school counselors, provide one to your principal. He or she may insist that the district forms must be completed which is fine, but request that an appropriate appraisal be completed as well. It may be that your principal will begin to see the greater relevance of such an appraisal and advocate for such an appraisal at the district level.

Overview of the Book

Introduction Section: We begin our text with our Introduction, titled *How Culturally Competent Is Your School?* This chapter, by Drs. Judy A. Nelson and Rebecca M. Bustamante, looks at the environment or the organizational cultural competence of schools and how to assess and improve those environments. The editors of this book decided to lead with a chapter on multiculturalism and diversity. We believe that a school environment that invites all students to learn and to be successful is essential to sound educational practices. Additionally, we view the school counselor as the natural leader in creating a culturally competent learning environment and advocating for the opportunities that diverse school demographics provide to that environment. We believe that school counselors have the awareness, knowledge, and skills to work towards an environment that is culturally competent and to include the assessment of organizational cultural competence in the CSCP.

Section I: The first major section of the text is titled *Direct Counseling Services* and includes the following chapters: Implementing School Counseling Core Curriculum, Individual Student Planning, and Responsive Services. Counselors provide these direct services to students at all grade levels, and they should be incorporated into the yearly calendar of the CSCP. If we think about these services in terms of a pyramid, we would place the school counseling core curriculum along the base of the Figure. All students need information, and this is where the school counselor provides information in classrooms, in school assemblies, and in groups. Dr. Helena Stevens provides lesson planning devices, suggestions for core curriculum lessons, and ideas on how to plan and implement a total school counseling core curriculum.

Some students (or perhaps one group or grade level) will need more specific planning during individual planning conferences, and we place these services toward the middle of the pyramid because not as many students will be impacted by individual planning as by core curriculum. All students will receive information during classroom school counseling core curriculum lessons; however, only several students, one grade level, or one classroom will need individual planning services at any given time. Dr. Glenda Johnson includes tools that are vital to efficiency when working with individual students, and her Five-Minute Individual Planning Tool is one you will use often!

At the top of the pyramid, the school counselor responds to crises and the immediate needs of students in a variety of situations ranging from the death of a pet to the death of a parent. Drs. Robika Modak Mylroie and Kimberly McGough incorporate an excellent model for dealing with crises and enumerate the various crises that typically present to the school counselor. To minimize being overwhelmed by crises, we cannot stress enough how important it is for the school counselor to plan and implement a balanced CSCP. When all students have access to the school counselor through core curriculum, many crisis situations might be avoided.

Section II: This section is titled *Counseling Skills* and includes the following chapters: Individual Counseling Sessions, Group Counseling, and Consultation and Collaboration. The competencies and skills needed to work with students individually and in groups are essential to school counselors, are an integral part of their training, and are unique to the school counselor. These chapters offer current research and thinking regarding how those skills can be used most effectively. Models for working with individuals and in groups are provided. Additionally, you will find the major issues and themes that present to the school counselor over time. Case studies are included to give you examples of exactly how to use your counseling skills in a variety of situations. Dr. Kathy McDonald provides extensive information regarding the specialty of counseling children and adolescents, and Dr. Judy A. Nelson and Ms. Benny Malone explore the group counseling intervention as it relates to school-aged children. We encourage you to use the models that these authors have provided for you to make the most of your direct counseling time with students.

Collaboration and consultation are skills that are unique to the counseling profession. These interventions provide student support through other sources rather than directly to students. Written by Dr. Le'Ann Solmonson, Chapter 7 incorporates essential tools for using these important counseling skills to the students' advantage.

Section III: This section is titled *Programming* and includes the following chapters: Post-Secondary Opportunities, Advocating for Appropriate Roles, Technological Applications and Appropriate Uses, and Data and Assessment in School Counseling. With much focus currently on post-secondary opportunities, Drs. Lia D. Falco and Sam Steen have written a wealth of information on how to help students prepare for the future. Providing information to students and parents regarding future opportunities might include individual planning, the school counseling core curriculum, and group counseling, as well as consulting and collaborating with parents and outside agencies.

When school counselors advocate for appropriate roles, that means that they are spending more time with students and more time managing their programs than with activities that are not consistent with the mission and vision of the CSCP. Dr. Carleton H. Brown includes his own real-life experiences of how to get administrators on board with the CSCP, which will help counselors advocate for their appropriate roles. Additionally, the chapter on technological applications, written by Dr. Rachael Whitaker, provides a wealth of information on how to best use technology to implement and manage a 21st-century CSCP. And, finally, Drs. Tiffany Simon, Jana McLain, Ms. Letitia Powell, and Dr. Ernest Cox provide blueprints for assessing student needs and collecting data that will provide a rationale for the CSCP and the programs implemented by the school counselor.

Section IV: The final section is titled *Leadership, Professional Ethics, and Supervision* and includes the following chapters: School Counselor Leadership, Professional Issues in School Counseling, and Common-Sense Counseling. Drs. Lisa A. Wines, Carol Hightower-Parker, Lia Rosales, and Ms. Sharon D. Bey provide extensive information on leadership opportunities for school counselors that lead to systemic change. The focus of the chapter on professional issues, written by Drs. Lisa A. Wines, Kathy Ybañez-Llorente, Joydel Snook, and Judy A. Nelson, is on the ethical responsibilities of school counselors as they face difficult situations with children and their families in a school setting. Included in this chapter is the importance of clinical supervision and how to obtain it and how to navigate the maze of district policies, state licensure regulations, and codes of ethics.

As a final bonus to this text, we are pleased to include a chapter titled *Common-Sense Counseling* written from the direct experiences of a high school counselor and district guidance and counseling director in a large suburban school district, Franklin D. Sampson. Sometimes our knowledge, skills, and ethical concerns defy common sense! We want to make sure that you don't lose sight of the good thinking that you have as a person and as a professional. These final tips will help you navigate your job as a school counselor with grace and finesse.

Final Thoughts on the Importance of School Counselors

Throughout your training as a school counselor, you will study theories, competencies, ethics, specific counseling skills, and professionalism. The intent of our textbook is to place you and your new knowledge in the actual day-to-day functioning of school counseling from managing your program to working with students directly and indirectly. Every school district is unique in its demographics and how it functions in order to educate students, and each campus possesses its strengths and challenge areas. And, yet, all students deserve an excellent education among professionals who care about them. As the school counselor on your campus, you have the potential to be one of the most influential professionals to interact with all students. We believe our text will help you do just that! Best of luck in a wonderful and satisfying career.

Lisa A. Wines and Judy A. Nelson

Note

1 Parts of the CACREP Standards that Routledge reproduces in its Work represent only selected parts of the 2016 CACREP Standards; inclusion of the CACREP Standards in the Routledge Work is in no way intended to imply CACREP endorsement or approval of the Routledge Work; and use of the Routledge Work as a teaching tool does not establish or connote compliance with CACREP Standards for purposes of determining CACREP accreditation of any education program.

References

American School Counselor Association. (2012a). *The national model: A framework for school counseling programs* (3rd ed.). Alexandria, VA: Author.

American School Counselor Association. (2012b). *School counseling competencies*. Alexandria, VA: Author.

Goodman-Scott, E. (2015). School counselors' perceptions of their academic preparedness and job activities. *Counselor Education and Supervision*, 54, 57–67. https://doi.org/10.1002/j.1556-6978.2015.00070.x

Gysbers, N. C., & Henderson, P. (2012). *Developing & managing your school guidance and counseling program* (5th ed.). Alexandria, VA: American Counseling Association.

Texas Education Agency. (2018). The Texas model for comprehensive school counseling programs. Austin, TX: Author.

Appropriate Activities for School Counselors	Inappropriate Activities for School Counselors
individual student academic program planning	coordinating paperwork and data entry of all new students
interpreting cognitive, aptitude and achievement tests	coordinating cognitive, aptitude and achievement testing programs
providing counseling to students who are tardy or absent	signing excuses for students who are tardy or absent
providing counseling to students who have disciplinary problems	performing disciplinary actions or assigning discipline consequences
providing counseling to students as to appropriate school dress	sending students home who are not appropriately dressed
collaborating with teachers to present school counseling core curriculum lessons	teaching classes when teachers are absent
analyzing grade-point averages in relationship to achievement	computing grade-point averages
interpreting student records	maintaining student records
providing teachers with suggestions for effective classroom management	supervising classrooms or common areas
ensuring student records are maintained as per state and federal regulations	keeping clerical records
helping the school principal identify and resolve student issues, needs and problems	assisting with duties in the principal's office
providing individual and small-group counseling services to students	providing therapy or long-term counseling in schools to address psychological disorders
advocating for students at individual education plan meetings, student study teams and school attendance review boards	coordinating schoolwide individual education plans, student study teams and school attendance review boards
analyzing disaggregated data	serving as a data entry clerk

1101 King St., Suite 625, Alexandria, VA 22314 ▪ Phone: 703 683 ASCA ▪ **www.schoolcounselor.org**

1

How Culturally Competent Is Your School?

Dr. Judy A. Nelson and Dr. Rebecca M. Bustamante

ASCA NATIONAL MODEL THEME

Leadership

Advocacy

ASCA SCHOOL COUNSELOR PROFESSIONAL COMPETENCIES

I-B-1h. Demonstrates multicultural, ethical and professional competencies in planning, organizing, implementing and evaluating the comprehensive school counseling program

I-B-2. Serves as a leader in the school and community to promote and support student success

I-B-3. Advocates for student success

I-B-3e. Understands the process for development of policy and procedures at the building, district, state and national levels

I-B-4. Collaborates with parents, teachers, administrators, community leaders and other stakeholders to promote and support student success

I-B-4d. Understands and knows how to apply a consensus-building process to foster agreement in a group

I-B-4e. Understands how to facilitate group meetings to effectively and efficiently meet group goals

I-B-5. Acts as a systems change agent to create an environment promoting and supporting student success

I-B-5a. Defines and understands system change and its role in comprehensive school counseling programs

I-B-5b. Develops a plan to deal with personal (emotional and cognitive) and institutional resistance impeding the change process

I-B-5c. Understands the impact of school, district and state educational policies, procedures and practices supporting and/or impeding student success

ASCA PRINCIPLES

Principle 7: School counselors can help other adults enhance their work with students' academic/educational, career, and personal-social development and for the purpose of removing barriers to individual student success.

Principle 20: Leadership for the school counseling programs is a shared responsibility between school counselors and school principals.

ASCA ETHICAL STANDARDS FOR SCHOOL COUNSELORS (2016)

A.1.f. Respect students' and families' values, beliefs, sexual orientation, gender identification/expression and cultural background and exercise great care to avoid imposing personal beliefs or values rooted in one's religion, culture or ethnicity.

A.3.a. Collaborate with administration, teachers, staff and decision makers around school-improvement goals.

A.3.b. Provide students with a comprehensive school counseling program that ensures equitable academic, career and social/emotional development opportunities for all students.

A.3.c. Review school and student data to assess needs including, but not limited to, data on disparities that may exist related to gender, race, ethnicity, socio-economic status and/or other relevant classifications.

A.3.d. Use data to determine needed interventions, which are then delivered to help close the information, attainment, achievement and opportunity gaps.

CACREP STANDARDS 2016

Section 5-G, Entry-Level Specialty Areas, School Counseling

Contextual Dimensions

2. School counselor roles as leaders, advocates, and systems change agents in P-12 schools

2.d School counselor roles in school leadership and multidisciplinary teams

Practice

3.a Development of school counseling program mission statements and objectives

3.b Design and evaluation of school counseling programs

3.k Strategies to promote equity in student achievement and college access

Introduction

The editors of this book decided to lead with a chapter on multiculturalism and diversity. We believe that a school environment that invites all students to learn and to be successful is essential to sound educational practices. Additionally, we view the school counselor as the natural leader in creating a culturally competent learning environment and advocating for students who bring diverse identities and cultural experiences to the school setting. We believe that school counselors should have the awareness, knowledge, and skills to promote an environment that is culturally competent. This competence includes an ability to assess organizational, or school-wide, cultural competence as part of the Comprehensive School Counseling Program (CSCP).

Cultural competence in the school counseling literature primarily has focused on how to be effective when counseling culturally and ethnically diverse students (Bidell, 2012; Burnham, Mantero, & Hooper, 2009; Chao, 2013; Council for the Accreditation of Counseling and Related Educational Programs [CACREP], 2016; Holcomb-McCoy, 2004; Lewis & Hayes, 1991; Sue, Arredondo, & McDavis, 1992). Culturally competent school counselors, at one time, were expected primarily to be able to relate to culturally different clients with respect. These expectations included having awareness of one's own and the client's cultures, creating a culturally sensitive working alliance (Collins & Arthur, 2010), and relating to and appreciating students and families of diverse backgrounds. Being able to appreciate and embrace differences is a necessary character trait for people who work in public schools. People who do not value cultural competence might find that the role of the school counselor is not a good fit for them. However, in 21st-century school counseling, counselors must go beyond cultural competence to be advocates for marginalized students, families, and communities. They must be agents of change who are willing to take risks for the betterment of school environments, as well as have the capacity to self-reflect on their own competencies and motives.

According to the American School Counselor Association (ASCA) Code of Ethics (2016), in addition to respecting the values, beliefs, and differences of the students and families with which they work, school counselors also are required to work with administrators for continuous school improvement. Counselors are called upon to implement and manage CSCPs that are relevant to and serve all students regarding academics, career, and social and emotional development. School counselors should effectively use school and student data to assess needs and identify disparities in educational opportunities, as well as use data to develop interventions and programs that help close academic, information, achievement, and opportunity gaps among students. Additionally, *The School Counselor on Cultural Diversity* (ASCA Principles, 2015) states that "school counselors demonstrate cultural responsiveness by collaborating with stakeholders to create a school and community climate that embraces cultural diversity and helps to promote the academic, career and social/emotional success for all students" (p. 19). With these mandates in mind, we present an assessment process designed to enhance the school environment through improved organizational cultural competence. This chapter will provide school counselors with advocacy tools and systemic change procedures that are consistent with the ASCA National Model (2012a), the ASCA Code of Ethics (2016), and the ASCA Principles (2015) of cultural diversity.

In recent literature (Banks, 2008; Khalifa, Gooden, & Jones, 2016; Santamaria, 2014), educational researchers have expanded on similar concepts of cultural competence (Bustamante, Nelson, & Onwuegbuzie, 2009; Portman, 2009), cultural responsiveness (Gay, 2013; Santamaria, 2014), and cultural relevance (Aronson & Laughter, 2016; Dover, 2013; Ladson-Billings, 2014). Essentially, these related notions provide frameworks for how teachers, counselors, and school leaders might ensure that school environments reflect the needs of diverse student populations. Using these frameworks, educators are guided in their efforts to advocate for sound educational practices for all students and to work effectively with families and communities to support inclusion. In training school leaders, particularly school counselors, we identified the need for leaders to be skilled in assessing and promoting culturally competent schools (Bustamante, Nelson, & Onwuegbuzie, 2009; Nelson & Bustamante, 2009; Nelson, Bustamante, Wilson, & Onwuegbuzie, 2008).

Portman (2009) discussed the changing role of the school counselor as one of proficiency in cultural mediation. According to Portman:

> I define *cultural mediation* in school counseling as an intentional process through which a school counselor, in the role of the cultural mediator, engages in prevention, intervention, and/or remediation activities that facilitate communication and understanding between culturally diverse human systems (e.g., school, family, community, and federal and state agencies) that aid the educational process of all students. (p. 23)

In our work with school leaders, we have expanded the idea of cultural mediators to include the assessment and implementation of school policies, programs, and practices that enhance equity and ensure supportive school environments. We believe that this cultural mediator role for school counselors is consistent with the ASCA National Model (2012a) and the counselor as leader of a significant program that has the potential to affect all students, staff, and stakeholders in the school community. Once the assessment process is completed, school counselors can use this data to develop action plans with strategies for equity that also are integral to the CSCP. As stated in Nelson, Bustamante, and Watts (2013), we define the following skills as integral to the new role of school counselors as cultural mediators:

> (a) understand how the policies, programs, and practices of a school significantly impact the personal/social, academic, and career outcomes for every student; (b) facilitate inclusiveness of responsibility for an inviting learning environment, social advocacy and action, and cultural competence; and (c) use leadership, advocacy, and accountability skills to enhance school programs in terms of promoting the success of every student regardless of race, ethnicity, sexual orientation, ability, religion, and other differences. (p. 46)

Although these functions might represent new responsibilities for many school counselors, these roles seem appropriate when considering the tremendous responsibility that school counselors have in managing CSCPs (ASCA, 2012a; Nelson, Bustamante, Sawyer, & Sloan, 2015; Portman, 2009).

Defining Culture, Organizational Culture, and School-Wide Cultural Competence

In this chapter, we focus on the notion of school-wide cultural competence as a valuable approach that school counselors might incorporate in developing a CSCP. In general, cultural competence refers to an individual's capacity to interact cooperatively and appropriately with others who represent cultures and identities different from one's own (Deardorff, 2009). Most researchers describe cultural competence in terms of an individual's knowledge, skills, and attitudes. In reference to educators, the terms *cultural relevance* and *cultural responsiveness* also commonly refer to the individual behaviors of teachers (Aronson & Laughter, 2016) and school leaders (Khalifa, Gooden, & Davis, 2016). Dover's (2013) framework for culturally relevant education (CRE) builds on previous frameworks by Gay (2013) and Ladson-Billing (2014). Dover (2013) proposed four markers of culturally relevant education: (a) connecting students' cultural references to academic skills and concepts; (b) engaging self and students in critical reflection; (c) facilitating self and students' cultural competence; and (d) critiquing discourses of power. Additionally, Sue, Arredondo, and McDavis (1992) advocated for the inclusion of cultural competent counseling in the professional practice of all counselors, and Holcomb-McCoy (2004) advocated for school counselors' use of culturally competent counseling in working with students, parents, and school staff. Our notion of cultural competence extends beyond the individual educator and classroom to include school-level policies, programs, practices, and characteristics of school culture that tend to impede or support the needs and experiences of diverse populations in schools.

The ideas of cultural competence, cultural responsiveness, and cultural relevance must be rooted in an understanding of what is meant by both culture and organizational culture. For decades, anthropologists and other social science researchers have taken the view that culture concerns systems of common symbols and shared meaning among a group of people that reflect norms and assumptions about the world (Geertz, 1973; Martin, 2002). Typically, this shared meaning is developed over time and generations among people, yet sub-cultures form and individual within-group differences are always present (Ting-Toomey, 1999).

Organizational culture, however, is best defined as the shared experiences, rituals, stories, espoused values, artifacts, and underlying assumptions of groups of people who work together (Schein, 1992). Organizations, or in this case schools, exist as shared systems of meaning and a sense of commonality to ensure continual organized activity, provide structure and predictability, and avoid confusion. Culture then is both cognitive (inside people's heads) and observable in symbols and meanings expressed through publicly shared language and artifacts (Alvesson, 2011). Much of culture, however, is a *taken-for-granted* aspect of social life and human behavior (Alvesson, 2011; Schein, 2011). Although aspects of culture are closely related to language and communication, many aspects of culture are not directly espoused or expressed and call for more in-depth observation and interpretation to bring subtle aspects of culture to levels of consciousness and expression (Alvesson, 2011). Organizational cultural competence, therefore, refers to an organization's ability to perform effectively in cross-cultural situations through a congruent set of behaviors, attitudes, and policies (Cross, Bazron, Dennis, & Isaacs, 1989; Pederson, 2000; Sue, 1999). We apply this idea to school settings and define school-wide cultural competence as "how well a school's policies, programs, practices, artifacts, and rituals reflect the needs and experiences of diverse groups in the school and outer school community" (Bustamante, 2006, p. 1).

In focusing on accountability data, counselors and school leaders easily can overlook characteristics of school culture that influence the academic and social engagement of students. However, school leaders often do not have the tools needed to observe aspects of school culture, and counselors frequently are unaware of aspects of school culture that students and staff might experience as exclusive or inclusive. Few counselors receive training in how to promote inclusive practices in schools, particularly when underlying norms and assumptions reinforce inequitable practices, are deeply embedded in school culture, and are reinforced by societal expectations and power differences. School counselors are often unaware of their own implicit biases and, therefore, might be oblivious to exclusive or discriminatory practices that are embedded in school settings. We recommend that ongoing assessment of the degree of inclusiveness reflected in a school culture be an essential component of the CSCP. This approach to assessment would allow for the identification of barriers and opportunities relevant to organizational cultural competence in the school environment. For this reason, we advocate that observations be conducted in schools to uncover implicit and expressed beliefs and practices by using an instrument titled the *School-wide Cultural Competence Observation Checklist* (SCCOC)[2007] as a guiding tool.

Assessing School-Wide Cultural Competence

School counselors need tools to assist them in identifying underlying organizational values and beliefs in the school culture that contribute to inequitable policies and practices. We find that by focusing on an organizational level of analysis, counselors can gain a more holistic view of how culturally responsive school practices might be to the experiences and needs of students in the school. Organizational cultural competence, as a guiding framework, provides a useful approach to examining how well a school or district's policies, programs, practices, traditions, underlying values, artifacts, and other essential indicators of culture truly reflect the values, experiences, and perspectives of culturally diverse groups in the school and school community (Bustamante, 2006; National Center for Cultural Competence, n.d.).

Although educators and counselors might consider themselves to be culturally competent individuals, our prior research results indicated that educators often struggle when conducting school-level equity or culture audits because they do not know how to focus their observations (Bustamante, Nelson, & Onwuegbuzie, 2009). We also found that although many school leaders theoretically understood the concept of school-wide cultural competence and proficiency, school leader participants reported that they did not know how to go about assessing cultural competence in actual school settings (Bustamante, 2005). To guide school leaders in reviewing their cultural environments, we developed the SCCOC as a mixed-methods approach to assessing the strengths and challenges of a culturally competent school by observing the total school environment. It is important to emphasize that the SCCOC was designed to be used as part of a culture audit and complemented by surveys, interviews, field observations, and preexisting data available from school, district, and state databases.

The School-Wide Cultural Competence Observation Checklist

The SCCOC has been used in our training of educators, including teachers, administrators, and school counselors, for more than a decade. We have found it to be instrumental in teaching our students how to assess and manage their programs to be useful in creating affirming educational environments and in advocating for all students. Qualitative feedback from our students and additional research studies have provided reliability and validity to our instrument (Bustamante, 2005; Bustamante, Nelson, & Onwuegbuzie, 2009; Nelson, Bustamante, Wilson, & Onwuegbuzie, 2008; Nelson & Bustamante, 2009; Onwuegbuzie, Bustamante, & Nelson, 2010). The SCCOC is a hands-on assessment procedure and a development process that allows faculty and staff to focus honestly on the strengths and challenges that are characteristic in any school environment.

Thirty-three items make up the instrument, which includes a Likert-type scale (1 = never, 2 = almost never, 3 = sometimes, 4 = almost always, 5 = always) to indicate the degree to which culturally competent practices, policies, and/or programs can be observed in the school setting. Observers can also make field notes in the spaces allotted for evidence, artifacts, and specific observations. These notes are important as they verify or define how the observer arrived at the score. Bustamante (2005) developed the SCCOC items based on domains and indicators that emerged from a previous Delphi study of cultural proficiency conducted with international school leaders.

Onwuegbuzie, Bustamante, and Nelson (2010) outlined how the instrument was constructed utilizing a series of both quantitative and qualitative data collection processes and analyses. Ultimately, the researchers established instrument validity and fidelity beginning with an interdisciplinary review of the literature and a Delphi study to determine the domains and potential items of the checklist. The checklist items were developed and grounded in intercultural, cross-cultural, and multicultural areas of research and practice. Culturally responsive policies, practices, and programs were studied, including social justice and advocacy issues, culturally relevant pedagogy, inclusive schools, equity audits, diversity, and cultural competence in human service organizations, particularly those in the field of professional counseling (Bustamante, 2005). The research team conducted an exploratory factor analysis that yielded strong support for the domains indicated on the checklist. They then pilot-tested the instrument with students in master's and doctoral-level counseling and educational administration programs, as well as practitioners who were superintendents, principals, counselors, and teachers. These groups (students and practitioners) used the SCCOC to assess the organizational cultural competence of their schools and then provided extensive feedback on the instrument through participating in focus groups and completing open-ended questionnaires. Following the piloting process, the research team made revisions, and the instrument was field-tested again.

The Role of the School Counselor in the Assessment Process

School counselors have a responsibility to ensure equitable educational environments for all students. The unique consultation and collaboration skills of school counselors allow them to assist in the creation of schools that are accepting of culturally diverse student groups. Using these unique skills, school counselors can facilitate the cultural awareness, knowledge, and skills of the entire school staff. When counselors guide teachers and administrators in collecting and reflecting upon culture-related data and students' sense of belonging, in addition to test score data, educators more likely can achieve inclusive environments that reflect greater cultural competence. Assessing the organizational cultural competence of the school is a practical starting point, and the school counselor has the leadership and advocacy skills to initiate the assessment process and move it to its logical conclusion, which is "What systemic changes do we need to make to become more culturally competent?"

School counselors historically have been advocates for students with academic struggles and disabilities, for English Language Learners, and for those who feel isolated and bullied. Students who are from violent and abusive homes and those who experience grief and loss often rely on the school counselor for support. In addition, according to the competencies and standards of the profession, the school counselor assists students who feel marginalized due to sexual orientation, race, ethnicity, or any other differences. Creating affirming environments for these students and for every student is appropriate and necessary for the school counseling profession, as stated in the ASCA Code of Ethics (2016) and position statements (ASCA, 2012b, 2014, 2015).

As noted by Lindsey, Robbins, and Terrell (2003), partnerships created by strong leaders create the potential for systemic change that leads to positive learning environments. Additionally, other researchers (Constantine, Hage, Kindaichi, & Bryant, 2007; Hipolito-Delgado & Lee, 2007) have documented how social justice, advocacy, and systemic change can be promoted in schools and communities consisting of predominantly poor and minority families when school counselors and school administrators collaborate. School counselors have the training and can take the initiative in this type of collaboration, and they have a professional, ethical, and humanistic responsibility not only to conduct a continual assessment of their own individual cultural competence but also to include as part of their CSCPs the assessment and changes needed in the organizational cultural competence of their schools.

ASCA Ethical Codes and Competencies

Education scholars suggested that school counselors ideally are positioned to identify policies and practices that potentially disadvantage people from traditionally marginalized groups (ASCA, 2012b; Nelson, Bustamante, & Watts, 2013; Studer, 2015). School counselors design and manage CSCPs, and these CSCPs clearly should address the needs of all students, particularly those who are marginalized and underserved (ASCA, 2015). Assessing and integrating organizational cultural competence in a school environment mainly encompasses two of the four themes in the ASCA National Model (2012a): advocacy and systemic change. Although leadership and collaboration are important to the success of the assessment and integration process, advocating for the success of all students is the major goal of organizational cultural competence, and this can usually only be accomplished through systemic change.

School counselors often act on behalf of students or provide indirect services, which is one way of advocating for the success of all students. Needs assessments and action plans are indirect services and the impetus for systemic change. When outdated educational theories, outdated teaching methods, and "the way we have always done it" attitudes are maintained, there is great risk of marginalizing certain populations or individuals. Changing demographics and social norms simply will not tolerate stagnation in the field of education. When school personnel and other stakeholders become aware that certain parts of the system are no longer functional, they may not know what to do about it. School counselors can provide the leadership and knowledge of conducting a full-scale assessment to determine what can be done to create a more culturally competent environment. Once the assessment process is completed, the school counselor can produce media that explains the results to the staff. As the staff begins to understand and accept the new vision, the action planning begins. We provide the SCCOC assessment process in the following sections.

The SCCOC Assessment Process

Step 1: School counselors begin the assessment process by enlisting the support of their administrative teams, particularly their principals. We recommend conducting a mini-session for administrators and staff that defines the purpose of the SCCOC. Teaching modules are available at the end of this chapter for use in this type of informational presentation. It is important that the counselor is transparent about what the process is and how it can be helpful. Not all staff will be *on board* with this process, but we have found that principals and most teachers welcome the opportunity to improve their schools and to work toward continuous improvement.

Step 2: The next step is to form an assessment team of about six to eight members who represent different groups in the school. Some possible choices for team members are an administrator, the counselor (of course), teacher leaders, department chairs, the nurse or librarian, a parent, and a student leader. The school counselor can ask for volunteers or personally ask individuals to serve on the team. Diversity is important to the assessment team, so counselors should think about being inclusive and even consider members who might have difficulty in making changes to the learning environment. Principals may want to assist in choosing the team or may leave those decisions up to the school counselor.

Step 3: Step 3 involves meeting with the team and explaining the instrument to them so they understand how they are to utilize the SCCOC. In groups, team members identify three strengths and three challenge areas of their respective schools and discuss possible action plans for improvement.

There is no official scoring of the instrument. Team members look at the data collection process as a qualitative assessment even though each item is assigned a score on a scale with 1 = never; 2 = almost never; 3 = sometimes; 4 = almost always; 5 = always. Those numbers simply provide a gauge for determining how the team members view the implementation of each item in the domains. Again, the teaching modules might be used at this point to help the team members understand the process from start to finish. If the counselor has conducted his or her own SCCOC before the meeting, that instrument can be an example to show the other team members. It is important to emphasize that each team member will conduct his or her own SCCOC without consulting other team members to enhance reliability. The counselor will give the team a time frame and a meeting date when individual results will be compared. Two weeks is generally an appropriate amount of time to complete the observations and the checklist.

Step 4: During step 4, the counselor meets with the team to compare results and to reach consensus on the strengths and challenges that emerged from the assessment process. The counselor should ask each team member to provide his/her top three strengths and top three challenge areas to identify areas for continuous improvement in school-wide cultural competence. Team members discuss the strengths and needs of the school and think about actions that might help create a more culturally competent learning environment based on the challenges they identified. This process may take one or several meetings with the team, but the outcome should be a final list of the three strengths and challenge areas that the team agrees they will address in the action plan. It is important to stress that the initial list is simply the beginning of systemic change. As team members strive for continual improvement, they can address other challenge areas during the next school year or once some of the current goals are met.

Step 5: As the team leader, the counselor now synthesizes the team's suggestions and creates a cultural competence action plan based on the identified strengths and challenges. The counselor writes the action plan and presents it to the team for review and discussion of implementation strategies. The action plan should be consistent with the CSCP. The counselor chooses action strategies with care. How much or how little will the staff support the new plan? Is it better to start with goals that are easily attainable and move to more difficult changes once the staff is comfortable with smaller changes? Every school is different. Some schools might require immense changes, and others will need only moderate strategies to improve the school environment. Some staff will welcome changes, but others will be resistant. School counselors are equipped with the skills to make decisions based on the needs of their students, their school environments, and their faculty and staff. An example of an action plan with recommendations for systemic change is included in the SCCOC template at the end of the chapter.

Step 6: The team now creates a multimedia presentation (e.g., PowerPoint, Prezi, podcast, role-play, social media venue, etc.) that explains the action plan and that can be used in staff development and with other constituency groups in the school community. The school counselor should incorporate other data sets into the presentation to help the staff see how the SCCOC data fits into a total picture of the school. Examples of these supporting data sets are grades, graduation rates, discipline reports, standard test scores, numbers of students in special programs, and so forth. The presentation of systemic change can be tricky. School counselors have the skills and can assist staff members in accepting action plans. If a counselor has wisely placed the bulk of the strategies in the CSCP, then teachers and other staff will not feel overwhelmed with *more things to do*. At this point, the counselor can ask volunteers to help with the plan, and those who are most interested will volunteer. It is important not to be discouraged by objections. School counselors can admit that there are barriers to any systemic changes and ask for help in addressing those challenges. See the following section titled *Barriers and Challenges to Culturally Competent School Environments* for more information.

Step 7: To ensure continuous improvement, we recommend that the team conduct the SCCOC at least one time every school year. If it is conducted at the beginning of the school year, team members can assess how well the action plan was implemented the previous year and begin to look at other systemic changes for the current year. Additionally, counselors can infuse the other data sets mentioned earlier to see what impact the action plan might have had on student success.

Barriers and Challenges to Culturally Competent School Environments

As with all leadership initiatives, particularly those involving systemic change, there are barriers and challenges with which to contend. Regardless of the awareness, knowledge, and skills of school counselors, they will most likely experience some deterrents to such systemic changes. The following discussion focuses on these deterrents: finding the time and support to manage a CSCP that works toward a culturally competent environment, managing the teachers and other staff who are opposed to making changes, and working on the personal threat of the *nice counselor syndrome* (Bemak & Chung, 2008).

Time and Support for the CSCP

First, in a variety of studies and articles, school counselors are encouraged to be agents of change (Singh, Urbano, Haston, & McMahan, 2010), advocate for students (Bemak & Chung, 2008), and use a social justice approach to school counseling (Griffin & Steen, 2011). In addition, the ASCA National Model (2012a) calls for school counselors to advocate for more counseling-related roles rather than administrative duties. However, many counselors continue to struggle with watered-down CSCPs due to the myriad other demands that administrators place on them. Please see Chapter 9 for thorough discussions of appropriate roles for school counselors. The current recommendation for school counseling duties is that 80% of a counselor's time is spent in direct and indirect services to students. That leaves 20% of the counselor's time for system support or management of the CSCP and non-counseling duties (sometimes described as fair share duties). Chapter 9 provides excellent descriptions and rationales for the appropriate roles for school counselors and how to achieve the ability to perform these roles rather than roles that do not focus directly on the mental health of the students in our schools. Educating administrators and teachers about the appropriate school counselor roles and collecting data on the impact of the appropriate roles will go a long way toward achieving the dynamic CSCP that school counselors are trained to develop and manage.

Coping With Those Who Do Not Want Change

Second, all agents of change (in this case, the school counselor) encounter apprehension and sometimes outright refusal to cooperate when advocating for systemic change. Generally, the first step in making systemic change is to enlist the support of the principal and the administrative team. Conducting the SCCOC assessment is a good place to start, and principals are usually interested in how their schools *score* on various instruments. School counselors can take advantage of this interest and make some *selling points* on the efficacy of making changes that will improve student success. Once the principal is on board, the counselor can begin to train the staff on organizational cultural competence and the benefits of a culturally competent environment for students. Short training sessions during faculty meetings can lead up to introducing the results of the SCCOC and the subsequent action plan. Choosing the action plan items is important so that teachers do not feel overwhelmed with changes and allow for staff input because teachers are creative and can offer excellent ideas. In some instances, it might be prudent to reveal one piece of the action plan at a time so as not to overwhelm faculty and staff. Ultimately, there will still be those who do not support change; however, if most others are supportive, the counselor can move forward and hope that the few who are against the changes will eventually come along.

The Nice Counselor Syndrome

Finally, Bemak and Chung (2008) described what they called *nice counselor syndrome* (NCS) in their work. This syndrome describes well-intentioned school counselors who truly believe in equal access and educational equity for all students, but who cannot advocate appropriately for these students. The NCS phenomenon occurs when school counselors cannot place more importance on social justice and advocacy than on avoiding conflict with administrators and teachers at all costs. These *nice* counselors want to project and maintain an image of getting along with everyone and to avoid the type of conflicts that typically develop during shifts in organizations. It is our belief that pre-service training is the best opportunity to have students reflect on the characteristics of NCS and to provide prospective school counselors with the leadership skills needed to implement and manage a strong CSCP as well as to manage conflict situations. Additionally, when counselor educators train graduate students to assess the organizational cultural competence of their schools, they develop skills needed to present systemic changes to school staff in a non-threatening way.

School counselors who are trained to assess the school's cultural competence promote a culturally competent environment in several ways. First, school counselors who model their own cultural competence for teachers and other staff, who make a point of publicly valuing differences, and who observe the environment carefully to seek out those who are also good role models can begin to encourage thinking about culture in a way that is opportunistic and helpful. Second, they can also help the administration understand how critical staff development is to systemic change, and school counselors are adept at helping people make changes with the least amount of discomfort. Third, school counselors know their faculty, staff, and administrators and how to encourage the most participation in change as possible as well as how much change a school can tolerate at any given time. Last, school counselors have training and knowledge regarding the measurement of change and how to use the assessment process in continuous improvement. These important skills will be essential in guiding teachers and staff through the change process.

Please watch the four teaching modules on how to conduct the SCCOC that you will find in the online companion to this text. These modules will help you understand the process as well as how to present the process to administrators, faculty, other staff, and even community members. Each module is only 15 minutes in length, and counselors are encouraged to use them in their training and staff development. The PowerPoint presentation and the SCCOC instrument are also available in the online companion and may be copied. Additionally, the instrument and an action plan follow the references in this chapter.

Activities

1. Discuss the changing role of the school counselor. How will you advocate for this new role?
2. In your words, what is a cultural mediator or cultural consultant? What tasks would a school counselor engage in as an advocate of this role?
3. Think of some school district policies that might impede equity for all students. Discuss the steps a school counselor might take to address these issues and possibly change them.
4. What are some programs for students and staff to better understand the opportunities that a diverse school provides to the learning community?
5. Brainstorm a list of possible staff development topics to help teachers understand the concept of organizational cultural competence.
6. From your list above, choose one topic and complete an outline of a presentation for staff development.
7. How is organizational cultural competence different from individual cultural competence? Why are both important to an equitable school setting?
8. Using the steps provided in this chapter on conducting the SCCOC, role-play the initial meeting with your assessment team. How would you explain the instrument and the process?
9. Now role-play the final steps of the SCCOC in which you meet with your team after the assessment has been completed. How would you help them reach consensus on the three most challenging and the three strengths that will drive the creation of the action plan?

Resources

Webinar:

Atkins & Olglesby (2017), "Interrupting Racism: Race & equity in your program." www.youtube.com/watch?v=B7ry2qAC3Zk&feature=youtu.be

Colorado Department of Education:
www.cde.state.co.us/postsecondary/equitytoolkit

National Education Association:
www.nea.org/home/39783.htm

References

Alvesson, M. (2011). Organizational culture: Meaning, discourse, and identity. In N. Ashkanasy, C. P. M. Wilderom, & M. F. Peterson (Eds.), *The handbook of organizational culture and climate* (2nd ed., pp. 11–28). London: SAGE Publications.

American School Counselor Association. (2012a). *The ASCA national model: A framework for school counseling programs* (3rd ed.). Alexandria, VA: Author.

American School Counselor Association. (2012b). *The professional school counselor and equity for all students.* [Position statement]. Alexandria, VA: Author. Retrieved from www.schoolcounselor.org/asca/media/asca/PositionStatements/PS_Equity.pdf

American School Counselor Association. (2014). *The professional school counselor and gay, lesbian, bisexual, transgendered, and questioning youth.* [Position statement]. Alexandria, VA: Author. Retrieved from www.schoolcounselor.org/asca/media/asca/PositionStatements/PS_LGBTQ.pdf

American School Counselor Association. (2015). *The school counselor and cultural diversity.* [Position statement]. Alexandria, VA: Author. Retrieved from www.schoolcounselor.org/asca/media/asca/PositionStatements/PS_Cultural Diversity.pdf

American School Counselor Association. (2016). *Ethical standards for school counselors.* Retrieved from www.schoolcounselor.org/files/ethical%20standards.pdf

Aronson, B., & Laughter, J. (2016). The theory and practice of culturally relevant education: A Synthesis of research across the content areas. *Review of Educational Research, 86*(1), 163–206. doi:10.3102/0034654315582066

Banks, J. A. (2008). *An introduction to multicultural education* (4th ed.). Boston, MA: Allyn & Bacon.

Bemak, F., & Chung, R. (2008). New professional roles and advocacy strategies for school counselors: A multicultural/social justice perspective to move beyond the nice counselor syndrome. *Journal of Counseling and Development, 86*, 372–381. doi:10.1002/j.1556-6678.2008.tb00522.x

Bidell, M. P. (2012). Examining school counseling students' multicultural and sexual orientation competencies through a cross-specialization comparison. *Journal of Counseling & Development, 90*(2), 200–207. doi:10.1111/j.1556-6676.2012.00025.x

Burnham, J. J., Mantero, M., & Hooper, L. M. (2009). Experiential training: Connecting school counselors-in-training, English as a Second Language (ESL) teachers, and ESL students. *Journal of Multicultural Counseling & Development, 37*(1), 2–14.

Bustamante, R. M. (2005). *Features of cultural proficiency in American International Schools in Latin America: A Delphi study*. Doctoral dissertation, University of San Diego, San Diego, CA.

Bustamante, R. M. (2006). *The "culture audit": A leadership tool for assessment and strategic planning in diverse schools and colleges*. Retrieved February 10, 2017, from http://cnx.org/content/m13691/latest/

Bustamante, R. M., & Nelson, J. A. (2007). *The school-wide cultural competence observation checklist*. Unpublished manuscript.

Bustamante, R. M., Nelson, J. A., & Onwuegbuzie, A. J. (2009). Assessing school-wide cultural competence: A tool for school leadership preparation. *Educational Administration Quarterly, 45*, 793–827. doi:10.1177/0013161X09347277

Chao, R. C. (2013). Race/ethnicity and multicultural competence among school counselors: Multicultural training, racial/ethnic identity, and color-blind racial attitudes. *Journal of Counseling & Development, 91*(2), 140–151. doi:10.1002/j.1556-6676.2013.00082.x

Collins, S., & Arthur, N. (2010). Culture infused counselling: A fresh look at a classic framework of multicultural counselling competencies. *Counseling Psychology Quarterly, 23*, 203–216. doi:10.1080/09515071003798204

Constantine, M. G., Hage, S. M., Kindaichi, M. M., & Bryant, R. M. (2007). Social justice and multicultural issues: Implications for the practice and training of counselors and counseling psychologists. *Journal of Counseling and Development, 85*, 24–29. doi:10.1002/j.1556-6678.2007.tb00440.x

Council for the Accreditation of Counseling and Related Educational Programs. (2016). *Accreditation procedures manual and application*. Alexandria, VA: Author.

Cross, T. L., Bazron, B. J., Dennis, K. W., & Isaacs, M. R. (1989). *Towards a cultural competent system of care, Vol. 1: A monograph on effective services for minority children who are severely emotionally disturbed*. Washington, DC: Georgetown University, Child Development Center, Child and Adolescent Services System Program, Technical Assistance Center.

Deardorff, D.K. (2009). Synthesizing conceptualizations of intercultural competence: A summary and emerging themes (pp. 264–271). In D.K. Deardorff (Ed.), *The SAGE handbook of intercultural competence*. Thousand Oaks, CA: Sage.

Dover, A. G. (2013). Teaching for social justice: From conceptual framework to classroom practices. *Multicultural Perspectives, 15*, 3–11. doi:10.1080/15210960.2013.

Gay, G. (2013). Teaching to and through cultural diversity. *Curriculum Inquiry*, 43, 48–70.

Geertz, C. (1973). *The interpretation of cultures*. New York: Basic Books.

Griffin, D., & Steen, S. (2011). A social justice approach to school counseling. *Journal for Social Action in Counseling and Psychology, 3*, 74–85.

Hipolito-Delgado, C., & Lee, C. (2007). Empowerment theory for the professional school counselor: A manifesto for what really matters. *Professional School Counseling, 10*, 327–332.

Holcomb-McCoy, C. C. (2004). Assessing the multicultural competence of school counselors: Checklist. *Professional School Counseling, 7*, 178–183.

Khalifa, M. A., Gooden, M. A., & Davis, J. E. (2016). Culturally responsive school leadership: A synthesis of the literature. *Review of Educational Research, 86*, 1272–1311.

Ladson-Billings, G. (2014). Culturally relevant pedagogy 2.0: a.k.a. the remix. *Harvard Educational Review, 84*, 74–84.

Lewis, A. C., & Hayes, S. (1991). Multiculturalism and the school counseling curriculum. *Journal of Counseling and Development, 70*, 119–125. doi:10.1002/j.1556-6676.1991.tb01571.x

Lindsey, R. B., Robbins, K. N., & Terrell, R. D. (2003). *Culturally proficiency: A manual for school leaders*. Thousand Oaks, CA: Corwin Press.

Martin, J. (2002). *Organizational culture: Mapping the terrain*. Thousand Oaks, CA: Sage Publications.

National Center for Cultural Competence. (n.d.). Georgetown University Center for Child and Human Development. Retrieved from https://nccc.georgetown.edu/

Nelson, J. A., & Bustamante, R. M. (2009). Preparing professional school counselors as collaborators in culturally competent school administration. *International Journal of Educational Leadership Preparation, 4*. Retrieved from http://cnx.org/contents/ c0ecc347-3778-4225-b891-c06bfc40c2d0@2/Preparing_Professional_School

Nelson, J. A., Bustamante, R. M., Sawyer, C., & Sloan, E. (2015). Cultural competence and strength-based school counselor training: A collective case study. *Journal of Multicultural Counseling and Development, 43*, 221–235.

Nelson, J. A., Bustamante, R. M., & Watts, R. (2013). Professional school counselors as cultural consultants. *Journal of Professional Counseling: Practice, Theory, & Research, 40*, 45–59.

Nelson, J. A., Bustamante, R. M., Wilson, E., & Onwuegbuzie, A. J. (2008). The schoolwide cultural competence observation checklist for school counselors: An exploratory factor analysis. *Professional School Counseling, 11*, 207–217.

Onwuegbuzie, A. J., Bustamante, R. M., & Nelson, J. A. (2010). Mixed research as a tool for developing quantitative instruments. *Journal of Mixed Methods Research, 4*, 56–78.

Pederson, P. (2000). *Handbook for developing multicultural awareness* (3rd ed.). Alexandria, VA: American Counseling Association.

Portman, T. (2009). Faces of the future: School counselors as cultural mediators. *Journal of Counseling and Development, 87*, 21–26. doi:10.1002/j.1556-6678.2009.tb00545.x

Santamaría, L. J. (2014). Critical change for the greater good: Multicultural perceptions in educational leadership toward social justice and equity. *Educational Administration Quarterly, 50*(3), 347–391. doi:10.1177/0013161X13505287

Schien, E. (1992). Organizational culture and leadership (2nd ed.). San Francisco, CA: Jossey-Bass.

Schein, E. (2011). Preface. In N. Ashkanasy, C. P. M. Wilderom, & M. F. Peterson (Eds.), *The handbook of organizational culture and climate* (2nd ed., pp. xi–xiii). London: SAGE Publications.

Singh, A. A., Urbano, A., Haston, M., & McMahan, E. (2010). School counselors' strategies for social justice change: A grounded theory of what works in the real world. *Professional School Counseling, 13*, 135–144.

Studer, J. R. (2015). *The essential school counselor in a changing society*. Thousand Oaks, CA: SAGE Publications.

Sue, D. W. (1999). Creating conditions for a constructive dialogue on "race": Taking individual and institutional responsibility. In J. Q. Adams & J. R. Welsch (Eds.), *Cultural diversity: Curriculum, classroom, & climate* (pp. 15–20). Chicago, IL: Illinois Staff and Curriculum Developers Association.

Sue, D. W., Arredondo, P., & McDavis, R. J. (1992). Multicultural counseling competencies and standards: A call to the profession. *Journal of Counseling & Development, 70*, 477–486.

Ting-Toomey, S. (1999). *Communicating across cultures*. New York: Guilford.

Appendix 1.1

The School-Wide Cultural Competence Observation Checklist

School District:	
School:	
Principal:	
Researcher(s):	
Review Date:	

Instructions: Rate on a scale of 1 to 5 (1 = Never, 2 = Almost Never, 3 = Sometimes, 4 = Almost Always, 5 = Always) the extent to which you observe each of the following criteria for cultural competence. Please note or provide evidence or documentation to support your rating.

	Observation Area/Domain and Criteria	Scale	Evidence/Documentation
School Vision/Mission			
1	There is a school Mission Statement or Vision Statement that includes a stated commitment to diversity and/or global citizenry.	**1 2 3 4 5**	
Curriculum			
2	Literature selections in the curriculum reflect a variety of cultural perspectives (classrooms and library).	**1 2 3 4 5**	
3	Global perspectives are integrated into curricula at all grade levels (world history and geography, culture studies, languages).	**1 2 3 4 5**	
4	Linguistic and content objectives are addressed for second language learners.	**1 2 3 4 5**	
Student Interaction and Leadership			
5	Racial/ethnic representation in advanced placement classes, honors classes, and gifted programs is balanced.	**1 2 3 4 5**	
6	Youth "voice" is considered in decision-making by regularly meeting with randomly selected groups of students to obtain feedback.	**1 2 3 4 5**	
7	There is a variety of student leadership opportunities for all students.	**1 2 3 4 5**	

8	Students of different groups integrate socially outside of the classroom.	**1 2 3 4 5**	
9	There are identified support programs to promote achievement and retention of lower-achieving groups.	**1 2 3 4 5**	
10	Students are involved in community service and service learning activities.	**1 2 3 4 5**	
11	There is a program in place to facilitate the adaptation of NEW students into the school and classroom.	**1 2 3 4 5**	
Teachers			
12	Teachers representing diverse groups are actively recruited by the principal and the district.	**1 2 3 4 5**	
13	New teachers are formally inducted through orientations and structured mentoring and support programs.	**1 2 3 4 5**	
14	Teachers team vertically and horizontally according to individual strengths, leadership abilities, and interests.	**1 2 3 4 5**	
15	Efforts are made to consciously integrate diverse teacher teams.	**1 2 3 4 5**	
16	Professional development is offered that addresses: a) race/ethnicity/nationality b) sexual orientation c) special needs d) language and dialect	 **1 2 3 4 5** **1 2 3 4 5** **1 2 3 4 5** **1 2 3 4 5**	
17	Informal teacher leadership roles are recognized.	**1 2 3 4 5**	
18	Professional development is focused and long term.	**1 2 3 4 5**	
Teaching and Learning			
19	Instruction is differentiated to address students with special needs, while challenging all students.	**1 2 3 4 5**	
20	Researched strategies that account for various learning styles are used in classrooms.	**1 2 3 4 5**	
21	Connections are made to students' culture and prior knowledge.	**1 2 3 4 5**	

22	Teaching strategies accommodate the needs of culturally and linguistically diverse learners using a variety of grouping strategies, hands-on activities, visuals, oral language development, reading/writing workshops, etc.	**1 2 3 4 5**	
Parents and Outer Community			
23	Community outreach programs regularly survey the perspectives of various local community constituency and stakeholder groups, including parents.	**1 2 3 4 5**	
24	Parent involvement programs exist for all culture groups.	**1 2 3 4 5**	
25	National and global ties are established through partnerships with similar organizations.	**1 2 3 4 5**	
26	The electronic community is realized and utilized for relationship building and sourcing best practices.	**1 2 3 4 5**	
Conflict Management			
27	The inevitability of intercultural conflict is recognized by peer mediation programs and/ or other proactive approaches to conflict resolution.	**1 2 3 4 5**	
28	Practices to ensure classroom and school safety for all are in place (e.g., including systems for addressing bullying or developing positive student relations).	**1 2 3 4 5**	
Assessments			
29	Authentic student assessments are used to complement standardized tests.	**1 2 3 4 5**	
30	Formative and summative program evaluations are conducted to ensure continual improvement.	**1 2 3 4 5**	
31	Teachers and administrators are evaluated by various constituency groups (other teachers, students, colleagues, self, supervisor, etc.).	**1 2 3 4 5**	
32	Organizational traditions are examined periodically to check for exclusive/inclusive practices.	**1 2 3 4 5**	
33	Celebrations reflect various cultures and introduce the community to new cultures. Representation at events and celebrations is diverse.	**1 2 3 4 5**	

General Observations: Strengths and Challenge Areas

The following is an example of strengths and challenge areas that may emerge during the assessment process in a middle school in which 30 percent of the students are Latino/Latina, 10 percent are African American, and 60 percent are White. Generally, the families in this area are middle-income families with only about 10 percent on free lunch and 5 percent on reduced lunch. Most own their homes and most are families in which two parents are working.

Strengths:

The librarian does an excellent job of including books in the library that reflect a variety of cultural perspectives. As our team members talked with her about the important role that these books play in the cultural competence of our school, on her own, she committed to including a committee of students of all ethnicities to assist her in the book-choosing process. This is a great example of how the assessment process itself can lead to immediate change!

New teachers are formally inducted through orientations and structured mentoring and support programs. Each new faculty is assigned a mentor who works closely with the new teacher throughout the year. Orientations are provided at the district and school building level throughout the year. Usually working with culturally diverse students is addressed during one or more of these trainings.

Practices to ensure classroom and school safety for all are in place (e.g., including systems for addressing bullying or developing positive student relations). Because laws in this particular state mandate that schools address bullying and student conflict, the staff has worked hard to put in place guidance lessons, interventions, and strategies to address these issues.

Challenges:

There is no program in place to facilitate the adaptation of NEW students into the school and classroom. This school receives about 5 to 10 new students a month. There has never been a program for them, and frequently the new students end up needing crisis intervention, and the counselors don't even know who these students are.

Youth "voice" is rarely considered in decision-making by regularly meeting with randomly selected groups of students to obtain feedback. The team found that student input is lacking and felt that this would be an important area for improvement.

Parent involvement programs exist for all culture groups. The PTO at this school is made up of mostly White parents. The team felt that it was essential to get other cultural groups involved.

Action Plan:

1. The school counselor will work closely with the principal and prepare a 20-minute staff development to give the entire staff the information regarding the SCCOC assessment including the strengths and challenge areas.

2. (addresses the first challenge area) The team agreed that, in general, teachers are well trained, work well on their teams, and provide culturally responsive teaching to students. However, the team saw some serious deficits in the areas of inclusivity for students. The first and easiest (remember low-hanging fruit) is for the school counselor to host a weekly meeting for new students. Traditionally, middle school is a tough transition for many students, particularly if they are new to an area. Therefore, every Friday, the school counselors will have all new students during that week come to the counseling suite to meet the counselors, to discuss being in a

new school, to ask questions, to meet a "buddy" who may have been new last year, and to have a special lunch or treat (whatever the schedule can accommodate). Since this is a middle school, there are three counselors who can alternate being the "host," or, if time permits, all three can attend the newcomers meeting.

3. (addresses the second challenge area). Continuing with the theme of focusing on students, the team liked the idea of having a group of students from different grade levels, races, ethnicities, and backgrounds to meet once a month with the administrative team. This could mean that one month the administrators would meet with 7th-grade Hispanic boys, another month African American girls, and another month with special education students. These are just examples. Again this intervention is relatively easy to implement. The counselor should be included in these meetings and can advocate for students to be honest in an appropriate way.

3. (addresses the third challenge area). The team was very interested in helping minority parents have a presence in the PTO and other facets of their children's school lives. This intervention will be more of a challenge and require more effort on the part of faculty and staff. The team decided to begin with a survey of parents to see what they need and want and how the staff can be helpful. Based on the feedback from the survey, next steps will be decided.

NOTE: While there are other challenge areas that the team would like to address, they were pleased with their current action plan and felt that it was "doable." The school counselor reminded the team that if these strategies could be implemented successfully during the current school year, then the team could move on to other projects for the following year.

Section I

Direct Counseling Services

2

Implementing the School Counseling Core Curriculum

Dr. Helena Stevens

ASCA NATIONAL MODEL THEME

Leadership

Collaboration

ASCA SCHOOL COUNSELOR PROFESSIONAL COMPETENCIES

IV-B-1. Implements the school counseling core curriculum

IV-B-1a. Identifies appropriate curriculum aligned to ASCA Student Standards

IV-B-1b. Develops and presents a developmental school counseling core curriculum addressing all students' needs based on student data

IV-B-1c. Demonstrates classroom management and instructional skills

IV-B-1d. Develops materials and instructional strategies to meet student needs and school goals

IV-B-1e. Encourages staff involvement to ensure the effective implementation of the school counseling core curriculum

IV-B-1f. Knows, understands and uses a variety of technology in the delivery of school counseling core curriculum activities

IV-B-1g. Understands multicultural and pluralistic trends when developing and choosing school counseling core curriculum

IV-B-1h. Understands and is able to build effective, high-quality peer helper programs

CACREP SECTION 5-G, ENTRY-LEVEL SPECIALTY AREAS, SCHOOL COUNSELING

Contextual Dimensions

2.a school counselor roles as leaders, advocates, and systems change agents in P-12 schools

2.c school counselor roles in relation to college and career readiness

2.d school counselor roles in school leadership and multidisciplinary teams

Practice

3.c core curriculum design, lesson plan development, classroom management strategies, and differentiated instructional strategies

3.k strategies to promote equity in student achievement and college access

3.l techniques to foster collaboration and teamwork within schools

3.m strategies for implementing and coordinating peer intervention programs

3.n use of accountability data to inform decision making

Introduction

Students in society are faced with navigating significant developmental life tasks. These tasks include, but are not limited to, identity development, peer interactions, relationships (romantic and friendship), self-esteem building, body image awareness, drug and alcohol use, pressures to perform academically and socially, and deciding post-secondary directions. These tasks and interactions inherently affect the social, emotional, and academic progress of a student. The school counselor develops classroom lessons and school counseling core curriculum to address and respond to, both preventatively and interventional, the life tasks and challenges that student encounter. School counseling core curriculum and classroom lessons curriculum are direct services in a comprehensive school counseling program that fall under the delivery quadrant of the ASCA National Model (2012a), and this quadrant should account for 80% of the school counselor's working time. Therefore, school counselors will want to carefully divide their calendar into measurable time slots to calculate the total number of minutes per week or month that are dedicated to school counseling core curriculum.

An essential function of the school counselor is to manage comprehensive school counseling core curriculum and to strategically plan and implement the direct services that will provide an impact on students' academic and personal success (Van Zandt & Hayslip, 2001). Schools with comprehensive school counseling programs that implement classroom lessons report higher grades, better prepared and informed students for future goal planning, and safer school climates (Sink, 2005). School counselors create school counseling core curriculum that is comprised of school-wide, classroom, group, and individual plans and lessons. School counseling core curriculum is inherently developmental in nature and targets the three main foci of student development: academic, career, and social/emotional. The school counselor must also take into account cultural, ethical, and school climate considerations when creating school counseling core curriculum (Van Zandt & Hayslip, 2001). This chapter will provide direction on the best practices to use when developing school counseling core curriculum as well as templates and examples that can be used in school counseling practice.

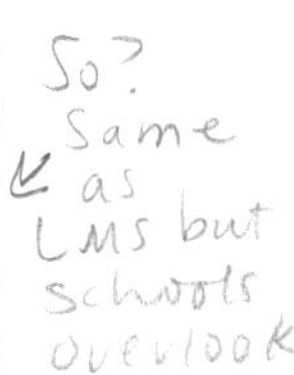

ASCA National Model

The American School Counselor Association (ASCA) has been on the forefront of advancing the field to keep pace with education reform and accountability standards. *The ASCA National Model: A Framework for School Counseling Programs* (ASCA, 2012a) provides a solid foundation for school counseling programs to be comprehensive in nature while addressing the needs of all students. The model provides the framework for developmental and preventive programming that is directed by data (Hatch, 2014). The ASCA National Model includes a foundation of professional competencies for program focus; student competencies and school counselor competencies; management that incorporates organizational assessments and tools that address school needs; delivery services for students, school staff, parents, and the community; and an accountability system to demonstrate effective programming (ASCA, 2012a).

There are four domains of the ASCA National Model (2012a) that pertain to the role of the school counselor: Delivery, Accountability, Management, and Foundation. Management is the school counselors' incorporation of "organizational assessment tools that are concrete, clearly delineated and reflective of the school's needs" (ASCA, 2012a, p. 41). School counseling core curriculum and lessons are tools in the Management domain. Delivery relates to the direct and indirect services a school counselor provides to students, parents, and school staff (ASCA, 2012a). The implementation of the curriculum and lessons, which can be individual, group, classroom, or school-wide, falls under the direct services in the Delivery domain.

ASCA provides the *School Counselor Competencies* (2012b) to serve as a guide for school counselors to use in their practice to ensure effective program implementation. The competencies "outline the knowledge, abilities, skills and attitudes that ensure school counselors are equipped to meet the rigorous demands of the profession and the needs of pre-K-12 students" (ASCA School Counselor Competencies, 2012b, p. 1). The Abilities and Skills of the *School Counselor Competencies* (Section IV-B, 2012b) detail the competencies school counselors need to be effective in developing and delivering core curriculum. See Resources for a link to the full document. Inherently, school counselors are charged to implement curriculum that appropriately correlates with the ASCA student standards and addresses all students' needs based on data (ASCA, 2014; Erford, 2015). As well, school counselors encourage staff participation in implementation of school counseling core curriculum, utilize technology, and understand multicultural and pluralistic trends when choosing the curriculum (ASCAb, 2012).

The American School Counselor Association supports using developmental, prevention, and intervention services that target the desired student mindset and impact achievement, behavior, and attendance. Managing effective school counseling core curriculum includes using data to inform decision-making; planning weekly, monthly, and annual calendars; using program assessment to evaluate the efficacy of the services; and using practices that will help close the achievement gap.

Leadership and Advocacy in School Counseling Core Curriculum

School counselors are uniquely positioned to impact equitable treatment and academic success for all students. As identified in the ASCA School Counselor Competencies (ASCA, 2012) in several areas, school counselors are to apply the themes or leadership and advocacy to their work in schools, including the school counseling core curriculum. Providing essential information to all students through classroom lessons for individual classes, an entire grade level, or the whole school population is one way to advocate for all students by allowing them access to the counseling program. School counselors should be competent in the areas of advocacy theory, application, and its use to close the achievement gap. As leaders of the comprehensive school counseling program, school counselors help to close the academic gap between under-achieving students and their affluent peers (Dollarhide, 2003; Bemak & Chung, 2005). Credentialed school counselors lead in the planning, implementing, and evaluating comprehensive counseling program for their schools that is for all students (ASCA, 2012b).

Advocacy efforts in curriculum development are those that use the school counseling core curriculum in all areas to identify, address, and remediate areas of unmet social, emotional, and academic needs in students, institutional and systemic barriers impeding student success, and/or lack of equitable access to resources (Brown & Trusty, 2005). Through needs assessments, behavior reports, observations, and parent interactions, school counselors are able to identify the specific needs and whether or not there is a lack of access to services to meet those needs. For example, a teacher may send a student to the office for behavior misconduct due to disruption or disrespect. The external behavior is what is seen rather than the internal issues that may be occurring such as family conflicts, anxiety, abuse/neglect, malnutrition, bullying, and so forth. Through identifying underlying issues, school counselors act as leaders when they use curriculum and classroom lessons to address unmet or unidentified student needs like coping, resilience, self-advocacy, and positive school climate.

ASCA Student Mindsets

The ultimate goals for students in primary and secondary settings are academic achievement and career and college readiness. For those goals to be met, the social/emotional aspects of a student need to be addressed as well. The ASCA Student Mindsets (ASCA, 2014) comprise 35 standards that school counselors can reference when determining topics and themes for school counseling core curriculum and lessons. The standards were developed based on a review of research and college/career readiness artifacts that identified strategies deemed to make the most impact on students' personal and academic success.

There are two categories listed in the ASCA Student Mindsets (ASCA, 2014). The first is *Mindset Standards* and relates to "psycho-social attitudes or beliefs that students have about themselves in relation to academic work" (p. 1). The second category is *Behavior Standards* and includes learning strategies, self-management skills, and social skills. See *Resources* for the full document. When developing curriculum, whether school-wide, group, or individual, the school counselor uses the Mindsets as a guide for choosing appropriate topics or content. The curriculum developed around these Mindsets will target increasing social skills and emotional well-being in students in order that they make successful academic and social choices.

Determining School Counseling Core Curriculum Topics: Needs Assessment

The needs of each school site vary depending on the developmental level, social system, community, and cultural factors that influence the students who attend the school. Although there are constant themes in student development everywhere in the nation, a school counselor needs to carefully consider how the school counseling core curriculum reflects the specific needs of his or her site. Differences can include social economic status impact, access to community services (clubs, sports, health, nutrition), cultural influences, family education influences, and emotional needs in students.

Identifying the needs is a critical beginning point for the school counselor when creating school counseling core curriculum for the month or year. It is imperative that data is used to inform practices (Dimmit, Carey, & Hatch, 2007). Data include, but are not limited to, needs assessments, behavior reports and referrals, school counseling office intake forms, and school climate reports. The school counselor may have an idea from walking around their site or from stepping into classrooms what the needs are, but this is a limited form of data collection to inform the services. A needs assessment is a formal way of identifying student, parent, staff, and school-wide needs. School counselors utilize needs assessments to seek input and further understand the school climate status, student needs, and parent and staff concerns about the students. School counselors can disseminate surveys or assessments, either paper or electronically, that ask questions related to feelings of safety, social-emotional well-being (depression, anxiety, self-esteem), teacher relationships and interactions, access to items that serve basic needs (toiletries, food, shelter), teacher and administration opinions about school counseling services, and many other topic areas.

By allowing school-wide personnel and services to provide input, school counselors connect themselves to the reported needs of the people they serve. Needs assessments can be both formative and summative, and by using them, school counselors can then identify major themes and needs and decide how those needs can best be addressed: individual, group, class, or school-wide interventions. Although not every need can be met, many can be identified and addressed. Example needs assessments can be found in the Appendix and in the Resources section.

Evidence-Based Practices

After identifying the needs and before developing the school counseling core curriculum, school counselors must ensure that they are incorporating evidence-based practices into their curriculums (Dimmit, Carey, & Hatch, 2007). Curriculum and lessons need to have an identifiable link between what is known to be efficacious and what counselors are doing so that student, parent, or staff outcomes are attainable and valid. Evidence-based practices integrate the best evidence of expertise, for the given construct, and the values of the person(s) being served to formulate a reliable plan of action. The plan of action in this case is the school counseling core curriculum.

Carey and Dimmit (2008) identified a model for using evidence-based practices in school counseling that includes (a) using data to identify the needs (needs assessment), (b) finding interventions and practices that have been shown to lead improvement in the identified area, and (c) determining whether the intervention or practices were effective. School counselors often must choose from programs that are known to be effective and programs that have not yet been evaluated. Best practices can be found in research literature, textbooks, training manuals, or online credible sources. See the Resources section at the end of the chapter for examples.

School counselors need to be conscious consumers when using packaged curriculum materials (i.e., Character Counts, Mind-Up, Second Step, PBIS, Peace Builders), pre-written lessons, or social-media-posted ideas. School counselors should do further research on the packaged program or suggested activities and critically analyze pre-written lessons for the inclusion of development, cultural, and ethics issues before delivering the curriculum at their sites. The *What Works Clearinghouse* is a government-sponsored program that provides a list of programs that have been empirically validated in research and are deemed to be recommended evidence-based practices (Institute of Education Services, n.d.).

Evaluating School Counseling Core Curriculum Programs

Program evaluations are a final critical component for using evidence-based practices. School counselors need to know the impact of their programs in order that they can continuously revise, update, and transform their school counseling core curriculum. Evaluations can be summative or formative and provide information about whether or not interventions, preventions, or education efforts (group, classroom, teaming, or individual) are working. These evaluations can be school climate and needs surveys (beginning and end of year) and help the school counselor track changes in the school climate and perceive if unmet needs are being met. Pre- and post-assessments (group and individual counseling) and satisfaction surveys (classroom guidance, parent and staff surveys) aid the school counselor in tracking learning outcomes and program impacts, and allow participants to provide suggestions for future programs/sessions.

Behavioral referral forms (tracking systems) can depict trends and frequencies for the amounts and types of behaviors students are referred for throughout the year. For example, if students are frequently referred for

Table 2.1 Examples of Evaluations

Level	Frequency	Methods	Use
School-wide	Beginning, middle, end of school year	Climate surveys, needs assessments, school counseling program satisfaction surveys, program implementation rates, behavior referrals	Identify if: desired outcomes are achieved, programs are being implemented efficiently, unmet needs are being met, school climate has changed
Classroom/Group	Pre and post group, after each session, beginning and end of lesson sequence	Assessments (based on construct being delivered), satisfaction surveys, teacher observations, behavior referrals	Identify if: desired outcomes are achieved, students are employing new learning, teachers observe different behaviors
Individual	Pre and post intervention, after each counseling session	Assessments (based on construct: self-esteem, organization, anger, etc.), behavior referrals, satisfaction survey	Identify if: desired outcomes are achieved, change in behavior has occurred, there are areas for improving curriculum or delivery
School Counselor	Beginning, middle, and/or end of year	*ASCA School Counseling Program Assessment*	Identify: areas for growth, areas of the model not being met

bullying and disruptive class behavior, a school counselor can focus school counseling core curriculum efforts on those topics. Throughout the year, the school counselor can use referrals to track if counseling efforts are contributing to a decrease in those referral areas. Lastly, school counselor performance evaluations (done by students, administration, or staff) aid the school counselor in considering areas of professional competency on which to increase focus and development (Henderson & Gysbers, 1998). The school counselor will determine the information needed and the appropriate method for gathering that information to evaluate the services they offer.

Table 2.1 provides examples of Evaluations, adapted from *The Program Evaluation Standards* (1994). Refer to the entire document (see Resources section) for a more detailed explanation of program evaluation.

Development, Culture, Ethics, and Learning Considerations

School counselors will need to do further research and professional development for all of the areas addressed in this section. When finding and developing school counseling core curriculum, the school counselor must incorporate learning theory, developmental theory, multicultural theory, and ethical considerations into their plans to provide comprehensive evidence-based approaches. The ASCA School Counselor Competencies (ASCA, 2012b) supports that school counselors need to have knowledge of developmental theory, learning theories, social justice theory, multiculturalism, counseling theories, and career counseling theories (ASCA, 2012b). As well, school counselors need to have knowledge of legal, ethical, and professional issues in preK–12 schools (ASCA, 2012b).

Developmental theory is used as a lens and framework for identifying the physical, emotional, social, cognitive, cultural, and linguistic stage in which a child or adolescent is positioned. The school counselor translates developmental and learning theories into practical applications for activities and lessons (Erford, 2015). Culture includes race, ethnicity, gender, socioeconomic status (SES), religion, politics, popular culture, family structure, and other systemic factors that influence child and adolescent development. To provide lessons that are pluralistic and inclusive, the school counselor must be reflective of cultural tenets to be addressed and considered in school counseling core curriculum. Lastly, in unison with development and culture, ethical standards (ASCA Code of Ethics, 2016) must be adhered to, to their fullest extent. School counseling core curriculum topics can be sensitive and can stir individuals emotionally. School counselors must pay close attention to creating and maintaining safe environments, keeping parents and administration informed of core curriculum topics and activities, and maintaining an appropriate neutral position in the school given any potential political influences.

Development

To provide effective counseling programs, development should be a foundation and lens when considering curriculum and lesson planning and implementation (Borders & Drury, 1992). School counselors are considered experts in the developmental stages of children and are entrusted with choosing curriculum that is necessary for children to grow and develop. Therefore, school counselors must be familiar with lifespan development theory when planning and developing school counseling core curriculum.

School counseling core curriculum needs to be flexible, sequential, and inclusive of developmental issues. What works for one age group may not work for another given the emotional, social, physical, language, and cognitive development of the age group being addressed. School counselors should be knowledgeable of developmental theories and use the theoretical tenets when developing school counseling core curriculum. Goals and strategies in curriculum will be developed in reflection of the current developmental (theory based) stage of the age group being addressed. The interventions and activities need to reflect appropriate goals and learning strategies for the targeted age group based on their developmental level. The goals will reflect an achievable outcome for the age group. The strategies will reflect feasible, realistic, and manageable tasks for the age group.

Examples of topics for different developmental levels can include the following. Topics mentioned at one level may be appropriate for other levels depending on the topic and how it is presented.

Early elementary (K–2): Self-control, friendships, positive behaviors, and kindness

Later elementary (3–5): Self-esteem, friendships, boundaries, bullying prevention, identity exploration, and safe choice making

Middle school and High school: Career exploration, friendship and romantic relationships (safe and appropriate behaviors), cultural identity awareness, moral decision-making, depression, anxiety, suicide, self-esteem, life skills, time management, organization, empathy, respect, sexual identity, drug/alcohol prevention and intervention, and coping

Culture

Culture refers not only to the racial and ethnic makeup of a student but also refers to the social, political, and economic culture of the system in which a student lives. School counselors need to be mindful of how their own cultural perspective influences the development of school counseling core curriculum (Chung & Bemak, 2011). Chosen core curriculum topics and activities need to be developed and delivered in such a way that is inclusive for all students. School counselors need to be not only multiculturally competent but also familiar with the dominant culture as well as sub-cultures (SES, political, religious, social, family structures) that influence students at their school. School counselors should continuously assess their level of multicultural competency and seek continuing education for further training and development (Ratts, Singh, Nassar-McMillan, Butler, & McCullough, 2015). The *Multicultural and Social Justice Counseling Competencies* (2015) is a resource tool that offers counselors a framework for understanding areas of competency for their professional work.

When providing counseling lessons on cultural awareness and cultural identity exploration, school counselors should be mindful of the messages they send via their activities and consider how their lessons will communicate diversity as an opportunity for learning, growth, and a contribution to life (Roaten & Schmidt, 2009). As well, lessons should be reflective of communicating that differences are valuable, and all persons deserve respect regardless of their differences. School counselors must be mindful of their own biases, privilege, and preconceived notions to avoid constructing or delivering a lesson that is not reflective of the aforementioned ideals (Lee & Picano, 2013). Lessons may reflect and include teaching empathy and positive regard for differences, acceptance of others in lieu of different beliefs, and conflict management.

Ethics

The ASCA School Counselor Competencies (ASCA, 2012b) advises that the school counselor must navigate school and district policies, state laws and regulations, and professional ethics when demonstrating a professional attitude (ASCA, II-C-4, 2012b). The ASCA Code of Ethics (ASCA, 2016) details the areas of practice that school counselors need to be competent in and aware of. School counseling core curriculum and activities avoid putting students in positions of physical and emotional harm. Additionally, school counselors are charged to "Develop and maintain professional relationships and systems of communication with faculty, staff and administrators to support students" (ASCA Code of Ethics, 2016, p. 6). When developing school counseling core curriculum, ethical practice includes collaboration and support from teachers and administration when school counselors determine topics, activities, and time schedules for delivery.

Learning

Learning styles of students differ based on development level, cognitive ability, intelligence style, cultural influences, and learning preferences. School counselors need to be aware of the influence of the aforementioned areas and intentionally plan their school counseling core curriculum while incorporating these influences. The school counselors' competencies need to include using technology for delivery aspects of their programming. Therefore, it is important to be familiar with using media in school counseling core curriculum, appropriate computer and cell phone apps that support the learning concepts, online technology such as shared files, online classrooms, and school-wide management platforms. As students become more involved and affected by technology, it is imperative that school counselors know how to integrate technology into their school counseling core curriculum plans.

Delivery Methods

Delivery of school counseling core curriculum depends on several factors: school level, weekly and monthly schedules, daily job functions of the school counselor, and access to materials and technology. School counselor caseloads are often out of the recommended ratio of 1:250 (ASCA, 2012a). Direct services have a decreasing trend in the progression from elementary to high school (Studer, Diambra, Breckner, & Heidel, 2011). School counselors meet with administrators and teachers to determine a schedule for classroom, group, and individual counseling services. Consistency of delivery is important for optimal attainment of constructs delivered. School counselors need to consider how they will maximize their efforts to deliver aspects of their school counseling core curriculum. Posters in hallways, e-newsletters, morning announcements, videos in classrooms, PowerPoint presentations sent to staff and faculty, shared drives for students, parents and staff to access resources, and guest speakers are some examples of how school counselors provide important information to the learning community.

Elementary school counselors spend more time providing classroom lessons, group counseling, and individual support for students (Wittmer & Clark, 2007). Lessons range between 20–60 minutes in duration depending on the ages of the children. More often lesson times are about 30 minutes, but they may be only 20 minutes for very young children and 60 minutes for high school students. School counselors work with administration and teachers to develop a time schedule for each grade and/or class of students to be seen on a consistent basis. School counselors utilize monthly topics—core development constructs (self-esteem, bullying, boundaries, etc.), character education topics, or identified targets (as identified in needs assessments including depression, divorce, and social skills)—to guide the scheduling and structuring of their lessons. Utilizing community partners (e.g., police officers, career representatives, health profession representative) maximizes the preventative efforts school counselors employ when delivering school counseling core curriculum.

Middle school counselors provide classroom, group, and individual interventions, taking into consideration their daily job function responsibilities (Wittmer & Clark, 2007). Caseloads of students can increase as the school levels progress, affecting a counselor's ability to deliver core curriculum lessons. As social/emotional/academic topics increase in depth for older students, the school counselor provides group counseling and individual counseling for interventions. School counselors work with teachers and administration to identify classes that, when missed, provide the least academic infringement for students. School counselors also utilize outside resources and collaboration for school-wide efforts to deliver aspects of school counseling core curriculum: community mental health agencies, drug/alcohol prevention programming, college and admissions representatives, and so forth.

High school counselors provide similar services and take similar approaches as mentioned for middle school counselors. High school counselors focus more intentionally on college and career readiness as students are nearing the completion of secondary education and preparing to enter the adult and working world (Wittmer & Clark, 2007) [see Chapter 8]. School counseling core curriculum strongly connects the personal and social aspects to job and college readiness, family and life planning, self-management, and healthy life choices. Classroom lessons are taught less frequently due to the needs of academic and career planning. High school counselors utilize community collaboration and resources to maximize their school-wide school counseling core curriculum delivery similarly as middle school and elementary school counselors do. A community resource book that encompasses information on licensed professional counselors, marriage and family therapists, social workers, drug and alcohol counselors, treatment facilities, nonprofits that provide essential services to families, faith-based social services, and so forth is essential for all counselors to have available to make appropriate referrals to students and their parents.

Developing Curriculum

Efficiently written curriculum, whether for classrooms, specific grade levels, or school-wide programming, should contain the areas listed as follows. These areas are constructed and written into individual, group, and comprehensive curriculum lessons. See Appendix 2.2 for examples of lesson templates.

- Topic
- ASCA Mindsets Addressed
- Purpose
- Rationale
- SMART Goal/Objective
- Time Length (minutes, weeks, months): School counselors work with teachers and administration to determine appropriate days/times for delivery of core curriculum lessons.
- Intended Audience: classroom, grade-level, and school-wide
- Delivery Procedures: Determine if using; lectures, individual work, pair-work, worksheets, books, materials and space available.
- Learning and Developmental Considerations: ages of students, learning styles, intelligence levels, ideal method of delivery for ages and construct
- Materials Needed/Technology Used
- Resources for Parents and Teachers: to reinforce learning.
- Evaluation Methods

Topics are chosen according to students' developmental level, school needs, referral reasons, assessment reports, and state-mandated school counseling core curriculum. The Mindsets (ASCA, 2014) serve as a foundation for core competencies that students should hold and rationale for the chosen construct or topic. The purpose and rationale provide the evidence and support for the chosen topics and lesson. School counselors will benefit from researching their topic to identify the recommended practices and gain knowledge of what works best for the topic on which they are providing support or interventions. The goal or objective is what the school counselor wants the students to walk away with after the lesson, series of lessons, or target intervention. Goals and objectives are clear, specific, measurable, and realistic to achieve. When planning a series of lessons, the school counselor identifies one larger goal or objective from which to operate. The series of lessons all work towards attaining the object or goal and act as curricular threads and are in alignments with the comprehensive school counseling program.

A clearly identified lesson plan aids the counselor in staying organized, considering classroom management needs (spacing, student needs, behavior), and allows the counselor to generate a post-lesson plan. The steps in the procedure are the intentional activities a school counselor chooses to implement and meet the goals or objectives. Activities and action items in a lesson reflect development, cultural considerations, and ethical boundaries. Being conscious of time allotted in a lesson is important to avoid overcomplicating a lesson or planning for too much to do.

Materials and technology needs reflect the items that will aid in delivery of the activities identified to attain the goal or objective. The materials and technology chosen depend on what is available at the site, budgets to purchase items, and items that best aid the lesson. School counselors are charged to be competent in technology as well as execute ethical boundaries when using technology or social media in their lessons (see ASCA Code of Ethics, 2016). Identifying evaluation methods ensures the school counselor is assessing lessons for successful attainment of the identified objectives or goals and aiding in editing or restructuring school counseling core curriculum. See Appendix 2.3 for examples.

Conclusion

School counselors develop and deliver school counseling core curriculum school-wide, in classrooms, and with groups and individuals to support student success and decrease the achievement gap. School counseling core curriculum can be used as a platform to advocate for and provide emotional, social, and academic services that students need, and may otherwise not be getting, to have access to healthy holistic development. School counselors assess the climate and needs of students, parents, and staff when determining curriculum topics. School counselors are intentional and deliberate in incorporating best practices and developmental, ethical, cultural, and learning considerations into their curriculum development. Evaluating for efficacy is a critical component when determining continued school counseling core curriculum efforts.

Activities

1. Divide the class into small groups and assign an assessment to each group (e.g., secondary assessment for parents, elementary assessment for teachers, etc.) to create. Assessments can be found on the Internet for examples of questions to ask.
2. Using the template in Appendix 2.2., create a school counseling core curriculum lesson for a specific grade level.
3. Investigate several websites for companies that sell pre-packaged school counseling core curriculum. Create a rubric to evaluate the appeal of each of the curricula (e.g., cost, reviews from counselors who have used the product, trial period, number of students who would be impacted by the product, etc.).
4. Brainstorm community partners who could assist with school counseling core curriculum. Name the partner and how it could help.
5. Discuss how school counselors can find the time to deliver lessons during the school year. Think about the academic calendar and the other tasks in which school counselors engage.
6. Create a staff development that could be presented in 15 or 20 minutes at a faculty meeting that explains to teachers and administrators why school counseling core curriculum is an integral function of the school counseling program.

Resources

The ASCA Competencies:

www.schoolcounselor.org/asca/media/asca/home/SCCompetencies.pdf

The ASCA Code of Ethics:
www.schoolcounselor.org/asca/media/asca/Ethics/EthicalStandards2016.pdf

Multicultural and Social Justice Counseling Competencies:
www.counseling.org/docs/default-source/competencies/multicultural-and-social-justice-counseling-competencies.pdf?sfvrsn=20

West Virginia Department of Education:
http://wvde.state.wv.us/forms/counseling-assessment/?level=m
http://wvde.state.wv.us/forms/counseling-assessment/

What Works Clearinghouse:
https://ies.ed.gov/ncee/wwc/

References

American School Counselor Association (2012a). *The ASCA National Model: A framework for school counseling programs* (3rd ed.). Alexandria, VA: Author.

American School Counselor Association (2012b). *School counselor competencies.* Retrieved from www.schoolcounselor.org/asca/media/asca/home/SCCompetencies.pdf

American School Counselor Association (2014). *Mindsets and behaviors for student success.* Retrieved from www.schoolcounselor.org/asca/media/asca/home/MindsetsBehaviors.pdf

American School Counselor Association (2016). *Ethical standards for school counselors.* Retrieved from www.schoolcounselor.org/asca/media/asca/Ethics/EthicalStandards2016.pdf

Bemak, F., & Chung, R. C. (2005). Advocacy as a critical role for urban school counselors: Working toward equity and social justice. *Professional School Counseling, 8*(3), 196–202.

Borders, L. D., & Drury, S. M. (1992). Comprehensive school counseling programs: A review for policymakers and practitioners. *Journal of Counseling and Development, 70,* 487–498.

Brown, D., & Trusty, J. (2005). *Designing and leading comprehensive school counseling programs: Promoting student competence and meeting student needs.* Belmont, CA: Thomson/Brooks/Cole.

Carey, J. C., & Dimmitt, C. (2008). A model for evidence-based elementary school counseling: Using school data, research, and evaluation to enhance practice. *The Elementary School Journal, 108*(5), 422–430.

Chung, R. C-Y., & Bemak, F. (2011). Multicultural social justice leadership strategies: Counseling and advocacy with immigrants. *Journal for Social Action in Counseling and Psychology*, *3*(1), 86–102.

Dimmitt, C., Carey, J. C., & Hatch, T. (2007). *Evidence- based school counseling: Making a difference with data-driven practices*. Thousand Oaks, CA: Corwin Press.

Dollarhide, C. T. (2003). School counselors as program leaders: Applying leadership contexts to school counseling. *Professional School Counseling*, *6*(5), 304–309.

Erford, B. T. (2015). *Transforming the school counseling profession*. Upper Saddle River, NJ: Pearson.

Hatch, T. (2014). *The use of data in school counseling*. Thousand Oaks, CA: Corwin Press.

Henderson, P., & Gysbers, N. C. (1998). *Leading and managing your school guidance program staff*. Alexandria, VA: American Counseling Association.

Institute of Education Services. (n.d.). *What works clearinghouse*. Retrieved from https://ies.ed.gov/ncee/wwc/

Lee, C., & Picano, K. E. (2013). Accommodating diversity by analyzing practices of teaching. *Teacher Education and Special Education*, *36*(2), 132–144.

Ratts, J. M., Singh, A. A., Nassar-McMillan, S., Butler, S. K., & McCullough, J. R. (2015). *Multicultural and social justice counseling competencies*. American Counseling Association. Retrieved from www.counseling.org/docs/default-source/competencies/multicultural-and-social-justice-counseling-competencies.pdf?sfvrsn=20

Roaten, G. K., & Schmidt, E. A. (2009). Using experiential activities with adolescents to promote respect for diversity. *Professional School Counseling*, *12*(4), 309–314.

Sink, C. A. (Ed.). (2005). *Contemporary school counseling: Theory, research, and practice*. Boston, MA: Houghton-Mifflin.

Studer, J. R., Diambra, J. F., Breckner, J. A., & Heidel, R. E. (2011). Obstacles and successes in implementing the ASCA national model in schools. *Journal of School Counseling*, *9*(2), 1–26.

VanZandt, Z., & Hayslip, J. (2001). *Developing your school counseling program: A handbook for systemic planning*. Belmont, CA: Brooks/Cole.

Wittmer, J., & Clark, M. A. (2007). *Managing your school counseling program: K-12 developmental strategies* (3rd ed.). Minneapolis, MN: Educational Media Corporation.

Appendix 2.1

Staff Assessment

Dear Staff of X Elementary,

I want to let you know I will do my best in offering my assistance to you in order to help our students succeed.

My number-one goal is maintaining the counseling program so to serve our students on academic, social, and emotional levels. I would love to have some feedback from you about the needs you see in these areas. Below you will find a needs assessment, and your input would be very helpful for me in planning the year and "critical areas" of focus. If you could fill this out and return it to my box or my room, I would greatly appreciate it! At anytime, feel free to give ideas, a student referral, feedback, or a "heads up."

Looking forward to this year,

Counselor

Your Name: ______________________

Position ____________________

1. How do you feel I should access students with needs (e.g., staff referral, student self-referral, sign-up sheet)? ____________________
   ____
   ____
2. Students need to know more about . . . ________________________
   ____
   ____
3. (please answer a, b, and c if applicable) **Would everyone please answer d even if you will not be having class meetings.** I would like to know what you see as pertinent issues to our students.
   a. I would like the counselor to have classroom meetings? Yes No

b. How often ____________? (once a month, once a week, 8 weeks total, etc.)
c. When _______________?
d. Topic requests: Check the 10 topics you would like the counselor to do in Counselor Corner (classroom meetings). Then number them by which one is your favorite, number one to ten, one being your top pick. Please note, if you would like more topics covered, please let me know.

Topic	✓	1–10
Abuse		
Anger Management		
Children of Alcoholics		
Conflict Management (Talk it Out)		
Dealing with Grief and Loss (covers several types of loss)		
Dealing with Divorce		
Families (Sibling Order)		
Feelings		
Fitting In		
Friendship		
Learning Styles		
Listening Skills		
Nonverbal Communication		
Self Esteem		
Social Skills		
Stress Management		
Test-Taking Skills		
Work and Study Habits		
Goal Setting		
Drugs and Alcohol		
Personal Safety		
Respecting Differences in Others and One's Self		
Other Suggested Topics:		

In addition, certain topics are federal mandates that need to be covered, such as bullying and various forms of harassment. I will work with you to schedule these mandatory trainings.

4. I hope to also conduct counseling groups for special needs that arise. Please list group topics you would like to see me offer or any other program you would like me to look at offering:
   ____
   ____
   ____

   If you have a student you would like to SST, please let me know and I will get the paperwork to you. Also, if there is a project with which you would like the peer helpers or middle school aides to help, let me know. Keep me updated on peer helpers' behavior so I can tweak it if we need to.

Appendix 2.2

Lesson Plan Template

School Name:	
Contact:	
Benchmarks & ASCA Mindset & Behaviors Addressed	
Standard(s) addressed:	
Instructional Development	
Grade Level(s):	
Title:	
Summary/Purpose	
Time Frame:	
Procedure:	
How will mastery of the counseling standard(s) be evaluated?	
Learning Resources	
Resources needed: (e.g., technology resources, media resources, books, web sites)	
Citation(s): You may include copyrighted materials in "resources needed," but do not reproduce copyrighted materials in your lesson plan. Non-copyrighted materials need to be reproduced and included with your lesson plan. Cite sources here.	
Collaborative Partners: (e.g., advisory teachers, other teachers, community resource people)	
Contact information *(optional)*	
Telephone:	
E-Mail:	

Appendix 2.3

Student Lesson Feedback Form

Name ________________________________ Grade ______
Lesson being evaluated ___________________________
Date ____

Circle appropriate number: 1 = not at all 5 = extremely

This lesson topic was helpful.

1 2 3 4 5

The lesson held my attention.

1 2 3 4 5

The lesson was easy to understand.

1 2 3 4 5

What I liked about this lesson:

____

What I liked about this lesson:

____

What I did not like about this lesson:

____

I would suggest the following to improve the lesson

____

Additional comments:

3

Individual Student Planning

Dr. Glenda S. Johnson

ASCA NATIONAL MODEL THEME

Leadership

Advocacy

ASCA SCHOOL COUNSELOR PROFESSIONAL COMPETENCIES

III-A-3. Counseling theories and techniques in different settings, such as individual planning, group counseling and classroom guidance

III-B-2. Facilitates individual planning

III-B-2a. Understands individual student planning as a component of a comprehensive program

III-B-2b. Develops strategies to implement individual student planning, such as strategies for appraisal, advisement, goal-setting, decision-making, social skills, transition or post-secondary planning

III-B-2c. Helps students establish goals, and develops and uses planning skills in collaboration with parents or guardians and school personnel and uses various career assessment techniques to assist students in understanding their abilities and career interests

III-B-2d. Understands career opportunities, labor market trends, and global economics

III-B-2e. Helps students learn the importance of college and other post-secondary education and helps students navigate the college admissions process

III-B-2f. Understands the relationship of academic performance to the world of work, family life and community service

III-B-2g. Understands methods for helping students monitor and direct their own learning and personal/social and career development

IV-B-3g. Uses school data to identify and assist individual students who do not perform at grade level; and do not have opportunities and resources to be successful in school

ASCA PRINCIPLES

Principle 10: The delivery component dividing program activities into program components of direct services (school counseling core curriculum, individual student planning and responsive services) and indirect services (referrals, consultation and collaboration) is the most effective and efficient means for organizing the program

Principle 11: The elements and strategies described as the delivery component for the school counseling program include all the means to have an impact on students' academic, career and personal/social development: direct student services (school counseling core curriculum, individual student planning and responsive services) and indirect student services (referrals, consultation and collaboration)

A.I. Responsibilities to Students

School counselors:

b. are concerned with the educational, academic, career, personal, and social needs and encourage the maximum development of every student.
d. are knowledgeable of laws regulations and policies relating to students and strive to protect and inform students regarding their rights.
e. promote the welfare of individual students and collaborate with them to develop an action plan for success.
f. consider the involvement of support networks valued by the individual students.

ASCA CODE OF ETHICS

A.2. Confidentiality School counselors:

a. inform individual students of the purposes, goals, techniques and rules of procedure under which they may receive counseling. Disclosure includes the limits of confidentiality in a developmentally appropriate manner. Informed consent requires competence on the part of students to understand the limits of confidentiality and therefore, can be difficult to obtain from students of a certain developmental level. Professionals are aware that even though every attempt is made to obtain informed consent it is not always possible and when needed will make counseling decisions on students' behalf. Recognize their primary obligation for confidentiality is to the students but balance that obligation with understanding of parents'/guardians' legal and inherent rights to be the guiding voice in their children's lives, especially in value-laden issues. Understand the need to balance students' ethical rights to make choices, their capacity to give consent or assent and parental or familial legal rights and responsibilities to protect these students and make decisions on their behalf.

A.3. Academic, Career/College/Post-Secondary Access and Personal/Social Counseling Plans

School counselors:

a.provide students with a comprehensive school counseling program that parallels the ASCA National Model with emphasis on working jointly with all students to develop personal/social, academic and career goals.

c.provide and advocate for individual students' career awareness, exploration and post-secondary plans supporting the students' right to choose from the wide array of options when they leave secondary education.

CACREP 2016 STANDARDS

Foundations

b. models of school counseling programs

Contextual Dimensions

a. school counselor roles as advocates, leaders, and system change agents in P-12 schools
c. school counselor roles in relation to college and career readiness

Practice

d. interventions to promote academic development
i. approaches to increase promotion and graduation rates
k. strategies to promote equity in student achievement and college access

Introduction

Individual student planning (ISP) falls under the delivery component of the ASCA National Model (2012) and is defined as school counselors coordinating ongoing systemic activities designed to assist in establishing personal goals and developing future plans (ASCA, 2012). The two main categories of ISP are appraisal and advisement (ASCA, 2012; Perera-Diltz & Mason, 2008) in the areas of academic, career, and personal/social (ASCA, 2012). For example, school counselors assist students in developing individual learning plans and transitioning from one grade level to the next (ASCA, 2012). The ASCA model recommends that school counselors devote a certain amount of their time (5–10%/elementary, 15–25%/middle, 25–35%/high school) to providing ISP as part of their delivery services. However, the amount of time spent on ISP varies contingent upon many factors, such as (a) school counselors' school/district/state-defined roles, (b) number of school counselors in the building, and (c) student demographics, etc. For instance, in a study conducted with school counseling interns located at a small university in the Midwest, Leuwerke, Bruinekool, and Lane (2008) found that the ISP time was significantly less than the ASCA's recommendations.

School counselors' delivery of ISP is not limited to conferencing one-on-one with individual students, but often includes meeting with small groups of students, parents, and school personnel (ASCA, 2012; Zambrano, Castro-Villarreal, & Sullivan, 2012). As an example, school counselors at all levels often meet with teachers, school psychologists, administrators, and other support personnel to discuss prevention, intervention, and remedial academic and behavioral student concerns.

School counselors have an opportunity to receive training on delivering ISP during their pre-service training while completing their field experience practicum and internship placements. Pre-service programs often include field experience requirements designed for interns to obtain the necessary experience in order to provide effective ISP services when they enter the profession. For example, Gibson (2009) described one pre-service program's requirements in which the school counselor in training is required to attend a minimum amount of student assistance team (SAT) meetings and ISP meetings. The school counselor intern is also required to work with some of the identified students individually or in groups as part of the strategies the SAT recommended.

High School

As previously noted, in comparison to their peers, high school counselors spend the most time delivering ISP services. Activities include college and career planning, interpreting test scores, academic counseling, and goal setting. Students themselves may seek the services of their high school counselors as they prepare to graduate and enter a post-secondary institution or the world of work. Specifically, at this level, school counselors may spend quite a bit of time assisting students with the college application process, enrolling and proctoring tests (i.e., SAT, AP exams, etc.).

Middle School

Middle school counselors spend less time on ISP than do high school counselors. Activities revolve around academic advising, career planning, and goal setting. Trusty, Niles, and Carney (2005) viewed middle school education planning in relation to elementary, high school, and post-secondary education; they believed that this is a critical developmental stage and suggested that more time needs to be devoted in the area of career planning at this level. To that end, the authors provided an education-career planning framework for middle school that is supported by outcome research and practically useful for middle school counselors and students. Zyromski and Joseph (2008) suggested that school counselors use of cognitive-behavioral therapy interventions when delivering ISP is "the most logical and educationally applicable interventions school counselors can use to impact academic achievement" (p. 3).

Elementary School

The least amount of time spent on ISP is at the elementary level. At this level, elementary school counselors spend more of their time on additional delivery services (i.e., school counseling core curriculum, individual and small group counseling). Academic achievement and college and career awareness are often the foci of these services. As previously mentioned, ISP services can be delivered to individuals, small groups, and may include parents as well as other school personnel. Some school counselors describe services delivered to all students as individual student planning. For example, in a qualitative study conducted by Johnson, Nelson, and Henriksen (2011), the participants were asked what is easy about delivering ISP services. One school counselor responded, "They love that . . . they love college day, career day" (p. 25). Her response indicated a belief that college and career day events presented to all students falls under the category of ISP.

Depending on the state/county/district, some school counselors may be assigned the role of coordinator for various programs. Johnson (2012) found that in several large districts, elementary school counselors were assigned the coordinator's role of various programs that included (a) gifted and talented, (b) dyslexia, (c) response to intervention (RtI), and (d) section 504. As part of the screening process and often throughout their enrollment in the programs, school counselors met with identified students for individual sessions.

The specific role played by the counselor will vary depending on districts/schools. For example, the school counselor may be assigned the role of gifted and talented coordinator. Duties involved with this role could include (a) attending a required number of staff development sessions; (b) administering academic screening instruments; (c) collecting referrals from teachers, parents, and students; (d) distributing inventories to teachers and parents; (e) organizing the information and completing a matrix; (f) submitting the information to the district coordinator and/or school committee for review; and (g) notifying the students, parents, and teachers of the committee's determination.

When delivering ISP services regardless of the school level (i.e., elementary, middle, high), counselors are reminded to use effective interventions (i.e., research-based, best practices) to obtain positive student outcomes (Fraser, 2012). In addition, Nelson, Tarabochia, and Koltz (2015) recommend the use of a model of student well-being, the PACES model. The authors provide suggestions that can be used when delivering ISP services to students. This model focuses on the use of strategies considering the five domains of Physical, Affective, Cognitive, Economic, and Social.

State Initiative and Federal Mandates

National Initiatives

Several states have their own comprehensive school counseling models (e.g., Texas, Missouri, and Utah), whereas other states (e.g., North Carolina, Nebraska) adopt the ASCA National Model (2012) as a guide for their comprehensive school counseling programs. Nonetheless, most, if not all, models include the delivery service of ISP as part of their respective models.

College and career readiness/awareness/planning is a focus of ISP at all levels. Preparing all students to have the option to enter post-secondary education/training when they graduate high school is a national/state focus. For example, the Dream 2020 campaign, initiated by former President Obama, called for the United States to regain its position of having the highest proportion of college graduates among nations. In response, Mrs. Obama's Reach Higher Campaign was created and called for the support of school counselors and mentors, as they are instrumental in assisting students transitioning from high school to college, especially underrepresented students and first-generation college students (Reach Higher Campaign, 2015).

The National Consortium for School Counseling and Post-Secondary Success (NCSCPS, 2017) was created to increase low-income and first-generation college students' access to higher education. This organization was created in response to the Reach Higher Campaign and continues its goal of equitable access for all students. School counselor leadership and strategic partnerships are the main focus of the NCSCPS, and include five critical areas for school counselors and college access professionals to be aligned and collaboratively implemented. These five areas are (1) research, (2) pre-service and in-service training, (3) standards and credentialing, (4) practice, and (5) policy—all designed to produce effective student post-secondary outcomes (NCSCPS, 2017).

District Policy

The amount and type of ISP services a school counselor provides can be impacted by district policy. ISP services can sometimes be a shared responsibility between the school counselor and other school personnel, such as the assistant principal or academic specialists. This collaborative approach can be used to allow more students to receive the individualized services that they need.

On the other hand, some districts require school counselors to coordinate a variety of programs (i.e., Section 504, Dyslexia, etc.), thus limiting the amount of time that school counselors can spend providing ISP. One school counselor reported that she was responsible for coordinating as many as five such additional programs (Johnson, 2012).

Some states (e.g., Wisconsin) require districts to provide academic student planning to all students (Wisconsin Department of Public Instruction, 2017). Teachers are often involved in this process, and many schools have instituted academic advising periods in the students' school schedule. These activities are delivered by the classroom teacher and have yielded positive student outcomes (2017).

Recommended Experiential Performance Discussion Points

This next section focuses on describing some of the activities that school counselors may typically conduct when delivering ISP services. The activities presented are taken from the literature, best practices from the field, and the author's school counseling experience at varying levels (i.e., elementary, middle, high) and in varied positions (i.e., general and special education counselor).

How to Conduct an Academic Review of Progress

School counselors have access to data that informs the need to provide ISP services in academic advising. Using the district's data management system, school counselors can run a report of their students' grades at various points during the semester to identify students who are not making adequate progress. Requests for academic advising are often made by teachers, parents, or students themselves.

When providing ISP services for academic review of progress, the school counselor can schedule 20-minute individual sessions with students. During this session, the school counselor reviews the limits of confidentiality with the student just as they would in any counseling session. As part of the session opening, the counselor would inform the student of the purpose of the session and the referral source, if any. The student's assent would then be obtained. Next, the counselor would review the student's grades. The school counselor could then ask the student to share the struggles they are experiencing in any course. The school counselor will listen intently to identify the cause of the academic struggles to identify the type of services (i.e., academic tutoring, intrapersonal conflicts within or outside of class/school, assistance with supplies, etc.) that may benefit the student. Once the cause has been identified, the school counselor and the student can brainstorm ways to address the concerns. Lastly, collaboratively, the school counselor and student develop a plan of action that includes a follow-up plan/date. The number of sessions the counselor and student has should be determined by the progress the student makes toward reaching their goal.

Meeting with all students individually may present a challenge for school counselors in a high school setting due to the number of students on their caseload. This further demonstrates the need and benefit of involving other school staff (i.e., skills specialists, assistant principals, etc.) to assist with advising and monitoring students' academic progress in order to develop planned interventions. One model I observed at a high school involved the school counselor, her intern, an assistant principal, and the college access coordinator. The students at this particular school were taking courses at the neighboring community college while simultaneously enrolled in high school. The four school personnel scheduled a time to visit classrooms and meet briefly one-on-one with individual students. Each professional carried a laptop to view the students' current academic information in their college courses. The school personnel (a) noted the student's academic progress, (b) collaboratively created a plan with the student, if needed, to address low or missing grades, and (c) documented the information on the student's monitoring form. This model provides a time-efficient way to meet with all students and demonstrates the collaborative role that school counselors and other professionals can share in addressing the needs of all students in academic ISP.

How to Conduct the Next Year's Planning and Registration

At the middle school level, counselors coordinate transitioning to high school and high school course selections. These tasks may be completed in a variety of formats. For instance, high school counselors may travel to the middle school and provide transitioning and high school course selections to the eighth-grade students in a prearranged format. Depending on the number of students, time available, and the needs of the student population, these presentations are presented in a whole-group format, two or three classes combined, individual classrooms, or individual groups of students, such as English Language Learner students. Regardless of the format, the middle school counselors often follow up with some students during an individual advisement session.

Whether this information is delivered by the high school counselors from the feeder school or the middle school counselors at the current schools, transition topics are covered. Topics often include (a) varying graduation plans, (b) required and elective courses, (c) high school credits and GPA, (d) structure of class periods, (e) joining clubs, and (f) scheduling specialty periods (i.e., athletics, dance team, swim team, honor choir, etc.). Schedule requests are often distributed to the students to complete with a deadline for submission to their middle school counselor.

Just as in middle school, student course selection and scheduling at the high school level can be completed in a variety of formats. The following example is one process school counselors can use when scheduling high school students for the following year. High school counselors can choose a two-week window in which to obtain students' requests for courses. School counselors can prepare a PowerPoint presentation that describes in detail the course selection process. This PowerPoint presentation can be delivered to all students by the school counselors and/or classroom teachers. If the presentation is delivered by the school counselors, classes can be combined and the presentation can be delivered in a place such as the cafeteria or auditorium. If the presentation is to be delivered by teachers, the school counselors could ask all of the first period teachers to deliver the presentation.

Prior to the scheduling presentations, the school counselors can prepare course selection forms for each student. Each form will have the required courses listed, space for electives, and a line for both the student and parent signatures. These forms can then be distributed to each student after they have viewed the presentation.

During the second week of the scheduling process, students can be provided a given time to report to the technology lab, where school counselors will be available. The counselors will verify each student's course selection, and students will then be asked to enter their selections into the scheduling program. Once all students have entered their courses, a query can be run to identify missing student's schedules. The school counselors can call for those students to come to the counseling suite to assist with entering their courses into the system.

How to Utilize the Master Schedule

Creating the master schedule is not typically the school counselor's responsibility. The master schedule is usually created by the assistant principal or another designee such as the technology specialist; however, in some schools and districts, the counselor is involved. As noted in the previous section, the most appropriate school counselor's role during registration procedures is to provide students and their parents with grade-specific course requirements and electives options and the process for choosing and submitting course requests. However, counselors may find themselves involved in creating the master schedule, if requested. The main information needed to create a master schedule is information regarding the number of course sections needed, the periods in a day, and the available teachers to teach those specific courses. With this information a matrix is created that involves, among many things, assigning teachers to specific courses, providing the teachers with a planning period, and avoiding conflicts. This information is entered into a scheduling program, or in some cases may be done by hand.

Hand Scheduling

In the previous sections, scheduling students and the master schedule, computer software programs are used by districts to handle this process. However, there are times when school counselors encounter students who need a schedule created by hand. An example of this can occur when the computer system is down. A hard copy of the master schedule is usually kept as a back-up for times such as these. After determining the courses the student needs, the counselor would then need to confer with the person in charge of the master schedule to find available seats open in the courses that the student needs. The school counselor then creates the student's schedule that lists the courses and time periods. Once the computer system is available, the counselor can enter the information into the system or provide a copy of the hand schedule to the person in charge of the master schedule.

How to Participate in Annual Individual Education Plan Meetings

Individual Education Plan (IEP) meetings are held for students who receive special services based on an identifying disability that requires accommodations that would not be received as a part of regular instruction and/or processes in the school day. A school counselor's involvement in this process can vary from no involvement at all to being a part of every IEP meeting held for a student. The counselor's role in IEP meetings could be as the chair of the Admission Review and Dismissal (ARD) meeting or simply as a member. If the counselor is the chair, he/she would follow the pre-determined agenda used in all ARD meetings. Sometimes the counselor acts as the person who provides empathy and understanding for parents who may be confused or alarmed that their student requires help outside of the mainstream programming.

Possible Counselor Roles in the IEP Process

As previously mentioned, before students are referred for the identification of their need for special services, they are referred to a committee to develop tiered interventions to address the students' challenges, whether behavioral or academic. This process is known as the Response to Intervention (RtI) process. A school counselor may be a part of the committee to address a student's inappropriate behavior. In this case, the school counselor could serve as a consultant as a child development specialist or may be more involved, such as developing a behavior intervention plan for the student.

The basic steps in completing a behavior intervention plan are as follows. Based on the information obtained in the committee meeting regarding the student's inappropriate behavior, the school counselor would determine the best time to observe the student. During the observation, the school counselor would make descriptive notes regarding the targeted behavior, the frequency of the behavior, and what happens before and after the behavior occurs. The school counselor would then meet with the student individually to discuss the behavior with the student. During this discussion the school counselor can look for (a) student strengths, (b) exceptions for when the behavior does not occur, and (c) student positive reinforcers to inform the development of a behavior plan. If enough specific information regarding the student's behavior was not obtained during the committee meeting, the school counselor may need to speak with the teacher and the parents to obtain additional information regarding the student.

Once this information has been obtained, the school counselor can develop the draft of a behavior plan. The behavior intervention plan should, at a minimum, contain (a) a behavioral description of the appropriate behavior expected, (b) under what conditions the targeted behavior is expected, (c) how data will be measured and collected, (d) the roles of persons involved in the plan, and (e) a follow-up date. This draft can then be shared with the committee and the student for input, revisions, and acceptance. It is important that as many stakeholders as possible be involved in the process of creating and implementing the behavior intervention plan to aid in the student's success.

Response to Intervention

Additionally, the school counselor may be involved in RtI process for students to determine if a referral for an IEP is warranted. Parents or school personnel may initiate this process. Federal guidelines require a timely response to the request. The process of identifying students who need special services is federally mandated with specific guidelines that need to be followed to ensure that students receive the appropriate services based on their disability. All persons involved with this process receive the necessary training to ensure their compliance with their respective roles. The goal of this section is to briefly discuss some of the roles the school counselor may have in regard to the IEP process.

Communicating With Parents and Guardians

How to Place and Respond to Parent Phone Calls

School counselors will often find themselves placing phone calls to parents and receiving phone calls from parents. Having a specific time of day to return and make phone calls will alleviate the stress of trying to stop in the middle of other tasks and respond to parents. Generally, it is acceptable to return and make phone calls at the end of the day when students have been dismissed. A voice message on your phone can indicate that phone calls will be returned at the end of the day. The nature of the phone call will determine the appropriate counselor's approach to effectively communicate with the parent. If the counselor initiates the call, it is important to begin the call by expressing the counselor's genuine interest in working with the parent in the best interest of the student. For example, the counselor may say, "Hello, Mrs. Brown, my name is Glenda Johnson and I am the school counselor at Smith High School. How are you today? I am calling to discuss our current academic concerns with Javier. Before I share my concerns, I was wondering if you have any concerns regarding his academic progress at this time." Based on the response, the counselor determines the best approach. If the parent has identified a concern, but is unsure as to how to assist their child, the counselor provides the parent with information regarding resources that can be provided by the school (e.g., tutoring, teacher conference, etc.). If the parent is not aware of any student concerns, behaviorally or academically, the school counselor would then provide the parent with factual information while simultaneously accessing whether a face-to-face parent conference would be the best approach. Regardless of the parent's response, the school counselor will always want to convey an interest in working with the parent in addressing the student's concern.

How to Provide Test Results to Students and Parents

School counselors engage in test interpretation with individual students, small groups of students, or during core curriculum classroom lessons. Some school counselors' caseloads may prevent them from meeting with each student individually. However, academic testing is confidential, and students may not be able to maintain these confidences due to age and immaturity, and they may not understand the actual meaning of the test results. Therefore, conducting informational sessions with parents regarding how to interpret test results might be more appropriate and can eliminate many individual phone calls and appointments. Most standardized tests include individual and group results, which include significant information on student strengths and weaknesses. These reports also contain directions for interpreting the results, which are fairly user friendly.

Results from interest inventories and career readiness types of assessments are more appropriate for students to share with each other if they so desire. Also, students are more able to understand the meaning of such assessments. Therefore, using a small-group approach or classroom lessons may be a more time-efficient practice in these cases. Infused within these activities are the college and career preparedness.

Career, College, and Technical/Trade Readiness

The high school counselor's role in delivering ISP in college and career preparedness is vital to student's post-high-school success (Reese, 2010), and often involves teachers (see Chapter 8 for extensive information on post-secondary opportunities). For example, the school counselor can collaborate with the career and technical education (CTE) teachers at the high school level, or other subject area teachers at the middle school level, to assist all students in developing a four-year plan for high school (grades 9–12) based on their chosen career. The students' interests can be assessed using interest inventories, achievement tests, and their own personal goals and extracurricular activities. Although these plans often change before the students graduate, the school counselor can identify the student's current post-secondary plans and provide information to the students based on their personal goals.

ASCA Ethical Considerations

Within the 2016 ASCA Ethical Standards for School Counselors (ASCA, 2016) document are many codes that are relevant to school counselors and the delivery component of ISP. The list of codes taken from the ASCA Ethical Standards (2016) that are applicable to ISP and provide guidelines for school counselors to follow when providing this service can be found at the beginning of this chapter.

Responsibilities to Students

When providing ISP, it is a best practice to provide services to all students in collaboration with their support system. Always seek to obtain the student's assent, regardless of age, when providing ISP services. In addition, it is imperative for school counselors to remember that the students' support system may involve members outside of, or in addition to, their parents/guardians. Therefore, school counselors are advised to be mindful of who has a right to the student's written or verbal information according to FERPA (2015), state, and district guidelines. Many times, in my practice as a school counselor, grandparents, foster parents, the parents' current partners, and step-parents were genuinely concerned about the student's welfare. While I embraced all the support others were providing for the student, I had to remain diligent in checking students' records to ensure that I had permission to speak with the person regarding a student's academic, personal/social, and college and career concerns. When working with high school students, always check your state's statutes regarding if, or at what age, students can give permission for you to share their information with members of their support system who are not their parents/guardians.

Confidentiality

It is wise to discuss confidentiality with students before beginning the ISP sessions. When delivering these services to a small group of students, be sure to stress the importance of keeping confidential information that is shared, but always include a statement explaining that confidentiality, although expected, cannot be guaranteed. Because ISP often involves academic advisement and test interpretation (especially at the middle and high school levels), school counselors are to safeguard individual students' information when working with small groups. Always allow the students to decide if they want to share their individual grades/scores with other students. I often shared with my students that if they discussed information shared in the group with students outside of the group that they would not be allowed to continue meeting as a group. At the elementary level, students sometimes reported back to me that one of the group members shared information about their classmates with other students who were not a part of the group. When this occurred, the first time the student who shared the information was given a warning. If it happened again, the student was not allowed to return to the group. Confidentiality is important to members in a group at all school levels (i.e., elementary, middle, and high), especially when discussing school performance, grades, and academics.

Academic, Career/College/Post-Secondary Access and Personal/Social Counseling Plans

School counselors are trained to advocate for equitable access for all students regardless of differences. This includes advocating for access to advanced course work, career options, and students' personal goals. When reviewing data, goal setting, and exploring career options during ISP activities, school counselors can identify any perceived barriers and advocate for the removal of those barriers, as well as teach students to become self-advocates.

Addressing Diversity in Individual Student Planning

School counselors are called to provide a comprehensive school counseling program to serve all students (ASCA, 2012). However, some students, based on certain characteristics (i.e., ethnicity, sexual orientation, etc.), may experience unequal treatment in the school setting. In reviewing the literature, some of these inequities were found among (1) students receiving special services (Adkison-Bradley et al., 2007; Mayes, Hines, & Harris, 2014; Milsom, 2007); (2) students from minority backgrounds (Martinez, 2013; McLeod, 2005); and (3) potential first-generation college students (Bryant & Nicolas, 2011), thus demonstrating the need for school counselors to intentionally focus on providing equitable service to all students. This can be done through ISP (Dipeolu, Storlie, & Johnson, 2014; Studer, 2016; Vela, Flamez, Sparrow, & Lerma, 2016). More importantly, school counselors have an ethical responsibility to intentionally focus on students' attainment of equitable access to academic, personal/social and career knowledge/choices/services (ASCA, 2016).

As a counselor of students who were deaf or hard of hearing, in ISP, I met with students to identify their specific interests and abilities. Once identified, I served as an advocate to obtain their access to the extracurricular activities afforded to their hearing peers. My advocacy efforts included meeting with sponsors, communicating with the director to acquire interpretation services, communicating with the transportation department, and most importantly facilitating communication among students, home, and school. These students were given the same opportunities as their hearing peers to participate in athletic team tryouts (e.g., basketball, soccer), student social groups (e.g., a ninth-grade girls' group), and electives of their choice as opposed to what was scheduled for them. This inclusive environment afforded the students an opportunity to feel a sense of belonging to the entire school environment.

As an elementary-level counselor in a district that served mostly Title I students that included English Language Learners, the teachers and parents were included in creating a college-going culture (i.e., speakers, community college van visits, printed information provided about ways to pay for college). Services that I viewed as ISP were provided in a school-wide format.

As a high school counselor enrolling English as a Second Language students in my district, I spent time with each student individually, taking a detailed school history and assessing the students' English fluency using a test to determine their appropriate course placement based on state and district guidelines. During this one-on-one time with students, I got to know the students to ascertain any other needs they may have as they transitioned to our school and their new community.

When I became a school counselor, I continued this focus on celebrating diversity by supporting student groups, clubs, and organizations, including decorating my office with culturally relevant news articles, pictures, books, and so forth, to create a culture-rich, inviting environment. The delivery service of ISP to students from various backgrounds provides a way for school counselors to address some of the inequities these students face in the school setting. Although it is imperative to learn about differences, it is also important to note within-group differences. This can be accomplished by getting to know students as individuals and identifying their interests, skills, and abilities to account for this during advisement and planning.

Conclusion

Individual student planning (i.e., advising, goal setting, career planning) is a delivery component of a comprehensive school counseling plan. The national emphasis on preparing all students to graduate career-college ready, regardless of their background, provides guidelines for states to adopt to ensure that this focus is addressed. School counselors are in a unique position to assist students, parents, teachers, administrators, and other stakeholders in addressing this focus.

Providing ISP is an important component of a comprehensive school counseling program delivered by school counselors at all levels. These services can be delivered to individual students, small groups of students, and can often include teachers, other school personnel, and parents. Academic advising, personal/social concerns, and career services are the focus of ISP. The amount of time school counselors spend on delivering these services can vary depending on the level and the demographics of the students being served. As previously noted, high school counselors spend more time on ISP than their middle and elementary school counterparts. Although the time spent in this area varies according to school counselors' level (i.e., elementary, middle, and high school), the importance of providing this service to all students remains the same and is a vital component to the school counseling program.

Variables such as (a) the delivery format (i.e., meeting with individual students, small groups of students, whole school activities [i.e., career day, college week, etc.]); (b) the type of interventions (i.e., one-on-one student scheduling meetings, five-minute meetings, student assistance team meetings, etc.); (c) the demographics of the student body (e.g., students from low-SES households, English Language Learners, etc.); and (d) the assigned counselor's roles (e.g., scheduling) determines exactly how school counselors approach individual student planning. Continued professional development, the literature, research, and best practices enable school counselors to advocate for their roles in ISP and to provide the best counseling services to their clients.

Activities

1. Using the 5-Minute Meeting Format, role-play the counselor's role with both an elementary student and a secondary student.
2. Create a school counseling website page that addresses the important issues for individual student planning. Brainstorm what to include on your page with your peers, and then create your page either in a group or individually.
3. Role-play an individual student planning session with an eighth-grade student and her parents. You are helping the student plan for the transition from middle school to high school. What items will you have on your list of bullet points to discuss in this session?
4. A high school senior has come to you for advice about the following year. Should he stay at home and attend the local community college or move about five hours away from his home and attend a state university? He has been accepted at both.

Resources

Achieve Texas:

https://txcte.org/counselors/

National Career Development Association:

www.ncda.org

References

Adkison-Bradley, C. R., Kohler, P. D., Bradshaw, E., Applegate, E. B., Cai, X., & Steele, J. (2007). Career planning with students with and without disabilities: A study of Illinois school counselors. *Journal of School Counseling, 5*(11). Retrieved from www.jsc.montana.edu/articles/v5n11.pdf

American School Counselor Association. (2012). *ASCA national model: A framework for school counseling programs* (3rd ed.). Alexandria, VA: Author.

American School Counselor Association. (2016). *ASCA ethical standards for school counselors*. Alexandria, VA. Retrieved from www.schoolcounselor.org/asca/media/asca/Ethics/EthicalStandards2016.pdf

Bryant, J. K., & Nicolas, J. (2011). Supporting and preparing future first-generation college students in the high school environment: Implications for school counselors. *Michigan Journal of Counseling, 38*(2), 17–26, 10.

Council for Accreditation of Counseling and Related Educational Programs. (2016). Retrieved from www.cacrep.org/wp-content/uploads/2012/10/2016-CACREP-Standards.pdf

Dipeolu, A. O., Storlie, C., & Johnson, C. (2014). Transition to college and students with high functioning autism spectrum disorder: Strategy considerations for school counselors. *Journal of School Counseling, 12*(11). Retrieved from www.jsc.montana.edu/articles/v12n11.pdf

Family Education and Privacy Act (FERPA-2015). Retrieved from https://ed.gov/policy/gen/guid/fpco/ferpa/index.html

Fraser, D. (2012). College and career readiness and the ASCA model. In *ASCA national model: A framework for school counseling programs* (3rd ed.). Alexandria, VA: Author.

Gibson, D. M. (2009). Transforming internship: The use of contracts in school counselor education. *Journal of School Counseling, 7*(4). Retrieved from www.jsc.montana.edu/articles/v7n4.pdf

Gysbers, N., Stanley, J. B., Kosteck-Bunch, L., Magnuson, C. S., & Starr, M. F. (2011). *Missouri comprehensive guidance and counseling program*. Retrieved from https://dese.mo.gov/sites/default/files/Manual_2.pdf

Johnson, G. S. (2012). *Mentoring experiences and needs of novice professional school counselors: A qualitative study*. Doctoral Dissertation. Retrieved from ProQuest Dissertations and Theses Global (1318857980).

Johnson, G. S., Nelson, J., & Henriksen, R. C. (2011). Experiences of implementing a comprehensive guidance and counseling program at the elementary level. *Journal of Professional Counseling: Practice, Theory, and Research, 38*(3), 18–32.

Leuwerke, W. C., Bruinekool, R. M., & Lane, A. (2008). School counseling intern roles: An exploration of activities and comparison to the ASCA National Model. *Journal of School Counseling, 6*(8). Retrieved from www.jsc.montana.edu/articles/v6n8.pdf

Martinez, M. A. (2013). Helping Latina/o students navigate the college choice process: Considerations for secondary school counselors. *Journal of School Counseling, 11*(1). Retrieved from www.jsc.montana.edu/articles/v11n1.pdf

Mayes, R. D., Hines, E. M., & Harris, P. C. (2014). Working with twice-exceptional African American students: Information for school counselors. *Interdisciplinary Journal of Teaching and Learning, 4*(2), 125–139.

McLeod, K. (2005). Principals release these people! *Journal of School Counseling, 3*(6). Retrieved from www.jsc.montana.edu/articles/v3n6.pdf

Milsom, A. (2007). School counselor involvement in postsecondary transition planning for students with disabilities. *Journal of School Counseling, 5*(23). Retrieved from www.jsc.montana.edu/articles/v5n23.pdf

The National Consortium for School Counseling and Post-Secondary Success (NCSCPS). (2017). Retrieved from www.ncscps.org/

Nelson, M. D., Tarabochia, D. W., & Koltz, R. L. (2015). Paces: A model of student well-being. *Journal of School Counseling, 13*(19). Retrieved from www.jsc.montana.edu/articles/v13n19.pdf

North Carolina School Counselor Association. (2017). *Professional development ASCA model*. Retrieved from www.ncschoolcounselor.org/page-1535554

Perera-Diltz, D. M., & Mason, K. L. (2008). Ideal to real: Duties performed by school counselors. *Journal of School Counseling, 6*(26). Retrieved from www.jsc.montana.edu/articles/v6n26.pdf

Reach Higher Campaign. (2015). *The first lady's reach higher campaign*. Retrieved from https://obamawhitehouse.archives.gov/reach-higher

Reese, S. (2010). A leading role for career guidance counselors. *Techniques*, 16–19. Retrieved from www.actonline.org

Studer, J. R. (2016). *A guide to practicum and internship for school counselors-in-training* (2nd ed.). New York: Routledge.

Trusty, J., Niles, S. G., & Carney, J. V. (2005). Education-career planning and middle school counselors. *Professional School Counseling, 9*(2), 136–143.

Utah comprehensive counseling and guidance: Planning for Utah's future one student at a time. Retrieved from www.schools.utah.gov/cte/ccgp/

Vela, J. C., Flamez, B., Sparrow, G. S., & Lerma, E. (2016). Understanding support from school counselors as predictors of Mexican American adolescents' college-going beliefs. *Journal of School Counseling, 14*(7). Retrieved from www.jsc.montana.edu/articles/v14n7.pdf

Wisconsin Department of Public Instruction (WDPI). (2017). *Academic and career planning*. Retrieved from https://dpi.wi.gov/acp

Zambrano, E., Castro-Villarreal, F., & Sullivan, J. (2012). School counselors and school psychologists: Partners in collaboration for student success within RTI and CDCGP frameworks. *Journal of School Counseling, 10*(24). Retrieved from www.jsc.montana.edu/articles/v10n24.pdf

Zyromski, B., & Joseph, A. E. (2008). Utilizing cognitive behavioral interventions to positively impact academic achievement in middle school students. *Journal of School Counseling, 6*(15). Retrieved from www.jsc.montana.edu/articles/v6n15.pdf

Appendix 3.1

Elementary Five-Minute Meetings

Name:	Grade:
Date:	Teacher:

Academics

1. Do you like school?
2. Do you believe your teacher likes you?

College and Career

1. What job would you like to have when you grow up?
2. Who is your role model?

Personal/Social

1. Do you have many friends at school?
2. How are you feeling today? (Use feelings chart)

Follow-up Notes

____

____

____

____

Circle delivery services needed

Academic Individual Planning
Individual Counseling
Group Counseling
Consultation with Teacher/Parent/Administrator and/or Other Support Personnel

Appendix 3.2

High School Five-Minute Meetings

Student's Name:	Grade Level:
Date/Grading period:	Class Period:

Academics

1. What are your current grades in each of your courses?
2. Do you need any academic assistance at this time?

College and Career

1. What are your plans after high school graduation?
2. Do you need any assistance at this time in pursuit of your post-secondary goals?

Personal/Social

1. Do you have any personal/social problems at this time? If so, would you like to discuss those problems with me?

Follow-up Notes

____

____

____

____

____

Circle delivery services needed

Academic Individual Planning
Individual Counseling
Group Counseling
Consultation with Teacher/Parent/Administrator and/or Other Support Personnel

Appendix 3.3

Case Studies

Elementary

The school counselor contacted Mrs. Brown, a second-grade teacher, via email to schedule a time to conduct five-minute independent student planning sessions with the 22 students in her class. Mrs. Brown communicated that third period on Wednesday would be an optimum time for the counselor to visit. At the designated time, the school counselor set up a desk outside of Mrs. Brown's classroom and promptly began her five-minute individual planning sessions with each student. The school counselor completed a form (see Appendix 3.1) after meeting with each student.

The school counselor used the brief sessions to identify students who may benefit from follow-up services. Brian, an African American male student, required follow-up in the area of academics and behavior. When asked if he liked school, Brian reported that he did not like school. When asked why, he reported that neither his teacher nor the students liked him. Additionally, he stated that he always gets in trouble for not completing his in-class and homework assignments. When asked what he wanted to be when he grows up, he responded that he wanted to be a policeman.

Based on the information the school counselor gathered during the five-minute meeting with Brian, the school counselor asked if Brian would be interested in meeting for individual counseling sessions. He agreed, and the school counselor sent home a form requesting parent permission for counseling. Brian returned the signed form to the counselor the next day.

The school counselor met with Brian for four individual counseling sessions. During the first session, Brian and the school counselor cooperatively developed the goals of staying on task and completing in-class and homework assignments. In cooperation with Brian, the teacher, and his parent, the school counselor developed a behavior intervention plan.

The school counselor used the four counseling sessions, over the next four weeks, to teach, role-play, and reinforce the skills of staying on task and completing assignments. Additionally, a chart was completed by the teacher that measured Brian's on-task and completion behavior. The parent reviewed and signed the behavior chart daily. Brian's teacher and parent agreed to reinforce Brian's progress toward goal completion both at home and at school. At the completion of four weeks, Brian was making progress

toward his stated goals and reported that he liked school and was beginning to make friends now that he was not getting into trouble as much.

High School

The school counselor emailed the ninth-grade English teacher, Mrs. Jones, to schedule a time to meet with each of her classes during the following week. Mrs. Jones provided the counselor with times and days that she could meet with each section of her English course. The next Thursday, the counselor set up a desk outside of Mrs. Jones's door in preparation for five-minute meetings with each student.

The school counselor met Carla, a ninth-grade Latina student, during her second period class. Carla shared that she was passing all of her courses; the school counselor confirmed this information on her laptop computer, which she took with her to all of her class meetings. However, when asked about personal/social concerns, Carla shared that her family's apartment building caught on fire two months ago and that they now live with relatives in another school district. Carla shared that she has accumulated a couple of absences because she is sometimes unable to secure a ride to her previous bus stop for the 6:00 a.m. pick-up. After three unexcused absences, Carla will not be able to receive credit in her current courses. The school counselor asked if Carla would like to work with her on a plan to ensure that Carla was able to attend school every day. Carla expressed interest in working with the counselor and shared that she was unaware of the counselor's ability to assist her with concerns regarding absences.

The school counselor, in conjunction with the school's homelessness coordinator, communicated with Carla's parents, the administrative staff, teachers, and district transportation and identified Carla as a student who qualified for services under the McKinney Vento Homelessness Act. Bus transportation was provided for Carla that enabled her to board the bus at her temporary address with her family members.

4

Responsive Services

Dr. Robika Modak Mylroie and
Dr. Kimberly McGough

ASCA NATIONAL MODEL THEMES

Leadership

Advocacy

Collaboration

Systemic Change

ASCA SCHOOL COUNSELOR PROFESSIONAL COMPETENCIES

IV-B-3. Provides responsive services.

IV-B-3a. Lists and describes interventions used in responsive services, such as individual/small-group counseling and crisis response.

IV-B-3c. Demonstrates an ability to provide counseling for students during times of transition, separation, heightened stress and critical change.

IV-B-3d. Understands what defines a crisis, the appropriate response and a variety of intervention strategies to meet the needs of the individual, group or school community before, during and after crisis response.

IV-B-3e. Provides team leadership to the school and community in a crisis.

IV-B-3f. Involves appropriate school and community professionals as well as the family in a crisis situation.

IV-B-3g. Understands the nature of academic, career and personal/social counseling in schools and the similarities and differences among school counseling and other types of counseling, such as mental health, marriage and family and substance abuse counseling, within a continuum of care.

IV-B-3h. Understands the role of the school counselor and the school counseling program in the school crisis plan.

ASCA PRINCIPLES

Principle 3: Some students need more assistance in accomplishing the age-appropriate academic, career, and personal/social developmental tasks. These students benefit from preventative or remedial interventions specifically designed to help them achieve tasks appropriate to their developmental level.

Principle 4: School counselors are qualified to make contributions to all students' development in the areas of academic (educational), career, and personal/social development.

Principle 5: School counselors can design and deliver interventions to meet students' developmental needs and to meet students' needs for prevention and remediation, thereby helping to close gaps between specific groups of students and their peers.

Principle 6: School counselors' interventions in students' academic, career, and personal/social development help students acquire and apply knowledge, skills, and attitudes promoting development in those three dimensions of human growth.

Principle 7: School counselors can help other adults enhance their work with students' academic/educational, career, and personal-social development and for the purpose of removing barriers to individual students' success.

Principle 10: The delivery component dividing program activities into program components of direct services (school counselor core curriculum, individual student planning and responsive services) and direct services (referrals, consultation, and collaboration) is the most effective and efficient means for organizing the program.

ASCA ETHICAL STANDARDS FOR SCHOOL COUNSELORS (2016)

A.9.a. Inform parents/guardians and/or appropriate authorities when a student poses a serious and foreseeable risk of harm to self or others.

A.9.b. Use risk assessments with caution. If risk assessments are used by the school counselor, an intervention plan should be developed and in place prior to this practice.

A.9.c. Do not release a student who is a danger to self or others until the student has proper and necessary support.

A.9.d. Report to parents/guardians and/or appropriate authorities when students disclose a perpetrated or a perceived threat to their physical or mental well-being.

CACREP STANDARDS 2016

Section 5-G, Entry-Level Specialty Areas, School Counseling

Foundations
1.d. Models of school-based collaborations and consultation

Contextual Dimensions
2.b. School counselor roles in consultation with families, P-12 and post-secondary school personnel, and community agencies

2.e. School counselor roles and responsibilities in relation to the school emergency management plans, and crises, disasters, and trauma

2.g. Characteristics, risk factors, and warning signs of students at risk for mental health and behavioral disorders

2.i. Signs and symptoms of substance abuse in children and adolescents as well as the signs and symptoms of living in a home where substance abuse occurs

2.k. Community resources and referral resources

2.n. Legal and ethical considerations specific to school counselors

Practice
3.d Interventions to promote academic development

3.f. Techniques of personal/social counseling in school settings

3.l. Techniques to foster collaboration and teamwork within schools

Introduction

Responsive services are activities designed to meet students' immediate needs and concerns (ASCA, 2016). Counselors deliver responsive services to students who are facing problems that hinder their personal, social, career, or educational development. In essence, responsive services are provided to all students who may be referred to the school counselor or who seek help from the school counselor. Moreover, Dollarhide and Saginak (2017) stated: "responsive services are activities used to address barriers to learning what prevent students from maximizing their academic and career, and personal/social experience in the school, and focus on the short term, goal-focused nature of developmental counseling" (p. 132). Responsive services include counseling in individual or small group settings or crisis response (Dollarhide & Saginak, 2017). It is essential to note that although responsive services encompass crisis counseling, responsive services are to be employed often and to many in a school setting.

The term *crisis* is "an event that exceeds the organism's ability to cope" (Dollarhide & Saginak, 2017, p. 142). During the last 20 years, there has been an increased awareness of the need for crisis intervention in schools. Crises in school settings range from affecting a single student to a majority in the school community (Erford, 2015). Suicide, loss of a student or faculty member, medical emergencies, family trauma, school shootings, gang activities, and natural disasters are among the crises that can affect a school community. Erford (2015) concluded: "[i]t is essential to note that an event that is perceived as relatively minor by one student, such as failing an exam or being 'dumped' by a girlfriend, may be perceived as a crisis by another student" (p. 330). In other words, a crisis can be one's perception and can be enough to hinder the learning experiences of a student; thus, school counselors must respond whether or not they perceive the event as a crisis.

Responsive services are inclusive of referrals, consultation, and collaboration (Erford, 2015). The school counselor usually makes referrals when a student or family's needs exceed the resources of the school counselor and school district. School districts often have an assembled referral list including, but not limited to, licensed professional counselors, psychiatric services, food pantries, utility assistance, and homeless shelters. Although school districts usually have vetted these resources, it is best practice for the school counselor to be aware of the resources available and to be familiar with key people within the organizations and resources on the list. Resource lists, appropriately designed, should incorporate the name of the agency, an address, phone number, fax number, point of contact, website, and email address. The effective school counselor provides the resource list to the student's family and highlights three to five resources with which the family can seek assistance. Optimally, the resources highlighted should have been contacted by the school counselor and up-to-date. As a follow-up, the school counselor should check on the family after the referral has been made to ascertain whether or not further referrals need to be made and to make sure that the family has received the assistance they need or have requested.

State Initiatives, Federal Mandates, and District Policies

Based on the organization of each state's government, initiatives and policies under the umbrella of responsive services vary. These initiatives are district mandates set forth by each state board of education. Examples of initiatives at the state level include child abuse prevention awareness and suicide prevention awareness. Decisions regarding how each child is educated are left to each individual state as well as the federal government. Some gaps exist between the lack of federal mandates and the need for programs in critical areas that have created a space for national awareness and education programs. These national awareness and education programs include, but are not limited to, Red Ribbon Week, National Teen Dating Violence Awareness Month, and National Bullying Prevention Awareness Month.

The policies of local school districts across the nation originate from state education codes and guidelines. School boards of school districts take into account their community stakeholders when developing and adopting local policy. In addition, the level of implementation of the ASCA National Model (ASCA, 2016) and the state's school counseling model varies by district. Therefore, like a fingerprint, no two school districts have the exact same organization of responsive services. School district websites and directors of counseling in school districts are a starting place when conducting research to determine the concentration of the district's responsive services.

School districts often have policies regarding the following situations: suicide risk, threat to others (threat assessment), self-harm, bullying and cyberbullying, and student pregnancy. Many policies call for involving other staff members. For example, threat assessments often include assistance from the student resource officer/campus police and the school psychologist. When the aforementioned occur, paperwork often needs to be filled out and kept on file at the district level. In cases such as threat assessments, tracking and proper documentation is essential so that school personnel can be vigilant and aware in case a student transfers schools. This can be rather tricky while maintaining student confidentiality.

Three-Tier Approach to Responsive Services

When thinking about Responsive Services, the three-tiered Response to Intervention (RTI) model is a framework that describes how achievement and behavioral issues are handled in a school environment. This model can serve to organize the school counselor's interventions with other individual cases that require responsive services. The school counselor plays an integral role throughout the RTI process; thus, this process mirrors how other responsive situations can be handled.

The first tier in the RTI process is geared toward all students and is preventative and proactive in nature. During this tier, a universal screener is administered to all students, often in the areas of reading and math. Regarding behavior, the school counselor may conduct guidance lessons on cyberbullying as prevention to all students in the school. According to Schmidt (2014), as new social concerns develop, novel preventative methods will be necessary. It is essential that school counselors are equipped to assess students' needs accurately and plan programs that promote healthy and sound decisions about the challenges before them.

The second tier in the RTI process targets students with some level of risk. Students who did not perform satisfactorily on the screening for math and/or reading may be given strategic interventions to improve their achievement, such as tutorials. Likewise, students who have frequent office visits to the principal for behavior may receive strategic interventions by the school counselor, such as an individual or group counseling.

The third tier in the RTI process encompasses students who have not been successful after receiving interventions at the second tier. These students are high risk and, therefore, individual interventions are put into place. Academic interventions that are often put into place include tutorials with individualized instruction. Behavioral interventions sometimes include an individualized behavior plan and continued counseling. Assistance for remedial concerns are concentrated and specialized for those needing the most assistance.

According to the RTI network, school counselors, as outlined by ASCA, assist in the academic and behavior development of students in various capacities including the following:

- Delivering a school counseling core curriculum to all students addressing academic, career, and social development
- Analyzing data to target struggling students in both academics and behavior
- Researching and collaborating intervention strategies implemented by school staff
- Making referrals to school and community resources (when appropriate)
- Working with campus administration on RTI design and implementation
- Advocating for equal education for all students and working to remove barriers of the system

Confidentiality and Informed Consent

As a school counselor, confidentiality is a cornerstone to building a student's trust and respect. Students often expect school counselors to maintain confidentiality no matter what is shared in session. They often have expectations for the school counselor not to disclose the content of the counseling session as a part of their rights, privacy, and often secrecy. However, there are some instances when a counselor will not be able to keep information that has been disclosed confidentially. According to Erford (2015), state and federal statutes affect the counselor-student relationship in school settings. Furthermore, if a student is under the age of 18 years, parents maintain the right to privileged information. Three areas that must be disclosed to parents or an outside agency that limit confidentiality include (1) an individual being harmed by someone, (2) an individual harming him/herself or thinking about harming him/herself, or (3) if the individual plans to harm someone else. These three areas should be communicated with the students on the front end of the conversation. Furthermore, it is important to have an age-appropriate sign posted in the counselor's office where students can easily see and read it and tell the student upfront about the three exceptions to confidentiality each time he/she receives counseling. It is the counselor's professional responsibility to stay well-informed and up-to-date regarding state statutes and exceptions to privilege or confidentiality (Erford, 2015).

Many school districts address informed consent in a blanket statement in the student handbook that is sent home at the beginning of the year. Parents and guardians are informed of the services that the counselor provides. If parents or guardians do not want their child to be seen by the school counselor, it is incumbent on the parents or guardians to provide a letter to the school stating that their child is not to receive counseling services. In cases of group counseling, it is wise to send out permission slips or consent forms to parents, which includes the limits of confidentiality in a group setting.

Responsive Services: Child Abuse and Neglect

According to the Centers for Disease Control and Prevention (CDC) website, self-reported statistics consistently indicate that more than 1 in 10 children and youth experienced at least one form of child abuse or neglect in 2014. Child abuse and neglect include all types of abuse or neglect of a child under the age of 18 by a parent or caregiver that results in harm or potential harm.

There are four common types of abuse (www.cdc.gov/features/healthychildren/):

- **Physical abuse** is the use of physical force, such as hitting, kicking, shaking, burning, or other shows of force against a child.
- **Sexual abuse** involves engaging a child in sexual acts. It includes behaviors such as fondling, penetration, and exposing a child to other sexual activities.
- **Emotional abuse** refers to behaviors that harm a child's self-worth or emotional well-being. Examples include name-calling, shaming, rejection, withholding love, and threatening.
- **Neglect** is the failure to meet a child's basic physical and emotional needs. These needs include housing, food, clothing, education, and access to medical care.

School counselors have many roles and responsibilities in recognizing and reporting child abuse and neglect. In some cases, the school counselor is the school personnel receiving the initial outcry from a student in an abusive situation. In other instances, it may be a teacher or a staff member on campus that either receives the outcry from the student or suspects abuse or neglect. It is essential that the school counselor be well-versed and be aware of the proper protocol in these situations.

In most states, child abuse recognition training for teachers and staff members is mandatory as teachers are sometimes the first person that the student tells about the abuse. It is vital that teachers are properly trained on the proper protocol established in the school because their reaction can impact a child abuse outcry. Counselors often provide the training for teachers and staff and maintain training attendance records. Common areas covered in the child abuse recognition training include the following:

- Factors indicating that a child is at risk of sexual abuse or maltreatment
- Warning signs indicating that a child is a victim of sexual abuse or maltreatment
- Procedures for seeking assistance within the school and outside of the school for a child that is at risk for sexual abuse or other maltreatment

Additionally, counselors provide a support system to teachers and staff when a teacher suspects or when a student discloses that they are being abused or neglected. School counselors often provide a user-friendly quick reference guide to teachers with the reporting website and phone number. Furthermore, it is prudent for the school counselor to sit with the teacher making the report as they guide the teacher through the reporting process.

Agencies vary in each state. Common agencies are Child Protective Services (CPS), Department of Children and Families (DCF), Department of Children and Family Services (DCFS), and Department of Social Services (DSS). Some websites have a portal in which the child abuse or neglect report can be made online. However, if the case is severe, the best rule of thumb is to call the hotline and speak directly to someone on the phone. In severe cases in which a child's immediate safety is in question, it is important to know that the campus police officer or student resource officer can be brought in to help as they have a special priority hotline to most agencies. Furthermore, it is important to know that most agencies rank cases as priority one and priority two cases. A priority one case requires the investigation to begin within 24 hours. Priority two cases require that the investigation begin within 72 hours.

Campus administration must be made aware that an agency has been called and a report has been made so they are not caught off guard when the agency comes to visit the student or when a parent calls the school requesting to find out who made the report and why. A summary including the student's name and the name of the accused abuser can be provided to the administration, as maintaining confidentiality is essential and administrators should be informed only on a need-to-know basis. It may be wise to involve the principal or police officer on campus if the student is afraid to go home or if his or her safety at home is questionable. Holding the student on campus until the agency arrives, in some cases, is necessary when the student may be going home to an unsafe environment. It is also critical that the counselor, or any adult at the school, make a promise that the child will be able to stay with a parent or a safe person. Once the agency is involved, individuals at the agency make decisions.

Establishing a positive rapport with students will create a welcoming and positive environment where students will feel safe to disclose situations of abuse. As previously stated, being honest in the beginning about what can and cannot be kept confidential is key when working with students in a school setting. By establishing a warm environment and being upfront with what can be kept confidential, students will understand that the process of counseling is ultimately there for their best interest.

After a student has disclosed the abuse, it is important to praise the student for being brave and reporting the abuse to an adult. It is essential to not lead the child with questions that might put the idea in his or her head about abuse. Rather, the school counselor should be open and establish him/herself as a safe person who will advocate for the student. It is essential to support the child in telling the truth, making it safe for the student to be vulnerable. The job of the school counselor is not to investigate; it is to objectively report facts obtained and to refrain from making judgments. School personnel are never part of an ongoing investigation and generally are not privy to the results of the investigation unless the agency determines that it is in the child's best interest for school personnel to obtain such information.

The school counselor may want to take brief notes, using a SOAP, SOAPIE, or SOAPIER note format (e.g., subjective, objective, assessment, planning, implementing, evaluating, and reassessing) while the student is describing the abuse; however, the bulk of the notes taken should be written down once the student is no longer present. It is also essential to gather required information from the school information management system or the student's cumulative file before making the report. This practice lessens the anxiety experienced by the counselor or the individual making the report and ensures thorough documentation. At this time, the counselor will need to decide who will make the anonymous report: the counselor or the person who received the outcry. Some agencies prefer to hear from the person who first heard the outcry. When making the report to the agency, it is essential to write down the name of the agency representative and the employee number for follow-up purposes. Some agencies will not provide information once a report has been made and an investigation is underway. When the counselor is finished with the report, it is important to keep documentation in locked storage in the counselor's office.

Child abuse reporting agencies appreciate the following information in a report if it is available:

- ◆ Student's full name, date of birth, address
- ◆ Parent/guardian's full name, date of birth, address
- ◆ Siblings and other children who are in the home, their ages, and school/campus
- ◆ Names of other adults present in the home
- ◆ How the student gets to and from school
- ◆ What time the student arrives at school and leaves for home
- ◆ Summary of the disclosure using the student's words as much as possible, including descriptions of identifiable marks or evident bruises

Responsive Services: Substance Use and Abuse

Substance use is a substantial problem in society and has reached an alarming level among children and adolescents. According to the Center on Addiction, the use of addictive substances, including tobacco/nicotine, alcohol, and other drugs, during adolescence inhibits brain development, diminishes academic performance, and increases the risk of accidents, homicides, suicides, and health conditions, including addiction. Teens and young adults are more likely than adults to take risks, including smoking, drinking, or using other drugs. Use of any addictive substance during brain developmental periods such as adolescence increases the chances of future use of that and other addictive substances. In fact, nine out of ten people with substance problems started using by age 18 (www.centeronaddiction.org/addiction-prevention/teenage-addiction).

Common substances that have infiltrated the lives of our students include, but are not limited to, alcohol, marijuana, synthetic marijuana, Molly/ecstasy, inhalants, cocaine, and heroin. In some cases of substance abuse, adolescents misuse prescription medication prescribed to family members, friends, or themselves. Opioids, depressants, and stimulants are three different types of prescription medication that adolescents misuse. Information was gathered from the National Institute of Drug Abuse for this chart (Table 4.1) on the three types of prescription drugs commonly abused by teenagers in the United States.

Table 4.1 Commonly Abused Prescription Drugs

Type	Nicknames	Effects
Opioids		Pain relief, drowsiness, euphoria, confusion, slowed breathing, and death
Codeine	Purple Drank (Syrup Sipping), Captain, Cody	
Fentanyl	Apache, China Girl, China	
Hydrocodone	Vike, Watson, 387	
Oxycodone	Oxy, Hillbilly Heroin, Percs	
Depressants		Drowsiness, slurred speech, poor concentration, problems with movement and memory
Xanex	Candy, Downers, Tranks	
Barbiturates	Barbs, Yellows, Pennies	
Sleep Medicine	Roofies, R2, Forget-me-pill	
Stimulants		Increased alertness and energy, increased blood pressure and heart rate
Amphetamines	Molly, Black Beauties, Speed, Truck Drivers Jif,	
Methylphenidate	MPH, Skippy, The Smart Drug	

Adapted and modified from www.drugabuse.gov/drugs-abuse/commonly-abused-drugs-charts

According to the CDC, alcohol is the most commonly used and abused drug among youth in the United States. The CDC's national Youth Risk Behavior Survey (YRBS) monitors priority health risk behaviors that contribute to the leading causes of death, disability, and social problems among youth and adults in the United States. According to survey results, 32.8% of 9th- to 12th-grade students surveyed in 2015 had consumed at least one alcoholic beverage within 30 days, and 17.7% consumed five drinks in a row in a couple of hours within 30 days of the survey.

If the school counselor suspects that a student is under the influence, proper protocol must be followed as outlined by the district or school counseling department. In cases such as these, the school nurse may evaluate the student for sobriety. The Student Resource Officer (SRO) and/or campus administration will most likely handle this situation. The school counselor may be called in to speak with the parents and provide resources once they arrive on campus.

Students may disclose to the school counselor that they use drugs or alcohol in their free time, away from school. If a student is under age 18, it is wise for the school counselor to inform the student's parents that he/she is using drugs as they are harming themselves and may require intervention. Before doing so, the school counselor should be aware of district policy, state, and federal guidelines regarding reporting such behavior to a child's parents. The school counselor can give the student two options: either the student tells the parents with the school counselor present or the school counselor informs the parents with or without the student present. Either intervention utilized requires documentation.

It is vital to request that the parents meet with the school counselor so that resources can be provided, and the student can get help. Contacting parents after the resources have been provided is fundamental to parental follow-up and support. Resources may include, but are not limited to, substance abuse rehabilitation programs, drug testing facilities, interventionists, Alcoholics and Narcotics Anonymous programs, and local churches with recovery programs. All too often, substance abuse is a symptom to a multilayered cluster of systemic issues. Should the school counselor discern that a student's parents are willfully supplying drugs to the student, a report to Child Protective Services should be in order.

A comprehensive list of resources and a keen ability to perceive the many layers of substance abuse and use can make a lasting impact on the student and the family. The voice of the school counselor is usually the voice of reason and can help parents understand that substance abuse is a disease and should be treated as such.

Responsive Services: Risky Sexual Behaviors

In 2015, 41% of the high school students surveyed by the CDC using the YRBS indicated that they had engaged in sexual intercourse. Moreover, 30% of the teenagers surveyed indicated that they had sexual intercourse within the previous three months (www.cdc.gov/healthyyouth/sexualbehaviors/index.htm). As a result of this sexuality among youth in the nation, many perspectives exist regarding students engaging in risky sexual behavior. It is essential that the school counselor be aware of ethics, state laws, and district policy regarding the protocol that dictates where confidentiality ends and proper reporting begins. Most importantly, no matter the action taken, the school counselor must maintain a non-judgmental stance providing a safe and supportive environment free from shame. The following are common situations the school counselor might encounter.

Student Discloses Sexual Activity

When students under the age of consent (varies by state) disclose to the school counselor that they are engaging in sexual activity including, but not limited to, oral, anal, object use, and vaginal sex, the school counselor shall inform the parents or guardians of the student. The school counselor can give the student an option to disclose this information to his or her parent or guardian with the counselor present as a support system. This disclosure should be done in person and not over the phone. The student may not want to tell the parent or guardian and may want it to come from the school counselor. Informing parents and documentation of such is essential so that the parents have the option to seek the medical attention that is appropriate for the family's value system (i.e., testing for STDs, birth control).

Minors Having Sex With Adults

Should a school counselor be informed that a student under the age of consent is having sexual relations with someone older, proper protocol must be followed, which involves reporting to law enforcement, commonly referred to as statutory rape. The age gap varies by state, as does the age of consent. For example, in some states statutory rape is where students are only two years apart in age. It is wise for the school counselor to be aware of state laws that regulate sexual behavior.

Students Having Sex on Campus

A school counselor who discovers that a student has engaged in sexual activity on campus must alert campus administration so that further investigation can take place and they can follow administrative protocol. This protocol may involve checking for school surveillance evidence and taking statements from those engaging in or aware of the sexual activity. Parents are called and disciplinary action is applied. If there is a significant gap in age (according to state law) between the individuals engaging in sexual activity, law enforcement might be involved, and charges might be filed. Depending on the gravity of the situation, students and parents might be distraught. School counselors might be asked to provide on-site crisis counseling for the students and parents and/or provide names of those in the community that can assist the family.

Student Discloses a Diagnosis of a Sexually Transmitted Disease

If a student under age 18 informs the school counselor that he or she has a sexually transmitted disease (STD), it is essential that the school counselor maintain a non-judgmental stance, free from shame. In cases such as these, the school counselor should be there for the student and convince the student to inform the parents so that medical attention can be sought. Additionally, it is essential for an action plan to be developed and implemented with the student, including writing down the names of sexual partners so that they can be informed. The school nurse can often be a useful resource when talking to students about sexually transmitted diseases.

Responsive Services: Teen Pregnancy

All too often, students confide in the school counselor and teachers that they suspect they might be pregnant due to a missed menstrual period or a positive home pregnancy test. In these situations, it is important that school counselors provide a safe environment free from judgment and advice. In most cases, the expectant mother's parents or guardians shall be informed about the pregnancy, especially if the student is under age 18. It is critical that parents be notified because the expectant mother will need monetary and emotional support. The male counterpart is often neglected and even overlooked in the process of support and parent notification. It is important not to isolate or treat the male student differently in terms of interventions and supports offered. The male student's process should be no different from the female involved.

If the pregnant student is planning on keeping her child, the physician providing pre-natal care will fill out paperwork initiated by the school district in order for the pregnant student to receive pregnancy-related services. The services may include homebound services, which provide a teacher to deliver instruction for the student while she stays home with her child after birth. In some cases, homebound services may be necessary if the student becomes bedridden before the baby is born. These services are extremely important because they prevent teenage mothers from getting behind in school, thus preventing expectant mothers from dropping out of school. According to the CDC, "only 38% of teens who gave birth at age 17 or younger earned high school diplomas by their 22nd birthday versus 60% of teen who were 18 or older when they gave birth. Among teens not giving birth, 89% earned high school diplomas" (www.cdc.gov/vitalsigns/young-teen-pregnancy/index.html).

Responsive Services: Teen Dating Violence

The CDC defines teen dating violence as the physical, sexual, psychological, and emotional violence within a dating relationship, also known as intimate partner violence (IPV). It can occur in person or electronically and might occur between a current or former dating partner. Teen dating violence is synonymous and inclusive of these terms: relationship abuse, dating abuse, domestic abuse, and domestic violence. According to the CDC, teen dating violence includes the following types of abuse (www.cdc.gov/violenceprevention/pdf/teen-dating-violence-factsheet-a.pdf):

- **Physical**: Occurs when a partner is pinched, hit, shoved, slapped, punched, or kicked.
- **Psychological/Emotional**: Means threatening a partner or harming his or her sense of self-worth. Examples include name-calling, shaming, bullying, embarrassing on purpose, or keeping him/her away from friends and family.
- **Sexual**: This is forcing a partner to engage in a sex act when he or she does not or cannot consent. This can be physical or non-physical, like threatening to spread rumors if a partner refuses to have sex.
- **Stalking**: This refers to a pattern of harassing or threatening tactics that are unwanted and cause fear in the victim.

According to the 2015 YRBS, 9.6% of U.S. high school students reported physical victimization, and 10.6% of high school students reported being sexually victimized in the last 12 months by their partner (www.cdc.gov/healthyyouth/data/yrbs/results.htm). Likewise, the CDC revealed that teenagers who are susceptible to teen dating violence have common risk factors. These factors include a belief that domestic violence is acceptable. Depressed and anxious teenagers are also more likely to experience teen dating violence, as well as teenagers who have conflicts with their parents and witness or experience violence in their homes. Furthermore, teenagers who engage in early sexual activity and have had multiple sexual partners are also more susceptible to teen dating violence.

The consequences or results of teen dating violence include, but are not limited to, symptoms of depression and anxiety, unhealthy behaviors (tobacco use, drug and/or alcohol abuse), antisocial behavior, poor academic performance, and thoughts of suicide. According to the youth.gov website, 65% of teenagers keep dating violence a secret. A majority of teenagers never obtain mental health services, seek protection in shelters, or pursue legal help. Therefore, it is essential for school counselors to be aware of the predispositions, signs, and consequences of teen dating violence so that they can pick up on behaviors that students may be exhibiting. Reaching out to these students and knowing what to say is key when trying to gain a victim's trust and disclosure.

When students tell school counselors that their partners are physically abusing them, it is essential that the counselor remain calm and empathetic while letting the students tell their stories. Additionally, the school counselor should praise students for having the bravery to tell their story. The disclosure of teen dating violence is something that cannot be kept confidential by the school counselor. The school counselor must alert the parents or guardians of the abused student. School counselors can then offer additional support by providing resources and proper protocol for reporting the abuse to the authorities.

Teen dating violence prevention efforts have been put in place by several state governments, and February has been designated as Teen Dating Violence Awareness Month nationwide. School counseling programs in school districts design prevention programs in order to inform students about healthy and unhealthy behaviors in relationships.

Responsive Services: Suicide and Self-Harm

In the K–12 setting, suicide is a difficult subject to broach with students, faculty, and staff. School counselors are faced with crisis counseling students who threaten suicide at school or at home, and the caregiver is seeking help. Ideally, the school has a suicide plan in place. It should be reiterated that school counselors are to lead the crisis team or, at the least, be a member of the team. This will enable the counselor to give knowledgeable feedback from a therapeutic perspective.

There are several reasons that a child might consider suicide. Some may see it as an attention-seeking device, but *all* threats should be taken seriously. The school counselor should emphasize this point to faculty and staff. Attention seeking or not, it is not for the counselor to decide at that time. There is a reason that a child is making such a serious threat, and understanding the rationale behind it is not necessary during the crisis, but rather action is needed. Once the crisis has been resolved, the reasons and preceding events should be investigated and resolved. The leading cause of suicide among children and adolescents is bullying, according to the CDC. Although it may be more accepted currently, children who are LGBTQ may find it difficult to be themselves or may get harassed by those who are not accepting of them. This bullying can lead to thoughts and attempts of suicide as well.

School counselors, faculty, staff, and caregivers should be aware of the possible signs of suicide. According to bullyingstatistics.org, these include the following:

- Showing signs of depression, like ongoing sadness, withdrawal from others, losing interest in favorite activities, or trouble sleeping or eating
- Talking about or showing an interest in death or dying
- Engaging in dangerous or harmful activities, including reckless behavior, substance abuse, or self-injury
- Giving away favorite possessions and saying goodbye to people
- Saying or expressing that they can't handle things anymore
- Making comments that things would be better without them

School counselors must act as soon as a child has made a threat of suicide (see Appendix 4.1). Most importantly, the crisis team should have a procedure in place to make sure that the child's well-being is addressed. The child's caregiver should be contacted right away, and a school official should be with the child at all times until the caregiver has come to receive the child. Remember that, in all cases, the school counselor must be sure that a child's caregiver will not hurt the child. It may be behaviors of the caregiver that have such a negative impact on the child's life that causes thoughts of suicide. School counselors can do a risk assessment on the child and see how immediate the danger is. Once the caregiver has come to get the child, the school counselor should be proactive in talking about options for the child. This should include giving resources for mental health counseling and/or behavioral inpatient facilities for the child to receive 24/7 care.

As a school counselor, one may follow up with the student once he or she returns to school. Remember that the child may have some anger or feelings of betrayal toward the counselor because confidentiality had to be broken. Therefore, it is essential for counselors to reiterate the confidentiality exceptions every time they meet with students. The counselor should be prepared to address these feelings. Additionally, school counselors should make suicide prevention part of their program by providing awareness workshops, pamphlets, and classroom guidance on this issue. Being knowledgeable and informed can help others who are not in the counseling field to understand risk factors.

Responsive Services: Completed Suicides

There may be times when the school counselor must respond to an entire school or grade level due to a child completing a suicide. This can be an overwhelming task since the school counselor may have been very involved with the student and his or her family and teachers. One major concern here is the effect of suicide contagion, which is the immediate result of successfully completed suicides. Many school districts have crisis teams in place that can respond to the school community, allowing the school counselor to simply supply information and not be directly involved in the response. If the district does not have a crisis team, the school counselor should create one, including counselors from other schools in the district and perhaps counselors from the community who are willing to help. Once the team is formed, the school counselor can supply information but does not have to do the actual responding.

Responsive Services: Self-Harm

Self-harm or self-injurious behavior is described as that behavior in which a person intentionally injures oneself regularly without fatal consequences (Bennardi, McMahon, Corcoran, Griffin, & Arensman, 2016; World Health Organization, 2015; mentalhealthamerica.net, n.d.). These behaviors include, but are not limited to, cutting, burning, scratching, hitting oneself, and drinking liquids that are not meant to be ingested. Self-harm has been reported to be common among young people, especially adolescents, with about 13.2% engaging in this behavior (Bennardi et al., 2016; Evans, Hawton, Rodham, & Deeks, 2005). Self-harm has been found to be associated with suicide, meaning that a person who attempts or completes suicide has most likely also engaged in self-injurious behavior (Carroll, Metcalfe, & Gunnell, 2014, as cited by Bennardi et al., 2016). Self-harm has also been associated with repeated use of alcohol, drugs, depression, behavioral problems, and problems in school (Bennardi, 2016; Hawton et al., 2012; Hawton & James, 2005).

This self-injurious behavior can stem from many factors affecting a child. Mental health concerns such as low self-esteem, depression, and anxiety are associated with causes for self-injury (Viana, Dixon, Berenz, & Espil, 2016). It is also used as a coping method because of these emotional and mental health issues (Viana et al., 2016). Responsive services for self-injurious behavior are similar to suicidal children, but the school counselor must decide what kind of threat level this may be: non-suicidal self-harm or deliberate self-harm. Counselors, faculty, and staff should also be aware of the signs of this behavior, which can include the following:

- Scars
- Fresh cuts, scratches, bruises, or other wounds
- Excessive rubbing of an area to create a burn
- Keeping sharp objects on hand
- Wearing long sleeves or long pants, even in hot weather
- Difficulties in interpersonal relationships
- Persistent questions about personal identity, such as "Who am I?" or "What am I doing here?"
- Behavioral and emotional instability, impulsivity, and unpredictability
- Statements of helplessness, hopelessness, or worthlessness

source: www.mayoclinic.org/diseases-conditions/self-injury/symptoms-causes/dxc-20165427

According to Bubrick, Goodman, and Whitlock (n.d.), the student either discloses or it is witnessed by staff or faculty that self-injurious behavior has occurred. This is confirmed through identifiable signs and symptoms, making the school aware of the issue. The school nurse should utilize expertise, assess lethality, treat wounds, and immediately contact emergency services if the harm is life-threatening. Additionally, the school counselor should meet with the student, following outlined process and procedures, and decide the level of risk. Finally, the school counselor contacts parents, makes referrals, and follows up no more than two weeks later.

Responsive Services: Bullying

According to Stopbullying.gov, *bullying* is defined as repetitious, aggressive behavior that involves an imbalance of power whether real or perceived. Bullying can be classified as verbal, physical, relational, and cyberbullying. Each of these types will be discussed briefly. School counselors face the challenge of recognizing what bullying looks like and how to work with it. School-wide programs should not only incorporate interventions with the bully and victim but should also address the role of bystanders and the impact they could have on bullying. It is important that counselors advocate for groups that may fall victim to bullying and encourage faculty, staff, students, and caregivers to become advocates as well.

Verbal and Physical Bullying

Verbal and physical bullying are the most easily recognizable forms of bullying. Verbal bullying can include name-calling, threatening, and/or slurs. Physical bullying is not necessarily outward violence, though counselors may see it as such. It can be a push or shove into a wall or a slap on the back of the head when the teacher is not looking. Bullies might have been able to do this for a while and are able to keep their abuse inconspicuous, and they pick on those who will not speak up. Bullies have often been thought to be the people in class who do not feel good about themselves; however, recent studies have shown that this is not necessarily the case. In some cases, bullies are the students in school who have a very high opinion of themselves. They may even be those who are well liked by the teachers.

Relational Aggression

Crick and Grotpeter (1995) defined the term *relational aggression*. This is commonly referred to as *girl bullying*, but boys participate in this type of behavior as well. Relational aggression behaviors are those concealed behaviors that damage peer relationships, such as exclusion and manipulation (Crick & Grotpeter, 1995). This can be difficult to catch as well because these bully behaviors are often unseen. Exclusion, rolling eyes, and rumor spreading are just a few of the ways that the perpetrator can hurt the victim.

Cyberbullying

Cyberbullying is an extension of relational aggression, which involves using technology or social media to hurt others (Erford, 2015). Aliases are often created on social media, making it more difficult to identify perpetrators. The dangerous piece of this behavior is that those children who were victims of bullying can become the perpetrators. These people are known as bully-victims. Hiding behind the mask of a screen makes it easier for victims to become aggressive as there are no immediate reactions, and they do not have to face the repercussions of those who have bullied them. In recent years, much of the bullying seen on the news involves cyberbullying, where people taunt and tease children on social media. Some results have been fatal, as those children who are attacked ultimately committed suicide. School counselors should be aware of the signs of those children who are being bullied and those who are the bullies.

Signs a Child Is Being Bullied

According to stopbullying.gov, the following are signs of both those who bully and those who are bullied. Look for changes in the child. However, be aware that not all children who are bullied exhibit warning signs. Some signs that may point to a bullying problem are as follows:

- Unexplainable injuries
- Lost or destroyed clothing, books, electronics, or jewelry
- Frequent headaches or stomach aches, feeling sick or faking illness
- Changes in eating habits, like suddenly skipping meals or binge eating. Kids may come home from school hungry because they did not eat lunch
- Difficulty sleeping or frequent nightmares
- Declining grades, loss of interest in schoolwork, or not wanting to go to school
- Sudden loss of friends or avoidance of social situations
- Feelings of helplessness or decreased self esteem
- Self-destructive behaviors such as running away from home, harming themselves, or talking about suicide

Signs a Child Is Bullying Others

Kids may be bullying others if they do the following:

- Get into physical or verbal fights
- Have friends who bully others
- Are increasingly aggressive
- Get sent to the principal's office or to detention frequently
- Have unexplained extra money or new belongings
- Blame others for their problems
- Don't accept responsibility for their actions
- Are competitive and worry about their reputation or popularity

The school counselor should follow procedures for bullying responsive services. Prevention should be the first course of action by providing an understanding to the school's faculty, staff, and students about the forms of bullying. A district-wide anti-bullying policy should be implemented, and it must address all forms of bullying. Informing the bystanders as to how to help other children who are being bullied can be one of the most positive prevention methods. This, in turn, can impact the intervention method where adults and peers step in when they see bullying occurring (Erford, Lee, & Rock, 2015).

Teaching skills such as advocacy, assertive behavior training, actively ignoring, and walking away can be extremely impactful for victims of bullying and their peers. Bystanders can learn how to be assertive when standing up to a bully for a peer, taking the peer away from the bully, and teaching them how to talk to an adult about the situation. Once again, making sure there are stringent rules in place for those who are bullies as well as any staff who knows about the situations but fail to report them is imperative (Erford et al., 2015).

Crisis Management and Response

School counselors should be either a crisis team leader or part of the team. It is important that a crisis manual is in place and that school faculty and staff are continuously informed about the procedures and updates in the crisis manual. Each member of the team should have specific duties and procedures, which are outlined in the manual, including what to do in each threat assessment, risk assessment, crisis, who to call, and how to return to normal procedures. Districts often select members based on established professional relationships, principal recommendation, and years of experience working in the district.

Procedures of Threat Assessment for Harming Others

A school counselor should be able to assess the level of threat of a situation, if a student or anyone else is making a threat to a student or the school. There are different types of threats defined by the Federal Bureau of Investigation (FBI) (Albrecht, 2010). Within these types of threats, the FBI notes different levels of threats from low, medium, to high. *Indirect threats* are vague but imply violence; *veiled threats* suggest the possibility of violence; *conditional threats* demand certain conditions or violence may occur; and *direct threats* are specific and clear, often naming the act and the target. The following descriptions of low-level, medium-level, and high-level threats can be found on the websites of the National Association of School Psychologists (NASP) and the FBI.

Low Level of Threat

- Poses a minimal risk to the victim and public safety
- Is vague and indirect

- Information is inconsistent, implausible, or lacks detail
- Lacks realism
- Content suggests person is unlikely to carry out the threat

Medium Level of Threat

- Could be carried out, although it may not appear entirely realistic
- More direct and more concrete than a low-level threat
- Wording suggests the individual has given some thought to how the act will be carried out
- Includes a general indication of place and time, but signs still fall well short of a detailed plan
- No strong indication that the individual has taken preparatory steps
- Statements seek to convey that the threat is not empty: "I'm serious!" or "I really mean this!"

High Level of Threat

- Direct, specific, and plausible
- Appears to pose imminent and serious danger to safety of others
- Suggests concrete steps have been taken (i.e., stalking or acquisition of a weapon)
- Always requires bringing in law enforcement.

It is imperative to have a protocol for threat assessment. The FBI recommends having a threat assessment team (TAT), which would probably include those who would be on the crisis team. Possible team members would be the principal, assistant principal, teachers counselors, campus security, and maintenance workers.

Procedures of Risk Assessment for Suicide

Risk assessment involves evaluating students who threaten to harm themselves through suicide or self-injurious behavior. When meeting with a student who is at risk, school counselors should assess the child's affect and how immediate the level of threat is. For example, if the child is threatening suicide, does he or she have a detailed plan as to how it is going to happen? If so, this would be an immediate threat. In any case, a child's caregiver would need to be contacted immediately, and someone would need to stay with the child at all times as noted in the suicide section. Other behaviors that are considered risks are as follows:

- Social isolation or withdrawal
- Giving away possessions
- Talking or reading about death
- Deliberate self-injurious behavior
- Engaging in risky behavior such as sex, drugs, or alcohol
- Change in appearance
- Change in eating or sleeping habits
- Writing suicide notes
- Access to weapons
- Family issues/dynamics/history
- Recent attempts or hospitalizations
- Recent death or loss in the family and/or recent death in family or friend by suicide

Crisis Intervention Plan for Schools

A school district's crisis intervention plan is imperative. The school counselor should be on the crisis team with other administrators, teachers, staff, community agencies, and parents. According to Garofalo and Erford (2014), the team should have specific jobs when the school is in crisis. This will lessen the likelihood of confusion as to who does what if there is a crisis in the school. The Virginia Department of Education has a well-laid-out plan that can be viewed online. Some of the information that will be discussed will come from that model, but consider your school and community and what resources are available. In this section, the basic pieces of a crisis manual are presented.

First, a crisis team should be established. As mentioned earlier, this team should be made up of faculty, staff, administrators, school counselors, and parents. Other members should include a police officer, firefighter, and a local mental health service provider. Each member of the crisis team should have a task and role, which is outlined in the crisis manual, as well as phone numbers listed. For example, the team will need someone to record information during meetings, someone to distribute material to schools and to community resources participating in the action plan, and someone to go over the plan in detail with faculty in each school.

The plan should be divided into sections: pre-planning, intervention, and post-crisis management. Some aspects within these sections should include the following:

- Risk and threat assessments
- Establishing headquarters for the team
- Outlining the chain of command

- Spokesperson for the media
- How information will be dispersed to school and community when in crisis
- Support systems available: this can include neighboring school districts, mental health facilities, religious organizations, emergency services, and community outreach groups
- Phone number of the National Crisis Hotline

Types of crises should also be outlined: intruder, natural disasters, suicide, death of a student/faculty/staff, fire, and bomb threats. Under each type of crisis, protocol for what the procedures are should be listed. There should also be a section for what administration, faculty, and staff are responsible for in times of crisis.

An example of protocol and procedures would be school lockdown in case of an intruder in the school. Schools should always consider keeping front doors locked and/or have entry codes so that visitors must be *buzzed* in through the office before entering the building. Cameras in and around the school are also necessary. However, if an armed intruder was to come into the school, a possible protocol may look as follows:

1. An announcement is made over the loud speaker. The announcement should only be known to faculty and staff as the intruder announcement. The administrator may say, "The lights are out in the gym." It must be generic so as not to alarm the students or alert the intruder.
2. Teachers should keep doors locked, turn off lights, and move students to a corner of the room where they are not seen through windows or doors (curtains may need to be put up in all rooms as to cover windows).
3. Teachers should account for all students.
4. Teachers must tell students to be quiet and remain seated in the corner of the room until a signal (much like the announcement to warn of an intruder) has been given.

Teachers should have emergency kits in their classrooms. Protocol for all types of crises should be practiced with students.

In an age of technology, it is difficult to keep information confidential until the after-crisis protocol has been established. Be aware that information (and sometimes second-hand information) will get out, but the crisis team should continue to follow protocol and have a spokesperson to discuss the incident. In any crisis that involves death, remember that many people will be in shock. Have support teams present and be aware of who will be most affected.

Ethical Standards

There are several ethical considerations brought forth by the American School Counselor Association's (ASCA) ethical standards regarding responsive services. School counselors should review the ASCA Code of Ethics, as the most recent edition was published in 2016. Within each standard there are several principles that apply to responsive services. However, the following are specific standards that apply to this section.

A.9: Serious Foreseeable Harm to Self and Others

School counselors establish that confidentiality must be upheld; however, if a student is threatening to harm him/herself or others, then confidentiality must be broken. School counselors should be aware of the school's legal codes and laws as well as the protocol for any kind of responsive situation. What happens when the caregiver is the issue for the child? Standard A.9.d (ASCA, 2016) stipulates that school counselors should report to Child Protective Services.

A.10: Underserviced and At-Risk Populations

Although this standard does not strictly represent responsive service situations, if an underserviced or at-risk child was in crisis and needed immediate help, school counselors should be ready to respond. Prevention and intervention methods can be beneficial for these groups. Teaching other students about these populations can also serve as a prevention tool. A child who has gender identity issues might be contemplating suicide, and peers can help. School counselors must be ready to call Child Protective Services if the environment at home is not safe for these children. Reaching out to *all* students is imperative. Remember that those students who are excelling may also be at risk for suicide, depression, and other issues. There may be extreme amounts of pressure that these children put on themselves or someone else puts on them. Children in the gifted and talented programs may also be underserved because they are seen as the bright children in the school who should not have problems, but they are still at risk of failure or face that extreme pressure.

A.11: Bullying, Harassment, and Child Abuse

All cases of bullying and harassment should be reported to administration, and child abuse and/or neglect should be reported to Child Protective Services. School counselors should be able to recognize the signs of these issues. Again, prevention methods should be in place, so bystanders are able to spot bullying and harassment or let an adult know when a child is being hurt. School counselors should know the laws in their state about bullying and cyberbullying and be in contact with the local police department in case there are laws protecting victims in the state.

Counselors should consult the ethical standards as well as other counselors and resources when faced with an ethical dilemma. The American Counseling Association (ACA) and the ASCA have ethical and legal departments, so counselors can call and consult. School counselors often have the luxury of having an attorney who represents the school district and can provide legal expertise when the school is faced with a situation.

Multicultural Considerations

When working with students who need responsive services, multicultural considerations should always be at the forefront of the counselor's mind. Multicultural considerations include, but are not limited to, ethnicity, race, culture, gender, age, sexual orientation, disabilities, and religion. Counselors should always be aware of their own values, beliefs, and knowledge. The ASCA Ethical Standards (2016) also state the school counselor's obligation toward multicultural awareness in Standards B.3.i, B.3.j, and B.3.k Responsibilities to Self.

School Counselors

B.3.i:

> Monitor and expand personal multicultural and social-justice advocacy awareness, knowledge and skills to be an effective culturally competent school counselor. Understand how prejudice, privilege and various forms of oppression based on ethnicity, racial identity, age, economic status, abilities/disabilities, language, immigration status, sexual orientation, gender, gender identity expression, family type, religious/spiritual identity, appearance and living situation (e.g. foster care, homelessness, incarceration) affect students and stakeholders.

B.3.j:

> Refrain from using services to students based solely on the school counselor's personally held beliefs or values rooted in one's religion,

culture or ethnicity. School counselors respect the diversity of students and seek training and supervision when prejudice or biases interfere with providing comprehensive services to all students.

B.3.k:

Work toward a school climate that embraces diversity and promotes academic, career and social/emotional development for all students.

School counselors should be aware of how to talk with students and parents/guardians who are of a different background in responsive service situations. A student who is gay who has not come out yet may be fearful when approaching his parents about his thoughts of suicide. How do school counselors approach this situation with parents as part of an ethical obligation without putting the student in danger? Learning about the different groups within the school can be a proactive way to create a safe environment for students in case a crisis situation were to arise. Of course, through professional development and training, school counselors can learn a lot about groups other than their own in order to meet the needs of their students.

Activities

1. Discuss with your classmates how you might respond to a crisis such as a student expresses suicidal thoughts, a student reveals ongoing sexual abuse, a minor admits to having sex with an adult, and a student describes ongoing violence in the home between parents. What will your feelings be when working through any of these issues with a student, and how will you cope?
2. Role-play a session with a student who expresses suicidal thoughts. Study the steps in the chapter first, and use those steps to practice this type of intervention. Next, role-play the conversation with the parents of the student. How will you support the family?
3. With your classmates, brainstorm the various referral mental health supports that are available in your area. Start compiling contact information that will eventually be used as your referral book for students, parents, and families.
4. Discuss the various ethical issues surrounding the problems of minors and drug and alcohol abuse, teen pregnancy, sexual acting

out, and intimate partner violence. Remember to weigh the legal implications with school district policy and the best interests of your clients.

5. Bullying and cyberbullying have been in the national news due to some students committing suicide over these problematic behaviors. Create a school-wide intervention for your chosen grade level or school. Plan the steps you will take to make an impact on students. Who will you enlist for support? How will the intervention be delivered? How will you assess the success of the intervention? What data will you collect? Remember that you are only one person. A school-wide intervention will take many people to make a difference.

Resources

Centers for Disease Control and Prevention:
www.cdc.gov/features/healthychildren
www.cdc.gov/vitalsigns/young-teen-pregnancy/index.html
www.cdc.gov/healthyyouth/sexualbehaviors/index.htm
www.cdc.gov/violenceprevention/pdf/bullying_factsheet.pdf
www.cdc.gov/violenceprevention/pdf/teen-dating-violence-factsheet-a.pdf

References

Albrecht, S. (2010). *Threat assessment: Workplace and school violence prevention.* Retrieved from https://leb.fbi.gov/2010/february/threat-assessment-teams-workplace and-school-violence-prevention

American School Counselor Association. (2016a). *The ASCA national model: A framework for school counseling programs.* Alexandria, VA: Author.

American School Counselor Association. (2016b). *Ethical standards for school counselors.* Retrieved from www.schoolcounselor.org.

Bennardi, M., McMahon, E., Corcoran, P., Griffin, E., & Arensman, E. (2016). Risk of repeated self-harm and associated factors in children, adolescents, and young adults. *BMC Psychiatry, 16,* 1–12.

Bubrick, K., Goodman, J., & Whitlock, J. (n.d.). *Developing and implementing school protocol for non-suicidal self-injury (NSSI).* Retrieved from www.selfinjury.bctr.cornell.edu/perch/resources/school-protocol.pdf

Bullying definition. (n.d.). In stopbullying.gov. Retrieved from www.stopbullying.gov/what-is-bullying/definition/

Carroll, R., Metcalfe, C., & Gunnell, D. (2014). Hospital presenting self-harm and risk of fatal and non-fatal repetition: Systematic review and meta-analysis. *PLoS one*, *9*, 526–533.

Center on Addiction. (2016). Teen substance abuse. Retrieved from www.centeronaddiction.org/addiction-prevention/teenage-addiction

Centers for Disease Control and Prevention. (2016a). *Child abuse prevention*. Retrieved from www.cdc.gov/features/healthychildren

Centers for Disease Control and Prevention. (2016b). *Preventing pregnancies in younger teens*. Retrieved from www.cdc.gov/vitalsigns/young-teen-pregnancy/index.html

Centers for Disease Control and Prevention. (2016c). *Sexual risk behaviors*. Retrieved from www.cdc.gov/healthyyouth/sexualbehaviors/index.htm

Centers for Disease Control and Prevention. (2016d). *Understanding bullying fact sheet*. Retrieved from www.cdc.gov/violenceprevention/pdf/bullying_factsheet.pdf

Centers for Disease Control and Prevention. (2016e). *Understanding teen dating violence*. Retrieved from www.cdc.gov/violenceprevention/pdf/teen-dating-violence-factsheet-a.pdf

Council for Accreditation of Counseling and Related Educational Programs. (2016). *CACREP standards*. Retrieved from www.cacrep.org/for-programs/2016-cacrep-standards/

Crick, N. R., & Grotpeter, J. K. (1995). Relational aggression, gender, and social psychological adjustment. *Child Development*, *66*, 710–722.

Dollarhide, C. T., & Saginak, K. A. (2017). *Comprehensive school counseling programs: K-12 delivery systems in action* (3rd ed.). Upper Saddle River, NJ: Pearson.

Erford, B. T. (2015). *Transforming the school counseling profession* (4th ed.). Upper Saddle River, NJ: Pearson.

Erford, B. T., Lee, V. V., & Rock, E. (2015). Systemic approaches to counseling students experiencing complex and specialized problems. In B. T. Erford (Ed.), *Transforming the school counseling profession* (4th ed.). Upper Saddle River, NJ: Pearson.

Evans, E., Hawton, K., Rodham, K., & Deeks, J. (2005). The prevalence of suicidal phenomena in adolescents: A systematic review of population-based studies. *Suicide Life Threat Behavior*, *35*, 239–250.

Garofalo, M., & Erford, B. T. (2014). Emergency preparedness and response in schools and universities. In L. R. Jackson-Cherry & B. T. Erford (Eds.), *Crisis assessment, intervention, and prevention* (2nd ed.). Upper Saddle River, NJ: Pearson.

Hawton, K., Bergen, H., Kapur, N., Cooper, J., Steeg, S., Ness, J., & Waters, K. (2012). Repetition of self-harm and suicide following self-harm in children and adolescents: Findings from the multicentre study of self-harm in England. *Journal of Child Psychology and Psychiatry, 53*, 1212–1219.

Hawton, K., & James, A. (2005). Suicide and deliberate self harm in young people. *BMJ, 330*, 891–894.

National Association of School Psychologists. (2002). *Threat assessment: Predicting and preventing school violence*. Retrieved from http://www.naspcenter.org/factsheets/threatassess_fs.html

National Institute of Drug Abuse. (2016). *Commonly used drug charts*. Retrieved from www.drugabuse.gov/drugs-abuse/commonly-abused-drugs-charts

Schmidt, J. J. (2014). *Counseling in schools: Comprehensive programs of responsive services for all students*. Upper Saddle River, NJ: Pearson.

Self-injury (Cutting, self-harm, or self-mutilation). (n.d.). In mentalhealthamerica.net. Retrieved from www.mentalhealthamerica.net/self-injury

Viana, A. G., Dixon, L. J., Berenz, E. C., & Espil, F. M. (2016). Trauma and deliberate self-harm among inpatient adolescents: The moderating role of anxiety sensitivity. *Psychological Trauma: Research, Practice, and Policy, 9*, 509–517.

Warning signs. (n.d.). In stopbullying.gov. Retrieved from www.stopbullying.gov/at

World Health Organization. (2015). *Assessment for self harm/suicide in persons with priority mental, neurological and substance use disorders*. Retrieved from www.who.int/mental_health/mhgap/evidence/suicide/en/

Appendix 4.1

Steps to Take When Responding to Suicidal Thoughts

1. When there is a threat, speak with the student about his or her thoughts, feelings, and hardships in life. This student should not be left alone. If needed, consider having someone stay with the student while you step out.
2. Within that, search for risk factors, a plan (e.g., giving away belongings, journaling, use of pills or a weapon), ask who is aware of the plan (friends or family), any previous thoughts or feelings, any previous attempts, the length of time these feelings have been present, physiological symptomology, cutting or burning behaviors, and any experienced isolation from friends/family. Inquire about the other places or ways he/she has expressed interest in suicide (e.g., music, journaling, drawing, internet). Ask the student to describe situations, places, or events that make him/her feel most suicidal or cause cutting.
3. Inquire about reasons to live, motivations for continued life or success, and positive attributes in the student's life. Discuss who he/she believes would be most impacted by his or her departure, and that death is final. Strongly emphasize there is no way of reverting or changing this decision if successfully done. Rate suicidal risk (low, moderate, or high).
4. After gauging this student's current emotional and psychological state, explain his/her need for support. Describe what is going on with him or her and why it is a dangerous state to be in. Explain your obligations to help and that to maintain confidentiality would risk your professional security. If there has been cutting or burning, please refer to the nurse for documentation of the self-inflicted injury(ies). Create a safety plan.
5. Gather and complete five forms/processes of documentation: (1) Suicide Contract with a number for a crisis hotline, (2) Parent Emergency Conference Form, (3) Referral book, (4) Nurse's Report, and (5) Rapid Report. Consult with a lead counselor/administration if needed.
6. Devise a plan with the student for contacting the parents. Call the parent. If the parent is not available, do not leave an alarming message. However, do say on the voicemail that you are the counselor, that their child is with you, and that both of you are awaiting a

returned phone. When you speak to the parents, describe that you have obtained some information and need to meet face to face with them and their child. The parent will probably insist on a conversation over the phone. Redirect them and ask when they can arrive at the school.

7. When the parent arrives, remain calm. Embrace the atmosphere that may be very sad and driven with emotion. Depending on the devised plan between you and the student, you can begin explaining to the parents the chain of events leading up to their child being in your office. If agreed between you and the student, request that the parents listen to their child until they have heard all the information. Allow the student to describe what they are feeling to the parents. Be sure to inject other facts that the student has failed to communicate once he or she has completed the story.
8. Invite the parents to respond. Be aware, it could be anger, sadness, frustration, or fear present in the room. This may or may not be the first they have heard of this issue. If not, ask for their prior interventions or attempted solutions to the problem. Be prepared to manage the environment, and perhaps, for others to join in on the conversation, such as the other parent/step-parent or maybe even grandparents or older siblings. Be sure to cover all of numbers 2, 3, 4, and 5.
9. Cover all of number 3's information.
10. Cover numbers 4 and 5's information. Read the contract and provide a hotline number to the student in case he or she feels suicidal and has no one around. Obtain all signatures. Make two copies: one for your personal file and one for the parent's file. Discuss referral and follow-up options if needed.

Section II

Counseling Skills

5

Individual Counseling Sessions

Dr. Kathy McDonald

ASCA NATIONAL MODEL THEME

Leadership

Advocacy

ASCA SCHOOL COUNSELOR PROFESSIONAL COMPETENCIES

II-C-1. Has an impact on every student rather than a series of services provided only to students in need.

IV-B-3. Provides responsive services.

IV-B-3a. Lists and describes interventions in responsive services, such as individual/small group and crisis response.

IV-B-3b. Theories such as REBT, RT, CBT, Adlerian, SFBC, and PCC

IV-B-3c. Ability to provide counseling in times of transition, separation, heightened stress, critical change

IV-B-3g. Difference between school counseling and other types of counseling

IV-C-3. Developmental *and* short-term responsive counseling

ASCA PRINCIPLES

Principle 2 All students can benefit from interventions designed to assist their academic, career and personal/social development

Principle 6 School counselors' interventions in students' academic, career and personal/social development help students acquire and apply knowledge, skills and attitudes promoting development in those three dimensions of human growth

Principle 9 The work of school counselors should be organized as a program

Principle 11 The elements and strategies described as the delivery component for the school counseling programs include all the means to have an impact on students' academic, career and personal/social development: direct student services (school counseling core curriculum, individual student planning and responsive services) and indirect student services (referrals, consultation and collaboration)

ASCA ETHICAL STANDARDS FOR SCHOOL COUNSELORS (2016)

A.1.b. Aim to provide counseling to students in a brief context and support students and families/guardians in obtaining outside services if the student needs long-term clinical counseling.

CACREP STANDARDS 2016

Section 5-G, Entry-Level Specialty Areas, School Counseling

Foundations

1.b. Models of school counseling

Contextual Dimensions

2.a. School counselor roles as leaders, advocates, and systems change agents in P-12 schools

2.f. Competencies to advocate for school counseling roles

2.g. Characteristics, risk factors, and warning signs of students at risk for mental health and behavioral disorders

2.n. Legal and ethical considerations specific to school counseling

Practice

3.c. Core curriculum design, lesson plan development, classroom management strategies, and differentiated instructional strategies

3.d. Interventions to promote academic development

3.f. Techniques of personal/social counseling in school settings

3.h. Skills to critically examine the connections between social, familial, emotional, and behavior problems and academic achievement

3.n. Use of accountability data to inform decision making

Introduction

School counselors serve all students, but they remain keenly aware of the disparities in achievement and opportunity for diverse populations (Hannon, 2016). In 2012, the number of White students in U.S. public schools had decreased to a slim majority, accounting for 51% of the student population, while Asian and Hispanic student populations increased. Also, the 2012 data collected included a suspension rate for African American male students doubling that of any other racial or ethnic group (U.S. Department of Education, 2016). The National Center for Children in Poverty stressed that students who have lesser resources are at greater risk for behavioral and social problems. School counselors, fortunately, are in a unique position to be among the first to hear of serious student concerns (Kaffenberger & O'Rorke-Trigiani, 2013).

The National Association on Mental Illness Mental Health Fact Sheet (2016) estimated that:

- 20% of youth ages 13–18 live with a mental health condition
- 11% have a mood disorder
- 10% have a behavior disorder
- 8% have an anxiety disorder
- Suicide is the third leading cause of death among youth ages 10–24.

Hays, Craigen, Knight, Healey, and Sikes (2009) included other prominent mental health issues in schools, such as dating violence, self-injury, eating disorders, and bullying. The LGBT youth are twice as likely as their peers to say they have been assaulted (Human Rights Campaign, 2012). Unaddressed needs lead to devastating consequences for our youth. DeKruyf, Auger, and Trice-Black (2013) suggested joining the school counselor roles of educational leader with that of mental health professional to respond to the profound personal/social needs of today's students. The unfortunate reality, according to DeKruyf et al. (2013), is that many students will not access mental health services outside of the school system, even when referred to appropriate resources. Therefore, individual counseling is a vital need as well as the school counselor's responsibility.

Therapy in Schools

The role of the school counselor is not one of a therapist (ASCA, 2012). It is true that school counselors do not offer therapy or long-term counseling, as these professionals are usually educated differently in their graduate program (i.e., taking psychopharmacology, clinical mental health, substance abuse, or a diagnosis course). Furthermore, the credential for these areas of specialization are different. For example, in Texas, in order to be a school counselor, you must be certified with teaching experience, as opposed to a licensed professional counselor, which allows the therapist to diagnose, work in a hospital setting, or even have a private practice. The educational environment and the diversity of roles limit the school counselor's time; therefore, ongoing weekly sessions are not appropriate. However, it is appropriate that a school counselor, in agreement with the student—and with consent from the parent(s) or guardian(s)—see a student for more than one session. These sessions can be to work on issues of grief and loss, academic progress, behavior monitoring, or interpersonal concerns. Additionally, follow-up visits or referrals may be a part of these visits as well.

The ASCA National Model (ASCA, 2012) created clarity in the roles and responsibilities of school counselors by outlining essential components, domains, themes, and standards (Cinotti, 2014; Dahir & Stone, 2007). The ASCA School Counselor Competencies (ASCA, 2012) emphasize the importance of distinguishing the similarities and differences between school counseling and other types of counseling, such as mental health counseling. The American School Counselor Association (ASCA) defines therapy as long-term treatment of a mental disorder. If a student has been diagnosed with a mental disorder, or has symptoms or characteristics equivalent to the appearance of such, then visits to the school counseling office are unlikely to manage or intervene in any manner related to the disorder.

Responsive Services

ASCA includes individual counseling as an element within responsive services. School counselors who implement a comprehensive program of services include individual counseling to meet the immediate needs of students (ASCA, 2012). School counselors who do not include individual counseling services as part of their program forgo the implementation of a comprehensive counseling plan.

Responsive services, on the other hand, are delivered in small groups or individual sessions, both of which are short-term and goal-focused (see

Chapter 4; ASCA, 2012). There are usually three levels of responsive services to consider: (1) prevention, (2) intervention, and (3) remediation. Responsive services, an element of the delivery domain, includes counseling in either small groups or individually. School counselors are highly trained professionals capable of evaluating a student's need and their own ability to serve that need (Gruman, Marston, & Koon, 2013). Referrals are to be made to therapists when the severity of a student's concern is beyond the scope of the counselor's training or the problem demands frequent sessions (Ethics, A.1.b).

Individual Counseling

Individual counseling sessions are reserved for students with very personal and private difficulties whose needs cannot be met in large or small groups and whose needs are determined to be within the counselor's scope of training. ASCA recommends a student-counselor ratio of 250:1, but as of 2012, the national average stood at 471:1 (ASCA Student to Counselor Ratio, 2013). Unfortunately, the number of students with critical needs is growing.

Once a need is determined to be relevant for an individual session, the counselor has a responsibility to be familiar with the school district's policy concerning parent permission. A student should be told if parent permission is required, thereby providing an opportunity for the student to withdraw the request for counseling. In the absence of district policy, it is advisable that the counselor seeks parent permission if the individual requires more than two or three sessions (Stone, 2009).

On occasion parents will refuse counseling services. Counselors recognize that parents have the legal right to consent or to refuse services on behalf of minor children. Counselors attempt to remove barriers to intervention by respectfully responding to parents' objections. If the parent still declines service, the wise counselor honors the parent's decision. A trusted teacher or administrator can monitor the student's well-being (Stone, 2009). If a student's concern involves abuse, however, no permission is needed. The counselor follows state and district guidelines in contacting the appropriate local or state authorities, as needed.

Approaches for Individual Counseling

The ASCA National Model emphasizes the importance of school counselors organizing their work in an effort to provide effective and efficient programs. School counselors who do not systematically plan for a comprehensive program will live in the land of responsive services. A disorganized counseling program results in large numbers of students stopping by to see the counselor. The number of drop-in students will be greatly reduced if the counselor makes a concerted effort to inform students of the counseling services available and how those services are accessed.

A comprehensive program begins with the collection of data that is then used for planning, organizing, and implementing all areas of service. Existing data sources in schools include attendance records, discipline logs, and grade reports. Another source for data-driven decision-making is behavioral observation. Observation of a student can be helpful in determining the level of a student's need (Gruman & Hoelzen, 2011). Information is also collected from stakeholders such as students, teachers, and parents in the form of a needs survey. Once data is collected and analyzed, the counselor begins to organize for direct or indirect services (ASCA Ethical Standards, 2016, A.3.e).

School counselors facing a plethora of need and large caseloads can use annual and weekly calendars to design functional programs. A sizable number of problems reported to the counselor are appropriate for preventive classroom lesson topics, such as bullying and conflict management. Classroom lessons are ideal for educating students about issues suitable for individual counseling, the protocol for referrals, and the limits imposed on confidentiality. Other problems are best served in small groups of students who share a common need. Concerns targeted through large or small groups saves the counselor's time but provides essential services to a large number of students.

Classroom teachers are essential allies in recommending students for appropriate service delivery. Teachers alert the counselor to distressed students who require prompt attention. They also remind concerned parents of the support offered through the counseling office. When parents are aware of available services, they will contact the counselor for consultation, counseling services, or referrals (Ethics, A.6.a; ASCA Ethical Standards, 2016, B.1.3). The best advocacy for the role of school counselor is the expectation of students, teachers, and parents that the counselor is delivering direct services to students.

School counselors advise stakeholders of program services through multiple sources, such as the school website, brochures, newsletters, or during public forums (see Appendices 5.1 and 5.2). Effective counselors do not simply advertise responsive services, but they explain the necessity of short-term, goal-oriented sessions for individuals, plus they clarify the ethical obligation to maintain student confidentiality (Huss, Norris, & Mulet, 2008; ASCA Ethical Standards, B.1.f). Culturally sensitive school counselors will have counseling program information and forms translated into languages represented at their schools. They serve *all* students.

Teachers, administrators, and parents can refer students to the school counselor, but students will also self-refer. Students are more willing to request help if the referral steps are made clear and the process is private. School counselors often create their own referral forms that ask for information pertinent to locating the student during the school day. A comment section can be included for the student to briefly explain the need to see the counselor one-on-one. Some referral forms include symbols or pictures for the student to indicate the level of urgency (Appendix 5.3). Knowing the student's level of need in advance allows the counselor to prioritize the requests. Students are informed early in the school year about the existence of counselor referral forms, how to access them, and how to return them. Most requests for individual sessions, even though they represent immediate concerns, can be assigned appointment times that fit well with both the student's schedule and the counselor's schedule. Students also need to know how they will be informed of appointment times. Once a student is scheduled, the classroom teacher should be informed of the appointment if it results in a student's absence from class. The student's need for counseling is kept confidential, but the student's location is not. Teachers will appreciate the counselor's awareness of frequent fliers who might be more interested in skipping classes than attending counseling sessions. School counseling programs are meant to enhance the educational system, not detract from it.

Confidentiality

School counselors offer emotional support and therapeutic activities for individual students, but in doing so, will find themselves walking a tightrope. Confidentiality is the tightrope stretched between parents' legal rights and the counselor's obligation to students' ethical rights (ASCA Ethical Standards, 2016, A.2.f; Stone, 2009). Counselors recognize an ethical obligation to protect students' privacy rights. A minor's privacy rights, however, legally belong to the parent. Preferably, the limits to confidentiality have already been explained to all students during core curriculum lessons early in the school year. Experienced school counselors go a step further by posting the limits in sight of students entering the counseling office and reviewing the limits before a session begins. Young children are more likely to understand if the limits are stated in age-appropriate terms (ASCA Ethical Standards, 2016, A.2.d). While confidentiality is an undisputed expectation of school counselors, the school counselor's reputation for trustworthiness looms large in the development of a therapeutic relationship. A school counselor is deemed trustworthy when the limits to confidentiality are made clear before information is shared (see Figure 5.1).

Stakeholders Referral for Counseling

Teachers and administrators who are aware of the personal/social issues of particular students might inquire about a student's visit to the counselor. Counselors can acknowledge that the inquiry is made out of concern, but the student's issue must remain confidential. Counselors are advised to think through this scenario and be prepared with a respectful, but resolute response to protect both the student's privacy and the counselor's reputation for trustworthiness. Information can entail acknowledgement of the referral, that the student was in for a visit, that a plan of action is in place, and recommendations for the teacher to implement or utilize, if appropriate. When clear rules have been established concerning student confidentiality, the counselor will face fewer intrusive questions. Prevention is the best course. School staff can be made aware of the legal and ethical standards concerning confidentiality at in-service training or through other means of communication (ASCA Code of Ethics, A.2.a).

When a parent or guardian makes referral for their child to see the school counselor, they too look forward to receiving feedback about the session. Similar to providing information to teachers and administrators, all steps should be followed. Sometimes parents are motivated for counseling services for different reasons, like proof the child is experiencing

Figure 5.1 Confidentiality: Young children may feel safe telling their troubles to Milo. He will keep their secrets unless someone is being hurt.

duress or stress related to the divorce, for example. Another motivation might be to provide evidence of behavioral or learning problems to a specialty area physician or psychiatrist. Regardless, it may be important to ascertain the parents' motivation for counseling services for their child ahead of time, especially if parents are in the midst of legal battles with one another.

Assent for Counseling Services

The ASCA code of ethics recommends that school counselors seek students' assent to share information relevant to their welfare. Assent for counseling services is not usually mandatory in school districts, but it does provide students with an overview of the types of services the school counselor can render, use of translators, and the limitations of such services when conveying harmful information.

Use of Translators

One limit to confidentiality, often overlooked, is the use of translators. School counselors in schools with diverse demographics use translators to counsel students and their families when they are not proficient in English. Some campuses are fortunate to find bilingual or multilingual counselors, but those counselors are in demand depending on the geographic region or area. Translators are useful when a student is in crisis, but they can be included in planned sessions, too, with the student's assent. Translators employed by the district might be educated on issues of confidentiality, but the counselor still reviews students' ethical rights to privacy and the importance of staying on message.

When training and preparing the translator for individual counseling sessions, there are several things to discuss. Translators must be aware that even though languages are not necessarily translated verbatim, that adding descriptors that alter the meaning, intent, or message tends to compromise the integrity of what the school counselor is conveying. Additionally, school counselors must verbally pace the session, taking time in between comments to allow translation to effectively take place. As a result of effective translation, parents will often begin to interact with the translator by requesting him or her when visiting the campus or calling the school and asking questions of the translator. Translators have to be mindful of the nature of their relationship as a result of serving as a support to the counselor. It is very easy to inadvertently situate into a role of the school counselor, not because they share a similar culture, but because the translator may be one of the few staff members to speak the language of the family. School counselors follow up with translators after distressing sessions, such as disclosures of abuse, to allow them the opportunity to vent emotional steam. In a session with a student, the school counselor does not talk to the translator; instead, the counselor maintains eye contact with the student and speaks directly to the student. The translator is important but peripheral to the student-counselor relationship.

Disclosure of Abuse or Neglect

Ultimately, an individual counseling session will result in a student choosing to disclose abuse or neglect. Needless to say, school counselors want to be fully prepared to act. These professionals are advised to be knowledgeable, not simply familiar, with their specific states' child protection laws and their district policies about reporting. In some states and in some instances, calls are not made to Child Protective Services (CPS), but are made to the local police department or 911. School counselors are not investigators, but they are reporters of information disclosed and observed. A report is required if even a suspicion of abuse arises. It is not only permissible to consult with another counselor if in doubt about making a report; it is encouraged by the Ethical Standards for School Counselors (ASCA, 2016).

Voluntary Disclosure

Students who voluntarily disclose depend on the outcry witness to respond with genuine concern and fortitude. A school counselor upholds this commitment to the student by receiving the information in a confident and composed manner. A student is less likely to feel undermined by the counselor reporting to CPS when the limits to confidentiality and the obligation to student welfare have been made clear before the disclosure.

During disclosure:

- Be a calming presence.
- Provide the student with a sense of safety and security.
- Listen closely to the words or terms the student uses—you will be using the student's own words later in filing the report.
- The student should do most of the talking while the counselor listens.
- Ask questions only to clarify the narrative; who, when, where.
- Do not help the narrative along by filling in information or making suggestions about people, places, or events.

- Use open-ended questions to allow the student to tell his/her narrative (What happened after that?)
- Try cued questions to gather more information (Tell me more about. . .).
- Mentally note the student's thought process, behavior, and affect.
- Notice the student's hygiene, manner of dress, and physical state.
- Ask the student about marks or injuries and note if the explanation is commensurate with the appearance of the injuries.
- Do not offer judgment on the accused person or event.
- Find out if the student is fearful of going home.
- Close the session by telling the student what steps you are going to take, such as reporting to CPS or consulting with a supervisor. Answer the student's questions.
- Thank the student for the display of courage and trust.
- Follow through with making the report to the correct agency or in seeking consultation.

Disclosure to Others

Teachers and administrators are watchful for signs of abuse in students, and, if they spot a concern, will ask the school counselor to speak to the student. In this instance, a student is not coming forward voluntarily to disclose. It is important that the counselor takes time to develop rapport before approaching the sensitive topic of abuse. Open-ended questions are the best approach to use in an interview because they allow the student the freedom to tell the narrative without prompting. A student might refuse to disclose or might disclose very little despite the counselor's efforts to make the student comfortable. A report should still be made based on the counselor's suspicion of abuse; include in the report if the student demonstrates a reluctance to talk. In some cases, the student provides a narrative that is inconsistent with injuries or observations and this, too, is critical to report to CPS. Mandated reporters are not investigators. School counselors provide the student the opportunity to talk, but they do not interrogate.

Impact of Disclosure on the Counselor

All disclosures of abuse or neglect tend to take an emotional toll on the school counselor, but some cases are unsparingly harsh. Physical abuse might be evident, with apparent injuries adding an unwelcome dimension to the student's story. The retelling of sexual abuse is particularly harrowing when it comes from the lips of a very young child. Neglectful actions of parents can stir up feelings of worry and anger. School counselors do well to remember during disclosure that the student is apprehensive and relies on the outcry witness for stability and empathy. They can offer strength and stability by focusing on the student's comfort rather than on their own discomfort. Once the student is cared for, the report is made, and work is done, self-care strategies should be employed to prevent burn-out or compassion fatigue by exercising, participating in yoga, reading, drawing, or listening to music—all of which helps heal the bruised spirit.

Managing the Counselor's Schedule During a Crisis

School counselors cannot always schedule individuals for appointments. Students in crisis must be seen immediately. Some student crises will happen at inopportune moments, and a few will take an inordinate amount of the time. The only way to plan ahead for these events is to inform the staff and students that, when a crisis occurs, other items on the counseling agenda will be on hold. Usually during a crisis, other staff members are willing to help the counselor get messages to those affected by sudden cancellations. Once the reason for the crisis becomes clear, it may be that the situation is an emergency to the student, but less of an emergency to the school counselor. School counselors take into account that a student can be deeply distressed over an issue that is of small importance to adults. However, if the student perceives the situation to be awful, then to the student it is awful. The student deserves empathy and a listening ear. A crisis of this sort can be resolved in a short time and the student returned to class in an improved mood, ready to learn, while proceeding with the day's agenda. Dismissal time seems to be a favored time for students to become distressed. Students are engaged during the day and are distracted from personal problems until it is time to go home and face them. If the distressed student indicates fear of abuse or neglect occurring at home, then the counselor attends to the student before allowing the student to be dismissed. A dismissal time disclosure provokes anxiety in the counselor and perhaps in the student. The school counselor does not hesitate to consult about the situation at hand, then weighs the risk to the student's safety and errs on the side of caution.

Progress Notes and Evaluations

Progress notes document interactions between the school counselor and the student. Large caseloads can hamper a school counselor's memory of previous contacts with students, making it a necessity to take notes about student visits to the office. Most states do not provide school counselors with the legal status of privileged communication. In the absence of privilege, then the courts can subpoena written records. Various methods can be used to record notes. The counselor must choose a format before seeing students. The method used for progress notes must be brief. SOAP is an acronym (subjective, objective, assessment, plan) that guides the writing of progress notes. SOAP notes are brief and efficient, but they adequately document the school counselor's competency in acting on behalf of students. SOAP notes then provide the school counselor with a memory aid and documentation of the school counselor's course of action. By documenting the school counselor's plan for addressing student need, the progress note legally protects in a court of law. Notes are concise, the names of other people mentioned by the student are unrecorded, and the date/time of sessions are included. Each individual session is documented (Cameron & Turtlesong, 2002). Progress notes are written with the assumption that they will be read.

S—*subjective*: refers to the student's perception of the problem

- *Sara stated that she is anxious about the upcoming SATs*

O—*objective*: includes the counselor's observation of the student's affect, behavior, and appearance

- *Twisted her fingers while talking and cried briefly*

A—*assessment*: includes the counselor's impression of the student's need

- *Needs intervention for test anxiety*

P—*plan*: refers to the action the counselor will take if subsequent sessions are needed

- *Individual session on relaxation strategies*

Harried counselors can easily forget to document a session. Counselors can train students to sign in and write the date and time of their sessions. Counselors can refer to the sign-in documents later to check that the writing of a progress note was not overlooked. If a sign-in method is used, consider that a document in list form destroys the privacy of students. Note cards can be used for individuals and then filed. Counselors are creative in finding ways to protect students' privacy while juggling documentation of sessions.

School counselors evaluate their work with students. Student evaluations of sessions are important for counselors to determine the effectiveness of an intervention. Session evaluations ask students for their perceptions and therefore are considered perception data. Session evaluations must fit the developmental level of the student being served. Perception data taken before and after sessions denote progress or lack of progress. Lack of progress indicates either the need to change interventions or the need for further sessions. An item that clarifies the student's perception of the intervention is included in evaluations if developmentally appropriate. Once the counselor has protocols in place for referrals, has scheduled individual appointments, and if required, has received parent permission, then the counselor is ready to choose a theoretical approach applicable to each student's need.

Theoretical Orientation

A broad knowledge of theories provides an abundance of interventions, while an understanding of child development guides the selection (ASCA, 2016). Effective school counselors research theories, attend workshops or courses, and learn multiple strategies and interventions that are useful for different ages. No theory is "one size fits all," but fortunately multiple theories are useful in the school environment (Erford, 2019). Therapeutic approaches that fit well into the education environment are available for the counselor to study and implement. Some of the approaches frequently used by school counselors are briefly discussed in the following sections.

Person-Centered Counseling

The person-centered counseling (PCC) approach assumes clients have the ability to find their own remedies to obstacles. The therapeutic relationship is fundamental in clients recognizing their inherent ability to affect personal change. The counselor's attitude of empathic understanding, congruence, and unconditional positive regard are foundational in establishing a healing, therapeutic relationship. School counselors offer all students the basic conditions for a therapeutic relationship, but person-centered principles are easily integrated with other approaches. Unconditional positive regard is currently incorporated into several therapies, such as dialectical behavior therapy (Sommers-Flanagan, 2015). Sometimes a student needs the undivided attention of a genuinely caring presence to find inner strength and healing.

Cognitive Behavioral Therapy

Cognitive behavioral therapy (CBT) is a broad theory that is a goal-oriented, short-term approach based on the idea that a change in distorted thinking will result in a positive change in mood and behavior (see Figure 5.2). Cognitive behavioral therapy has been well researched and is proven to be an effective choice for anxiety (Muris, Mayer, den Adel, Roos, & van Wamelen, 2009; Mychailyszyn et al., 2011), depression (O'Callaghan & Cunningham, 2015), and many other concerns. Multiple resources are available to counselors in the form of curricula, worksheets, activities, and books that apply CBT principles to different developmental levels. Due to its efficacy in addressing various needs and ages, CBT is a theory that has a lot to offer school counselors.

Solution-Focused Brief Therapy

Solution-Focused Brief Therapy (SFBT) is a time-limited and goal-oriented approach, making it a practical choice for use in schools. Rather than ruminating about past events or spotlighting the current problem and symptoms, the individual is guided to focus on the solution. The individual envisions a future where the problem does not exist, and then uses personal strengths and resources to achieve resolution. Techniques include the therapist's recognition of the individual's resiliency in the face of difficulty, giving compliments on the student's inner strengths, using the miracle question to promote a perception of life without the problem, and the use of scaling questions to determine progress. SFBT is quite useful for many concerns that individuals present to the school counselor, and research suggested the effectiveness of the approach in schools (Erford, 2019).

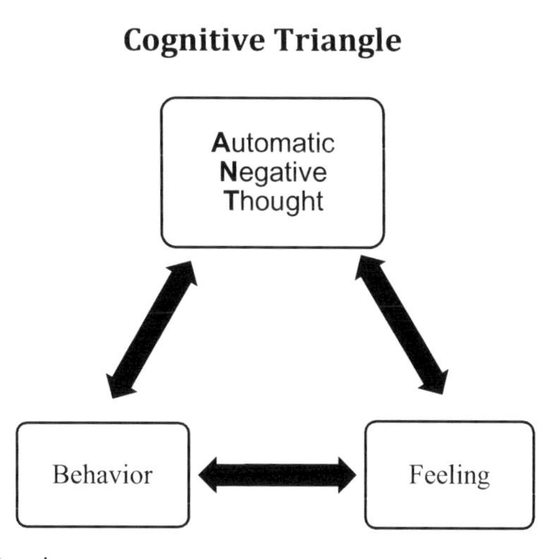

Figure 5.2 Cognitive Triangle

Play Therapy

Play therapy is a structured, developmental intervention that falls into the two broad categories, directed and non-directed. Both types are effective interventions (Ray, Armstrong, Balkin, & Jayne, 2015) and can be successfully incorporated into a school's counseling program. Counselors include a large assortment of toys and play items in the counseling room, and the students engage in play with items that represent their world. The counselor's role is to be a caring and engaged presence within the world the child creates (Landreth, 2002).

Narrative Therapy

Narrative therapy is based on the idea that individuals weave their identities from the myriad stories they tell about themselves. Individuals with problem-saturated narratives focus on negative, problematic events or statements from others. Positive parts of their life stories recede and become small, unnoticeable pieces of their life narratives. Externalizing the problem is central to narrative therapy. The individual is not the problem; the problem is the problem. If a student states that he or she is anxious, the counselor uses language that separates the problem of anxiety from the student's identity. An example is, "How long has anxiety been your enemy?" Counselors listen for exceptions to the problem that offer the individual a window to a successful outcome and a view of life without the problem (Nafziger & DeKruyf, 2013).

Trauma-Informed Counseling and Approaches

Trauma, broadly defined, includes many life events such as natural disasters, interpersonal violence, war, as well as devastating generational or historical experiences such as the Holocaust or racial oppression. Training in the area of trauma is important for counselors serving in every area of the mental health field and across all mental health settings. Unfortunately, training in the recognition of trauma symptoms and in effective approaches and interventions lags behind the enormous need. Individuals often do not report trauma as the presenting problem, but trauma often underlies problems that present (Goodman, 2015).

Mailloux (2014) emphasized the ethical underpinnings of counselors' need for trauma training. The counselor has an ethical obligation to avoid retraumatizing the client, as well as an ethical obligation for self-care to mitigate the effects of vicarious trauma. Little, Akin-Little, and Gutierrez (2009) researched trauma-focused cognitive behavioral therapy (TF-CBT) and found it to be an empirically effective approach to trauma, useful for children and their caregivers.

Trauma-focused cognitive behavioral therapy is a structured psychoeducational approach to trauma with specific components. Interventions include relaxation strategies, affect regulation, coping strategies, and processing of the trauma narrative. Parents and caregivers are important to the child's progress and receive information in parenting the traumatized child. Parents are included in some sessions. Coleman and Macintosh (2015) maintain that evidence-based practices ignore the power of creative expression. Art provides a client with the opportunity for expression without words, which is especially important for those who find the impact of trauma to be too difficult to articulate.

Animal-Assisted Therapy

Animal-assisted therapy (AAT) is an effective tool in building a quick rapport between students and counselor. Levinson (1969) wrote about his breakthrough with an emotionally distant autistic child. The child played with Levinson's dog in one session and then allowed Levinson to join in the activity. When student-counselor ratios are high, and the workload is heavy, the counselor provides less direct services to each student on the caseload. The use of a pet in a counseling program offers the counselor an outstanding identity among the school faculty. Students are attracted to both the pet and the counselor, resulting in a fast bond. School counselors have a duty to follow school and district policies concerning the presence of animals in schools. If animals are not allowed, then reasonable, respectful, and appropriate steps can be taken to request change. The counselor who relies on research can build a strong case on the effective use of therapy pets in the schools.

Any counselor who intends to use a therapy dog should first have the dog evaluated and registered through a reputable therapy dog organization. Smaller animals are useful as a therapeutic intervention and are often more acceptable to administrators. If a counselor is permitted to bring a therapy pet to school, the presence of the animal should be well advertised to parents, school faculty, and students (see Figure 5.3).

Friendly pets are ice breakers, encourage ease of conversation, and relieve anxiety (Fine, 2000); therefore, animals can be beneficial additions to school counseling programs. Pets fit nicely into a play therapy environment, and they can be used as rewards on behavior contracts. A comforting therapy dog can accompany a highly anxious student into the classroom, and they can bring laughter to a grief-stricken child. A therapy pet is a talking point that builds rapport and provides a tranquil focal point during disclosures of abuse. Animals relieve the apprehension of students who enter counseling

***Meet Milo**

Milo is a registered therapy dog that will be present in the counseling office on Tuesdays and Thursdays.

Research is clear. Those who like animals are comforted by friendly pets. Milo would like to fill the role of friendly pet for our students.

Milo also understands that people laugh, cry, feel embarrassed, and make mistakes. He has feelings, too, and he REALLY understands making mistakes.

Milo knows that not all students like dogs, even though he likes all students. He is willing to take his nap elsewhere so everyone can access the counselor.

**If you have any concerns or questions about the therapy dog, please contact the counselor.*

Ms XXX
School Counselor
Phone:

Figure 5.3 Meet Milo

for any reason, but they are especially appreciated during the discussion of sensitive subjects.

Even though AAT is a useful approach, it is not for everyone. If a student is allergic or fearful or culturally opposed, then the pet should be absent from sessions. The needs and safety of the therapy animal are additional responsibilities for the busy counselor, although the focus is always on the safety and success of students. Careful planning and foresight are essential for the effective inclusion of AAT into a comprehensive counseling program.

Conclusion

Individual counseling, as an element of Responsive Services, is included in the ASCA National Model of School Counseling. Counselors who aspire to a comprehensive program include individual counseling in direct delivery of services. School counselors plan and organize service delivery to meet the needs of all students; therefore, students with immediate and private needs are served in individual counseling. Planning includes educating the stakeholders about available counseling services, limits to confidentiality in counseling, and the protocols in place for referrals. Knowledge of federal and state laws that impact school counseling and students are imperative, and the ASCA Code of Ethics and the policies of the school district are thoroughly reviewed and frequently referenced. Interventions are chosen based on their effectiveness and their appropriateness for the developmental levels of the students served in counseling. School counselors are not therapists, but they provide a restorative therapeutic relationship along with therapeutic interventions that lead to student success.

Activities

1. Discuss the theory of your choice in working with students in a school setting. Explain how you would use your theoretical perspective in the following situations: an elementary student who complains about a teacher, a third-grade student who reveals that he/she is being bullied, a high school student who just lost a good friend to a suicide, a high school senior who has been tardy an excessive number of times to first period, or a high school girl who just found out that her boyfriend is cheating.
2. Role-play a counseling session in which a fifth-grade boy reveals that he has been sexually abused by a neighbor. Once the session is over, role-play the steps you would take to make the report.
3. Design your counseling space. Make a list of the furniture and accessories you would need to create the space you want for the grade level of your choice.
4. Role-play a counselor introduction to the students in your school. This will include what a counselor does, how students can make an appointment with the counselor, and the limits of confidentiality.
5. Make a sign that indicates the limits of confidentiality in the language appropriate for the students you will counsel. This sign would be posted on your door or some other location that is able to be viewed by all students as they enter your office.

Resources

National Alliance on Mental Illness:
www.nami.org/

References

American School Counselor Association. (2012). *ASCA National Model: A framework for school counseling programs* (3rd ed.). Alexandria, VA: American Counseling Association.

American School Counselor Association. (2013). *Student/counselor ratios.* www.schoolcounselor.org/school-counselors-members/careers-roles

American School Counselor Association. (2016). *ASCA code of ethics.* Alexandria, VA: American Counseling Association.

Cameron, S., & turtle song, i. (2002). Learning to write case notes using the SOAP format. *Journal of Counseling and Development, 80,* 286–292.

Cinotti, D. (2014). Competing professional identity models in school counseling: A historical perspective and commentary. *Professional Counselor, 4,* 417–425.

Coleman, K., & Macintosh, H. (2015). Art and evidence: Balancing the discussion on arts- and evidence-based practices with traumatized children. *Journal of Child & Adolescent Trauma, 8*(1), 21–31.

Dahir, C. A., & Stone, C. B. (2007). *School counseling at the crossroads of change (ACAPCD-05).* Alexandria, VA: American Counseling Association.

DeKruyf, L., Auger, R. W., & Trice-Black, S. (2013). The role of school counselors in meeting students' mental health needs: Examining issues of professional identity. *Professional School Counseling, 16*(5), 271–282.

Erford, T. E. (2011). *Transforming the school counseling profession* (3rd ed.). Upper Saddle River, NJ: Pearson.

Fine, A. H. (2000). *Animal-assisted therapy: Theoretical foundations and guidelines for practice.* San Diego, CA: Academic Press.

Goodman, R. (2015). Trauma counseling and interventions: Introduction to the special issue. *Journal of Mental Health Counseling, 37,* 283–294.

Gruman, D. & Hoelzen, B. (2011). Determining responsiveness to school counseling interventions using behavioral observations. *Professional School Counseling, 14*(3).

Gruman, D. H., Marston, T., & Koon, H. (2013). Bringing mental health needs into focus through school counseling program transformation. *Professional School Counseling, 16,* 333–341.

Hannon, M. D. (2016). Professional development needs of urban school counselors: A review of the literature. *Journal of Counselor Preparation & Supervision, 8,* 139–154.

Hays, D. G., Craigen, L. M., Knight, J., Healey, A., & Sikes, A. (2009). Duty to warn and protect against self-destructive behaviors and interpersonal violence. *Journal of School Counseling, 7,* 1–30.

Human Rights Campaign. (2012). *Growing up LGBT in America: HRC youth survey report key findings*, p. 16.

Huss, S. N., Bryant, A., & Mulet, S. (2008). Managing the quagmire of counseling in a school: Bringing the parents onboard. *Professional School Counseling, 6*, 362–367.

Kaffenberger, C. J., & O'Rorke-Trigiani, J. (2013). Addressing student mental health needs by providing direct and indirect services and building alliances in the community. *Professional School Counseling, 16*(5), 323–332.

Landreth, G. L. (2002). *Play therapy: The art of the relationship* (2nd ed.). New York: Brunner-Routledge.

Levinson, B. M. (1969). *Pet oriented child psychotherapy*. Springfield, IL: Charles C. Thomas.

Little, S. G., Akin-Little, A., & Gutierrez, G. (2009). Children and traumatic events: Therapeutic techniques for psychologists working in the schools. *Psychology in the Schools, 46*, 199–205.

Mailloux, S. L. (2014). The ethical imperative: Special considerations in the trauma counseling process. *Traumatology: An International Journal, 20*, 50–56.

Muris, P., Mayer, B., den Adel, M., Roos, T., & van Wamelen, J. (2009). Predictors of change following cognitive-behavioral treatment of children with anxiety problems: A preliminary investigation on negative automatic thoughts and anxiety control. *Child Psychiatry and Human Development, 40*, 139–151.

Mychailyszyn, M. P., Beidas, R. S., Benjamin, C. L., Edmunds, J. M., Podell, J. L., Cohen, J. S., & Kendall, P. C. (2011). Assessing and treating child anxiety in schools. *Psychology in the Schools, 48*, 223–232.

Nafziger, J., & DeKruyf, L. (2013). Narrative counseling for professional school counselors. *Professional School Counseling, 16*, 290–302.

National Alliance on Mental Illness. Retrieved from www.nami.org/get attachment/Learn-More/Mental-Health-by-the-Numbers/children mhfacts.pdf

National Center for Children in Poverty. Retrieved from nccp.org

O'Callaghan, P., & Cunningham, E. (2015). Can a targeted, group-based CBT intervention reduce depression and anxiety and improve self-concept in primary-age children? *Educational Psychology in Practice, 31*, 314–326.

Ray, D. C., Armstrong, S. A., Balkin, R. S., & Jayne, K. M. (2015). Child-centered play therapy in the schools: Review and meta-analysis. *Psychology in the Schools, 52*, 107–123.

Sommers-Flanagan, J. (2015). Evidence-based relationship practice: Enhancing counselor competence. *Journal of Mental Health Counseling*, *37*, 95–108.

Stone, C. (2009). *School counseling principles: Ethics and law*. Alexandria, VA: American Counseling Association.

U.S. Department of Education (DOE). *Status and trends in the education of racial and ethnic groups 2016*. Retrieved from https://nces.ed.gov/pubs2016/2016007.pdf

Appendix 5.1

ABC Middle School Counseling Program

Mrs. XXXX, M.Ed., SCS
Phone: 111–555–2222
Email: xx@xxx.xxx

The American School Counselor Association encourages school counselors to focus on three developmental levels of students: Academic Growth, Career Exploration, and Personal/Social Development. The four direct delivery methods are explained below:

1. Core Curriculum, conducted on a regular schedule in classrooms, focuses on topics appropriate for all students.
2. Individual Planning involves academic, career, and elective planning.
3. Responsive Services are direct counseling services provided to students on a short-term, goal-directed basis. The three types of counseling services available are:
   - Small group counseling (6 sessions): Group topics will be announced throughout the year. Written parent permission is required for student inclusion in a group.
   - Individual counseling provided on an as-needed basis for students with immediate needs. Students may self-refer or they can be referred by their parents or teachers
   - Crisis response

A student might see the counselor in small group or individual sessions for:

- Grief and loss issues; illness of a parent or sibling
- Family transition concerns (divorce, separation, remarriage, foster placement)
- Anxiety/worry
- Aggressive behavior, physical, verbal and nonverbal
- Withdrawn or passive behavior and many other concerns

The counselor is glad to provide a referral list to community resources if parents are interested in long-term therapy for their children.

**Limits of confidentiality include harm to self, harm to others, and harm to the student. Parents are asked to honor the counselor's ethical obligation to student confidentiality and the role that confidentiality plays in developing a therapeutic relationship. The counselor, above all, supports student safety and welfare.

Appendix 5.2

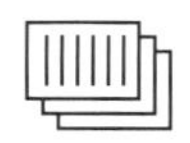

Dr. XXXX
6th grade counselor

Dr. XXXX has been in education for 27 years. Now relocated to XX, she has recently joined the district family. Her interests include childhood trauma, crisis response, and animal-assisted therapy.

XXX XXXX earned her Masters of Education in Counseling at X University. She earned her PhD in Counselor Education from X.

Sixth grade parents are invited to call, email, or make an appointment to address any concerns they might have about their children.

Mrs. XXXX
5th grade counselor

Mrs. XXXX has been in education for 17 years. She is a Licensed Professional Counselor and member of American School Counselor Association.

She graduated with her Masters of Education in Counseling at X University.

Please do not hesitate to contact Mrs. XXXX with any questions you may have regarding the Counseling Program.

Mrs. XXXX welcomes the opportunity to work with you and your student throughout the year.

Guidance and Counseling Program

Front Office:
XXX-XXX-XXXX

The American School Counseling Association encourages school counselors to focus on three developmental levels of students: Academic Growth, Career Exploration, and Personal/Social Development. The guidance program at JEI is comprehensive, encompassing all three developmental levels.

Three direct delivery methods are used to encourage student academics, career exploration and personal/social development:

Classroom Guidance is conducted on a regular schedule, and focuses on topics that are appropriate for all students.

Individual Planning involves academic, career, and elective planning.

Responsive Services include

- **Small group counseling** (4-6 sessions). Written parent permission is required for student inclusion in a group.
- **Individual counseling** is available for students who need to be seen individually, but only on a limited "as-needed" basis.

If an individual student needs a referral to a resource or therapist the counselors will consult with parents.

Ways students access the counselors:

- Self-referral
- Teacher referral
- Parent referral
- Administration referral

The counselors at XXX are available to consult with parents. Please call for an appointment.

Reasons students see the counselor

Grief and loss issues; illness of a parent or sibling

Family transition concerns (divorce, separation, remarriage, blended families, foster placement)

Anxiety/Worry

Aggressive behavior, both verbal and nonverbal

Withdrawn or passive behavior

Traumatic events- even those from the past

Recurring nightmares with a common theme

Guidance and Counseling Program

Appendix 5.3

Counselor Note

First and last Name: ___________________________________

Teacher: ____________________________ Date: _________

My Problem is:

Little	BIG	HUGE
See me this week	**See me tomorrow**	**See me now**

Comment: ____

Fold this note in half. Give it to your teacher. Your teacher will put it in my box.

Student Request Form

Appendix 5.4

Tips, Tricks, and Techniques

Counseling involves abstract ideas. Individuals of all ages benefit from the use of visual aids and behavioral practice.

Personal Space

The school counselor creates a circle of space on the floor using a long jump rope or hula hoop. The circle represents an individual's personal space or space bubble. The counselor steps inside the circle and then the student walks forward, stopping as soon as the circle is reached. The two make eye contact and have a short dialogue, then change places. The counselor points out that some people will have larger or smaller personal spaces than the one represented. Some people consider it a violation of personal space if an individual reaches into the imaginary circle. "Would you hand me the red map pencil in front of you, please?" is preferable to leaning into the individual's personal space.

Friendship

The same jump rope or hula hoop can represent a circle of friendship. Since all behavior is communication, our words, body language, and tone of voice either pulls people toward us in friendship or pushes people away. The student stands in the center of the circle and practices push/pull behavior with the counselor. The counselor responds by stepping close to the student's circle of friendship, or moving away, depending on the student's communication. Physical education teachers are a great source for borrowing hula hoops, jump ropes, and other items!

Apologizing

Many individuals, including adults, do not know how to apologize with sincerity. An apology is reparation for a misdeed that can be done in either written form or spoken directly to the injured party. A true apology contains four parts:

1. I'm sorry for (name the misbehavior).
2. It was wrong because . . .
3. Next time I will . . .
4. I hope you will forgive me.

The aggrieved individual should not be coerced into accepting an apology. Instead, the individual may choose to forgive only when the change in behavior is evident. A template of the four-part apology can be posted in classrooms as a helpful reminder.

The Cognitive Triangle

The cognitive triangle is useful for teaching an individual about the connection between thoughts, feelings, and behaviors. Individuals who recognize and challenge their own misperceptions can alter their attitudes. The student is taught to search for automatic negative thoughts (ANTs), challenge them, and then change them into positive thoughts (see Figure 5.2).

Parent Support

The American Academy of Child and Adolescent Psychiatry offers an online resource for parents called the Facts for Families Guide. The Guide includes printable information on multiple topics of concern in

English, Spanish, and Chinese. The counselor considers the ethical obligation to confidentiality before contacting the family.

Death

Young children have a hard time grasping the idea of death. The counselor often serves two simultaneous roles in situations that involve young children—counselor to the grieving student and consultant to the family. The counselor offers support to the student through individual counseling sessions and by offering the counselor's office as a private sanctuary where the student can grieve when overwhelmed. In rare situations, a parent might ask the counselor to inform a student about the death of a loved one. As hard as it is on the adult to witness their child's pain, this news must come from the parent, the caregiver, or someone in the family who is close to the student, and not the counselor. The counselor consults with the person who will be giving the death notification. The use of a glove or hand puppet can demonstrate the life force that leaves behind a motionless body. The parent or caregiver can use this technique to prepare a child who is attending a first funeral. An excellent online resource for both parents and counselors is The Dougy Center, a non-profit organization dedicated to helping grief-stricken children and families.

Anger

Anger creates intense energy that could result in someone being hurt. Focused deep breathing, a simple exercise, decreases emotional intensity, relaxes muscles, and slows the heart rate. A very angry individual benefits from a breathing coach. The counselor stands in front of the individual, if it is safe to do so, and states, "I am going to breathe for you." The individual typically falls into the same breathing rhythm. An individual in the throes of anger is not ready to learn anger control strategies. Once the person is calm, the counselor can teach effective techniques such as deep breathing, relaxation strategies, and positive self-talk. Free apps can be downloaded and used to teach students exercises such as slow breathing and relaxation strategies.

Styles of Behavior

Students who evaluate their own behavior gain insight into their personality. The continuum of behavior helps students analyze their own style and to recognize how they are seen by their peers (see Figure 5.8).

Resources

The Dougy Center, The National Center for Grieving Children & Families:

www.dougy.org

The American Academy of Child and Adolescent Psychiatry:

www.aacap.org

Appendix 5.5

Styles of Behavior

All behavior is communication to others. Most people do not fall on the extreme ends of the continuum, but somewhere along the line. Are you more passive, more aggressive, or more assertive in your behavior? Where would your classmates say you are on the continuum?

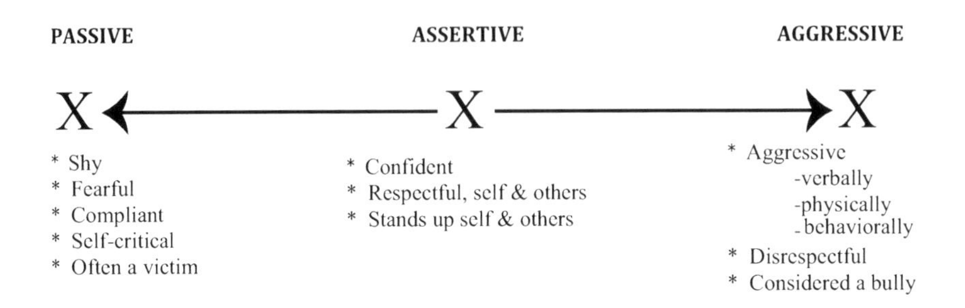

Body language communicates a person's style of behavior.

PASSIVE	ASSERTIVE	AGGRESSIVE
Stay away from me.	I am kind.	Stay away from me.
I'm afraid you will hurt me.	I am safe.	I'll hurt you.
	I am strong.	
	I take a stand.	

Styles of Behavior

Appendix 5.6

An Inviting Office Space

6

Group Counseling

Dr. Judy A. Nelson and Benny Malone

ASCA NATIONAL MODEL THEMES

Leadership

Advocacy and Social Justice

ASCA NATIONAL MODEL SCHOOL COUNSELOR PROFESSIONAL COMPETENCIES

III-B Management: Abilities and Skills:

III-B-6a. Uses appropriate academic and behavioral data to develop school counseling core curriculum, small-group and closing-the-gap action plans and determines appropriate students for the target group or interventions

III-B-6b. Identifies ASCA domains, standards and competencies being addressed by each plan

III-B-6c. Creates lesson plans related to the school counseling core curriculum identifying what will be delivered, to whom it will be delivered, how it will be delivered and how student attainment of competencies will be evaluated

III-B-6d. Determines the intended impact on academics, attendance and behavior

III-B-6e. Identifies appropriate activities to accomplish objectives

III-B-6f. Identifies appropriate resources needed

III-B-6g. Identifies data-collection strategies to gather process, perception and outcome data

III-B-6h. Shares results of action plans with staff, parents and community

IV-A Knowledge:

IV-A-7. Principles of working with various student populations based on characteristics such as ethnic and racial background, English language proficiency, special needs, religion, gender and income

IV-A-8. Principles of multi-tiered approaches within the context of a comprehensive school counseling program

IV-A-9. Responsive services (counseling and crisis response) including grief and bereavement

IV-B-3. Provides responsive services

IV-B-3a. Lists and describes interventions used in responsive services, such as individual/small-group counseling and crisis response

IV-B-3b. Understands appropriate individual and small-group counseling theories and techniques such as rational emotive behavior therapy, reality therapy, cognitive-behavioral therapy, Adlerian, solution-focused brief counseling, person-centered counseling and family systems

IV-B-3c. Demonstrates an ability to provide counseling for students during times of transition, separation, heightened stress and critical change

IV-B-3d. Understands what defines a crisis, the appropriate response and a variety of intervention strategies to meet the needs of the individual, group or school community before, during and after crisis response

CACREP 2016 STANDARDS

6a. theoretical foundations of group counseling and group work

6b. dynamics associated with group process and development

6c. therapeutic factors and how they contribute to group effectiveness

6d. characteristics and functions of effective group leaders

6e. approaches to group formation, including recruiting, screening, and selecting members

6f. types of groups and other considerations that affect conducting groups in varied settings

6g. ethical and culturally relevant strategies for designing and facilitating groups

6h. direct experiences in which students participate as group members in a small group activity, approved by the program, for a minimum of 10 clock hours over the course of one academic term

SCHOOL COUNSELING PRACTICE

3d. interventions to promote academic development

3e. use of developmentally appropriate career counseling interventions and assessments

3f. techniques of personal/social counseling in school settings

3g. strategies to facilitate school and postsecondary transitions

3h. skills to critically examine the connections between social, familial, emotional, and behavior problems and academic achievement

3i. approaches to increase promotion and graduation rates

3j. interventions to promote college and career readiness

3k. strategies to promote equity in student achievement and college access

Introduction

As we think about working with students directly, face-to-face, we believe group counseling to be a way to bring relatively small numbers of students together who struggle with similar issues and who could support each other during challenging times. While school counseling core curriculum provides direct student contact to large numbers of students in classrooms, grade-level meetings, or entire school assemblies, group counseling is a service that allows counselors to respond to students who need more than the core curriculum lessons presented to larger groups, and yet, serve more students than if counselors met with students individually. Also, group counseling can be preventive in nature, rather than crisis oriented, by remediating problem behavioral patterns that have been noticed by teachers and/or parents. Working in a group can teach students coping skills, social interactions, and decision-making skills as well as provide a safe place for practicing these new behaviors.

According to the American School Counselor Association (ASCA) [2014], group counseling is a necessary intervention in the Comprehensive School Counseling Program (CSCP) and provides an opportunity for students to adjust, cope, communicate, and collaborate in a safe environment.

Furthermore, academic, career, and social/emotional concerns can be addressed in group counseling. In our chapter, we will address theoretical perspectives and group processes in school counseling, the role of the school counselor in group counseling, parent consent, student referral and recruitment, coordinating times for groups, and suggested topics for elementary and secondary levels. Additionally, we will provide two case examples of group work that we have used in public schools.

Theoretical Perspectives and Group Process in Group Work in Schools

Choice theory (Glasser, 1998) is the underlying theoretical basis for reality therapy (Wubbolding, 2010), which used together in group counseling can be effective in teaching students that problem behaviors stem from their choices. Choice theory is based on the premise that everything we do is chosen and is designed to help us achieve what we want (Glasser, 2001). Working from a choice theory perspective, students can examine their current behaviors through their actions, thinking, and feelings in a safe environment. Ultimately, students identify what is important to them, create goals, and plan the actions necessary to reach the stated goals. In group work, individual students will have the support of the school counselor, but also of other students who also struggle with behavioral problems. Alternatively, reality therapy emphasizes the therapeutic relationship and helps students take control of their lives. Given the opportunity to learn how to make better choices, students can develop more satisfying relationships with peers, parents, and adult supervisors (Robey, Beebe, Mercherson, & Grant, 2011). According to Corey (2013), reality therapy is well suited for group work and has been researched in schools to document its effectiveness (Comiskey, 1993; Green & Uroff, 1991; Swenson, 1995).

Relational-cultural theory (RCT) can also be utilized in group work in school settings, particularly in middle schools, the years when navigating peer connections and individual identity development (including racial identity development and sexual identity development) are so critical (Tucker, Smith-Adcock, & Trepal, 2011). The RTC posits that humans have an intense need for connection, and yet, pre-teen and teenaged students often exhibit behaviors that paradoxically block these connections. The RCT focuses on development, wellness, and multiculturalism (Tucker, Smith-Adcock, & Trepal, 2011) and fits nicely with the needs of middle school students. Thus, adolescents can benefit from direct counseling services that assist them in examining their current relational behaviors and implement changes that will result in more satisfying relationships. School counselors who are trained in choice theory and/or RCT will have a sound foundation for working with diverse students and their various concerns in group work.

Student Recruitment, Referral, and Screening

Recruitment, referral, and screening are important procedures in establishing groups in any setting, including schools. The questions to ask are: Which students would benefit from group work? How can the school counselor locate group participants? What will the screening process look like? How many students should be in the group? Clearly, school administrators, teachers, parents, and staff can be helpful in identifying students who would benefit from group work.

Faculty and Staff Referrals

We have tried a number of ways to elicit the input of fellow educators. One way is simply to create a form that outlines the groups that the counselor plans to conduct throughout the school year and ask teachers to list students who might be appropriate for each group. This initiative is not without its problems! Without proper directions or training, teachers can list such large numbers of students that the school counselor could never begin to serve even a fraction of them. Providing teachers with some training about groups at a faculty meeting can help teachers understand the benefits of group work as well as assist them with making appropriate recommendations. These points are important to cover in the training of teachers and staff to identify potential group members:

- Introduce group work by citing the counselor competencies and codes of ethics relevant to group counseling. These are included at the beginning of this chapter. Be sure to explain the special training you have had in group counseling.
- Discuss the possible group topics that you are considering and explain the relevance of each one to school success.
- Explain how to identify students who may benefit from group counseling and what particular group may be appropriate for certain students. This step will depend on the groups you are planning to run. For example, explain to teachers that a group for children who have recently experienced divorce is not for every child who has experienced divorce. Teachers need to identify those students who are experiencing emotional distress due to the divorce. This distress would probably be affecting grades, relationships with teachers and peers, and possibly classroom behavior.

- Provide teachers with a handout with some reminders about referrals to group counseling and a place to write names of any students that the teachers would like to refer to your groups.

Parent Referrals

Additionally, parents often ask for help from the school counselor with their children's problems, thus making parents a reliable source for referrals to group work. School counselors should have a prominent place on the school website, the school newsletter, and other social media available to school staff. Announcing group work through these communication venues is one way to inform parents of upcoming events tasked by the school counselor, including groups that are being formed. Additionally, the counselor may simply contact parents by phone when the counselor is concerned about a particular student and feels that group counseling would be beneficial.

Additional Group Referrals

Also, the nurse, administrators, bus drivers, and cafeteria workers are in daily contact with students and may observe patterns of behavior that warrant screening for group work. The school counselor can include these support personnel in the teacher training or provide special training sessions for them. And, of course, as mentioned previously, the school counselor who interacts with and counsels students consistently will identify students who can benefit from group participation. Using assessment strategies including grades, testing data, and discipline reports can be helpful in identifying students who struggle academically or who have a sudden drop in grades or an increase in behavior problems.

Considerations for Group Work

The number of students in group work in schools varies depending on the ages, grade levels, and developmental levels of the students. Generally, the younger the students, the smaller the groups and the shorter the meeting time. Children in the early elementary grades (K-1) might meet for 20 minutes two or three times a week with a group size of three or four students (Henderson & Thompson, 2010). Preadolescent children might include five to seven group members and might meet once a week for around 30 minutes or even longer depending on the group and the students' availability (Dagley & English, 2013). Adolescent groups could include five to ten members and could last for an entire class period of 45 to 55 minutes.

The number of weeks that a group meets is often determined by the academic year. Some school districts are divided by six or nine weeks' grading periods; thus, group work might be accomplished within the grading periods. Districts are usually divided by quarters or semesters, which can also determine the length of time a group meets. Another option is to meet twice a week for three or four weeks. Scheduling group work in schools is ultimately one of the management tasks of school counselors, and plans should be made with care to make sure that group work is included in the yearly calendar of the CSCP. In addition to meeting times and group size, the decision to mix genders or to have a *boys only* or *girls only* group must be made. One variable to consider is the purpose of the group and the appropriateness of mixing genders, especially if topics discussed are extremely sensitive. There is not a consistent answer to this issue; thus, we recommend that counselors make this decision based on campus trends and the needs of the students.

Once students are identified and group times and meeting places are established, the school counselor begins the screening process. This process requires a face-to-face meeting with each potential participant, at which time the counselor explains what issues the group will address, why this particular student is invited to join the group, when and where the group will meet, and for how many weeks the group will meet. At this time, the school counselor also provides the student with a permission slip for the parents to sign. Students should not join a group without parent permission. In some school districts, it may not be mandatory to obtain parent permission, but we strongly recommend it due to sensitive topics and confidentiality issues. In addition to the student screening process, we recommend calling the parents to alert them to the nature of the group and the requirement of a parent signature to provide permission. All of these steps give the students and the parent(s) time to think about whether or not the student should participate in group work. These steps take time; thus, we encourage counselors to schedule group work throughout the semester in such a way that the screening process can work to everyone's benefit. We have included some helpful forms in the appendices of this chapter to assist with that process.

Coordination of Group Work in Schools

School counselors cite time constraints as the most common reason for not conducting groups in schools (Steen, Bauman, & Smith, 2007). In other words, the counselors who participated in the study noted that administrative duties consumed a great portion of their time, leaving little room for organizing and running groups. In order to address this particular barrier to group counseling, we refer readers to the Foreword and Chapter 9, which provide great detail about advocating for appropriate counselor roles and managing the CSCP effectively. Ultimately, administrators have a good deal to say about counselor activities; thus, principal buy-in is essential. We have found that education is one key way to help administrators and teachers understand the importance of group work, and we cannot emphasize enough the importance of collecting data to show that the students who attend group counseling make changes that are essential to their success in school. Another barrier in one study (Steen, Bauman, & Smith, 2007) was a lack of support among administrators who did not see the value of group work, teachers who were concerned about students missing instructional time, and parents who refused to sign the permission forms. Again, educating school staff and parents can help in promoting a positive attitude regarding group counseling. Starting small is another way to envision long-term goals for the CSCP and to provide the staff time to adjust to this particular counseling method.

As the counselor plans for group work, the logistics become important. Where will the group meet? What time during the school day will be appropriate for group work? How long will group sessions last? Generally, school counselors have offices to use for small groups. Schools may also have conference rooms or classrooms that are not being used at certain times of the day. Asking the staff to assist you in planning for your group work and finding the necessary space is one way to get them involved in the process and to get acclimated to the group work that is part of the school counselor's work. The time of day to hold groups is most likely the challenging part of running groups in schools. No matter how important school counselors believe that a student's participation in group work is, teachers and administrators do not want students missing instructional time. This challenge requires a great deal of creativity on the part of the school counselor. Here are some of the ways that school counselors have made it possible for students to fit group work into their schedules:

- Recess time for elementary students
- Lunch bunch where students bring their lunches to the counseling office
- Homeroom or advisory time
- Rotate students out of one class for a six-week group session; thus, students only miss one different class per week during the six-week period.
- Rotate students out of art, music, and P.E. so that students only miss each class two times in a six-week group session.

- Before or after school when transportation is available. Often middle and high schools offer late buses for sports and band practices, for tutoring, or for detention. Group attendees can use the late bus.

The last decision for school counselors to make regarding group work in schools is how long the group meeting will last. Often this decision is based on the time of day during which the group meets. For example, in elementary school, recess may last 20 to 30 minutes, which is an appropriate amount of time for counselors to meet with students in this age group. Also, the lunch period may be 30 minutes long, which again would work for all ages. Asking students to bring their lunches on group day and providing milk or juice in the counselor's office could allow for more time to conduct group work and less time going through the lunch line and getting lunch trays through the building and to the counselor's office. In some schools, students may not have the ability to bring a lunch from home, and the school counselor may want to provide a light and healthy lunch for students in the group.

If the counselor asks teachers to allow students to attend group during class time, the counselor must work out the timeframe with the teachers. If the class lasts 55 minutes, but the counselor wants to see the students for 30 minutes, will it be disruptive for the students to return to the teacher during the second half of the class? Showing respect and empathy for the teacher's time and role in educating children will make it possible for school counselors to collaborate to find the best way to fit group work into the school day. To this end, it may be workable to rotate students' group time each week so that they only miss a class one or two times for the duration of the group sessions. Again, creativity and collaboration skills will be necessary to obtain the best schedule for everyone involved.

Another option for older students is to have group sessions before or after school. Many middle and high schools provide late buses for sports or band practices, tutoring, and detention. Having groups meet for an hour after school is appropriate for older students if they have transportation home. Many students arrive at school 20 to 30 minutes before the doors open. This is another opportunity for group work. Providing students with special permission slips to enter the school before the official entry time can give the school counselor time to meet with students for 20 to 30 minutes. It is always a good idea to provide these students with an entry pass back to class to avoid problems with being tardy. Another helpful hint is to alert the first-period teachers to your group schedule and which students are involved. Many schools at all levels also have advisory or homeroom periods.

These classes can last from 15 minutes to a full class period and may be an appropriate time to have students attend group.

The Facilitator Role in Group Counseling

Directive or Non-Directive

Professional school counselors can be directive or more laissez-faire in group work. Bemak (2005) was critical of the group work that he often sees in schools, which involves a very controlled environment, almost like a classroom. Additionally, he stated that often the work included icebreakers, structured exercises, and pre-packaged guidance lessons. According to Bemak (2005), this trend does not allow for the often painful and difficult discussions that students need to have in a safe environment with a very skilled facilitator responding to and guiding the discussion in a way that frees students to discuss the most troublesome and heart-breaking issues that confront them. He attributes the training that counselors receive in group process for their inability to create a free, open, and inviting discussion in group work. School counselors may fear that they will lose control of the group, or that students will misbehave or abuse one another either verbally or possibly physically. Additionally, school counselors may avoid providing group counseling to the marginalized culturally diverse students for fear that they may not be able to handle the degree of frustration, anger, and hopelessness that may emerge in these group sessions.

Taking Bemak's (2005) critique into account and the genuine worries that school counselors have regarding group work in schools, we strongly urge school counselors to visit groups in psychiatric hospitals, discipline schools, and even in juvenile detention centers to learn how experienced counselors handle difficult situations and conversations in group work without squelching the needs of the clients. We believe that to truly address the needs of students and to empower them to make good choices and to be successful, school counselors must be willing to give up the power and allow the students to exert theirs.

Multicultural Considerations

Bemak, Chung, and Siroskey-Sabdo (2005) described a group intervention called Empowerment Groups for Academic Success (EGAS), which is designed to promote empowerment to marginalized students. This group counseling approach comes from a multicultural perspective and had profound effects on the group of seven at-risk African American girls who participated in the group experience. Although the group's purpose was to help in the girls' academic success, the leaders did not focus on grades or assignments, but rather allowed the participants to drive the focus of the group on their personal struggles and grievances. The facilitators believed that the open invitation to discuss their distress was what truly empowered them. The self-reported gains of the group work were as follows: the ability to share their feelings and resolve interpersonal difficulties, a continued support of the group members even after the group ended, knowing that their feelings were universal, more academic success, a new desire to continue their education after high school, and lastly a feeling of sadness and loss that the group ended. Learning about this model and others like it is strongly encouraged for the implementation of groups that really make a difference.

Types of Groups and Suggested Topics

Shechtman (2002) identified three types of groups: educational or guidance groups, counseling groups, and therapy groups. We believe that the information shared in an educational group would most likely be good for all students and should be reserved for classroom school counseling core curriculum, where many more students can be impacted than in a small group setting. The school counselor will probably conduct groups that provide counseling to students with social or academic challenges, whereas therapy groups should be reserved for students with problems such as eating disorders or severe mental illness and should be referred to community mental health agencies. Taking these recommendations into account, the following suggested topics would serve students who need more than classroom core curriculum, but whose problems are not severe enough for therapy groups outside of the school.

Suggested Group Topics

Here are some suggested group topics that can be tailored to the appropriate level. Can you think of some others for each grade level?

Elementary: Divorce, Blended Families, Making and Keeping Friends, Academic Success, Getting Along with Teachers, Bullying (for bullies and for those who are bullied), Teasing, Hygiene, Boundaries
Middle School: Divorce, Blended Families, Making Good Decisions, Choosing Friends, Academic Success, Bullying, Anger Issues, Negative Peer Pressure, Drugs and Alcohol in My Family, Executive Functioning or Organizational Skills, Self-Esteem

High School: My Career Interests, What's After High School?, Drugs and Alcohol in My Family, Dating Violence, Getting Along with Adults, Assertiveness Training (for girls), Anger Issues, Avoiding Dangerous Behaviors, Body Image, Sex and the Law

Confidentiality and Ethical Issues in Group Work in Schools

The Students' Responsibility

This issue of confidentiality in group work is difficult and cannot be guaranteed, particularly when working with children who may not understand the importance of confidentiality or how others may be impacted if they breach confidentiality. Explaining confidentiality in appropriate developmental language is the first step. Counselors can also have students sign an agreement of confidentiality or contract and should remind students of that agreement at the beginning and end of each group session. A group contract identifies the expected student behaviors and should include the following components:

- A statement of confidentiality
- An agreement to mutually respect all members of the group
- A promise not to hinder the group process
- An understanding that the group will achieve cohesiveness
- An awareness that group members will learn from and support each other

The Counselor's Responsibility

The school counselor's responsibility to confidentiality is exempt when other educators have a *legitimate need to know* or when the counselor has a *duty to warn or protect*. Parents have a right to their children's educational information, which includes counseling information according to federal laws (Family Educational Rights and Privacy Act). The school counselor can make a case with parents for not sharing detailed information by explaining the nature of trust in the counseling relationship and by assuring parents that if there were information that was vital to the safety of the child, the counselor would provide that information. If the parents have provided permission as we have suggested and have been given information about the themes and goals of the group, there may be fewer questions about what actually happens in each group session. However, the law is in favor of the parent in these cases, and if the parent insists on knowing details of his or her child's group counseling sessions, the parent has the right to know. Caution must be taken to protect the confidentiality of the other students in the group when supplying information to parents.

Our Final Thoughts: Tips for Success

- Call the group by a name that appeals to students rather than the adults, e.g., in elementary settings: Getting Along group as opposed to Social Skills Training; Keeping Your Cool group versus Stress Management or Anger Management group; Rising to the Top Group instead of Empowerment Group for Academic Success. In secondary settings: Not Too Cool for School group in place of Group for Academic Success; Girl Power group rather than Assertiveness Training group.
- Establish group ground rules at the first session. Elicit some ideas for rules from group members following the counselor's explanation of group purpose, duration, timing, etc. Write them down and post the rules at every session. Allows student buy-in to maintain appropriate behavior and understand that goals are personal and individual.
- Suggested rules (or commitments, agreements) in addition to confidentiality: Respect others, use courtesy/manners, take turns, proper tone of voice, right to pass rather than share, participate to best of my ability, prompt to arrive and prompt to depart. Counselor's rules should be listed too: communicate with teachers and parents for permission to attend, have activities prepared and ready to go quickly (due to short timeframe), same rules of respect, manners, and "facilitate" to best of my ability, etc.
- Alternate *structured sessions* (S) and *experiential sessions* (E), e.g., session 1(S): set rules and introduce short topical table game; session 2(E): the color of my feelings when . . . (paint, markers, crayons, chalk with individual paper or mural paper on wall or table); session 3(S): children's literature—counselor reads topical story and discusses themes with group members and how they may apply to the individual. Session 4(E): role-play scenarios provided by counselor, then debrief. This sets a routine for group and facilitates management of student behavior. (Demonstrating a balanced way of doing life.)
- It is okay for a student to repeat the same group in the following year if needed. A year of maturity may allow new insights to develop, or a student's need may continue to exist.

- Include a termination discussion at the last session. Ask students to evaluate the group: "Was it helpful to you? Do you think it would be helpful to another student in your situation? What was the best part of being in the group? What part of being in the group did you not like as much? What will you do if this situation is a problem for you in the future?" Hopefully, they will say "ask for help, tell someone, talk it over," etc. Pay attention to what they tell you.
- Never leave a teacher and student waiting for you and you fail to show up. Any emergency or crisis should be handled by another administrator while you are in group. A school runs on a tight schedule; all need to stay committed to their specialized assignments; teachers teach; counselors conduct group, teach school counseling core curriculum, and counsel individual students. You will kill your reputation and lose the cooperation of teachers if you fail to follow through on your program commitments. Move from being a reactive counselor to a proactive counselor. (Smiley face!)

Activities

1. Using the model presented in either Appendix 5.1 or 5.2, create a group counseling plan. Students can work in pairs or by themselves.
2. Choose the theory that you would use in group work with a certain grade level. Explain why you would use this particular theory.
3. Survey at least five school counselors who conduct group work and ask them about their group work. Ask them the following questions and add two of your own to ask:
   a. Why do you conduct groups here at your school?
   b. When do you schedule groups, and how many students are impacted by the group experience?
   c. What are some of the topics covered in your groups?
   d. How do you identify students who would benefit from group work?
   e. Do you get parent permission to include their children in group work?
4. Create a presentation to help teachers understand the importance of group work. Work with other students to create the presentation and present it to an audience.
5. Role-play a discussion with your administrators as you make the request to host group counseling sessions during the students' lunch periods. You would have to forego helping out on lunch

duty to do this. Be sure to approach your administrators with the appropriate ASCA competencies, appropriate and inappropriate school counseling duties, and any data that you have on the efficacy of group counseling in schools.

Resources

Association for Specialists in Group Work:
www.asgw.org

References

American School Counselor Association (2014). *The school counselor and group counseling*. [Position statement]. Alexandria, VA: Author. Retrieved from https://www.schoolcounselor.org/asca/media/asca/Position Statements/PS_Group-Counseling.pdf

Bemak, F. (2005). Reflections on multiculturalism, social justice, and empowerment groups for academic success: A critical discourse for contemporary schools. *Professional School Counseling*, *8*(5), 401–406.

Bemak, F., Chung, R., Siroskey-Sabdo, L. A. (2005). Empowerment groups for academic success: An innovative approach to prevent high school failure for at-risk, urban African. *Professional School Counseling*, *8*(5), 377–389.

Comiskey, P. (1993). Using reality therapy group training with at-risk high school freshmen. *Journal of Reality Therapy*, *12*(2), 59–64.

Corey, G. (2013). *Theory and practice of counseling and psychotherapy*. Belmont, CA: Thomson Brooks/Cole.

Dagley, J., & English, E. (2013). *Group work in schools* (Vol. 9). Thousand Oaks, CA: SAGE Publications.

The Family Educational Rights and Privacy Act (FERPA) (20 U.S.C. § 1232g; 34 CFR Part 99).

Glasser, W. (1998). *Choice theory: A new psychology of personal freedom*. New York: Harper Collins.

Glasser, W. (2001). *Counseling with choice theory*. New York: Harper Collins.

Greene, B., & Uroff, S. (1991). Quality education and at-risk students. *Journal of Reality Therapy*, *10*(2), 3–11.

Henderson, D., & Thompson, C. (2010). *Counseling children* (8th ed.). Belmont, CA: Brooks-Cole.

Robey, P. A., Beebe, J. E., Davis Mercherson, A., & Grant, G. (2011). Applications of choice theory and reality therapy with challenging youth. *International Journal of Choice Theory & Reality Therapy*, *31*(1), 84–89.

Shechtman, Z. (2002). Child group psychotherapy in the school at the threshold of a new millennium. *Journal of Counseling and Development, 80*, 293–299.

Steen, S., Bauman, S., & Smith, J. (2007). Professional school counselors and the practice of group work. *Professional School Counseling, 11*(2), 72–80.

Swenson, S. (1995). *Benjamin Franklin High School: What we are learning about teaching/learning strategies*. Orland Park, IL: Consolidated High School District 230.

Tucker, C., Smith-Adcock, S., & Trepal, H. C. (2011). Relational-cultural theory for middle school counselors. *Professional School Counseling, 14*(5), 310–316.

Wubbolding, R. E. (2010). *Reality therapy: Theories of psychotherapy series*. Washington, DC: American Psychological Association.

Appendix 6.1

Small Group Case Example: Elementary Divorce Group
(Suitable for Mixed-Gender Group, Grades 3–5)
Benny Malone, MSW
Certified School Counselor, Retired

Overview of Group Organization

Time Issues for Group Sessions

Younger students may have shorter group sessions (30 minutes) and attend a fewer number of sessions (six sessions); older students may have longer group sessions (45 to 60 minutes) and attend more sessions (eight sessions). Efforts should be made to complete Fall semester groups before the winter break. You may lose continuity if the groups carry over. Always remind the students that they can request a one-on-one visit with the counselor if needed after the group ends.

Group Space

Conduct the group in a space that is set up for both table activities and experiential activities. An excellent area is a self-contained classroom with two large rectangular tables with chairs; shelves or open storage for art materials, role-play props, and children's literature; chalkboard or large whiteboard; and open space for activities requiring movement.

Gender and Age/Grade Level

Preference should be given to mixed-gender groups since families are made up of both males and females. Since the group will be conducted during the school day, mixing ages/grade levels within a group is not practical. The same general activities can be used with any grade level with appropriate developmental adjustments.

Five-Step Format

1. Warm-up Activity—Group Rounds Check-in (timed, 1 minute each) or Ice Breaker
2. Topic Introduction—Counselor introduces topic for the session
3. Activity (Structured or Experiential; best to alternate from session to session)—materials, directions, sub-grouping/partners if needed, time limits

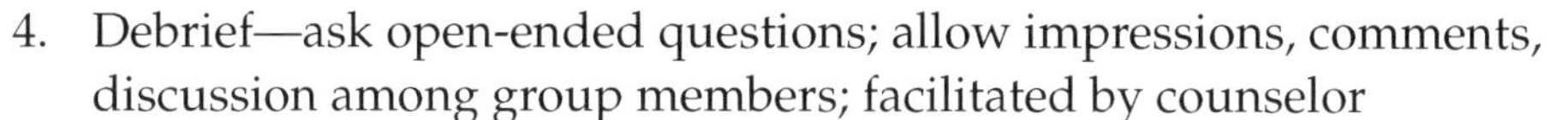

4. Debrief—ask open-ended questions; allow impressions, comments, discussion among group members; facilitated by counselor
5. Closing Routine—Remember students will be returning to an academic setting. May need to de-escalate behavior or activity levels of some students. Guide them in returning session materials to proper storage place. Establish a closing routine in Session 1. Suggestions—read short story; draw session-related individual picture with quiet background music; journal two to three sentences about feelings before/during/after group today; read two or three riddles; quick game of Hangman (Counselor chooses word or phrase that reinforces session topic.)

Elementary Divorce Group Topics Using Five-Step Format

Session 1: Orientation and Introduction

1. Warm-up Activity—Group purpose; member introductions, "Friendly Interview"
2. Topic Introduction—Group start-up tasks. Establish group commitment and rules; demonstrate Group Rounds Check-in
3. Structured Feelings Activity—Students take turns identifying pictures of feelings and describing, "A time I felt______ was when _______." Pull a feeling picture out of a basket; use feelings card deck; musical chairs, "Name the feeling" where you stopped with the music.
4. Debrief—What do you expect to get out of being in this group? Allows counselor to clarify purpose of the group.
5. Closing routine. Include next session date and time with explanation of whether students will be released by the teacher for group (older students) or picked up from class by the counselor/paraprofessional (younger students).

Session 2: Feelings—You Mean I'm Not Alone? Identifying and Understanding My Feelings

1. Warm-up Activity—Group Rounds Check-in
2. Topic Introduction—Introduce feelings in families, feelings between friends. What is a feeling? Where do they come from? What makes them change? Read and discuss *My Many Colored Days* by Dr. Seuss or other similar book tying feelings to colors.
3. Experiential Feelings Activity—Cover tables with butcher or art paper. Provide markers, crayons, and/or colored chalk. Remove

chairs so that students stand at the table. Designate large spaces on the paper for each student. Student will draw a personal feeling he or she is having now or has had in the past relating to a family experience.

4. Debrief—Group members take turns telling about their drawing—why that color, why that design, what was the feeling, what was the situation? After all have shared, ask group if anyone has had a similar feeling to someone else in the group. Discuss situations that may trigger certain feelings.
5. Closing Routine—Include complimentary comments regarding participation, following rules. Remind of responsibility of re-entering instructional area appropriately.

Sessions 3: What Is Divorce? Let's Have the Facts!

1. Warm-up Activity—Group Rounds Check-in
2. Topic Introduction—Elicit ideas from group members to gauge where each student is emotionally and factually. Students tell what divorce means individually.
3. Structured Reading Activity—Counselor reads a children's book about divorce. Allow group members to address issues as you turn pages. Do not rush through the reading and discussion.
4. Debrief—Ask open-ended questions. What part of the story seemed like what you have experienced? What stood out to you as the biggest problem kids might have when their parents decide to get a divorce? How did you try to handle that problem? Did any part of the story cause you to feel a certain way? What was happening and how did you feel when I was reading that page? Counselor should continue to hold the book and turn to pages that students reference. End debriefing with students holding hands in a circle and each identifying another group member that had a similar feeling, problem, or experience because of divorce. Objective is to encourage commonality of feelings, similarity of problems faced, and a general understanding that you are not alone.
5. Closing Routine—Since this is a heavy topic, consider reading two to three riddles or playing the Hangman game to lift students' moods, helping them rebalance for instructional time.

Sessions 4–7: Addressing Stressful Issues

By now your group routine should be well established, and students are more comfortable with sharing in the group. Choose some issues that group members identified in Session 3 and address these over the next four sessions. In Session 7 introduce the idea of the group creating its own book about divorce to help other kids like them.

Topics to address in addition to Identifying and Understanding My Feelings may include Telling Your Friends, Living with One Parent, Visiting Your Parent, Living with a Step-Parent, Mom's/Dad's Partner. The variations in your Five-Step Format will primarily occur in step 2: Topic Introduction, step 3: Activity, and step 4: Debrief—specifically the open-ended questions you will be asking.

Following are suggestions for steps 2, 3, and 4 associated with the Stressful Issues you plan to address in these four sessions.

Session 4: Stressful Issues

2. Topic Introduction—Telling Your Friends
3. Experiential Role-Play Activity—Using puppets or role-play, have group members act out how they might tell a close friend about the divorce. Coach students after a scenario is played and allow them to reenact how they would tell a friend this news. If using a role-play activity, have a few props available such as balls for a playground scenario, backpack or books for waiting at the bus stop, lunch box or tray for lunchtime conversation.
4. Debrief—Include open-ended questions about how the friend reacted; how group member felt before and after the telling; who might you want to tell and why this friend; what good thing might happen if you tell; what bad thing might happen if you tell.

Session 5: Stressful Issues

2. Topic Introduction—Stressful Changes—Living with One Parent/ Living with a Step-Parent
3. Structured Board Game Activity—Play card or board game about divorce. Discuss stressful events that happen in the game. Include stress management strategies in conversation while playing is facilitated by counselor.
4. Debrief—Gauge group members' understanding of vocabulary and facts of divorce. Clarify facts of divorce, e.g., separate living arrangements, court, judge, remarriage, step-parent relationship, step-sibling relationship, changes in routine (new child care, mom gets a job). Summarize and practice simple stress relief strategies. Include how stress influences how you feel and act.

Session 6: Stressful Issues

2. Topic Introduction—Visiting and Having Contact with the Other Parent
3. Experiential Group Writing Activity—Using a chalkboard, whiteboard, or large tablet, write a group letter to the "missed" parent. You may start out with a review of the divorce book you read in session 3 concerning the parent with whom the child has less contact. There are often feelings of loss that may be difficult for the group member to express to either parent. They may want to protect the feelings of both parents. This activity allows expression of these complex feelings. Counselor does the writing. Letter is addressed to My Missed Parent. Students can dictate what they want to say to the parent, how they feel about not seeing the parent as often, what they remember as some fun activity or event with the missed parent, and something the student is proud of or worried about that they want to tell the missed parent.
4. Debrief—This letter is not presented to anyone. It does not go home with the student. The activity represents a very safe time of sharing difficult feelings with others who understand and do not judge. Open-ended questions should include discussion of the student not being at fault for the divorce occurring and not having control over what parents decide. Remind group members that they are just now trying to understand the stressful divorce issues for kids, and parents are likely trying to Figure out the stressful divorce issues for adults. Relate this to other major changes they have experienced that no longer seem like a big problem, such as moving to a new school, having a baby brother or sister born into the family, or a parent or grandparent getting sick and going to the hospital. Encourage students to talk to their parents when they feel worried, scared, frustrated, or angry about any family situation. By sessions 6 and 7, the students should be gaining confidence in identifying how they feel in stressful situations and that it is helpful to talk to someone, especially their parents.

Session 7: Stressful Issues

2. Topic Introduction—Mom's/Dad's Partner
3. Structured Communication Activity—Using a chart demonstrate the Thought-Feeling-Action cycle. Do a practice activity. Matching three cards as a sequence.

Examples: Thought—made an A on a test; Feeling—happy, satisfied, proud; Action—do something nice for someone; do my homework without a reminder from Mom tonight. Thought—little brother will probably try to play with my big Lego project while I'm at Scouts tonight; Feeling—angry if he breaks it; worried that he might break it; Action—put Lego project away in a safe place. Thought—no one in this house likes me; Feeling—angry, sad; Action—yell at Mom and slam door when she tells me to start my homework.

4. Debrief—This topic is frequently the most stressful day-to-day issue the group members face. Allow for a range of feelings expression. The new special friend of a parent is an obvious threat to the hope the student has for the family to reunite. Communication is likely to go in the negative direction if the Thought is Mom's or Dad's new special friend is "no friend of mine!" As part of debriefing, do a simple Pros and Cons activity of this situation. Try to come from the parent's perspective as well as the student's perspective. Conclude the debriefing with the explanation of the group members writing a book to help other students experiencing divorce. Be aware of any group members who share potentially dangerous comments or actions by the parent's new special friend. This will warrant an individual meeting with the student to assess whether the child is at risk.

Session 8: Reaching Out

1. Warm-up Activity—Group Rounds Check-in
2. Topic Introduction—Writing a book about divorce to help others
3. Experiential Creative Writing Activity—This session requires materials: markers, plain 8 ½-x-11 paper, topic labels, construction paper for divider pages, list of topic prompts. Students will work individually creating drawings or writing about the various topics. It is a lengthy activity, and the counselor should be completely organized and start the activity quickly. Topic divider sheets may be prepared in advance. Students may choose to work on any or all topics. Simple content such as a page divided in half with illustrations or descriptions about the good and the bad, before and after, then and now, the best and the worst, etc., work very well.
4. Debrief—The counselor's job with this activity is to support by having ample materials and helping with specific questions a group member may ask about his or her design idea. The students should not put their name on their work. Instead, they

should write their grade level at the bottom of the page. After this session, the counselor should bind the booklet in some way. Laminating the pages/dividers will help preserve the students' work. The booklet can be shared one-on-one with students referred to you who are having significant difficulty with the news of a new divorce or separation of the parents. The growth in the group members in being able to cope with major family changes and their confidence in knowing how to express feelings and ask for help will be evident in each contribution to the group's book.

5. Closing Routine—If possible, plan a lunch bunch meeting of group members in the next two weeks as a check-in and to show them the finished and bound book. Congratulate all on their hard work and willingness to tackle difficult topics. Remind them that you are available to meet if they need to talk.

Appendix 6.2

Small Group Case Example: Secondary Group for Academic Success (Suitable for Same-Gender Group, Grades 6–9)

Judy A. Nelson, Ph.D.
Certified School Counselor, Retired

Overview of Group Organization

Time Issues for Group Sessions

Students in middle school may have shorter group sessions (30 minutes for sixth and seventh graders) and attend a fewer number of sessions (six sessions); older students may have longer group sessions (45 to 60 minutes for eighth and ninth graders) and attend more sessions (eight sessions). Efforts should be made to complete Fall semester groups before the winter break. You may lose continuity if the groups carry over. Always remind the students that they can request a one-on-one visit with the counselor if needed after the group ends. In many secondary schools, advisory or homeroom are at the beginning or the end of the day. This might be a good time to pull students for group, as many teachers allow students to use this time as a study hall.

Group Space

Depending on the size of the counselor's office or the counseling suite, groups can meet in one of these areas. If that does not allow adequate room for the students, perhaps an empty classroom would work. Be sure to get permission from the teacher and be respectful of the teacher's space. If you need equipment (e.g., computer, overheard projector, art materials, etc.) for any of the sessions, be sure to have it ready in advance.

Gender and Age/Grade Level

During the adolescent years, groups may be better suited to same-gender participants and accomplish more of their goals, but it is not a requirement. Since the group will be conducted during the school day, mixing ages/grade levels within a group is not practical. The same general activities can be used with any grade level with appropriate developmental adjustments. Depending on the grade and developmental level of your group participants, counselors should be able to accommodate between five and eight group members.

Five-Step Format

1. Warm-up Activity—Group Rounds Check-in (timed, 1 minute each) or Ice Breaker
2. Topic Introduction—Counselor introduces topic for the session
3. Activity (Structured or Experiential; best to alternate from session to session)—Materials, directions, sub-grouping/partners if needed, time limits
4. Debrief—Ask open ended-questions; allow impressions, comments, discussion among group members; facilitated by counselor
5. Closing Routine—Remember students will be returning to an academic setting. May need to de-escalate behavior or activity levels of some students. Guide them in returning session materials to proper storage place. Establish a closing routine in Session 1. Suggestions—journal two to three sentences about feelings before/during/after group today; ask students to go around and tell something they learned in group or something they want to accomplish during the week.

Secondary Academic Success Group Topics Using Five-Step Format

Session 1: Orientation and Introduction

1. Warm-up Activity—Group purpose; member introductions, "Friendly Interview"
2. Topic Introduction—Group start-up tasks. Establish group commitment and rules; demonstrate Group Rounds Check-in
3. Structured Activity—The counselor poses some introductory questions to the group to help them think about the purpose of the group and how they can benefit from participating. Some examples are: What are some of the things that you do well? How do you feel when you are successful at a task or an activity? Then segue way into feelings about how they are doing in school and how to improve that.
4. Debrief—What do you expect to get out of being in this group? Allows counselor to clarify purpose of the group.
5. Closing routine. Include next session date and time with explanation that students will be released by the teacher for group. Students will have a pass from the counselor for permission to leave class or lunch.

Session 2: Feelings—You Mean I'm Not Alone? Identifying and Understanding My Feelings

1. Warm-up Activity—Group Rounds Check-in
2. Topic Introduction—Introduce feelings. What is a feeling? Where do they come from? What makes them change? Name some times when it was difficult to control feelings and times when it was easy. Remind students of the feelings of success that they discussed in the first session.
3. Experiential Feelings Activity—Ask students to either draw or write about a time in a class of their choice in which they felt particularly successful. Have drawing and writing paper and pencils available.
4. Debrief—Group members take turns telling about their drawing or their written story—what was the feeling, what was the situation? After all have shared, ask the group if any of their experiences and/or feelings were similar. Discuss what about these situations triggered feelings of success.
5. Closing Routine—Include complimentary comments regarding participation, following rules. Remind of responsibility of re-entering instructional area appropriately.

Sessions 3: What Is Academic Success? Let's Find Out

1. Warm-up Activity—Group Rounds Check-in
2. Topic Introduction—Tell students that today they are going to embark on a type of treasure hunt to discover what it means to be successful in school. Elicit ideas from group members to gauge where each student is emotionally and factually. Students tell what academic success means individually.
3. Experiential Activity—"Clues" to the treasure hunt can be written on tag board and turned face down on the table. After the students have discussed what academic success means to them, the counselor turns over each "clue," and the students decide if they included that "clue" in their discussion. Don't rush the discussion. Give students plenty of time to talk about each one of these principles of success.
4. Debrief—Ask open-ended questions. What "clues" are similar to what you experienced in your story about success from the last session? What do you think might be some challenges of using these principles of success every day in all of your classes?
5. Closing Routine—Since this is a heavy topic, consider playing the Hangman game to lift students' moods, helping students rebalance for instructional time. Use words in the game that are related to academic success.

Sessions 4–7: Addressing Stressful Issues

By now your group routine should be well established and students are more comfortable in sharing in the group. Choose some of the challenge issues that group members identified in Session 3 and address these over the next four sessions. The topics to address in these last sessions might include getting along with teachers, asking for help, paying attention in class, and completing work. These are just examples. Make use of the challenges that the students named during their discussion and address those in the following section titled Stressful Issues.

The variations in your Five-Step Format will primarily occur in step 2: Topic Introduction, step 3: Activity, and step 4: Debrief—specifically the open-ended questions you will be asking.

Following are suggestions for steps 2, 3, and 4 associated with the Stressful Issues you plan to address in these four sessions.

Session 4: Stressful Issues

2. Topic Introduction—Getting Along with Teachers
3. Experiential Role Play Activity—Using role-play have group members act out how students should respond appropriately to following directions and accepting correction. Coach students after a scenario is played and allow them to reenact how they respond in these two cases. Using a role-play activity, have a few props available, such as a desk in a classroom, backpack or books, or lunch box or tray for lunch time. The vignettes are written on paper, and each student takes one to role-play. Examples might be: in math class the teacher has asked you to move to another seat because you are distracted by your friend who sits next to you; in the cafeteria, you take your tray back to the cleaning area, and the teacher on duty asks you to go back to your seat and clean the papers that you left there; during writing time in English, you ask the teacher if you can go to the library, and she says "no" because you are behind in your work.
4. Debrief—Include open-ended questions about how the student reacted to the directions or the correction; were the role-plays examples of new behaviors for the students, or do they always respond appropriately (this is an opportunity for challenge if the students believe that they are always appropriate)? What good things might happen if you respond to your teachers appropriately?

Session 5: Stressful Issues

2. Topic Introduction—Stressful Changes—Asking for Help
3. Activity—Ask students to generate times when they had to ask for help in situations other than school. How did that help or hurt the

student? Role-play is again a good way to help students prepare to ask for academic help from their teachers. Several scenarios can be practiced demonstrating the right way and the wrong way to ask for help.

4. Debrief—Ask students to generate some areas in their academics in which they know they need help. Then discuss when and where they could practice their new skills to get help for the problem area. Provide and practice simple stress-relief strategies to help students cope with anxiety. Include how stress influences how you feel and act.

Session 6: Stressful Issues

2. Topic Introduction—Paying Attention in Class
3. Activity—Using a chalkboard, whiteboard, or large tablet, ask students to generate some healthy living traits for school success. Examples would include getting proper sleep and nutrition, eating breakfast, getting outside every day to exercise, and so forth. Once the students have exhausted their list, the counselor may add to it if they have missed some important points. Help the students understand the relationship between healthy habits and doing well in school.
4. Debrief—Ask students to identify the areas on the list that they need to improve in order to be better able to be alert in school. In addition, have the students determine when it is the most difficult for them to pay attention (first thing in the morning, after lunch, a boring class, etc.) and what they can do about it (ask the teacher to move them to the front of the class or away from distractions, etc.).

Session 7: Stressful Issues

2. Topic Introduction—Completing Work
3. Activity—Using a chart, demonstrate the Thought–Feeling–Action cycle. Do a practice activity. Matching three cards as a sequence.

Examples: Thought—made an A on a test; Feeling—happy, satisfied, proud; Action—do something nice for someone; do my homework without a reminder from Mom tonight. Thought—little brother will probably try to play with my laptop while I'm at soccer tonight; Feeling—angry if he breaks it; worried that he might break it; Action—put laptop away in a safe place. Thought—no one in this house likes me; Feeling—angry, sad; Action—yell at Mom and slam door when she tells me to start my homework.

4. Debrief—This topic is frequently the most stressful day-to-day issue the group members face. Allow for a range of feelings expression. Not completing work is often the downfall of at-risk students. Ask

students to provide their own personal examples of the Thought–Feeling–Action cycle using the times they have not completed work. What were they thinking and feeling that led to not completing their work?

Session 8: Reaching Out

1. Warm-up Activity—Group Rounds Check-in
2. Topic Introduction—Making a short video to help other students learn about academic success.
3. Organizing the video—Ask each student to take one of the sessions and to say a few words about what he/she learned in that session. The counselor will have paper, markers, and other art supplies available for the students to create signs for their presentations. The counselor, using a cell phone, iPad, or video recorder, will record each student making key points about having success in school.
4. Debrief—The counselor's job with this activity is to support by having ample materials and helping with specific questions a group member may ask about his or her design ideas. The growth in the group members is that they will be able to exhibit behaviors that will bring greater academic success, cope with their feelings and express them appropriately, and ask for help when needed and will be evident in each contribution to the group's video.
5. Closing Routine—If possible, plan a lunch bunch meeting of group members in the next two weeks as a check-in and to show them the finished video. Congratulate all on their hard work and willingness to tackle difficult topics. Remind them that you are available to meet if they need to talk.

Appendix 6.3

Parent Permission Letter

August 27, 2018

Dear Parents:

Middle school is an exciting time for students! During their journey from childhood to adolescence, students experience many challenges, such as learning to make healthy choices and avoiding negative peer influences.

Awesome Middle School's counseling department is eager to provide your child with the necessary support to accomplish their academic, personal, and social goals. As part of the developmental guidance program at our school, we offer individual and small group counseling sessions. The purpose of these meetings is to help students to be more successful at school.

Following is a list of topics that can be discussed in an individual or group setting:

*Anger
*Grief
*Attendance
*Responsible Behavior
*Decision Making/Problem Solving
*Self-Esteem
*Communication Skills
*Achievement/Study Skills
*Divorce
*Cross-Cultural Effectiveness

Most meetings will be held two to four times monthly for a total of four to eight sessions on an as-needed basis. Each child who participates will receive an invitation that lists the schedule for the meetings.

If you think your child would benefit from these meetings with a counselor, please sign the form and return it to their advisory teacher by August 28, 2018.

Sincerely yours,
Counselor Name
Lead Counselor
School Name

____________________	______________	______________________
Name of Student	**Grade**	**Advisory Teacher**

_____ My child has permission to participate in individual counseling.
_____ My child does not have permission to participate in individual counseling.

_____ My child has permission to participate in group counseling.
_____ My child does not have permission to participate in group counseling.

____________________	____________	____________________________
Parent Signature	**Date**	**Telephone Number**

7

Collaboration and Consultation

Dr. Le'Ann Solmonson

ASCA NATIONAL MODEL THEME

Collaboration

ASCA SCHOOL COUNSELOR PROFESSIONAL COMPETENCIES

I-A-6 Collaborations with stakeholders such as parents and guardians, teachers, administrators, and community leaders to create learning environments that promote educational equity and success for every student

I-B-2d Identifies and applies components of the ASCA National Model requiring leadership, such as an advisory council, management tools, and accountability

I-B-4 Collaborates with parents, teachers, administrators, community leaders and other stakeholders to promote and support student success

I-B-4a Defines collaboration and its role in comprehensive school counseling programs

I-B-4b Identifies and applies models of collaboration for effective use in a school counseling program and understands the similarities and differences between consultation, collaboration, and counseling and coordination strategies

I-B-4c Creates statements or other documents delineating the various roles of student service providers, such as school social worker, school psychologist or school nurse, and identifies best practices for collaborating to affect student success

I-B-4d Understands and knows how to apply a consensus-building process to foster agreement in a group

I-B-4e Understands how to facilitate group meetings to effectively and efficiently meet group goals

I-C-5 Effective school counseling is a collaborative process involving school counselors, students, parents, teachers, administrators, community leaders and other stakeholders

III-B-2 Establishes and convenes an advisory council for the comprehensive school counseling program

III-B-2b Determines appropriate education stakeholders who should be represented on the advisory council

III-B-2c Develops effective and efficient meeting agendas

III-B-2d Reviews school data, school counseling program assessment and school counseling program goals with the advisory council

III-B-2e Records meeting notes and distributes as appropriate

III-B-2f Analyzes and incorporates feedback from the advisory council related to school counseling program goals as appropriate

III-C-3 Management of a school counseling program must be done in collaboration with administrators

IV-A-10 The differences between counseling, collaboration and consultation, especially the potential for dual roles with parents, guardians and other caretakers

IV-B-5a Shares strategies that support student achievement with parents, teachers, other educators and community organizations

IV-B-5b Applies appropriate counseling approaches to promoting change among consultees within a consultation approach

IV-B-5c Works with education stakeholders to better understand student needs and to identify strategies that promote student achievement

IV-B-6a Partners with parents, teachers, administrators and education stakeholders for student achievement and success

IV-B-6b Conducts in-service training and workshops for other stakeholders to share school counseling expertise

IV-B-6c Understands and knows how to provide supervision for school counseling interns consistent with the principles of the ASCA National Model

V-B-1f Works with members of the school counseling team and the administration to decide how school counseling programs are evaluated and how results are shared

V-B-3b Shares the results of the program assessment with administrators, the advisory council and other appropriate stakeholders

ASCA PRINCIPLES

Principle 7: School counselors can help other adults enhance their work with students' academic/educational, career, and personal-social development and for the purpose of removing barriers to individual student success.

Principle 8: School counselors work with others in the school on behalf of students to support accomplishment of the school's mission and to assist in the removal of systemic barriers to student success.

Principle 15: Collaborative, cooperative planning with parents/guardians, teachers, administrators, staff, and community members in developing a school counseling program results in the program being effective and an integral part of the total school mission.

Principle 20: Leadership for the school counseling programs is a shared responsibility between school counselors and school principals.

CACREP 2016

1.d models of school-based collaboration and consultation

2.b school counselor roles in consultation with families, P-12 and postsecondary school personnel, and community agencies

3.l techniques to foster collaboration and teamwork in schools

Introduction

Consultation and collaboration are two key markers in the transformed school counseling profession. A traditional model of school counseling entails school counselors working in isolation as solo practitioners within the educational setting. Within this type of structure, school counselors are constantly in a state of triage trying to prioritize those students who are in the greatest need for services and interventions (Sink, 2011). Due to limitations on the counselor's time, there are often students who do not receive adequate attention or assistance because they have not been deemed to be a high enough priority (Johnson, Rochkind, Ott, & DuPont, 2010).

Pat Martin, Assistant Vice President for the National Office of School Counselor Advocacy, presents a wonderful analogy of a waterfall to demonstrate the need for a change in this historically traditional approach. Pat describes her early work as a school counselor like being in the pool at the bottom of a waterfall. She saw her students as babies falling over the cliff with the descending water. She believed it was her job to catch the babies before they fell into the pool. However, she realized very quickly that because she simply could not catch all the falling babies, she had to decide which ones to let drop into the pool. The frustration and feelings of inadequacy prompted her to devise a better solution than catching babies after they have already fallen. She used her skills to engage in collaboration and consultation and went to the top of the waterfall. The team she assembled worked together to build a fence to prevent most of the babies from falling in the first place (DeVoss & Andrews, 2005).

A school counselor who masters the art of collaboration and consultation has achieved a higher level of efficiency and effectiveness and increases the time available to work with all students (Clark & Breman, 2009). Collaboration is essential in developing, implementing, and evaluating a comprehensive school counseling program (ASCA, 2012). A team approach allows for multiple perspectives, ensures stakeholder representation, and assists in incorporating the program as an essential element of the overall academic program. Collaboration provides a synergy among a variety of interdependent systems for enhancing student development (Drew, 2004). The inclusion of collaboration as one of the four themes of the ASCA model provides evidence of the importance of engaging in partnerships within the school setting.

Before school counselors begin to work, we often ask them to consider what barriers they may face. By considering the barriers first, they have the opportunity to plan ahead and develop strategies to minimize or avoid any setbacks. Because consultation and collaboration involve active engagement with others, human factors are always at play. Some of those factors include inability to obtain buy-in from others, stakeholders not being on the same page, and lack of follow-through from collaborators. Luckily, counselors are skilled at working with resistance and have been trained to help groups reach consensus. When faced with these barriers, it is important for counselors to rely on their skills training and address the issues much like you would in a counseling session. Active listening, reflections, probing, and challenging are all skills that can be used to work through the human factors that can interfere with progress.

In a consultation situation, the consultee may have the expectation that the consultant is going to intervene, take control, and solve the problem. It is critical to ensure from the beginning what your role will be and what it will not be. Empowering the consultee through encouragement and expressions of confidence can help overcome any sense of inadequacy the consultee may have. Resistance can also be present in a consultation relationship. The signs are very similar to client resistance. Some of those signs are negative attitude toward suggested solutions—"that won't work" or "I've tried that before" statements—and failure to follow through with agreed-upon interventions. As a busy school counselor, you must resist the urge to step in just because your ideas will be more efficient. Remember, the benefit of consultancy is that you are developing skills that can be utilized by the consultee in the future. Your investment of time now will save you time in the future. Be patient and trust the process for the benefit of the consultee and yourself.

Collaboration and consultation are both included in the system support domain of a comprehensive school counseling program. Both involve indirect services that are intended to benefit the overall educational, personal, social, and career development of students. Collaboration is related to program management activities that engage multiple stakeholders and resources for the purpose of achieving identified student outcome goals. Consultation is a support service that provides indirect services to students through direct services to the consultee for the purpose of addressing concerns or issues that are interfering with student success. The successful school counselor will understand how consultation and collaboration fit into the big picture of a comprehensive school counseling program, recognize the benefits, and prepare for potential barriers.

Collaboration

The ASCA (2012) model draws on the work of Lawson (2003), an expert in the area of collaboration. Lawson suggests collaboration facilitates positive outcomes for students, but the process can be time consuming and difficult and must be nurtured, supported, and reinforced. He describes collaboration as an example of competent practice. "Basic competence related to collaboration entails doing the correct things, at the proper times, in the appropriate places, and for justifiable reasons, and achieving the desired results" (p. 45).

In addition, Lawson describes collaboration as "a never-ending developmental process" (p. 46) that requires connecting and communicating, cooperation, coordination, community building, and contracting. The ASCA model embraces 7 of the 10 types of collaboration identified by Lawson:

- Inter-professional collaboration
- Youth-centered collaboration
- Parent-centered collaboration
- Family-centered collaboration
- Intra-organizational collaboration
- Inter-organizational collaboration
- Community collaboration (pp. 6–7)

Inter-professional collaboration may also be referred to as a multidisciplinary collaboration. It occurs when different professionals within the school setting come together to address a problem or concern from within the framework of each professional specialization. This type of collaboration can include teachers, administrators, speech and language pathologists, diagnosticians, school psychologists, school nurses, social workers, and other professionals who provide services to students. A common place to see this type of collaboration is in a Special Education Admission, Review, and Dismissal (ARD) or 504 meeting. Each professional contributes to the development of the Individualized Education Plan (IEP) of the student and offers knowledge and services to address the identified disability. The role of the counselor includes ensuring that the student's social and emotional needs are met in relation to the disability, developing the student's graduation plan, and participating in transition planning related to post-secondary goals.

Youth-centered, parent-centered, and family-centered collaboration involve engaging those stakeholders in addressing the identified student goals. This type of collaboration would incorporate students, parents, and/or families as "partners and co-producers of principles, action theories, programs, and results, and who share responsibility and accountability for the results" (Lawson, 2003, p. 52). Lawson suggests this type of collaboration is empowering and democratic in nature.

Intra-organizational collaboration is similar to inter-professional collaboration in that it engages individuals from within the school system. The difference is that it includes paraprofessionals such as secretaries, instructional assistants, custodians, cafeteria workers, and bus drivers. An example of this type of collaboration would be a program to reward a specified behavior. All adults who interact with students are involved in achieving the desired outcomes.

Inter-organizational collaboration occurs when the school counselor engages with organizations outside of the school to work together on an identified goal. This could be local non-profits, faith-based organizations, or a corporate partner.

Finally, community collaboration involves all stakeholders in the area coming together to meet the needs and foster optimal development of students and their families. Collaboration facilitated by the school counselor can occur at differing levels based upon the needs of the campus, the presenting problem, or the goals that are being addressed. Figure 7.1 is a graphic representation that is helpful in considering the different levels of collaboration.

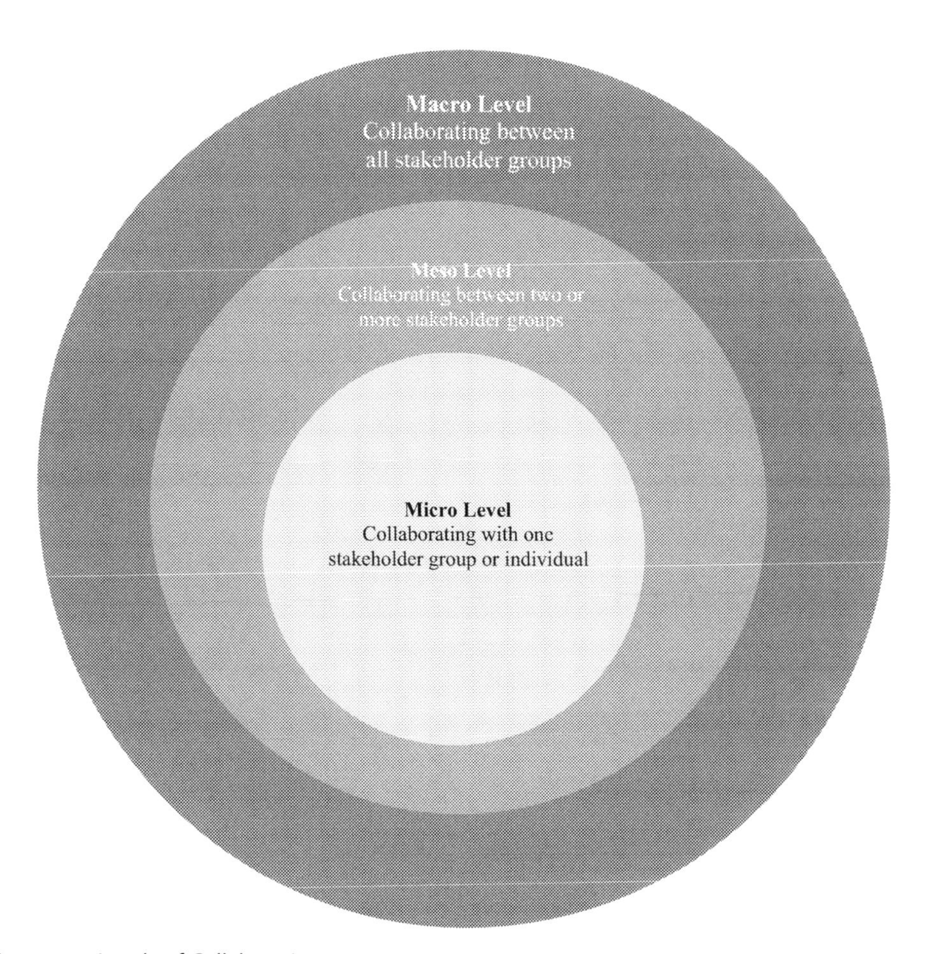

Figure 7.1 Levels of Collaboration

Levels of Collaboration

The micro level involves working with one stakeholder group or an individual in a collaborative manner to address an area of concern. The initial contact can originate from the counselor or the stakeholder group. If the contact originates with the stakeholder group, it may begin as a consultation request. The author experienced a situation as an elementary counselor that is an excellent example of this type of consultation and collaboration. The third-grade teachers came to the counselor to consult due to social problems that had become a distraction in the classroom. There had been an increase in conflicts among the students, tattling, and requests for the teacher to intervene. The counselor had recently attended a professional development seminar on the use of weekly class meetings to improve interpersonal relationships among the students. The counselor presented the information to the teachers and offered to train the teachers and the students on how to conduct the class meetings. The teachers were interested in utilizing the intervention. The counselor and teachers agreed to the counselor facilitating the first three meetings and co-facilitating with the teacher for the fourth meeting. After four weeks, the teacher would assume full responsibility for the meetings. The frequency of the conflicts decreased after the intervention. In the process, teachers obtained new skills in classroom management that could be utilized with future classes, and students developed new skills in conflict resolution so that less teacher intervention was necessary.

The meso level involves collaboration between two or more stakeholder groups. At this level, the school counselor identifies multiple stakeholder groups to assist in achieving a goal. An example is a high school counselor who has a goal to assist students in obtaining information related to post-secondary education opportunities. She is planning a college and career fair as one of the activities related to this goal. The stakeholders she will be collaborating with include the local community college, a local technical school, military recruiters, university alumnae groups in the area, and parents. The community college has agreed to present information on financial aid opportunities, degree and certificate programs available through the school, and advising on transferring credits to a four-year university. The technical school will provide details on the certificate programs offered and labor market information related to the associated careers. The military recruiters will provide information about training and careers available through the military branches. University alumnae will set up tables and provide information about their alma mater and discuss their college experiences with the students. Parents will assist in recruiting alumnae groups, advertising the event, and serving as hosts for a hospitality area available to the volunteer presenters. Through the collaborative efforts of the identified stakeholders, the counselor has provided a wealth of information to the students and has made progress in achieving the counseling goals related to college and career readiness.

The macro level involves collaborating with all stakeholders. The best example of this level is the use of an advisory council. Detailed information related to advisory councils will be provided later in the chapter. Table 7.1 provides examples of how to collaboratively work toward achieving goals at each level.

Table 7.1 Examples of Collaboration to Achieve Specific Goals

Goal Area	Micro Level	Meso Level	Macro Level
Career Development	Counselor collaboration with subject-area teachers (inter-professional) to plan activities and gather materials to assist students in connecting academic subject with career options	Counselor collaboration with teachers and local business partners (inter-organizational) to recruit guest lecturers and volunteer tutors related to specific academic subjects and organize job-shadowing opportunities for students	Counselor collaboration with Advisory Council (intra-organizational) to review data related to career activities associated with the comprehensive program and brainstorm ideas to increase career development opportunities among students
Improving Attendance	Counselor collaboration with attendance personnel (intra-organizational) to review data for patterns and identify specific groups for focused interventions Counselor collaboration with parent groups (parent-centered) to develop strategies for improving attendance	Counselor collaboration with teachers and community stakeholders (inter-organizational) to develop incentives for improving attendance	Counselor collaboration with Advisory Council (intra-organizational) to set goals for attendance and review data to determine effectiveness of interventions
Interpersonal Relationships	Counselor collaboration with student leadership (youth-centered) to plan activities aimed at increasing acceptance and respectful engagement across student groups	Counselor collaboration with student leadership, teachers, support personnel, and administration (intra-organizational) to develop expectations for acceptance and respectful engagement across student groups	Counselor collaboration with Advisory Council (intra-organizational) to set goals for improving interpersonal relationships and review data to determine effectiveness of interventions

Advisory Councils

An effective method of engaging in macro collaboration is through the creation of an Advisory Council, which comprises representatives of all stakeholder groups, including teachers, other school professionals, administration, parents, students, community members, and community agencies. The Advisory Council brings all stakeholders together for a collaborative macro focus on the overall program designed to facilitate student development.

The identification of council members should take into consideration the different types of collaboration listed and the representation of all populations within the school. The purpose of this council is to provide input related to the development of program goals, review program results, assist in program improvement, provide support for the program, and assist in publicizing the program. The first step in creating an Advisory Council is to determine who will be invited to participate. Prior to this process, the school counselor needs to determine what the level of engagement will be for the group. The following questions are things to consider:

1. What type of advisory council is being developed?
2. Will the group meet one to two times a year to serve only in an advisory capacity or will it be a working group that is fully engaged in the activities of the comprehensive counseling program?
3. What groups should be represented from within the school and outside the school? Be sure to consider the different types of collaboration in which you plan to engage.
4. Who are the individuals from that group that can provide helpful and constructive feedback?
5. Do those individuals have a positive influence within the group represented?
6. Are they individuals who could participate in capacity building for the program?

Once the counselor has generated a list of several people from each stakeholder group, he or she will determine how invitations to join will be presented. The invitation should include information on the purpose of the council, the time commitment involved, the scope of responsibility, the training that will be provided, and the desired outcomes (see Figure 7.2).

After securing the commitment of the members, preparation for your first meeting begins. Consider the type of training your group may need.

1. Do they need further training on the role of the Advisory Council?
2. Do they know what a comprehensive school counseling program is?
3. Do they need assistance in how to read and understand the data you will be presenting?

4. Do they know how to create SMART goals based upon data?
5. Do they understand the process of continuous improvement based upon data-driven decisions?

As the group begins to work together, it is important to remember the stages of group development and draw upon knowledge of group dynamics. Consider how to facilitate the development of a working relationship among the stakeholders that honors and values the input of each member. If the group only meets once or twice a year, this may not be as critical as it would be for more frequent meetings. A group that functions in an oversight and advisory capacity may not meet as frequently as a council that is hands-on and engaged. A working Advisory Council will meet more frequently and may include organized committees to focus on specific aspects of the program and be more actively engaged in the actual work. Regardless of the structure of the council, the school counselor should be organized and well prepared for meetings in order to honor the time of the council members. In preparation of the agenda, consider the following questions:

Sample invitation letter

Dear Stakeholder,

The counseling department at Palmer Middle School is forming an Advisory Council to serve as support for achieving counseling-related student outcomes. Our desire is to have representation from all stakeholder groups, including teachers, administrators, parents, students, community members, and community agencies. We recognize each of these groups is a vital influence in the overall development of our students.

The council will meet once every 6 weeks to assist in the development of program goals, review of program data, and recommendation for continued improvement of the counseling program. In addition, the Advisory Council will assist in the implementation of counseling-sponsored events held twice a year.

The counselors are hosting an informational meeting on Tuesday, April 14, from 5:30–7:30 in the school library for individuals who have been identified as prospective council members for the next academic year. At this meeting, we will provide initial training on the role of Advisory Council members, the scope of responsibility, and the time commitment involved. You will have the opportunity to ask questions and provide input on future training needs of the council members. We hope you will consider attending the meeting and joining the Advisory Council.

Please RSVP by calling 123–456–7891 or emailing counselors@palmerms.org

Sincerely,

Connie Counselor
Lead Counselor
Palmer Middle School

Figure 7.2 Sample Invitation Letter

1. What are the goals for this meeting?
2. What information needs to be shared with the council?
3. What assistance is needed from the council?
4. What feedback is needed from the council?
5. What decisions need to be made by the council?
6. How will the work of the council be documented?

For the Advisory Council to truly be useful and collaborative in nature, it is critical to be intentional about encouraging feedback and input. If the program holds an annual meeting simply for sharing information, an annual report would be presented, and the meeting would not be collaborative in nature. However, when collaboration is the intent of the meeting, the time spent should be focused and structured in such a manner as to provide for collaboration to occur. When you are working with volunteers, it is critical that they feel like they are contributing, and they see the fruition of those contributions. When meetings are simply to impart information, attendance might wane, and collaborators might drop out. The key to maintaining strong collaborative relationships is to have everyone engaged in setting goals and committed to the desired outcomes. Being intentional about identifying ways to connect, communicate, cooperate, and engage in community building will facilitate the collaborative process.

Consultation

Consultation is a form of collaboration in which a school counselor engages. Students, parents, teachers, and administrators often see the school counselor as a resource person. When a problem arises, and they are unsure of the solution, they may come to the school counselor to seek assistance. Common issues include academic or behavioral assistance, understanding normal as opposed to abnormal development, social and emotional difficulties, parenting challenges, conflict resolution, and decision-making. The counselor may be seen as an expert, a mediator, or an advocate. Consultation can occur in both formal and informal manners. It may be a phone call from a parent seeking advice or a brief conversation with a teacher in the workroom. For more formal approaches to consultation, there are models to utilize depending upon the knowledge and skills of the individuals involved and the purpose of the consultation.

Consultation is a process that involves individuals coming together to solve a problem, seek information from someone with expertise, or make a decision. The problem may be related to an individual, a group, or a system.

The individuals involved in the process include the consultant (school counselor), the consultee (teacher, parent, student, administrator), and the concern (individual, group, or system). The counselor is providing a direct service to the consultee for determining an intervention to address the concern (Studer, 2015). Erford (2015) acknowledged the power and efficiency of consultation is that it assists the consultee in developing new knowledge and skills that will allow for assuming responsibility for independently solving similar problems in the future. When the intervention effectively addresses the concern, the consultee feels successful, empowered, and confident in his or her ability to resolve similar issues.

Consider the following scenarios:

- A first-grade teacher comes to the school counselor to discuss problematic behaviors that are interfering with a student's ability to learn.
- A tenth-grade student talks to the school counselor about what she believes to be unfair treatment by her math teacher.
- A seventh grader's parent calls the school counselor after progress reports are sent home indicating the student has a failing grade in three subjects.

A counselor functioning in a traditional role would assume an attitude of "I will handle it." This counselor would begin to work with the first-grade student on school success skills, talk to the math teacher, and talk to the failing student. While the counselor may still be successful in remediating the problem, the next time the teacher has a student with behavior problems, a student feels she is being mistreated by a teacher, or the student is failing, the same process is likely to be repeated. A more collaborative method would be to take on the role of consultant to assist with each of the problems. Let's explore what that process might look like.

Behavioral Consultation

Ms. Andrews is a second-year first-grade teacher who is struggling to manage the behavior of Christopher. Her frustration level is clear when she arrives in the counselor's office with Christopher, who is crying, in tow. She indicates that Christopher cannot remain in the classroom because he has been so disruptive, and she asks the counselor to allow him to take a time-out in her office. Because the situation has escalated to this point, the counselor determines it may be best for Ms. Andrews and Christopher to allow him to stay with her to assist with de-escalation of emotions. However, the counselor also invites the teacher to come back after school to talk about how to assist Christopher in developing the skills to be successful in the classroom.

Ms. Andrews returns after school, and the school counselor is prepared to begin the consultation process. She asks Ms. Andrews to describe the behaviors that are concerning and disruptive and how often they are occurring. She uses her counseling skills of reflection, empathy, and clarification to ensure she has a good understanding of the problem, and Ms. Andrews feels validated. She asks about the classroom management system in place and what interventions Ms. Andrews has already tried. Because Ms. Andrews has presented numerous disruptive behaviors, the school counselor asks her to identify the two most concerning behaviors to target for intervention. The counselor explains the need to set manageable goals so as not to overwhelm Christopher and help him experience success. Which behaviors could possibly be ignored initially in order to assist Christopher in finding success?

Together, the school counselor and Ms. Andrews identify strategies for gathering baseline data that will assist in determining how often the behavior is occurring so that they will be able to assess the effectiveness of interventions. They also develop a system for continuing to collect data through the intervention period. The school counselor assists Ms. Andrews in developing different strategies for addressing the disruptive behavior and a system for rewarding Christopher for demonstrating more appropriate behaviors. They schedule a time to meet again in two weeks to review the data in order to determine how Christopher is responding to the interventions.

The school counselor makes a note to check in with Ms. Andrews in the next few days to make sure she feels supported and to see how Christopher is progressing. When they come back together in two weeks, if it is determined the intervention is being successful, the school counselor would encourage the teacher to continue the process with the other identified behaviors. If the data indicates the interventions are not successful, they would brainstorm other ways to intervene. After several cycles of this process, they would determine whether there is a need to refer Christopher for a higher level of intervention or assessment. The process described should be formally documented as a response to intervention (RTI). This is especially important in the event that Christopher has to move to a higher level of intervention. This process benefits both the teacher and the student. The teacher learns new management skills for misbehaving students, and the student learns more self-control and achieves more classroom success.

Mediation as Consultation

Leslie is a tenth-grade student who schedules an appointment with the school counselor to discuss what she believes to be unfair treatment by her math teacher, Mr. Walker. Leslie says that Mr. Walker yells at the entire class and is not helpful when they do not understand something. Leslie has not turned in several homework assignments because she does not understand how to complete them. When asked if she has gone to tutorials or talked to Mr. Walker about the problem, Leslie states she has not because she does not think Mr. Walker likes her and does not think it will help. She also says she is afraid to talk to Mr. Walker by herself.

The counselor has several things to consider in this consultation. Does Leslie have the ability to have the conversation one-on-one with Mr. Walker? Does the school counselor have knowledge or experience with Mr. Walker to determine how he might respond to a conversation with Leslie? If the counselor believes Leslie has the ability to have the conversation one-on-one and Mr. Walker would respond to her in a positive manner, the consultation may simply involve role-playing with Leslie. The school counselor would assist her in articulating her concerns and feelings in a respectful manner that is more likely to be well received. However, the school counselor may feel it would be more beneficial for Leslie and Mr. Walker to have a mediator to facilitate the conversation. If so, the following steps would assist in achieving a positive outcome:

- Assist Leslie in identifying her main concerns and being able to articulate her feelings in a respectful manner.
- Meet with Mr. Walker to allow him to voice his concerns and prepare for how to respond effectively to Leslie. Inform him that Leslie would like to talk to him about some concerns, but do not articulate them for her.
- At the agreed-upon meeting time, remain neutral. Use counseling skills to reflect, facilitate dialogue, and clarify the concerns of both parties.
- Ask both parties what they need to happen to be able to work together effectively. Facilitate compromise if necessary.
- Document the agreed-upon resolution and provide both parties with a copy of the agreement. If necessary, obtain signatures of both Leslie and Mr. Walker as a sign of their commitment to work together.
- Follow up with both Leslie and Mr. Walker to evaluate the effectiveness of the agreement.

Parent-Teacher Conferences as Consultation

Mr. Thompson calls the school counselor after receiving his seventh-grade daughter's progress reports. Rene has failing grades in history, science, and English. Mr. Thompson is concerned and would like to schedule a

conference with all of Rene's teachers. The counselor agrees to facilitate the conference. She coordinates with Mr. Thompson and Rene's teachers to schedule the day and time. A traditional method of facilitating parent-teacher conferences would involve each teacher identifying problematic behaviors and missing assignments. This can result in a student feeling attacked and discouraged. A conference that begins with the student perspective allows the student to feel more in control and assume responsibility for his or her academic performance. The following agenda is an example of a solution-focused, student-led conference.
[[Comp: The following Agenda should be inserted in a Box.]]

Agenda for Facilitation of Parent Conferences

Introductions

Statement of Purpose of Conference
Acknowledge Who Called the Conference

> We are here because the seventh-grade team had concerns regarding academic progress. Mr. Thompson requested the conference after receiving Rene's first report card.

Define the Intended Outcome of the Conference

> We are all interested in helping Rene to improve her performance at school and want to see what we can do to help her with that. We want to come up with a plan that will make Rene more successful at school and feel better about herself.

Student's Understanding of the Problem (By beginning with the student, hopefully he or she will put the information on the table. This is intended to make the student feel less vulnerable and defensive than when adults are naming the problem(s). If appropriate, the counselor may want to meet with the student prior to the conference to prepare.)

Ask the Student What Is His/Her Perception of School Performance

- Gather general information regarding adjustment to school:
  - Are you happy at school?
  - What do you like about school?
  - What have you found to be the most difficult?

- How would you describe your academic performance?
  - What are you doing well at school?
  - What is difficult for you?
  - Which classes seem to be causing the most difficulty?

Ask the Student What Types of Things Are Preventing Him/Her From Being Successful at School

- Explore learner behaviors:
  - How often are you working at home?
  - How do you spend your work time at school?
  - How are you keeping track of your assignments?
  - How would you describe your level of organization?
- Explore affective areas:
  - When you think about the work that you need to do, how do you feel?
  - Do you feel overwhelmed?
  - Do you avoid work because you are unsure of where to begin?

Teacher's Perception of the Problem

(It is very important in this phase that teachers build upon the information that the student has identified and provide positive reinforcement for any insight the student has demonstrated.)

Provide information regarding behaviors that are inhibiting student success.

- Validate information student has shared:
  - I agree that Rene often struggles with meeting deadlines.
  - Rene is right in that she does the work and gets it turned in the first time, but then does not follow through with corrections.
- Provide additional information on other observations regarding issues impeding success:
  - I have noticed that Rene does very well when she has a group assignment. However, she does not show the same level of engagement on individual assignments.
  - Rene is very bright; however, she is often off-task in class and then does not understand the directions for completing the assignment.
- Be sure to identify student strengths, as well as challenges.

Provide information regarding current status in class.

- Provide parents with a current progress report.

- Summarize missing assignments without going into great detail. Remember, everyone needs to provide this information and time is limited:
  - Rene is currently missing three homework assignments.
  - Rene has two tests that she needs to retake and will need to make arrangements for tutoring before she can schedule the retake.

Parent's Perception of the Problem

If parents have been contributing throughout the conference, this may not be necessary. Give parents the opportunity to ask clarifying questions.

Plan for Improvement

Establish a written plan for improvement (see Figure 7.3).

Be specific in stating the objectives of the plan. (Commitment Statements) Be sure that you do not identify more than two or three things for the student to work on. If you have too many goals, the student may be overwhelmed and fail at all of them.

Include parent responsibility in the plan.

- Rene will do one hour of homework every day.
- Rene will keep a "to-do" list of her assignments.
- Rene will decrease socializing in class.
- Mom and Dad will monitor Rene's "to-do" list.
- Mom and Dad will e-mail teachers on Thursday for a weekly update.

Plan for follow-up

- Who will be monitoring her success?
- Who will communicate progress (or lack of) to parents?
- What will improvement look like?

Referrals as Consultation

A school counselor may receive or make referrals. Referrals may be received from the student, teachers, parents, or other school personnel who are interacting with a student and believe there is a problem or issue that is beyond their level of expertise. A referral may also come from another student who is concerned about a classmate. When a referral is received, it is important for the counselor to have some basic understanding of the problem. Many school counselors have had the experience of a student arriving in the office and being told, "My teacher told me to come see you." When asked why the teacher sent the student, he or she is unable to articulate the reason. The

STUDENT IMPROVEMENT PLAN

Student Name ______________________________ Date ________________

Areas to Focus on for Improvement

1.

2.

3.

Commitment Statements

1.

2.

3.

4.

5.

Follow-Up Plan

1.

2.

3.

Signatures

______________________________ ______________________________

______________________________ ______________________________

______________________________ ______________________________

Figure 7.3 Student Improvement Plan

counselor must become a detective in order to determine how to help the student. This can easily be resolved by having a referral form that provides information about the reason for the referral. The form should be developmentally appropriate and reflect the services that are provided by the school counselor. An example of a form is provided in Figure 7.4.

Depending upon the nature of the referral, information regarding classroom or behavioral observations may be needed. This form can be utilized to provide information to the school counselor or to an outside professional (see Table 7.2).

The school counselor should have post-referral procedures to follow up with the individual making the referral. Those procedures should include

School Counseling Referral Form

Student Name ____

Date____________________________ Grade Level __________________________

Individual Making Referral____

Reason for Referral

____ academic concerns ____behavioral concerns

____social concerns ____personal concerns ____other concerns

Please briefly describe the problem. (If you would prefer to discuss the problem with the counselor, please provide contact information.)

____

____

____

Figure 7.4 Student Counseling Referral Form

Table 7.2 Behavioral Observations

BEHAVIORAL OBSERVATIONS				
Child's Name **Date**	**Never or Rarely**	**Sometimes**	**Often**	**Very Often**
Fails to pay close attention to details or makes careless mistakes				
Fidgets or squirms more than is developmentally appropriate				
Difficulty sustaining attention during group activities				
Difficulty sustaining attention during independent work				
Appears to not listen when spoken to directly				
Doesn't follow through on instructions or fails to finish work				
Appears to drift off				
Moves from one activity to another prior to completions				

BEHAVIORAL OBSERVATIONS				
Child's Name	**Never or Rarely**	**Sometimes**	**Often**	**Very Often**
Date				
Difficulty with organization, prioritizing, or getting started on activities				
Easily overwhelmed/shuts down				
Avoids activities that require sustained attention or are not of interest				
Talks excessively/interrupts or intrudes on others/ blurts out answers before questions have been completed				
Has difficulty waiting his/ her turn				
Easily distracted				
Loses things necessary for tasks or activities				
Forgetful				
Appears anxious or nervous				
Difficulty in following rules				
Difficulty with peer relationships				
Appears sad and withdrawn				
Expresses physical complaints (stomachache, headache, etc.)				
Difficulty managing emotions				
Angers easily				
Daydreams				
Pouts or sulks				
Demands immediate attention				
Overly sensitive to feedback				
Mood changes drastically				
Makes inappropriate noises				

the limits on what may or may not be shared with the individual due to confidentiality. In a school setting, the disclosure of information should be on a need-to-know basis. These questions can help guide you in making decisions about what information to share:

- Who are the individuals that need to know the information in order to work effectively with the student?
- What information do these individuals need to know?
- How will the information assist these individuals in working with the student?
- Can these individuals be trusted to keep the information confidential?
- Do I need parent permission to share the information?
- Do I need student permission to share the information?

Protecting the counseling relationship should always be a priority. For the last two questions, the school counselor should consider the impact of sharing information on the level of trust in the counselor-counselee relationship. If the school counselor believes it would benefit the student if others were aware of the information, a candid conversation with the parent or student in which the benefits are described can be helpful. When a student or parent views other school personnel as a part of the overall team that can be of assistance, he or she may be more willing to agree with the need-to-know requirement. Ultimately, the school counselor must respect the right to privacy of the student and/or parent.

When a student concern exceeds the capacity of school resources or the problem is not directly related to school success, an outside referral may be necessary. Having a list of referral sources assists the school counselor in being prepared for this situation. A school social worker may be able to assist in creating a comprehensive list of referral sources, including sliding-scale or free services. If possible, the list should include a minimum of three professionals in each category (counselor, psychologist, psychiatrist, counseling clinics, health clinics, inpatient services, residential services, etc.) Providing multiple referral options is important from a legal and ethical standpoint. It allows the parent to make a choice and prevents any assumption that the counselor was a part of the decision-making process.

School counselors may be targeted for marketing efforts of professionals seeking referrals. Prior to making a referral, the school counselor would want to feel comfortable with the quality of services being provided and that the standards for ethical practice are being met. It would also be unethical for the school counselor to receive any type of compensation or benefit from the referral. There are several things to keep in mind when making an outside referral. The first is whether the parent/student can utilize the referral. Making a referral to an outside counselor is not beneficial if financial resources or necessary transportation are not available. The referral has no value if the parent is unable to utilize it. Another consideration is whether the parent is planning on utilizing insurance benefits to pay for services. If so, referring the parent to the list of approved providers may be appropriate. The school counselor can review the list with the parent to determine if the counselor has any information about specific providers. However, it is wise to refrain from recommending a specific provider.

For some referrals, it may be helpful or necessary for the professionals to exchange information. An outside counselor may want information related to how the student is functioning in the school setting. The school counselor may want information on how the school can support the goals of counseling. In order for the two professionals to be able to exchange information for the purpose of coordinating, collaborating, or consulting, a signed release of information must be obtained. The release must include the following:

- The information that can be shared
- Who can share the information
- The individuals with whom the information can be shared
- A date range during which the information can be shared
- The parent's right to withdraw permission to release information

The release of information can be one-way or two-way. The school may have permission to release information with an outside professional related to academic performance, assessments, attendance, and/or behavioral issues. However, the parent may not agree to the outside professional sharing information related to the services provided with the school. This should be detailed in the release of information. The parent may agree to sharing information with the school counselor, but not other school personnel. A sample release of information is provided in Figure 7.5.

In the example release form, both counselors have permission to share information with each other. In addition, either counselor can share information with the teacher and the assistant principal. If the parent only wanted information to be shared by the school with the outside counselor, the names would be removed from the appropriate places on the form. School districts may have release forms that have been approved by legal counsel. The Special Education Department may also have forms that can be utilized. If forms are not available, a counselor-created form may need to go through administrative processes to be approved. Until a signed release is in place,

RELEASE OF INFORMATION

I, *Patty Parent*, parent or guardian of *Sam Student*, date of birth, *01–02–2006*, give permission for the following release of information for the purpose of providing and coordinating services to my child.

Information can be shared by the following individuals:

Name/Title	Phone Number
Conrad Counselor, School Counselor	*987–654–3210*
Rene Referral, LPC	*123–456–7890*

The information may be shared with the following individuals:

Name/Title	Phone Number
Conrad Counselor, School Counselor	*987–654–3210*
Rene Referral, LPC	*123–456–7890*
Anne Assistant Principal	*987–654–3210*
Thomas Teacher	*987–654–3210*

Name/TitlePhone Number

Information that may be shared includes:

_x__academic records __x_discipline records_ x__attendance records
___assessment information __x_counseling goals x__counseling interventions
___other (please list)________________________________

This release of information will expire one calendar year after the date of signature. The parent has the right to revoke permission at any time.

______________________________ ______________________

Parent Signature Date

Figure 7.5 Release of Information

the school counselor should never provide confidential student information that is protected by the Family Educational Rights and Privacy Act.

Referrals may take the form of consultation and collaboration. A school counselor may want to consult with someone who has more experience or expertise who can assist in working with a student. A school counselor may want to collaborate with an outside professional to provide continuity in services being provided to a student.

Conclusion

Collaboration and consultation are essential to an efficient and effective model of school counseling. A school counselor must be able to develop and engage in professional working relationships necessary to facilitate collaboration and consultation. As with all aspects of the profession, the school counselor must be mindful of cultural considerations and ethical practice. As a leader in the school, the school counselor should model practices that encourage effective collaboration among all stakeholders in order to provide the most positive outcomes for students.

Activities

1. Role-play a meeting designed to help a fifth-grade student with behavioral problems. One person will play the role of the school counselor, the facilitator of the meeting. Other possible attendees are the student's parents, the teachers who work directly with the student, and an administrator. Complete the appropriate forms.
2. Role-play a meeting designed to assist a ninth grader who is failing three courses at the end of the first semester of the academic year. One student will play the role of the school counselor, the facilitator of the meeting. Other possible attendees are the student's parents, the teachers who work directly with the student, and an administrator. Complete the appropriate forms.
3. Create an agenda for a school counselor's first Advisory Council meeting. What types of assistance do you want from this group; how often will you meet and when; what type of training might they need to fulfill their responsibilities on the Council (confidentiality, the Comprehensive School Counseling Program, the job roles of the school counselor)?
4. You are a school counselor who works in an inner-city high school. Many students in your school do not have appropriate after-school activities in which to participate. You decide to meet with several community agencies to see if they would be willing to have students engage in service-learning activities several days a week after school. Make a list of the agencies you would contact and create an agenda for the meeting. In advance of the meeting, brainstorm with your administrators and teachers some activities you could suggest to this group of community members.

Resources

The School Counselor and School-Family-Community Partnerships:
www.schoolcounselor.org/asca/media/asca/PositionStatements/PS_Partnerships.pdf

References

American School Counselor Association. (2012). *The ASCA national model: A framework for school counseling programs* (3rd ed.). Alexandria, VA: Author.

Clark, M. A., & Breman, J. C. (2009). School counselor inclusion: A collaborative model to provide academic and social-emotional support in the classroom setting. *Journal of Counseling and Development, 87*(1), 6–11.

DeVoss, J., & Andrews, M. (2005). *School counselors as educational leaders.* Belmont, CA: Wadsworth Publishing.

Drew, S. (2004). The power of school-community collaboration in dropout prevention. In F. P. Schargel & J. Smink (Eds.), *Helping students graduate: A strategic approach to dropout prevention* (pp. 65–77). Larchmont, NY: Eye on Education.

Erford, B. (2015). *Transforming the school counseling profession* (4th ed.). Upper Saddle River, NJ: Pearson.

Johnson, J., Rochkind, J., Ott, A., & DuPont, S. (2010). *Can I get a little advice here? How an overstretched high school guidance system is undermining students' college aspirations.* Retrieved from www.publicagenda.org/files/pdf/can-i-get-a-little-advice-here.pdf

Lawson, H. A. (2003). Pursuing and securing collaboration to improve results. *Yearbook of the National Society for the Study of Education, 102*(2), 45–73. doi:10.1111/j.1744-7984.2003.tb00065.x

Sink, C. (2011). School-wide responsive services and the value of collaboration. *Professional School Counseling, 14*(3), ii–iv. doi:http://dx.doi.org/10.5330/PSC.n.2011-14.ii

Studer, J. (2015). *The essential school counselor in a changing society.* Thousand Oaks, CA: SAGE Publications.

Appendix 7.1

Counselor Referral Form

____________	____________	____________	____________
Student's Name	Grade	Date	Person Referring

Academic performance in your class:

Pass or Fail______%

REASON FOR REFERRAL:

____

____

____

____

____

CHECKLIST (Previous Action Taken):

_____Talked with student about the problem

_____Talked with parent about the problem

_____Progress report reflected problem

_____Academic/Behavioral adjustments

_____Nurse referral

_____Behavioral contract

_____Changed seating arrangement

_____Previous counseling referral

_____Previous Assistant Principal Referral

_____Other

What would you like to see happen:______

____

____

____

____

____

Referring Person/ Recorder **Date**

cc: Counselor's File: White
Counselor's Secretary: Yellow
Referring Person's File: Pink

COUNSELOR'S ACTION

_____Counseled with student

_____Parent contact initiated

_____Teacher/student conference

_____Observation

_____Individual sessions (PPR)

_____Group (PPR)

_____Informal Consultation (Psych)

_____Referral to outside resource

_____Other

____

COMMENTS:

____

____

____

____

____

____

____

____

____

FOLLOW-UP SCHEDULED:

____

____

Counselor's Signature **Date**

(PPR) Parent Permission Required

Section III

Programming

8

Post-Secondary Opportunities

Dr. Lia D. Falco and Dr. Sam Steen

ASCA NATIONAL MODEL THEME

Advocacy

ASCA SCHOOL COUNSELOR PROFESSIONAL COMPETENCIES

I-A-5 Individual counseling, group counseling and classroom guidance programs ensuring equitable access to resources that promote academic achievement; personal, social and emotional development; and credibility including the identification of appropriate post-secondary education for every student

I-C-3 School counseling programs promote and support academic achievement, personal and social development and career planning for every student

III-A-5 Principles of career planning and college admissions, including financial aid in athletic eligibility

III-B-2d Understands career opportunities, labor market trends, and global economics, and uses various career assessment techniques to assist students and understanding their abilities and career interests

III-B-2e Help students learn the importance of college and other post-secondary education and helps students navigate the college admissions process

III-B-2g Understands methods for helping students monitoring and direct their own learning an personalized/social and career development

ASCA PRINCIPLES

Principle 1: As with other dimensions their development, students benefit from assistance in accomplishing the age-appropriate task related to their academic, career and personal/social development

Principle 2: All students can benefit from interventions designed to assist academic, career and personal/social development

Principle 3: Some students need more assistance in accomplishing the age-appropriate academic, career and personal/social developmental tasks. These students benefit from preventative or remedial interventions specially designed to help them achieve task appropriate to the development level

Principle 4: School counselors are qualified to make contributions for all students' development in the area of academic (educational), career and personal/social development

Principle 6: School counselors' interventions in students' academic, career and personal/social development help students acquire and apply knowledge, skills and attitudes promoting development in those three dimensions of human growth

CACREP STANDARDS 2016

Section 5-G, Entry-Level Specialty Areas, School Counseling

Foundations

1.c models of P-12 comprehensive career development

Contextual Dimensions

2.b school counselor roles in consultation with families, P-12 and postsecondary school personnel, and community agencies

Practice

3.e use of developmentally appropriate career counseling interventions and assessments

3.g strategies to facilitate school and postsecondary transitions

3.i approaches to increase promotion and graduation rates

3.j interventions to promote college and career readiness

3.l strategies to promote equity in student achievement and college access

Introduction

In many respects, the role of a professional school counselor in post-secondary planning has remained somewhat constant over the past 20 years. Yet, the U.S. faces a rapidly changing socio-political climate. The professional skills needed to be successful in the workplace, and workplaces themselves, are changing as a result (Gysbers, 2013). The publication of the American School Counselor Association's (ASCA) *The ASCA National Model: A Framework for School Counseling Programs* (ASCA, 2012) was a significant resource for clarifying the roles and functions of school counselors. It delineated areas of emphasis for school counselors that would lead to the development and implementation of comprehensive school counseling programs and, thereby, provided a structure to meet the needs of all K–12 students. Recently, a focus on "college and career readiness" (CCR) has come to the front and center of the school counseling profession. Much of this momentum is related to former President Obama and First Lady Obama's direct role in promoting the efforts of school counselors serving students, primarily in high schools, all over the nation (Schaefer & Rivera, 2012). The First Lady, in particular, was instrumental in creating the Reach Higher Initiative and communicated these efforts in a number of ways, including key-noting the ASCA National Conference in 2014, hosting the annual school counselor of the year award ceremony at the White House, facilitating webinars, promoting video competitions across the country that involved increasing the number of students who completed the FAFSA application, and inviting the school counselors, administrators, and counselor educators to the White House to participate in a day of advocacy for the profession. Although it is obvious that post-secondary opportunities are not limited to just attending college, picking a great career and being successful in these endeavors is also important, and school counselors can help with all of these aspects of post-secondary planning.

The former First Lady's Reach Higher Initiative targeted six areas, including the following: (1) higher education institutions ensuring preparation standards in College and Career Readiness (CCR), (2) strengthening partnerships between a university and school district on the training of practicing school counselors in CCR, (3) strengthening partnerships between a university and school district in the fieldwork placement of students in partnership with school districts, (4) creating state or school district policies and procedures for hiring of school counselors, (5) creating state or school district policies and procedures that allow non-profit college access professionals to work within a school district, and

(6) strengthening of non-profit organizations' training of direct service staff to meet state, district, or other credentialing requirements. This initiative expands the work of some states and school districts, and baffles others due to the limited resources and coordination that existed prior to this push. More specifically, an example of what still remains unclear is regarding how the work should unfold to meet the needs of students navigating our public schools. Nevertheless, this Reach Higher Initiative fostered a positive public perception of the important roles school counselors have in college and career development, and the momentum has continued (Schaefer & Rivera, 2012).

In addition to highly publicized actions on behalf of the White House initiatives, there is some emerging research that shows a positive link between what school counselors do with high school students and the students navigating the college process (Bryan, Moore-Thomas, Day-Vines, & Holcomb-McCoy, 2011). At the same time, there has been some major criticism because school counselors have not been fully prepared to engage in this work, as graduate preparation programs have focused too much on clinical and content areas such as vocational development and psychology (Public Agenda, 2010; Savitz-Romer, 2012). Scholars have collaborated with the help of the College Board to come up with eight components of CCR that must be applied at various levels (e.g., elementary, middle, and high) [College Board, n. d.]. These include college aspirations, academic planning for college and career readiness, enrichment and extracurricular engagement, college and career exploration and selection processes, college and career assessments, college affordability planning, college and career admissions, and transition from high school to college enrollment. The research is scarce, but some of these topics will be covered later in this chapter.

The professional standards established by the ASCA called the *ASCA National Standards for School Counseling Programs* were published in 1997. More recently, the *ASCA Mindsets and Behaviors for Student Success: K-12 College and Career Readiness for Every Student* replaced these standards and emphasize CCR ideals more specifically. The *ASCA Mindsets and Behaviors for Student Success* (ASCA, 2014) include the same domains as the ASCA National Model (personal-social, academic, and career development) and are grounded in general educational research and literature on non-cognitive factors such as cooperation, grit, resiliency, goal setting, motivation, self-control, and work habits. Although ASCA has taken on a much stronger position on career development, post-secondary planning, and CCR, the Council for Accreditation of Counseling and Related Educational Programs (CACREP) supports these areas of career development training in counselor education programs.

For instance, CACREP—the national organization responsible for accrediting Master's and doctoral-level programs—has detailed a curriculum that includes standards relevant to career development. These standards include:

(a) the theories and models of career development, counseling, and decision-making;
(b) approaches for conceptualizing the interrelationships among and between work, mental well-being, relationships, and other life roles and factors;
(c) processes for identifying and using career, avocational, educational, occupational, and labor market information resources, technology, and information systems;
(d) approaches for assessing the conditions of the work environment on clients' life experiences;
(e) strategies for assessing abilities, interests, values, personality, and other factors that contribute to career development;
(f) strategies for career development program planning, organization, implementation, administration, and evaluation;
(g) strategies for advocating for diverse clients' career and educational development and employment opportunities in a global economy;
(h) strategies for facilitating client skill development for career, educational, and lifework planning and management;
(i) methods of identifying and using assessment tools and techniques relevant to career planning and decision-making; and
(j) ethical and culturally relevant strategies for addressing career development.

This list, while exhaustive, does not specifically refer to school counselors. However, there are some school counseling–specific standards that suggest school counselor educators should prepare trainees to

(a) develop models of P–12 comprehensive career development;
(b) function effectively when consulting with families, P–12 and post-secondary school personnel, and community agencies;
(c) understand their role in relation to college and career readiness;
(d) use developmentally appropriate career counseling interventions and assessments;
(e) create strategies to facilitate school and post-secondary transitions;
(f) develop approaches to increase promotion and graduation rates;
(g) use interventions to promote college and career readiness; and
(h) employ strategies to promote equity in student achievement and college access.

The fact that CACREP endorses career development within the curricula when preparing both counselors in general and school counselors reiterates the importance of post-secondary planning initiatives.

The purpose of this chapter is to explore what school counselors need to know and be able to do to provide effective career development and career counseling services to K–12 students. We focus on high school (e.g., secondary public schools) because it is, arguably, the most salient time during K–12 schooling for post-secondary planning. It is also the age group that receives a great deal of attention in the literature. However, we would be remiss if we did not stress the importance of applying this information across the developmental spectrum (e.g., elementary and middle schools), in other schools outside of public schools (e.g., parochial and charter schools, etc.), and with the understanding that this work is not innovative or new, but the philosophy of supporting success for all students despite their racial, ethnic, cultural, socioeconomic, religious, or gender backgrounds is an endeavor that must continue.

Theories of Career Development

Many important career development theories can assist school counselors in their work with students. A strong theoretical foundation gives school counselors a better understanding of particular strategies, counseling approaches, and tools by helping determine how, when, and why to use them. Having the ability to use a number of theories and approaches better positions school counselors to determine and meet the needs of each individual student. In a high school setting, where counselors may be spending more time assisting students with educational and post-secondary planning than in other contexts, certain theories of career development may be more applicable. In this section, we have chosen to provide an overview of four major career development theories that, we believe, are particularly useful for understanding the experiences of school-aged individuals and assisting them with important decision-making.

Holland's Theory of Vocational Personalities

Holland's theory is considered an extension of earlier trait-factor approaches that emphasize the "person-environment fit" in career counseling and vocational planning. It focuses on individual characteristics (personality traits) and occupational tasks (environmental factors) and is grounded in the basic assumption that there is an optimal vocational or career "match" for individuals based on one's personality (Holland, 1959). Holland's theory asserts that personalities fall into six broad categories: Realistic, Investigative, Artistic, Social, Enterprising, and Conventional (often referred to as the RIASEC typology). Because individuals with certain personalities are attracted to certain kinds of jobs, the work environments, then, reflect this personality and can be grouped into six similar clusters (RIASEC). Although each individual is made up of all six types, one type is usually dominant. Most personalities tend to resemble up to three of the six personality factors.

Personalities can be matched with similar combinations of work environments using a problem-solving approach, and the closer the match of personality to the job, the greater the satisfaction one will experience in that occupation (Holland, 1997). For example, someone with a "Realistic" personality type may be well-suited for jobs in law enforcement, construction, or agriculture, whereas someone with a "Social" personality type may be well-suited for jobs in teaching, coaching, or nursing. This theoretical framework allows the school counselor to help students understand their personalities and consider post-secondary options through exploration of associated career pathways.

Theory of Work Adjustment (TWA)

The theory of work adjustment (TWA) [Dawis & Lofquist, 1984] is also considered a theory of "person-environment fit." Like Holland's theory, TWA assumes that individuals seek out environments that are congruent with their personal characteristics, and the degree of fit between individuals and work environments will be associated with important, positive outcomes such as satisfaction, achievement, performance, and stability (Swanson & Fouad, 1999). Whereas Holland's theory places more emphasis on vocational choice, TWA emphasizes vocational adjustment (Dawis, 1994). Rather than relying on a typology to assist individuals with decision-making, TWA describes two sets of common dimensions: individuals' abilities in relation to those required of a particular job, and individuals' work values in relation to rewards associated with a particular job.

Both Holland's theory and the TWA contribute to an understanding of the transition from school to work by ensuring that both individual and environmental characteristics are fully considered in the vocational decision-making process (Swanson & Fouad, 1999). School counselors can help students develop a sense of their own skills, interests, and values as they make vocational choices and begin post-secondary planning. This may be particularly important for work-bound youth who will have less time for trial and error than their college-bound peers. Both Holland's theory and the TWA have been very influential in vocational counseling by contributing a wealth of information about the types of skills and abilities necessary in the world of work. Holland's theory has been employed by popular assessment tools such as the *Self-Directed Search (SDS)*, *Vocational Preference Inventory*, and the *Strong Interest Inventory (SII)*. Holland's theory has also resulted in practical resources like the *Dictionary of Holland Occupational Codes and Career Clusters*, which apply Holland's personality typology to major occupations. Research within the framework of TWA has contributed substantial evidence about the patterns of rewards that typify different occupations, particularly those that do not require a college degree. Information about these reward patterns are very useful for school counselors working with students who will be entering the world of work upon graduation. It is important for students to understand not only how to secure a job but also how to stay in a job. Thus, school counselors can help students clarify their needs and then help them determine which types of jobs are better able to provide them with appropriate rewards (e.g., flex-time, salary, benefits, etc.).

Social Cognitive Career Theory

Social Cognitive Career Theory (SCCT) [Lent, Brown, & Hackett, 1994] is derived from Albert Bandura's (1986) general social cognitive theory. It is a widely supported model and is particularly useful for understanding students' self-beliefs and career-related choices. SCCT posits that career choice behavior is influenced by outcome expectancies, interests, and career self-efficacy. The theory proposes an interactional influence of external/environmental factors and individual/cognitive variables on individuals' career development. Within this model, one's background influences one's learning experiences, which influence self-efficacy. Self-efficacy shapes interest and outcome expectations, which, ultimately, influence career choice (Lent, Brown, & Hackett, 2002). The outcomes that young people anticipate in taking coursework necessary for certain vocations or careers is closely connected to their self-efficacy beliefs in related subject areas. Perceived barriers such as those related to gender, ethnicity, age, socioeconomic status, or family constraints may create negative outcome expectations, even when students have had previous success in the given area.

SCCT provides a mechanism for understanding students' career-related choices through its focus on self-efficacy and the ways in which self-efficacy influences behavior. Four sources of information (mastery experiences, vicarious learning experiences, physiological states/emotional arousal, and verbal persuasions) lead to domain-specific self-efficacy beliefs within individuals, which are closely related to behavioral outcomes (career choice). Thus, it is particularly useful for understanding the career development of diverse students because it allows for examination of social-cognitive variables as a function of many aspects of identity, including race, gender, sexual orientation, etc. (Betz, 2007).

Within the SCCT, the emphasis on the cognitive aspects of motivation allows school counselors to view students as active agents, or shapers, of their own decision-making and career development. School counselors who utilize a social-cognitive framework can help students understand how they are able to shape their own career outcomes; that their beliefs about themselves, their environments, and possible career paths play a prominent role in the decision-making process. One of the most useful features of the SCCT is that the sources of information that are postulated to lead to the development of self-efficacy beliefs can be readily used to guide the development of interventions (Betz, 2007). In other words, school counselors can utilize information from a variety of sources to improve students' self-efficacy while simultaneously facilitating experiences that give rise to career-related interests. Helping students develop specific skills, providing them with opportunities to take a variety of coursework, pairing them with mentors, and teaching them stress management strategies are all concrete ways that school counselors can improve student self-efficacy within the SCCT framework (Falco, 2016).

Gottfredson's Theory of Circumscription and Compromise

The theory of circumscription and compromise is a developmental theory of career choice. It focuses on how students become aware of and eventually navigate the array of vocational choices available within their societies (Gottfredson, 1981, 2004). Similar to other theories of career development, circumscription and compromise views choice as a matching process, whereby individuals seek occupations that align with their interests and goals and for which they possess relevant skills and dispositions. Children's growth and development affects their behavior in many ways. According to the theory, in the vocational realm two major developmental outcomes are the formation of a "cognitive map of occupations" and the "self-concept." The theory posits that most individuals will eventually develop the same or similar cognitive map of occupations, but everyone will develop increasingly individualized self-concepts. As they develop, children's conceptions of people and occupations develop in parallel as they perceive various dimensions of difference and begin to form stereotypes (Gottfredson, 2004).

Gottfredson's theory views individuals as unique and agentic, who simultaneously influence and are influenced by the environment. In other words, we become who we are through the experience of engaging with the world around us, and we affect the direction of our development by exposing ourselves (accidentally or purposefully) to certain formative experiences rather than others (Gottfredson, 2004). As children mature, they take an increasingly more active role in choosing, influencing, and interpreting their experiences, which—in turn—leads to the creation of self-concept.

Within this framework, the concept of circumscription refers to the narrowing of possible options. In other words, vocational choice begins as a process of eliminating occupational alternatives that do not align with one's self-concept. Early in life, students begin to rule out entire categories of occupations as socially unacceptable or not possible, generally based on the stereotypes they form about people, workers, and jobs. According to Gottfredson (2004), children rule out progressively more sectors of the occupational realm as they become more perceptive about increasingly abstract dimensions of jobs in relation to the compatibility with how they view themselves as future workers. Most of this process is unconscious, as circumscription occurs often without their knowing much about what workers actually do in the jobs they prematurely fail to consider as a possibility. Therefore, within this framework, an important task for the school counselor is to ensure that students are exposed to a wide range of possible career options, beginning early in schooling, and to provide occupational information to stimulate interest and exploration.

Compromise is the process whereby students begin to rule out preferred occupations for ones they view as most accessible. As Gottfredson (2004) explains, weighing the relative benefits of the higher-ranking options available is considered vocational *choice*. When later forced with a decision to select among the remaining acceptable options, the choice becomes *compromise*. When viewed this way, career development and decision-making focuses more on barriers to choice. For school counselors, helping students uncover opportunities and reducing the need to compromise becomes essential. Students vary greatly in the personal traits that enable them to explore, remain optimistic, and persist in the face of barriers, but school counselors have many opportunities to empower students to improve facets of their self-concept and promote a range of realistic, accessible vocational aspirations. To summarize, the theory suggests that effective career counseling will (a) provide coaching in lifelong skill development and self-agency (Savickas, 1996); (b) provide information and instruction about the world of work commensurate with students' cognitive development and capabilities; (c) optimize experiences that expose students to a wide range of vocational possibilities, including those that challenge stereotypes; and (d) optimize personal growth and self-awareness in the interest of helping students develop positive, accurate self-concepts (Gottfredson, 2004).

Career Assessments

Given the complex array of career options available in contemporary society, one of the most important tasks for school counselors is to help students through the use of career assessments. Assessment can provide a focus to career exploration and post-secondary planning as counselors help students develop insights about themselves and the world of work (Prediger, 1995). Suffice it to say that the major role of assessment in post-secondary planning is self/career exploration (a parallel process). Assessment in career development harks back to the person-environment framework discussed in the previous section, where the primary focus was on matching individuals with appropriate careers. Thus, the primary purpose of many career assessments is to gather quantifiable information or data that could be used to guide individuals into specific vocations. It is important to always keep in mind that results from career assessments are just one piece of information in a large, complex puzzle, and many variables influence post-secondary planning and career choice. In this section, we describe different types of assessments that we believe are most useful when doing post-secondary planning with students in K–12 settings.

Types of Assessments

Broadly speaking, career assessments fall into two main categories. The first category contains assessments that measure aspects of individuals such as interests, values, needs, abilities, and personality (Betz, 1992). The second category includes assessments that measure aspects of the career development process, such as self-efficacy, decision-making, or career maturity (Swanson & Woitke, 1997). Assessments can be viewed as addressing the *what* and *how* questions related to post-secondary planning and career decision-making (Swanson & Fouad, 2015). What difficulties are present? What options are available? What are the students' primary interests or strongest skills? How do students' interests align with their skills? How do students' values compare with the demands of specific occupations? Within these categories, different assessments yield different kinds of data, and all results should be considered within the context of other available information. It is important for school counselors to use high-quality, valid, and reliable instruments and to know the limits of the assessments they use (Swanson & Fouad, 2015).

Interests

For school counselors who want to assist students with assessing their vocational interests, several measures are currently available and widely used. Indeed, vocational interests are the most frequently assessed construct in career counseling (Hansen, 2005). Recall also that interests are also prominent in each of the theories described in the previous section of this chapter. Examples of assessments that measure interests include the Strong Interest Inventory (SII), the Self-Directed Search (SDS), and the Kuder Career Search. Each of these are commercially available and can be purchased by individuals or institutions, but many interest inventories have been developed/adapted for specific purposes and may be more widely available on career planning websites. The SII provides information related to individuals' career vocational and leisure interests. The measure consists of four scales: general occupational themes, basic interests, occupational scales, and personal style. Students respond to a battery of questions, 291 total, and scores provide proportion of preferences that the individual chose for the various SII items/scales. Individuals respond using a five-point scale from strongly like to strongly dislike. The scores from the SII can be used to examine students' responses to the entire SII as well as within specific scales.

The Interest Profiler Short Form (Rounds, Su, Lewis, & Rivkin, 2010) is a shorter version of the 180-item original (Lewis & Rivkin, 1999) and was developed to be a valid, reliable measure of Hollands' RIASEC interest themes. This assessment can be self-administered in both paper and pencil and computer-based format and takes about 30 minutes to complete. Items contain questions about students' interests in a variety of occupations of varying skill levels. Response options include like, dislike, or unsure—and scores are calculated by totaling the likes in each subscale. Results from this assessment can be used to explore related occupations in the O*Net database.

Values

From the previous section on theories, it is clear how skills and interests are important variables in post-secondary planning and, ultimately, the selection of a career. The theory of work adjustment (Dawis & Lofquist, 1984) introduced the concept of *work values* by describing the ways in which people balance their own needs with the perceived rewards of various positions. Although we did not cover Super's theory of career development (Super, 1953; Super, Savickas, & Super, 1996), he is largely credited with further clarifying the construct of work values in the context of vocational planning. The first formal assessment of work values was the Work Values Inventory (WVI; Super, 1970). Subsequent measures of work values include the Minnesota Importance Questionnaire (MIQ; Rounds, Henly, Dawis, Lofquist, & Weiss, 1981) and the Work Aspect Preference Scale (WAPS; Pryor, 1983). Other assessments such as the SIGI-PLUS (Educational Testing Service, 1993), DISCOVER (American College Testing, 1984, and ASVAB Career Exploration Program (Wise et al., 1992) all incorporate work values.

There is not an optimal, agreed-upon format for conceptualizing or measuring work values. Many of the assessments described here rely on what is called a "paired comparison" format, which presents two value statements, and each statement is compared to every other statement—or a rank format where value statements are presented in groups and respondents are asked to rank order the statements within each group. Counselors can help students use this information to compare their scores with known "reinforcer" patterns of various professions. For example, a student who scores relatively high in areas of time flexibility, predictable income, and helping others might consider professions such as teaching or nursing. Other approaches incorporate self-report measures, including interview or narrative techniques, whereby the counselor asks students structured questions to help elucidate work values (Cochran, 1997). Creative ways to help students explore work values might include assessments such as the "Million Dollar Question," where the counselor asks the student, or a group of students in a class, to respond to the following question: If you could have any job in the world, what would you choose and why? Helping the students process their answers to a question like this can help them clarify their work values. A similar activity involves the use of card sorts where students are given a set of work values and asked to prioritize them, and the counselor can use follow-up questions to help students clarify their work values.

Self-Efficacy

Vocational planning and career development also focus on the process of choice, which includes such things as decision-making, self-efficacy, and career maturity. In contrast to assessments that measure interests, skills, and values, measures of career development process tend to be developed more often for research purposes rather than published commercially (Swanson & Fouad, 2015). For example, the Career Decision-Making Self-Efficacy Scale (CDMSE; Betz & Taylor, 1994) uses SCCT as a framework for assessing students' perceived self-efficacy for making career-related decisions. Information from this assessment can help guide appropriate interventions to improve student self-efficacy.

Maturity

The concept of career maturity emerged from developmental theories of career development and focuses on the process of career choice through its emphasis on individuals' "readiness" to make such a choice. The Career Maturity Inventory (CMI; Crites, 1978) measures individuals' ability to make appropriate career choices, including awareness of what is required to make a career decision and the degree to which one's choices are both realistic and consistent (Patton & Creed, 2001). It also measures attitudes toward the decision-making process. Information from this assessment can help the counselor identify areas of decision-making that may inhibit students in their future planning and ability to implement a career choice. A more specific aspect of career maturity is career decision status, which can also be thought of in terms of "certainty" or "indecision." The Career Decision Scale (CDS; Osipow, Carney, Winer, Yanico, & Koschier, 1976), which provides information about the specific issues that impact individuals' career decisions, can also be used to better understand students' decision-making skills.

In summary, assessment plays an important role in post-secondary planning, both formal and informal. At different stages in the post-secondary and career planning process, school counselors can use assessments to gather information about students' skills, interests, values, self-efficacy, maturity, and other career-related constructs. Additionally, use of state assessment results and school district selected career inventories (such as EXPLORE, Scholastic Aptitude Test, end-of-course exams, and American College Testing) are recommended. The use of various assessments is almost limitless if counselors use a little creativity. Other fun and interesting ways to engage students in the career planning process include the use of guided imagery, "idea journals," free writing, career genograms, career bingo, collage, timeline analysis, and life mapping, as discussed in Heppner, O'Brien, Hinkelman, and Humphrey (1994). These data are very useful for helping students gain the self-awareness that is crucial for making an informed decision about what to do with one's life after graduating from high school. Ideally, students should be able to make a choice that is aligned with their values, skills, and interests, along with their resources and available supports, so that they have maximum potential for success.

Post-Secondary Planning and the World of Work

What do school counselors need to know about current educational and occupational trends for post-secondary planning and the world of work? This is a difficult question to answer, first because the world of work is in constant flux. Second, the ever-evolving technological advances have made the world more interesting, while many jobs that require specific non–college degree skills cannot be easily filled because students are not prepared to do these jobs or are not aware that these would be viable career paths (e.g., plumbing, construction, automobile mechanics, and so forth). Third, this contrast between what constitutes traditional post-secondary planning (i.e., all students being ready and prepared for college) and the reality that not all students need to attend college or will be appropriate for a traditional college experience makes the role of the school counselor complicated. That being said, school counselors do help students plan for options that could include transitioning and gaining acceptance to a university, college, community college, and so forth, or specifically the pursuit of gainful employment.

To illustrate specifically what school counselors might be responsible for doing in particular, the following description is one ideal example of what a school counselor could be involved in K–12 and concerning post-secondary work within a comprehensive school counseling program. For example, a local job posting in a large urban school district that serves primarily high-poverty, high-risk populations of students, primarily identified as having English as a second language, outlines essential functions that are not exhaustive, but representative of what is expected as a potential member of the school counseling workforce. Specifically, these roles are noted as aligning closely with the ASCA as well as Comprehensive Competency Based Guidance. The counselor is expected to provide activities to meet the needs of the students; consult with teachers, staff, and parents to enhance their effectiveness in helping students; and provide support to other educational programs. Next, the school counselor is expected to guide and counsel groups and individual students through the development of educational and career plans. Counselors will also provide orientation activities for students who are new to the school, and ensure that families participate in orientation programs. Transition issues are critical, and the school counselor is expected to assist students in the transition from school to school, level to level, and school to work throughout the developmental/educational lifespan. Other duties include informing students and parents of test results and their implications for educational planning, while also providing resources and information to assist in career awareness and career exploration activities and help students take appropriate steps toward implementing their educational and career plans. Finally, the school counselor is expected to assist students in evaluation of their graduation requirements and in updating their four-year plans and career portfolios.

From this example, you may be wondering what specifically must the school counselor do to help a high school student prepare for college or the world of work? The following sections outline a decision-making model for helping students develop the skills necessary to establish a firm foundation in school as they prepare for their emerging young adulthood.

Decision-Making

Effective post-secondary planning requires focus on both the content (what) and process (how) of vocational decisions. Using cognitive information processing theory as a framework, researchers at Florida State University developed a very useful counseling tool called the CASVE decision-making cycle (Sampson, Peterson, Lenz, & Reardon, 1992), which integrates both content and process. It is a career decision-making model that focuses on action-oriented steps that school counselors can use to assist their students at each stage. This approach to post-secondary planning and career development is a way to link theory and practice in the delivery of effective services for students. The aim is to help individuals make an appropriate career choice and learn improved problem-solving and decision-making skills that will be needed for future choices.

The model uses a pyramid concept to understand what is involved in career choice (the content) and the CASVE cycle to help individuals understand how to make career choices (the process). Information processing domains related to career decision-making and job placement can be conceptualized as a pyramid. The foundation of the pyramid includes knowledge domains (self-knowledge such as values, interests, skills, and preferences—and occupational knowledge such as categories of employment and educational requirements). The middle of the pyramid includes decision-making skills (necessary steps in choosing a job or program of study). The top of the pyramid includes the executive processing domain (metacognitions such as self-talk, self-awareness, and self-regulation). CASVE stands for Communication—Analysis—Synthesis—Valuing—Execution. The CASVE cycle is situated in the middle part of the pyramid within the decision-making skills domain (see Figure 8.1). For school counselors assisting students with post-secondary planning, helping students become more skilled at decision-making may be a particularly effective strategy.

Problem solving and decision-making can be conceptualized in terms of the CASVE cycle. The cycle is essentially understanding how to make a career choice. In choosing a career path, it is important to think about many factors. Assuming the student has come to the point where he or she is ready to start making some choices, the school counselor can help students think about what kind of decision-maker they are, what decision-making style they use, and factors that might interfere with the decision-making process. Making a decision can be very easy or difficult depending on the amount of information available to make choices. CASVE is meant to provide individuals with exploratory questions during each step, helping them identify the gap between where they are now and where they want to be.

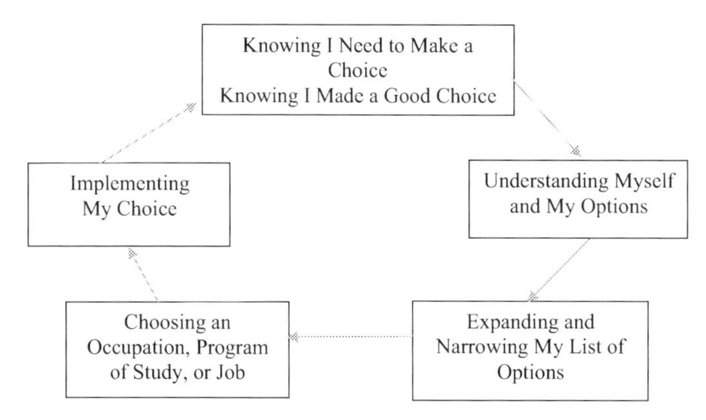

Figure 8.1 CASVE Cycle for Students

Adapted from Sampson, Peterson, Lenz, and Reardon (1992).

Communication involves both external demands (I need to choose a major) and internal states such as emotions, behaviors, or physiological distress (I'm so anxious I can't sleep). In this stage of the cycle, the individual communicates both within him- or herself through self-assessment and reflective thinking, and with others in their life. The purpose of this communication is to identify the gap between where they are now and where they want to be in the future through analyzing internal and external cues.

Analysis involves improving or enhancing self-knowledge (values, interests, skills, preferences) and occupational knowledge (structure of the world of work, programs of study, or jobs), the capacity to apply a decision-making model, and metacognitions. Analysis is a recurring process of learning, reflection, and developing a more complex view of oneself. All people have some information at the start of this process. School counselors should help students at this stage by asking them to reflect on the following questions: What motivates me? What are my skills and values? What do I enjoy doing? How do I envision myself in the future? This stage also requires students to understand how they make important decisions. To help students, school counselors should ask: what was an important decision you made recently and how did you make it?

Synthesis involves elaboration or expansion of possible options. During this stage, school counselors might utilize career assessments to help students generate vocational options and identify the maximum number of potential alternatives. After elaborating, crystallization allows for the narrowing of options to a manageable number. School counselors can help students eliminate inappropriate options by using assessment results and occupational information. Identifying two or three options is best for proceeding on to the valuing stage.

Valuing occurs when students begin to judge the costs and benefits of each option. During this stage, school counselors can help students judge the costs and benefits of each alternative to oneself, significant others, the cultural group, and the community and/or society at large. As students begin to prioritize alternatives, based on the valuing, they can begin to make tentative primary and secondary choices (plan A, plan B).

Execution involves formulating a plan for implementing a tentative choice. Examples of execution might be selecting a vocational training program or college major, exploring financial aid opportunities, completing education or training, and beginning a job search. Execution may involve formal education/training, engaging in full- or part-time work, volunteering, or seeking employment (the steps to apply for and get a job). The cycle comes full circle with communication. School counselors can help students review external and internal cues. Has the gap been closed? Have the negative emotions and physiological states improved? Is the student taking action to achieve a goal?

There are a few important considerations when using the CASVE cycle in post-secondary planning. First is the idea that career choice evolves over time and may involve many iterations. At times, individuals may cycle back and forth between stages before advancing in their decision-making. Others may proceed through the cycle many times as they meet smaller objectives in service of a longer-term goal. Chance and serendipity also play a role in the process. Sometimes unexpected events emerge in a person's life, and those events may eliminate previous options or provide new options that didn't exist previously. This may require cycling back through analysis and valuing. It is also important to keep in mind that, although CASVE utilizes a cognitive information processing model, emotions may be just as important as cognitions in decision-making. Intuition is also very important in the decision-making process. School counselors using CASVE should help students understand that intuition is a different way of knowing, and intuitive insights are as important as rational insights. Almost everybody uses both rationality and intuition, and they can be complementary in the decision-making process. Perceived discrepancies between rationality and intuition might simply be a signal that more problem solving is needed to move forward.

Application to Planning Sessions

Post-secondary planning with students should be a part of the services offered by school counselors. There are many considerations to be made when counselors meet with students regarding post-secondary planning. Knowing what the related mandates are from the district, the district requirements to host individualized or group meetings as a part of their transition or graduation planning, process for matriculation into college, or simply guidance in planning are critical to understanding in these sessions. Following are the phases of how to carry out a planning session with students assigned to school counselors on an annual basis with the focus on post-secondary planning.

Phase 1: Session Preparation

When the counseling session is scheduled ahead of time, the school counselor should be ready by having accessed the student's report card, assessment information, the course schedule, and current placement information. This reduces the amount of time hunting, gathering, and making copies that would take away from the session itself and create an appearance of disorganization. It would be helpful if the school counselor helped the student prepare by asking the student to bring goals, personal statements, and a journal to the planning session.

Phase 2: Session Exploration

The school counselor should seek to understand the student's interests, strengths, and desires post high school, which might include attending college, working, or maybe owning or starting a business. This process of exploration should be fluid and receptive. Next, it is essential to know how family members have influenced the preferences or the roles that personal values play in the choice of a career. Then, school counselors help students investigate the personal vision related to the type of lifestyle they desire and the greater contribution to society they would like to make. Finally, financial aid options, family resources, and scholarship/grant considerations should be discussed. Some families believe that garnering student loans is not an option, so this should be explored. Looking at the student's extracurricular abilities could work in securing college funding or what resources the family can contribute to post-secondary options.

Phase 3: Model Integration

As recommended in this chapter, integrating the CASVE model and following a theory of career development is pertinent. Strategies to accomplish this may be direct questioning or use of the million-dollar question. Model integration requires skill development on the part of the school counselor. Using elements of each helps make the session more solid and fulfills the necessary requirement that school counselors operate within a theory, which tends be a process that deserves refinement along the way.

Phase 4: Assessment and Data Integration

Next, looking at data collected from the student's career assessments, report cards, the course schedule, academic achievement results, and SAT/ACT scores should assist the school counselor in shaping the conversation. There should be a discussion about these various pieces of information and interpretation of the collective outcome data. Keep in mind that some students lack test-taking skills, may perform poorly, and it may not serve as a true reflection of their academic ability or their potential to succeed in the future. An exploration of skills and talents that have not been assessed during testing or because of grades in academic courses would be beneficial to understand the whole person.

Phase 5: Goal Setting

Goals should be established together, such as short-term or immediate defined as *here and now* and long-term goals that are focused on the next year through the senior year. These goals should be strengths-based, written down, and revisited often by the student.

Phase 6: Task Allocation and Evaluation

Students should be asked to reflect on the session and to explore YouTube™ videos or Internet sites about their post-secondary interests, preferably by a certain deadline. Students should have an idea of their earning potential and ability to be successful in their selected field or trade. Students should be asked to complete a brief evaluation for the school counselor to refine and improve the session planning processes.

Phase 7: Documentation Strategies

At the end of the session, school counselors should have a system in place to document each planning session. This system should be one that can be accessed from year-to-year, particularly if school counselors travel from grade-to-grade with the same assigned caseload of students. This system may need to be in place for all school counselors in the department versus just within the individual school counselor's office. Students should be encouraged to maintain a journal that they bring with them and keep year after year. Students have a high responsibility that comes with this process, and their organizational skills must be intact in order for the process to be effective over time.

Ethical Considerations

Previous sections have focused on individual career development and post-secondary planning, including the importance of different theoretical frameworks and their application to the career planning and decision-making process. Career interventions are a well-researched and effective way to help students engage in post-secondary planning (Whiston & Blustein, 2013). The ASCA identifies three areas, or domains, for student development, which include academic, personal/social, and career (ASCA, 2012), and the most recent student standards, referred to as the ASCA Mindsets and Behaviors for Student Success (ASCA, 2014), are specifically geared towards K–12 college and career readiness. Because of this and because of the school counseling profession's roots in vocational guidance (Pope, 2000), it follows logically that career development and post-secondary planning continue to be a large part of the services provided by school counselors. Knowledge of career development and career exploration is critical for effective and ethical practice (Swanson & Fouad, 2015).

In schools, career exploration and post-secondary planning is arguably one of the most important direct services provided by school counselors because academic development, personal/social development, and career development—the three domains defined by the ASCA National Model (ASCA, 2012)—overlap considerably. For example, one ASCA "mindset" for student success is that students understand that post-secondary education and life-long learning are necessary for long-term career success (ASCA, 2014, M4). One behavior for student success is that students are able to identify long- and short-term academic, career, and social/emotional goals (ASCA, 2014, B-LS 7). School counselors focus on career development activities, particularly at the high school level, by helping students plan for the future, navigate the process of choosing a college or major or post-secondary work setting, and understand the relationship between high school activities and future occupational goals (Swanson & Fouad, 2015). The ASCA Mindsets and Behaviors for Student Success are intended to be objectives and outcomes of a comprehensive K–12 counseling program, with many interventions and activities designed to build on one another as students progress through their schooling (ASCA, 2014). Subsequent sections provide a brief overview of career development interventions at the elementary, middle, and high school levels. For school counselors, knowledge of development as it relates to career and post-secondary planning is essential for ethical practice. We also recommend visiting the ASCA website (www.schoolcounselor.org) for additional resources to help deliver developmentally appropriate career interventions.

Professional Issues

School counselors providing career development and post-secondary planning services may face several professional and ethical challenges, including availability of resources (Schenck, Anctil, Smith, & Dahir, 2012), advocating for the importance of career interventions (Whiston, Fouad, & Juntunen, 2016), multiple demands (Schenck et al., 2012), and educational laws and policies that influence priorities in schools (Schenck et al., 2012). Recent and growing emphasis on academic achievement—and performance on state standardized tests—may have the unintended consequence of reducing the time spent on students' career or personal/social development. Teachers may be less willing to sacrifice classroom instructional time for non-academic activities or interventions, reducing the opportunities to collaborate on career exploration. As Swanson and Fouad (2015) point out, this could bring into conflict what school counselors know about effective practice and their own ethical obligations to be part of an interdisciplinary team. What might be considered "best practice" may not always be practical or feasible in a real-world setting, and school counselors must be equipped to balance their students' needs with the ideals articulated in the ASCA National Model.

Other ethical considerations school counselors must avoid, in what often feels like the absence of time, are the option of selecting courses or placing students in programs in order to complete a task or to set the master schedule for the current or upcoming year. Another issue that is often apparent for school counselors is their advocacy for a student's matriculation into a university and the tendency to promote students attaining a college degree. Although this may be difficult not to do, some families and individual students believe running the family business or generating self-employed revenue is how they wish to make their contribution to society. It is relevant to remember the student as our client and resist placing our values and beliefs onto them in a manner such as this.

Multicultural Competencies

School counselors' knowledge of how the world of work operates for individuals from diverse backgrounds is a key component of competent, ethical career counseling. It is critical for school counselors to consider how "career" is defined by individuals from varying cultural backgrounds and the relative importance of work in people's lives. Another important consideration is what occupations are over- or under-represented by individuals from particular demographic groups and what a member of a particular group might need to consider when contemplating a particular career choice (Flores & Heppner, 2002). It is possible that many racial/ethnic or other minority students may make career decisions based on their own stereotypes regarding appropriate options; therefore, helping students understand how their views were formed may help prevent premature foreclosure on possible career options. Lastly, school counselors must be aware of what assessments are appropriate to use with students from diverse backgrounds and to take caution when interpreting the results. For example, a counselor who wanted to use a career genogram or family tree would want to take into consideration that some students may not have a traditional, nuclear family structure. Or, a school counselor would want to consider how a student's gender may influence scores on an interest inventory. As noted earlier, it is important to consider the purpose of the assessment and to use assessment responsibly when assisting with career development and post-secondary planning.

Although not entirely applicable to school counselors in school settings, the reader should note that the National Career Development Association (NCDA) has published a set of recommendations for working with individuals at various stages of development. Additionally, the NCDA has also published a code of ethics (NCDA, 2007), which is a valuable resource for assisting career counselors in various settings with ethical decision-making. Please see the complete NCDA *Code of Ethics* (2007) for detailed guidance on professional issues related to career counseling and development.

Conclusion

School counselors can perform some specific tasks when working with students in middle and high schools to lay a foundation for students to be both college and career ready. That being said, elementary and middle school students must not be overlooked in this process, but the limited resources typically afforded to school districts for school counseling services means that some difficult choices on where funding is applied will need to be made.

The following specific educational and vocational focus can be taken by a school counselor with secondary students when reasonable resources are available, according to one's caseload, in order to help students prepare for life after high school. These steps include (a) four-year planning, (b) standardized testing, (c) choosing the right post-secondary option, (d) if appropriate, financial planning, (e) scholarships, (f) college and job applications, (g) cover letters, resumes, and personal statements, and (h) letters of recommendations. Furthermore, covering other more general school counseling administration duties, like testing or discipline needs, will also be necessary. A few of these issues are highlighted in the case illustration that follows.

A high school counselor referred to as Professor Johnson was responsible for a caseload of approximately 390 students, a ratio better than the state's recommendation of 450 to 1. Yet in this caseload there were a striking 120 seniors. The other part of the caseload consisted of 270 sophomores, who in two years would be seniors. On this particular Monday, or any day for that matter, Professor J's time spent in school consisted of any number of tasks. Professor J helped multiple students at different times on activities such as choosing the correct courses to take in the next term by looking up current or past academic and attendance history, or answering questions about the differences between the SAT and ACT college entrance exams using a basic Internet search and knowledge from a recent training delivered by the College Board. Another time, a student is meeting with Professor J, and it is discovered that this student is one of the first in his or her family to go to college, so assistance on things like exploring the differences between public and private colleges and universities, or the pros and cons of applying to a community college were discussed. In this case and with any student from any background entering the workforce directly or before transitioning into college, these pros and cons should be broached. This will only be a problem if a student who really needed to hear this information was not allowed to talk about it or wasn't asked by the school counselor for fear someone could be offended by considering a much less expensive approach to college attendance. Lastly, a less common situation encountered includes one in which a student wants to or should be considered for a trip overseas on a study abroad program, which although unique, is becoming more popular.

In most cases, Professor J is familiar with what is encountered daily, but offering some insight on things that are less familiar to the counselor will require some assistance to ensure the student is getting the help that they need. Not being able to serve every student in every case is not a problem, but failure to seek the help when it is needed is a problem our students cannot afford, as these mishaps can have dire consequences on one's future career and postsecondary outlook.

School counselors can be intentional about addressing obvious postsecondary developmental needs in public schools. This arduous role is not limited to just helping students gain admission to college or choosing and pursuing great careers. School counselors can help students be successful at various points, including graduation from high school and college, picking a career path that aligns with their life's purpose, or a combination of these two. In either case, these endeavors have positive implications, especially in light of the strengths provided in culturally diverse communities for the students and the emerging society in which they live.

Activities

1. Discuss with a partner how you would arrange registering students for classes for the following year: in a large suburban high school (2,000 students), in a small rural high school (500 students), and in an urban inner-city high school (850 students). Think about how many counselors would be involved; how the procedures would be

divided; other school personnel who might be involved; and, most importantly, what do you want students to think about before they register? Share your ideas with the large group.

2. Brainstorm the community partners that you could include in classroom curriculum that would help students in middle school think about college and career readiness. What types of presentations could they make to one grade level, to the entire school, to a specific group (e.g., students with special needs, students whose first language is not English, students in gifted classes, athletes, students in band, etc.)?
3. Find out what programs are available in your area through the community college system that prepare students to begin taking college courses immediately after high school. These programs might include speakers who will come to your school, high school classes that will count for college credit, and informational fairs that inform students and parents about the community college experience.
4. With a team, explore the many websites that are available to help students make decisions about post-secondary options. Look for online college fairs, interest and aptitude surveys for middle and high school students, four-year university websites, community college websites, and so forth. Prepare a resource guide based on your group's findings.
5. Some college campuses have summer programs for middle and high school students. Find out what is available in your area, the topics, the cost, and the dates.

Resources

Texas CTE Resource Center for Counselors:
www.txcte.org/counselors

The College Board:
www.collegeboard.org/

O*Net Online:
www.onetonline.org/

U.S. Department of Education, Gear Up:https://www2.ed.gov/programs/gearup/index.html

Duke TIP:
https://tip.duke.edu/

References

American College Testing Program (ACT). (1984). *DiSCOVER for schools*. Hunt Valley, MD: Author.

American School Counselor Association. (2012). *The ASCA national model: A framework for school counseling programs* (3rd ed.). Alexandria, VA: Author.

American School Counselor Association. (2012). *The ASCA national model: A framework for school counseling programs* (3rd ed.). Alexandria, VA: Author.

American School Counselor Association. (2014). *Mindsets and behaviors for student success: K-12 college- and career-readiness standards for every student*. Alexandria, VA: Author.

Bandura, A. (1986). The explanatory and predictive scope of self-efficacy theory. *Journal of Social and Clinical Psychology*, *4*(3), 359–373.

Betz, N. E. (1992). Career assessment: A review of critical issues. In S. D. Brown & R. W. Lent (Eds.), *Handbook of counseling psychology* (pp. 453–484). Oxford, England: John Wiley.

Betz, N. E. (2007). Career self-efficacy: Exemplary recent research and emerging directions. *Journal of Career Assessment*, *15*(4), 403–422.

Betz, N. E., & Taylor, K. M. (1994). *Manual for the career decision-making self-efficacy scale*. Columbus, OH: Department of Psychology, The Ohio State University.

Bryan, J., Moore-Thomas, C., Day-Vines, N. L., & Holcomb-McCoy, C. (2011). School counselors as social capital: The effects of high school college counseling on college application rates. *Journal of Counseling & Development*, *89*(2), 190–199.

Cochran, L. (1997). *Career counseling: A narrative approach*. Thousand Oaks, CA: SAGE Publications.

Crites, J. O. (1978). *Career maturity inventory*. Monterey, CA: CTB/McGraw-Hill.

Dawis, R. V. (1994). The theory of work adjustment as convergent theory. In M. L. Savickas & R. W. Lent (Eds.), *Convergence in career development theories: Implications for science and practice* (pp. 33–43). Palo Alto, CA: CPP Books.

Dawis, R. V., & Lofquist, L. H. (1984). *A psychological theory of work adjustment: An individual-differences model and its applications*. Minneapolis, MN: University of Minnesota Press.

Educational Testing Service (ETS). (1993). *SIGI PLUS*. Princeton NJ: Author.

Falco, L. D. (2016). The school counselor and STEM career development. *Journal of Career Development*, *44*, 359–374.

Flores, L. Y., & Heppner, M. J. (2002). Multicultural career counseling: Ten essentials for training. *Journal of Career Development*, *28*(3), 181–202.

Gottfredson, L. S. (1981). Circumscription and compromise: A developmental theory of occupational aspirations. *Journal of Counseling Psychology*, *28*(6), 545.

Gottfredson, L. S. (2004). *Using Gottfredson's theory of circumscription and compromise in career guidance and counseling*. Retrieved from www.udel.edu/educ/gottfredson/reprints/2004theory.pdf

Gysbers, N. C. (2013). Career-ready students: A goal of comprehensive school counseling programs. *The Career Development Quarterly*, *61*(3), 283–288.

Hansen, J. C. (2005). Assessment of interests. In S. D. Brown & R. W. Lent (Eds.), *Career development and counseling: Putting theory and research to work* (pp. 281–304). New York: Wiley.

Heppner, M. J., O'Brien, K. M., Hinkelman, J. M., & Humphrey, C. F. (1994). Shifting the paradigm: The use of creativity in career counseling. *Journal of Career Development*, *21*(2), 77–86.

Holland, J. L. (1959). A theory of vocational choice. *Journal of Counseling Psychology*, *6*(1), 35.

Holland, J. L. (1997). *Making vocational choices: A theory of vocational personalities and work environments*. Odessa, FL: Psychological Assessment Resources.

Lent, R. W., Brown, S. D., & Hackett, G. (1994). Toward a unifying social cognitive theory of career and academic interest, choice, and performance. *Journal of Vocational Behavior*, *45*(1), 79–122.

Lent, R. W., Brown, S. D., & Hackett, G. (2002). Social cognitive career theory. In D. Brown (Ed.), *Career choice and development* (4th ed., pp. 255–311). San Francisco, CA: Jossey-Bass.

Lewis, P., & Rivkin, D. (1999). *Development of the O* NET interest profiler*. Raleigh, NC: National Center for O* NET Development.

National Career Development Association. (2007). *NCDA code of ethics*. Broken Arrow, OK: Author.

Osipow, S. H., Carney, C. G., Winer, J. L., Yanico, B., & Koschier, M. (1976). *The career decision scale* (3rd revision). Odessa, FL: Psychological Assessment Resources.

Patton, W., & Creed, P. A. (2001). Developmental issues in career maturity and career decision status. *The Career Development Quarterly*, *49*(4), 336–351.

Pope, M. (2000). A brief history of career counseling in the United States. *The Career Development Quarterly*, *48*(3), 194–211.

Prediger, D. (1995). *Digests, E. R. I. C. assessment in career counseling*. Retrieved from https://www.counseling.org/resources/library/ERIC% 20Digests/95-18.pdf

Pryor, R. G. (1983). *Work aspect preference scale: Manual*. Melbourne: Australian Council for Educational Research.

Public Agenda. (2010). *Can I get a little advice here? How an overstretched high school guidance system is undermining students' college aspirations*. New York: Author.

Rounds Jr, J. B., Henly, G. A., Dawis, R. V., Lofquist, L. H., & Weiss, D. J. (1981). *Manual for the Minnesota importance questionnaire: A measure of vocational needs and values*. Minneapolis, MN: University of Minnesota.

Rounds Jr, J. B., Su, R., Lewis, P., & Rivkin, D. (2010). *O*NET interest profiler short form psychometric characteristics: Summary and supporting evidence*. Raleigh, NC: Department of Labor O*NET Resource Center.

Sampson, J. P., Peterson, G. W., Lenz, J. G., & Reardon, R. C. (1992). A cognitive approach to career services: Translating concepts into practice. *The Career Development Quarterly*, *41*(1), 67–74.

Savickas, M. L. (1996). A framework for linking career theory and practice. In M. L. Savickas & W. Bruce Walsh (Eds.), *Handbook of career counseling theory and practice* (pp. 191–208). Palo Alto, CA: Davies-Black.

Savitz-Romer, M. (2012). The gap between influence and efficacy: College readiness training, urban school counselors, and the promotion of equity. *Counselor Education and Supervision*, *51*(2), 98–111.

Schaefer, M. B., & Rivera, L. M. (2012). College and career readiness in the middle grades. *Middle Grades Research Journal*, *7*(3), 51.

Schenck, P. M., Anctil, T. M., Smith, C. K., & Dahir, C. (2012). Coming full circle: Reoccurring career development trends in schools. *The Career Development Quarterly*, *60*(3), 221–230.

Super, D. E. (1953). A theory of vocational development. *American Psychologist*, *8*(5), 185.

Super, D. E. (1970). Career development. In J. Davitz & S. Bass (Eds.), *Psychology and the educational process*. New York: McGraw-Hill.

Super, D. E., Savickas, M. L., & Super, C. M. (1996). The life-span, life-space approach to careers. In D. Brown & L. Brooks (Eds.), *Career choice and development* (3rd ed., pp. 121–178). San Francisco, CA: Jossey-Bass.

Swanson, J. L., & Fouad, N. A. (1999). *Career theory and practice: Learning through case studies*. Thousand Oaks, CA: SAGE Publications.

Swanson, J. L., & Fouad, N. A. (2015). *Career theory and practice: Learning through case studies*. Thousand Oaks, CA: SAGE Publications.

Swanson, J. L., & Woitke, M. B. (1997). Theory into practice in career assessment for women: Assessment and intervention regarding perceived career barriers. *Journal of Career Assessment*, *5*, 431–450.

Whiston, S. C., & Blustein, D. L. (2013). *The impact of career interventions: Preparing our citizens for the 21st century jobs*. National Career Development

Association. Retrieved from www.ncda.org/aws/NCDA/asset_manager/get_file/63826/ncda-svp_final_version_impact_of_21st_century.Pdf.

Whiston, S. C., Fouad, N., & Juntunen, C. (2016, August). *Professional practice guidelines for integrating the role of work and career into psychological practice.* APA council of representatives.

Wise, L., Welsh, J., Grafton, F., Foley, P., Earles, J., Sawin, L., & Divgi, D. R. (1992). *Sensitivity and fairness of the Armed Services Vocational Aptitude Battery (ASVAB) technical composites.* Monterey, CA: Personnel Testing Division, Defense Manpower Data Center, Department of Defense.

9

Advocating for Appropriate Roles

Dr. Carleton H. Brown

ASCA NATIONAL MODEL THEMES

Leadership

Advocacy

ASCA SCHOOL COUNSELOR PROFESSIONAL COMPETENCIES

I-B-2e. Creates a plan to challenge the non-counseling tasks that are assigned to school counselors

I-B-3. Advocates for student success

I-B-3a. Understands and defines advocacy and its role in comprehensive school counseling programs

I-B-3b. Identifies and demonstrates benefits of advocacy with school and community stakeholders

I-B-3c. Describes school counselor advocacy competencies, which include dispositions, knowledge and skills

I-B-3d. Reviews advocacy models and develops a personal advocacy plan

I-B-3e. Understands the process for development of policy and procedures at the building, district, state and national levels

II-B-4e. Advocates responsibly for school board policy and local, state and federal statutory requirements in students' best interests

III-B-4c. Creates a rationale for school counselor's use of time in the delivery component to focus on the goals of the comprehensive school counseling program

III-B-4d. Identifies and evaluates fair-share responsibilities, which articulate appropriate and inappropriate counseling and non-counseling activities

III-B-5. Develops calendars to ensure the effective implementation of the school counseling program

III-B-5a. Creates annual and weekly calendars to plan activities to reflect school counseling program goals

ASCA ETHICAL STANDARDS

B.2.c. Advocate for a school counseling program free of non-school-counseling assignments identified by "The ASCA National Model: A Framework for School Counseling Programs" as inappropriate to the school counselor's role.

B.2.h. Advocate for administrators to place in school counseling positions certified school counselors who are competent, qualified and hold a master's degree or higher in school counseling from an accredited program.

B.2.i. Advocate for equitable school counseling program policies and practices for all students and stakeholders.

CACREP STANDARDS

Foundations

G.1.b. models of school counseling programs

Contextual Dimensions

G.2.a. school counselor roles as leaders, advocates, and systems change agents in P-12 schools

Practice

G.3.o. use of data to advocate for programs and students

Introduction

During my first few months as an elementary school counselor, I spent much time conducting individual counseling, group counseling, providing character education

lessons, implementing prevention programing, and spearheading teacher assistant team meetings (i.e., assisting teachers with students with behavior issues). I thought I was fully addressing the requirements and the demands expected of a school counselor—until one day, my principal, a first-year building administrator, asked me into her office for a one-on-one chat. My principal acknowledged that I was doing some good work within the school, but she was worried that I was not being seen enough in the hallways and around the school. I replied to her that I was purposely spending time on the playground with students and engaging parents in the morning and afternoon during car pick-up. She stated that this was true, but this was not exactly what she was referring to. I asked her to be more specific. She finally stated that teachers were complaining that I was not participating in what we affectionately call "duty." Duty in this context meant mandatory supervision and possible discipline of children during certain times of the school day when students were not in the classroom (i.e., cafeteria or lunch duty, playground duty, bus duty, etc.). I mentioned to my principal that my professional ethics and best practices of school counseling promoted the counselor as a support person rather than being in the role of a disciplinarian. The principal stated that my performing such tasks is part of that "other duties assigned" clause in my contract. Needless to say, this part of our conversation ignited the first disagreement that my principal and I would embark on. I was not sure what to say next. I had in the past advocated for students, but I was not sure how to advocate for myself!

Brief History of Perceptions of School Counselors' Roles

Primary school stakeholders include students, teachers, administrators, and parents. These stakeholders have had strong perceptions regarding the appropriate role of the school counselor over the years. A brief history of stakeholders' perceptions of the school counselors' roles can be divided into two sections: Snapshot of the Early Years and Snapshot of Clarification Years.

Snapshot of Early Years

An article by Shertzer and Stone (1963) made clear that students during this time viewed school counselors as having a minor role in assisting them with personal issues. On the other hand, teachers perceived school counselors as administrative in nature and counselors of failing students. Administrators did not view school counselors as professionals who were able to deal with students, but mostly helpers in administrative tasks. Parents, on the other hand, perceived school counselors more as career counselors. The authors recommended how essential it was for school counselors to develop their professional identity and disseminate such information to school stakeholders.

Rippee, Hanvey, and Parker (1965) investigated stakeholder perceptions by assessing students' and teachers' perceptions before observing and experiencing counseling services, and then reassessing those perceptions after observing and experiencing counseling services. The authors learned that stakeholders' perceptions significantly changed after counseling services were provided. Initial perceptions of school counselors included primarily performing administrative duties; after observing and experiencing counseling services, students saw school counselors' essential duty as working with students and teachers. The authors also encouraged school counselors to develop their professional identity and explain it to stakeholders. In 1967, Hansen completed a study that focused on school counselors' perceptions. Results indicated that school counselors wanted to work more with teachers and counseling students rather than performing administrative tasks and completing paperwork. In 1970, Hart and Prince completed a study comparing school principals' and counselor educators' perceptions of the role of school counselors. Results indicated that school principals still considered school counselors as clerical workers, and counselor educators viewed any administrative tasks as inappropriate for the role of school counselors. The authors argued that building administrators had inappropriate expectations for school counselors.

Snapshot of Clarification Years

In 2004, Lieberman reviewed the literature regarding the school counselor's role, identified the need for role clarification, and identified the inappropriate duties forced upon school counselors (i.e., disciplinarian, administrative, record-keeping, etc.). The author made it clear that school principals needed to understand the appropriate roles of school counselors for the benefit of students. During the time of the 2004 article, the American School Counselor Association (ASCA) was in the process of redefining a statement of the counselor role. Lieberman (2004) was confident that ASCA's statement would assist in role clarification for the field. Monteiro-Leitner, Asner-Self, Milde, Leitner, and Skelton (2006) investigated the views of the role of the school counselor and found that most counselors agreed that administrative tasks took up too much time and were inappropriate for school counselors. In 2007, Chata and Loesh's study showed that aspiring principals were more in touch with the school counseling position; they concluded that over 240 principals-in-training were able to differentiate between appropriate and inappropriate roles of school counselors. But there was still much education and advocacy to be done. Scarborough and Culbreth (2008) completed a study to assess over 350 school counselors at various grade levels. Their results indicated high school counselors were least likely to practice in their preferred way, and elementary school counselors were more likely to practice in their preferred way. Additionally, school counselors with more years of experience were found to be more likely to practice in the way they preferred. Toporek, Lewis, and Crethar (2009) made it plain that although a small number of principals began understanding the role of the school counselor, continual research and the national ASCA model asserts that it is important that school counselors diligently continue to advocate and educate for appropriate roles in the school setting.

American School Counselor Association National Model

Before advocating for an appropriate school counselor role, it benefits school counselors to know what are appropriate and inappropriate roles for the profession. The previous section denotes the struggle over the years among stakeholders to agree on the appropriate roles of a school counselor (Chata & Loesch, 2007; Hansen, 1967; Hart & Prince, 1970; Lieberman, 2004; Monteiro-Leitner et al., 2006; Rippee, Hanvey, & Parker, 1965; Scarborough & Culbreth, 2008; Shertzer & Stone, 1963; Toporek, Lewis, & Crethar, 2009). Fortunately, ASCA has taken on the responsibility of defining a professional identity for school counselors. The ASCA has developed three editions of a national model to aid school counselors in making clear their professional identity and the comprehensive school counseling program (CSCP).

The latest (third) edition of the ASCA National Model (2012), is a framework for school counseling programs that covers national themes of school counseling leadership, advocacy, collaboration, and systems change as well as four critical components of building a CSCP: foundation, management, delivery, and accountability. The delivery component is a primary aspect of the model as it addresses the appropriate roles that school counselors exhibit to have a successful program. In fact, the delivery component is "80% or more of the activity in the ASCA National Model" (ASCA, p. 44). The authors of the third edition of the ASCA National Model adapted Campbell and Dahir's (1997) vision of appropriate and inappropriate roles for school counselors and listed them on page 45 of the text. Some examples of appropriate roles or activities for school counselors include planning individual student academic programs and providing individual and small-group counseling services to students. Some examples of inappropriate activities include coordinating paperwork and data entry of all new students, keeping clerical records, and serving as a data entry clerk. For a complete list of the ASCA appropriate and inappropriate roles, see the Figure in the Foreword of this text. ASCA's list has influenced state counseling departments such as that of Arkansas to adopt and build on the list to make it consistent to the school counseling programs in the state. In fact, the Arkansas Department of Education (2008) included in its Public School Student Services Program Planning, created by Act 908 of 1991, a list of ASCA's role expectations.

The ASCA also has developed school counselor competencies to assist in defining the professional identity of the school counselor. The school counselor competencies address "the knowledge, abilities, skills, and attitudes" to become effective school counselors and aligns with effective school counseling programs (ASCA, 2012, p. 148). Examples of school counselor competencies include the school counselor understanding and defining advocacy and its role in CSCPs as well as developing a personal advocacy plan. The school counselor competencies can be found in the appendix section of the third edition of the ASCA National Model.

Getting Started

School counselors are in a unique position as members of the school faculty. The primary interactions that take place within the school environment are arguably between the teacher and the student; however, school counselors provide support to students beyond this primary interaction. Unfortunately, when school districts are subject to financial distress, school support systems such as school counselors are sensitive to budget cuts (Graham, 2015; Khan, 2017; Lattanzio, 2013; Leal, 2017). The fear of job stability may lead some school counselors, especially beginning school counselors, to be hesitant to share their voice or advocate for themselves and their programs. In such cases, new school counselors may lean on seasoned counselors or mentors for professional advice (Bickmore & Curry, 2013). For instance, one of my mentors, Donna Wilchie, a veteran with 20 years of experience as a school counselor, states: "never be afraid" (personal communication, February 3, 2017) to advocate for yourself. A key to confidence in advocacy is knowledge. Wilchie explains further, "knowing what is required of your position on a state level and then on a local level will help you develop" a strong sense of professional identity for purposes of advocating.

In the beginning scenario of this chapter, I was presented with a difficult circumstance. The building principal was intent on having me perform *duty*. Fortunately, I was aware of my state rules and legislation. In the state in which I worked, school counselors were to spend no less than 75% of their time every month providing direct *counseling*-related activities to students. The other 25% could be administrative activities as long as it related to *counseling* services. Furthermore, I shared with my principal that our state association posted a list of appropriate and inappropriate roles on their website, and an inappropriate activity included assisting with duties such as lunch duty and bus duty; the list was adapted and modified from ASCA's list. After hearing this information, my principal verified the rules by reviewing them for herself and admitted that she was not aware of said information and changed her views in favor of me. I was greatly appreciative.

My situation is an example of what school counselors have been facing throughout the country, and it supports Wilchie's assertions that not only should school counselors "know . . . your state" requirements, but also join and keep up-to-date with "your state and national . . . professional organizations" (personal communication, February 3, 2017). By knowing or becoming the expert on the appropriate expectations of a school counselor, they can feel assured when relaying such information to stakeholders.

The Art of Communication With Stakeholders

Knowledge is important, but that knowledge must be communicated. Having the ability to positively relay advocacy concerns is essential to effective advocacy outcomes. School counselors are given the opportunity to interact with primary (students, teachers, administrators, and parents) and other significant school stakeholders (school support staff and community liaisons) in various avenues and levels (local and district): one-on-one, meetings, team collaborations, and presentations to name a few. In addition, school counselors should consider testifying before their state legislators in order to promote appropriate school counseling activities. Regardless of the venue, Hatch (2014) suggested some basic ideas to keep in mind that are helpful. The first suggestion is to use a "politically appropriate advocacy voice" (p. 188). For the situation, what voice inflection, pitch, and/or pace will benefit and move the conversation forward? Will sarcasm be appropriate or a distraction? Depending on the voice selections, the message spoken may change the dynamics of the conversation. For instance, if I stated in the earlier example to my principal in a physically intimidating, serious, or sarcastic tone the following, "regardless of the profession's expectations, school counselors just love to perform supervisory and disciplinarian duties," the principal may have taken offense and ignored my plea to reconsider assigning me such tasks. It benefits school counselors to be conscientious of their voice tone and their body language, particularly when suggesting change.

Another suggestion from Hatch (2014) is to be "prepared with a thorough analysis of the data" (p. 188). Although knowledge is critical, having numeric data, if the situation calls for it, is powerful. For instance, let us say that there is a school counselor who has implemented a program that addresses bullying within the school. The school counselor has collected data over time that shows the effectiveness of the program. A teacher complains that the program is a waste of time and takes away from valuable teaching time. The school counselor shares data that shows that bullying incidents have decreased and academic scores have increased since the bullying program has been in place. In sharing the data, the school counselor is advocating for his or her program through data analysis. The teacher is more likely to change his or her mindset about the program after hearing a thorough analysis of the outcome data. See Chapter 11 for an in-depth discussion of data collection and analysis.

The "Getting Started" section of this chapter highlights the importance of school counselors becoming the expert in their field for advocacy purposes (see Table 9.1). However, sometimes a situation requires school counselors to allow others to be the experts and to assist and support with suggestions or solutions. Hatch (2014) recommended school counselors be prepared with "thoughtful recommendations" and open to "consider new ways" to resolve an issue (p. 188).

An example of obtaining support from others is when a school counselor has been invited to attend a meeting of teachers and the administration regarding the behavior of a student that the school counselor has been counseling. The student was sent to the school counselor by his math teacher to *fix* the student's attitude and behavior in completing class assignments. After meeting with the student over time, the school counselor recognizes that the student actually completes his assignments quickly in class and is often bored for the remaining time of the class. The school counselor reviews the student's past grades in math and standardized test results in math. The student has a track record of positive achievements in math. The school

Table 9.1 Getting Started

"Getting Started" Key Concepts
Lean on mentors or experienced school counselors
Be confident and assured
Be knowledgeable
Join and participate in your professional organizations
Keep current with the profession

counselor discusses with the student and the student's parent regarding the student taking a more rigorous math class (i.e., algebra). Equipped with this information, the school counselor attends the meeting, and when the school counselor is faulted for not *fixing* the student, instead of going on the defensive, the school counselor carefully listens to each person's viewpoint of the matter, uses basic counseling techniques to acknowledge that he or she is listening (examples include reflection, tracking, summary, minimal encouragers etc.), before sharing facts that lead to a thoughtful recommendation that the student would benefit from being in a more challenging math class.

The overall idea of advocacy through communication to stakeholders is to be prepared and intentional when possible and use appropriate techniques, voice, and body language. The tips of using the appropriate voice and being thoroughly prepared with information and recommendations assist school counselors for advocacy conversations. If prepared, school counselors can be intentional in addressing pressing issues concerning students or inappropriate roles when the moment arises.

Communicating With the Principal

Advocating through communication to the principal can be intimidating. Research shows that principals do not view school counselors as leaders or advocates; however, when school counselors participate in advocacy efforts and have what Wilchie states as a good "rapport" with their principals, they have positive advocacy results (personal communication, February 3, 2017). In 2005, Amatea and Clark conducted a qualitative study examining building administrators' perception of the roles of school counselors. Results of the study found that fewer than 15% of participants consider school counselors as innovative leaders or advocates of the role of school counselor but more so as collaborative consultants.

Clemens, Milsom, and Cashwell (2009) conducted a study that included almost 200 school counselor participants, and found that school counselors who had a positive relationship with their administrator were more likely to advocate effectively for various school counselor roles. Other authors and researchers deem it important that school counseling programs place more emphasis on advocacy, leadership, and professional identity (Gibson, Dooley, Kelchner, Moss, & Vacchio, 2012; Lewis & Hatch, 2008; Moss, Gibson, & Dollarhide, 2014; Reiner, Dobmeier, & Hernandez, 2013), and school administrator programs should teach their students the integral role of the school counselor (DeKruyf, Auger, & Trice-Black, 2013).

A Personal Narrative

The need for school counselors to continue to advocate for appropriate roles is clear, but how might school counselors go about advocating to their principals? One way to successfully advocate to and educate school principals is to use advocacy tools. Julio Mascorro is a school counselor with five years of experience, and in that time he has quickly become a school counselor leader and advocate in the El Paso Independent School District. Mascorro states that during his first year as a school counselor, he found himself "doing tasks that were clearly not what a professional school counselor" is supposed to complete (personal communication, February 3, 2017). These tasks involved "running a school store, processing volunteer applications, organizing and running PTA functions such as dance and craft fairs, picking up literacy materials from Barnes & Noble, and many other non-counseling-related activities that took me away from serving the students' academic, career and personal/social needs." During his second and third years as a school counselor, Mascorro began reassessing his counseling program through the lens of the ASCA National Model (ASCA, 2012) and recognized, "it was time to start advocating for my program and for myself as a professional school counselor."

He worked with his district area director of guidance to formulate a list of appropriate and inappropriate activities and a tool that, although influenced by the ASCA National Model (ASCA, 2012), is specific to his school and district. The tool helps him to assess his program and effectively communicate his role to the building principal. The tool is entitled Counselors Performance Objectives (CPO). The CPO not only helps counselors plan out their goals and objectives for the year, but also is a "working timeline for us to know when to complete each identified goal." At the beginning of the academic year, Mascorro meets with his building principal to review and attain approval of a completed CPO. Mascorro states in his discussion with the principal, he goes "over the campus needs based on the data collected and articulate how my comprehensive guidance program and goals will address the campus' needs and how it aligns with the school's vision and mission." He states when having this discussion, it has been useful to communicate how he plans to allocate his percentage of time to student services as well as school support. Furthermore, he states that during this discussion, it is ideal to also share the list of "recommended and non-recommended activities" appropriate for school counselors in his district.

In summary, Mascorro discussed the importance of using such tools and advocacy:

> In outlining my plan and activities that would support my program for the year, I stressed the time and effort that it would require to complete these activities. This conversation with my principal was a great segue to address the other duties that even though not difficult to perform, they were time consuming and took away from my program goals and objectives . . . as professional school counselors . . . it is our responsibility to 'speak-up' [and show that] . . . we are valuable assets on any campus and . . . we must show our value through our program.

Conclusion

Advocating for appropriate school counselor roles has become an integral part of the profession. School counselors new to the profession should not be afraid to advocate for themselves and their school counseling programs. Beginning school counselors may get started in equipping themselves for advocacy work by getting to know their local, state, and national professional expectations. They would also benefit from understanding and practicing effective advocacy through prepared, intentional, and skilled communication with stakeholders. Also, school counselors can benefit from advocacy tools by starting with the use of ASCA materials or tools and then over time modify those tools to fit their situation, school, and/or district. Such ASCA tools include School Counseling Program Assessment, Use of Time Assessment, Annual Agreement, School Data Profile, and Lesson Plan Template, all found in the third edition of the ASCA National Model (ASCA, 2012).

Finally, school counselors should continue to add tools to their toolboxes to effectively advocate not only for themselves but also for their school counseling programs. For instance, Mascorro states that he advocates to faculty and staff through Professional Learning Community meetings and Campus Improvement Team meetings. Depending on the formal expectations of the school counselor, technology tools such as PowerPoint and Prezi presentations may be useful in communicating data and/or advocacy efforts. Also, according to Mascorro, other avenues of communicating advocacy talking points include having monthly counseling corner newsletters, sending guidance calendars to primary school stakeholders, and utilizing a school counselor webpage or website for disseminating information. There are many ways that school counselors advocate for their appropriate roles and their programs. It is important that school counselors continue to do the work of defining and educating others regarding the significant role of the school counselor.

Activities

1. School counselors may benefit from collaborating with other school counselors and/or their area director of guidance to create a list of inappropriate and appropriate activities for school counselors in their district. This list can be based on the ASCA list and vary depending on school level (elementary, middle, high). The list may be used as a tool to advocate for appropriate roles and/or against inappropriate roles. Choose a local school in your area in which you are familiar. Develop a list of appropriate and inappropriate activities that school counselors engage in your chosen school. How might you use this list to advocate for change if you were the school counselor?
2. An elementary physical education teacher is upset at a fourth-grade student for speaking inappropriately to her. She takes the student to the administration office for correction, but none of the administrators can be found. Therefore, she brings the student to your office (the school counselor). What is your verbal response? What actions might you take? Explain your communication style and your reasons for the actions you decided to take.
3. It is the beginning of the academic year. Although you (a school counselor) have worked hard to develop character education units for the students in your building, a couple of teachers refuse to allow you in their classrooms to conduct your lessons. The teachers are very protective of their time because they feel pressure to make sure their students do well on the standardized test that will be given later in the year. How might you go about advocating for your program? What tools might you employ from your toolbox? Give reasons for your decisions.

Resources

ACA Advocacy Competencies:
www.uwyo.edu/education/_files/documents/diversity-articles/ratts_2009.pdf

Advocacy Competencies- Endorsed by the ACA Governing Council:
www.counseling.org/Resources/Competencies/Advocacy_Competencies.pdf

Advocacy Competencies for Professional School Counselors:
www.schoolcounselor-ca.org/files/Advocacy/Advocacy%20Competencies%20for%20School%20Counselors.pdf

References

Amatea, E. S., & Clark, M. A. (2005). Changing schools, changing counselors: A qualitative study of school administrators' conceptions of the school counselor role. *Professional School Counseling Journal, 9*(1), 16–27.

American School Counselor Association. (2012). *ASCA national model: A framework for school counseling programs* (3rd ed.). Alexandria, VA: American Counseling Association.

Arkansas Department of Education. (2008). *Public school student services program planning*. Retrieved from http://arsca.k12.ar.us/documents/2008StudentServicesPlaning.pdf.

Bickmore, D. L., & Curry, J. R. (2013). The induction of school counselors: Meeting personal and professional needs. *Mentoring & Tutoring: Partnership in Learning, 21I*(1), 6–27. doi:10.1080/13611267.2013.78457.

Campbell, C. A., & Dahir, C. A. (1997). *Sharing the vision: The national standards for school counseling programs*. Alexandra, VA: American School Counselor Association Press.

Chata, C. C., & Loesch, L. C. (2007). Future school principals' views of the roles of professional school counselors. *Professional School Counseling Journal, 11*(1), 35–41.

Clemens, E. V., Milsom, A., & Cashwell, C. S. (2009). Using leader-member exchange theory to examine principal—school counselor relationships, school counselors' roles, job satisfaction, and turnover intentions. *Professional School Counseling Journal, 13*(2), 75–85.

DeKruyf, I., Auger, R. W., & Trice-Black, S. (2013). The role of school counselors in meeting students' mental health needs: Examining issues of professional identity. *Professional School Counseling Journal, 16*(5), 271–282.

Gibson, D. M., Dooley, B. A., Kelchner, V. P., Moss, J. M., & Vacchio, C. B. (2012). From counselor-in-training to professional school counselor:

Understanding professional identity development. *Journal of Professional Counseling: Practice, Theory, and Research*, *39*(1), 17–25.

Graham, K. A. (2015). School counselor layoffs overturned: District to appeal. *The Philadelphia Inquirer*. Retrieved from www.philly.com/philly/news/20150708_City_school_firings_overturned.html

Hansen, J. C. (1967). Job satisfactions and job activities of school counselors. *Personnel and Guidance Journal*, 790–794.

Hart, D. H., & Prince, D. J. (1970). Role conflict for school counselors: Training versus job demands. *Personnel and Guidance Journal*, *48*(5), 374–380.

Hatch, T. (2014). *The use of data in school counseling*. Thousand Oaks, CA: Corwin, A SAGE Company.

Khan, S. A. (2017). *Baltimore City schools to lay off 115 staff members*. WBALTV11. Retrieved from www.wbaltv.com/article/baltimore-city-schools-to-lay-off-115-staff-members/9961398

Lattanzio, V. (2013). *Nearly 4000 Philadelphia teachers, school staff losing jobs*. NBC10. Retrieved from www.nbcphiladelphia.com/news/local/Layoff-Notices-Looming-Over-Philadelphia-School-District-210577111.html

Leal, F. (2017). California teachers get layoff notices despite teacher shortages. *EdSource*. Retrieved from https://edsource.org/2017/california-teachers-get-layoff-notices-despite- teacher-shortages/578675

Lewis, R. E., & Hatch, T. (2008). Cultivating strengths-based professional identities. *Professional School Counseling Journal*, *12*(2), 115–118.

Lieberman, A. (2004). Confusion regarding school counselor functions: School leadership impacts role clarity. *Education*, *124*(3), 552–558.

Monteiro-Leitner, J., Asner-Self, K. K., Milde, C., Leitner, D. W., & Skelton, D. (2006). The role of the rural school counselor: Counselor, counselor-in-training, and principal perceptions. *Professional School Counseling Journal*, *9*(3), 248–251.

Moss, J. M., Gibson, D. M., & Dollarhide, C. T. (2014). Professional identity development: A grounded theory of transformational tasks of counselors. *Journal of Counseling & Development*, *92*, 3–12.

Reiner, S. M., Dobmeier, R. A., & Hernández, T. J. (2013). Perceived impact of professional counselor identity: An exploratory study. *Journal of Counseling & Development*, *91*, 174–183.

Rippee, B. D., Hanvey, W. E., & Parker, C. A. (1965). The influence of counseling on the perception of the counselor role. *Personnel and Guidance Journal*, 696–701.

Scarborough, J. L., & Culbreth, J. R. (2008). Examining discrepancies between actual and preferred practice of school counselors. *Journal of Counseling & Development*, *86*, 446–459.

Shertzer, B., & Stone, S. C. (1963). The school counselor and his publics: Problem in role definition. *Personnel and Guidance Journal*, 687–693.

Toporek, R. L., Lewis, J. A., & Crethar, H. C. (2009). Promoting systemic change through the ACA advocacy competencies. *Journal of Counseling & Development*, *87*, 260–268.

Appendix 9.1

Campus Snapshot

School Name

Demographics

Enrollment	African American	American Indian	Asian	Hispanic	White	Sp. Ed.	F/R	ESL
Total								
% of Enrollment								

Special Programs

(Place "x" for programs on your campus.)

Program	Grant Programs	Life Skills	Access **(Adaptive Behavior)**	Capturing Kids Hearts	New Arrival Center	Other **(List name of program(s) below.)**	

Cypress-Fairbanks ISD: Permission Granted

Appendix 9.2

Counseling Professional Staff

School Name

Counseling Staff	Education **Degree, Major & School**	Area of Special Interest/ Training/Licensure
Lead Counselor Name	Undergraduate Degree/ Institution **Masters Degree/Institution** **Doctorate Degree/Institution**	
Counselor #1 Name		
Counselor #2 Name		
Counselor #3 Name		
Counselor #4 Name		
School Psychologist		
Other (Sped Counselor)		

Cypress-Fairbanks ISD: Permission Granted

*Include all campus counseling staff—e.g., Campus Counselors, Intern, Itinerant Bilingual Counselor, YSS, Special Education Counselor, Psychologist

Appendix 9.3

Comprehensive Developmental School Counseling Program Calendar

School Name

Calendar items in **Bold** are required as listed. Schedule all other activities according to campus needs.

Month	School Wide Activities	Grade	Grade	Grade
August	**RS-ongoing**	Retention (gC)	Retention**(gC)**	Retention (gC)
	Building Better Relationships (BBR) (cT) (cC)	New Student Orientation (cC) Middle School Transition (cC)	New Student Orientation (cC)	New Student Orientation (cC)
	PBIS (cT) (cC)	Academic Success (gC)	Personal Goals; Decision Making and Responsibility; Effective Alcohol Education Program:; Drug Awareness; Tobacco Free Teens (cT)	Self Concept; Self Esteem; Decision Making; Goal Setting; Values; Peer Pressure; Positive Relationships (cT)
	Credit-by-Exam notice (IP)	Alcohol Education Program; Drug Awareness; Tobacco Free Teens (cT)	Duke Talent Search (IP)	Alcohol Education Program; Drug Awareness; Tobacco Free Teens (cT)
	Course Selection & Scheduling (IP)	**Meet the Counselor (cC)**	**Meet the Counselor (cC)**	Tolerance/ Diversity through LA (cT)
	Master Schedule Adj. (SS)			**Meet the Counselor (cC)**
	Teacher Inservice (SS)			
	Open House (SS)			
	Admission, Review, Dismissal Meetings (IP, SS)			
	Social Skills Lessons (cT)			
	Peer Mediation (gO)			
	Common Sense Parenting (SS)			

Month	School Wide Activities		Grade	Grade	Grade
	Cross-cultural Effectiveness through Social Studies and Reading (cT)				
	Course Selection & Scheduling for New Students (IP)				
	Academic Achievement Strategies through Language and Reading (cT)				
September		**RS-ongoing**	Lessons on Diversity (cT)	**Duke Talent Search (IP)**	Decision Making Skills PFD/SFL classes, **Goal Setting,**
		Master Schedule Adjustments (SS)	**Fall Study (SS)**	Conflict Resolution/ Peer Mediation/ Drug Awareness—ongoing through Skills for Adolescents (cT)	**Healthy Lifestyle** (cT)
		Admissions, Review, Dismissal Meetings (IP, SS)	**Goal Setting (cT)**	**Fall Study (SS)**	Tolerance/ Diversity through LA
		Write DGP (SS)		**Anger Management (cT)**	(cT)
		Building Better Relationships (cT) (cC)		**Goal Setting (cT)**	Dating Relationships; Personal Safety through PFD (cC) Mediation/ Drug Awareness—ongoing through Skills for Adolescents (cT)
		PBIS (cT) (cC)		**Healthy Lifestyle (cT)**	**4-year Plan Conferences (IP)**

Month	School Wide Activities		Grade	Grade	Grade
		Plan and schedule groups and classroom guidance (C)		**Skills for Living (cT)**	**Fall Study (SS)**
		Course Selection & Scheduling for New Students (IP)			**Classroom Presentation-Career Awareness and Survey cT)**
		Social Skills Lessons (cT)			
		Common Sense Parenting (SS)			
		Cross-cultural Effectiveness through Social Studies and Reading (cT)			
		Academic Achievement Strategies through Language and Reading (cT)			
		Meet the Counselor (cC)			
		MAC Study (SS)			
		RS-ongoing			Career Awareness (cC, cT)
October		Course Selection & Scheduling for New Students IP)	Drug Awareness (cC/T/O)	Drug Awareness (cC/T/O)	Goal Setting (cC)
		Master Schedule Adjustments (SS)	Anti-victimization (cC/T)	Bullying, Harassment, Teasing	Career Planning Survey (cCT)
		Admission, Review, Dismissal Meetings	Organizational Skills; Study Skills (gC)	(cC, cT)	Drug Awareness (cC/T/O)

Month	School Wide Activities		Grade	Grade	Grade
		(IP, SS)	Diversity/ Tolerance (cC)	Diversity Awareness (cC)	Tolerance/ Diversity through LA (cT)
		Building Better Relationships (cT)			
		Cross-cultural Effectiveness through Social Studies and Reading (cT)			
		PBIS (cT)			
		Social Skills Lessons (cT)			
		Red Ribbon Wk. (cT)			
		Counselor Inservice (SS)			
		PALS (gCO)			
		Academic Achievement Strategies through Language and Reading (cT)			
		Celebration of Success (SS**)**			
		RS-ongoing			
November		Course Selection & Scheduling for New Students (IP)	Decision Making; Goal Setting; Six-Year Plan (gC)	**Duke Talent Search (IP)**	Decision Making; Goal Setting (gC)
		Admissions, Review, Dismissal Meetings	Organizational Skills; Study Skills (gC)	Decision Making; Goal Setting (cT)	ROPES (cT) (O)
		(IP, SS)		Six-Year Plan Review (cC/T)	Tolerance/ Diversity through LA (cT)

Month	School Wide Activities		Grade	Grade	Grade
		Building Better Relationships (cT)		Self-Esteem Awareness (gC)	Four-Year Plans through AAS (cC, IP)
		Social Skills Lessons (cT)			Advisory Session; Goal-Setting (cC)
		Peer Mediation (gO)			
		TCA Conference (SS)			
		MAC Study (SS)			
		PALS (gCO)			
		Cross-cultural Effectiveness through Social Studies and Reading (cT)			
		PBIS (cT)			
		Stars Breakfast (SS)			
		Celebration of Success (SS)			
December		**RS-ongoing**	Organizational Skills; Study Skills (gC)	**Duke Talent Search (IP)**	Career Survey (cC)(cT)
		Building Better Relationships (cT)		Career Exploration through Keyboarding (cT)	Tolerance/ Diversity through LA (cT)
		Admission, Review, Dismissal Meetings			Career Exploration through Keyboarding (cT)
		(IP, SS)			
		Course Selection & Scheduling for New Students(IP)			

Month	School Wide Activities		Grade	Grade	Grade
		Master Schedule Adjustments (SS)			
		Social Skills Lessons (cT)			
		Peer Mediation (gO)			
		PALS (gCO)			
		Stars Breakfast (SS)			
		Cross-cultural Effectiveness through Social Studies and Reading (cT)			
		PBIS (cT)			
January		**RS-ongoing**	(SS)Academic Achievement Strategies (gC, cT)	Conflict resolution/ Mediation/ Drug Awareness—ongoing through Skills for Adolescents (cT)	Tobacco Free Teens (c/O)
		Course Selection & Scheduling for New Students (IP)	Anger Management (cG)	Academic Achievement Strategies (gC)	Academic Achievement Strategies (CT)
		Building Better Relationships (cT)	Organizational Skills: Study Skills (gC)	**TAKS Field Test-W (SS)**	Mediation/ Drug Awareness—ongoing through Skills for Adolescents (cT)
		At Risk Committees (IP)			Tolerance/ Diversity through LA (cT)
		Stars Breakfast (SS)			Career Opportunities (PFD) 175 students (cT)

Month	School Wide Activities		Grade	Grade	Grade
		Cross-cultural Effectiveness/ Diversity—ongoing through Social Studies (cT)			Advisory Session; Goal-Setting (cC)
		Admission, Review, Dismissal Meetings (IP, SS)			
		Master Schedule Adjustment (SS)			
		PALS (gCO)			
		Cross-cultural Effectiveness through Social Studies and Reading (cT)			
		PBIS (cT)			
		Celebration of Success (SS)			
February		**RS-ongoing**		Academic Success (gC)	**TAKS-W (SS)**
		Course Selection for Next Year (IP)	Academic Success (gC)	**TAKS/SDAAII-W (SS)**	Anger Management (gC)
		Building Better Relationships (cT)	Six Year Plan Presentation (cC)	**Six Year Plan Review (cC)**	Tolerance/ Diversity through LA (cT) (cO)
		MAC Study (SS)			Tobacco Free Teens (c/O)
		Electives Night (SS)			High School Registration (cC,)

Month	School Wide Activities		Grade	Grade	Grade
		Parent Night-Financial Aid-Higher Education (SS)			Academic Achievement Strategies (gC)
		PALS (gCO)			Four-Year Plan Presentation through AAS (cT)
		Stars Breakfast (SS)			Advisory Session; Goal-Setting (cC)
		Admission, Review, Dismissal Meetings (IP, SS)			
		Course Selection & Scheduling for New Students (IP)			
		Cross-cultural Effectiveness through Social Studies and Reading (cT)			
		PBIS (cT)			
March		**RS-ongoing**	Elementary Meeting. for 5th to 6th Transition(SS)	Cultural Awareness/ Diversity (cTO)	Advisory Session; Goal-Setting (cC)
		Course Selection for Next Year (IP)	Visits to Elementary Campuses (cC)	Registration (cC)	Tolerance/ Diversity through LA (cT)
		Building Better Relationships (cT)	Peer Pressure (gC)	**RPTE (SS)**	Cultural Awareness (cTO)
		Course Selection & Scheduling for New Students (IP)	Registration (cC)	**Anti-victimization Unit—Child Lures (cT)**	Registration (cC)

Month	School Wide Activities		Grade	Grade	Grade
		At-Risk Counseling (IP)			
		Admission, Review, Dismissal Meetings (IP, SS)			
		Stars Breakfast (SS)			
		PALS (gCO)			
		Cross-cultural Effectiveness through Social Studies and Reading (cT)			
		PBIS (cT)			
		Ropes (O)			
		RPTE (SS)			
April		**RS-ongoing**	Peer Pressure (gC)	**TAKS/SDAAII-M, R (SS)**	**High School Transition (cC)**
		Building Better Relationships (cT)	**TAKS/SDAAII-M, R (SS)**	WHO (cC)	**TAKS—M, R, SS, Sci. (SS)**
		MAC Study (SS)	Academic Success (gC)		**SDAAII-M, R (SS)**
		Admission, Review, Dismissal Meetings (IP, SS)			TAKS-I SS, Sci (SS)
		Stars Breakfast (SS)			Advisory Session; Goal-Setting (cC)
		PALS (gCO)			Tolerance/ Diversity through LA (cT)
		Cross-cultural Effectiveness through Social Studies and Reading (cT)			
		PBIS (cT)			

Month	School Wide Activities		Grade	Grade	Grade
		Celebration of Success (SS)			
May		**RS-ongoing**	Peer Pressure (gC)	Awards Nights (SS)	**High School Transition (cC)**
		Building Better Relationships (cT)	Elementary Visits to Thornton (SS)	Career Exploration through Keyboarding (cT)	Advisory Session; Goal-Setting (cC)
		Credit-by-Exam Notice (IP)	Awards Nights (SS)		Tolerance/ Diversity through LA (cT)
		Summer School Conferences (IP)			Awards Night (SS)
		TAKS info to Parents (SS)			Career Exploration through Keyboarding (cT)
		Master Schedule Adjustment (SS)			
		Placement Committees (SS)			
		PALS (gCO)			
		Admission, Review, Dismissal Meetings (IP, SS)			
		Cross-cultural Effectiveness through Social Studies and Reading (cT)			
		PBIS (cT)			

Month	School Wide Activities		Grade	Grade	Grade
June		**Guidance Program Evaluation (SS)**			HS transition materials delivered (SS)

Key

C: Guidance Curriculum by Counselor

T: Guidance Curriculum by Teacher

O: Guidance Curriculum by Other (Dare Officer, Nurse, etc.)

RS: Responsive Services (consultation, community referrals, crisis intervention, individual counseling)

IP: Individual Planning c: Classroom Session

SS: System Support g: Small Group Session

Appendix 9.4

Developmental Guidance Program

Guidance Curriculum Duties

The purpose of the Guidance Curriculum component is to help all students develop basic life skills. The curriculum has a scope and sequence for student competency development and is taught in units with planned lessons.

State-recommended percentage, Middle School = 35% to 40%

In the area of Guidance Curriculum, the counselors at *SCHOOL NAME* will:

1. Deliver classroom guidance activities or serve as a consultant to teachers conducting guidance lessons. *(required by TEC § 33.006)*
2. Plan and present lessons on the following guidance curriculum topics:
   - Self-confidence Development
   - Motivation to Achieve
   - Decision-making, Goal-setting, Planning, and Problem-solving Skills
   - Interpersonal Effectiveness
   - Communication Skills
   - Cross-cultural Effectiveness
   - Responsible Behavior
3. Identify appropriate resources and materials necessary for presenting the guidance curriculum.
4. Assist teachers in instructing students on how to interpret and utilize the results from the 8th-grade Career Planning Survey.
5. Coordinate classroom and small group guidance lessons with campus and district goals.
6. Prepare a monthly calendar of guidance curriculum activities that includes:
   - Topics/programs presented
   - Grade level receiving the presentation
   - Format of the presentation (classroom session or small group activity)
   - Lesson presenter (counselor, campus staff, or other person)

Cypress-Fairbanks ISD: Permission Granted

Appendix 9.5

Comprehensive Developmental School Counseling Program

School Name

Caseload Assignment of Counseling Staff

Beginning-of-Year Plan
(List each counselor by name, assignment and activities.)

Counseling Staff*	Grade Level Or **Alpha**	Enrollment **Per Caseload**	Number of Students on Needing Extra Support" List **Per Caseload**	Number of Small Groups Planned **(By Topic)**	Number of Students to be Served in Small Groups **(By Topic)**	Number of Planned Guidance Curriculum **Presentations by Counselor**	Number of Students to be Served in Guidance Curriculum Presentations
Lead Counselor							
Counselor #1 Name							
Counselor #2 Name							
Counselor #3 Name							
Counselor #4 Name							

School Psychologist							
CYS Worker							
Other (Sped Counselor)							
TOTAL							

Cypress-Fairbanks ISD: Permission Granted.

*Include all campus counseling staff—e.g., Campus Counselors, Intern, YSS, Special Education Counselor, Psychologist

Appendix 9.6

Comprehensive Developmental School Counseling Program

Middle School Name

Caseload Assignment of Counseling Staff

End-of-Year Evaluation
(List each counselor by name, assignment and activities.)

Counseling Staff*	Grade Level or Alpha	Enrollment **Per Caseload**	Number of Students on "Needing Extra Support" List **Per Caseload**	Number of Small Groups Conducted **(By Topic)**	Number of Students Served in Small Groups **(By Topic)**	Number of Guidance Curriculum **Presentations by Counselor**	Number of Students Served in Guidance Curriculum Presentations
Lead Coun-selor Name							
Counselor #1 Name							
Counselor #2 Name							
Counselor #3 Name							

Counselor #4 Name							
School Psychologist							
CYS Worker							
Other (Sped Counselor)							
TOTAL							

Cypress-Fairbanks ISD: Permission Granted

*Include all campus counseling staff—Campus Counselors, Intern, YSS, Special Education Counselor, Psychologist

10

Technological Application and Appropriate Uses

Dr. Rachael Whitaker

ASCA NATIONAL MODEL THEME

Leadership

Collaboration

Systemic Change

ASCA SCHOOL COUNSELOR PROFESSIONAL COMPETENCIES

I-B-1g. Uses technology effectively and efficiently to plan, organize, implement and evaluate the comprehensive school counseling program

II-B-4b. Understands the legal and ethical nature of working in a pluralistic, multicultural and technological society

IV-B-1f. Knows, understands and uses a variety of technology in the delivery of school counseling core curriculum activities

V-B-1i. Uses technology in conducting research and program evaluation

ASCA PRINCIPLES

Principle 5: School counselors can design and deliver interventions to meet students' developmental needs and to meet students' needs for prevention and remediation, thereby helping to close gaps between specific groups of students and their peers.

Principle 7: School counselors can help other adults enhance their work with students' academic/educational, career, and personal-social development and for the purpose of removing barriers to individual student success.

Principle 8: School counselors work with others in the school on behalf of students to support accomplishment of the school's mission and to assist in the removal of systemic barriers to student success.

Principle 9: The work of school counselors should be organized as a program.

Principle 11: The elements and strategies described as the delivery component for the school counseling program include all the means to have an impact on students' academic, career, and personal/social development: direct student services (school counseling core curriculum, individual student planning and responsive services) and indirect student services (referrals, consultation, and collaboration).

ASCA ETHICAL STANDARDS FOR SCHOOL COUNSELORS (2016)

A.2.m. Advocate for appropriate safeguards and protocols so highly sensitive student information is not disclosed accidentally to individuals who do not have a need to know such information. Best practice suggests a very limited number of educators would have access to highly sensitive information on a need-to-know basis.

A.2.n. Advocate with appropriate school officials for acceptable encryption standards to be utilized for stored data and currently acceptable algorithms to be utilized for data in transit.

A.2.o. Avoid using software programs without the technological capabilities to protect student information based upon currently acceptable security standards and the law

A.5.d. Do not use personal social media, personal e-mail accounts or personal texts to interact with students unless specifically encouraged and sanctioned by the school district. School counselors adhere to professional boundaries and legal, ethical and school district guidelines when using technology with students, parents/guardians or school staff. The technology utilized, including, but not limited to, social networking sites or apps, should be endorsed by the school district and used for professional communication and the distribution of vital information.

A.14.a. Demonstrate appropriate selection and use of technology and software applications to enhance students' academic, career and social/emotional development. Attention is given to the ethical and legal considerations of technological applications, including confidentiality concerns, security issues, potential limitations and benefits and communication practices in electronic media.

A.14.b. Take appropriate and reasonable measures for maintaining confidentiality of student information and educational records stored or transmitted through the use of computers, social media, facsimile machines, telephones, voicemail, answering machines and other electronic technology.

A.14.c. Promote the safe and responsible use of technology in collaboration with educators and families.

A.14.d. Promote the benefits and clarify the limitations of various appropriate technological applications.

A.14.e. Use established and approved means of communication with students, maintaining appropriate boundaries. School counselors help educate students about appropriate communication and boundaries.

A.14.f. Advocate for equal access to technology for all students.

A.15.a. Adhere to the same ethical guidelines in a virtual/distance setting as school counselors in face-to-face settings.

A.15.b. Recognize and acknowledge the challenges and limitations of virtual/distance school counseling.

A.15.c. Implement procedures for students to follow in both emergency and nonemergency situations when the school counselor is not available.

A.15.d. Recognize and mitigate the limitation of virtual/distance school counseling confidentiality, which may include unintended viewers or recipients.

A.15.e. Inform both the student and parent/guardian of the benefits and limitations of virtual/distance counseling.

A.15.f. Educate students on how to participate in the electronic school counseling relationship to minimize and prevent potential misunderstandings that could occur due to lack of verbal cues and inability to read body language or other visual cues that provide contextual meaning to the school counseling process and school counseling relationship.

CACREP STANDARDS 2016

Section 5-G, Entry-Level Specialty Areas, School Counseling

Foundations

1.b.—Models of school counseling programs

1.d.—Models of school-based collaboration and consultation

Practice

3.b. Design and evaluation of school counseling programs

3.c. Core curriculum design, lesson plan development, classroom management strategies, and differentiated instructional strategies

3.d. Interventions to promote academic development

3.k. Strategies to promote equity in student achievement and college access

3.n. Use of accountability data to inform decision making

Introduction

Technology can be described as an application or device to gain particular knowledge or accomplish a specific task. Technology in the schools can be defined as any device or material used to make the role of the school counselor easier. Specifically, online technologies are growing and changing tremendously. Steele, Jacokes, and Stone (2014) explained how school counselors are not immune to the cultural shift technology is bringing to the classrooms. From communication styles to delivery methods, technology is changing the face of school counseling. School counselors and their use of technology places school counseling programs at the realm of all things fun and innovative. In this chapter, you are introduced to various technology applications, formats, and ethical considerations that inform school counselors in efficient programming. This chapter aims to provide you with the conceptualization and knowledge of an optimal school counseling program deeply embedded in and technological advances for supporting a comprehensive school counseling program.

History of Technology in Schools

In order to understand why technology is so important in today's schools, we need to take a look back into the history. Long gone are the days when chalkboards were the essential school-based technology. Hallström and Gyberg (2011) wrote an article titled "Technology in the rear-view mirror: How to better incorporate the history of technology into technology education," which discussed three proponents to establishing effective technology in education settings. First, establish a knowledge baseline around technology in your current environment and how your specific geographic location has evolved around technology. What might your school be comfortable in using or what might be challenging in understanding technology? Second, base your decision on the selection of technology that is most relevant for your particular environment and the associated costs. Consider the grade levels, district policies, student, staff, and school counselor's needs as opposed to wants. Third, in the past, how has technology been beneficial or not in your particular environment? Understanding the history of technology in the particular school is going to help you decide on what would best benefit your school or district. Discussing with stakeholders, teachers, and staff their fundamental knowledge, wants, and needs surrounding technology can help in making the best possible choice.

Integration of Technology

What is technology integration and how does it help school counselors? Typically, integrated technology means advanced tools that are often used to demonstrate deeper educational concepts and are tools to engage, yet directly impact, one's accessibility to information. Although this might look different from school to school or even district to state, the idea of integrating technology into the job role of a school counselor have become widely supported. Classrooms and educational settings are quickly advancing in the same way, if not faster, with technology-integrated education platforms. Organizations, such as the American School Counselor Association (ASCA), state and national school counseling credentialing, and the National Board for Certified Counselors (NBCC), are in collective support of technology and how it advances the profession. In fact, several of these credentialing bodies require candidates from school counseling programs to demonstrate proficient use and understanding of technology in the p–12 environments before graduating. Another example of this available option is through the Center for Credentialing and Education (2014) [www.cce-global.org/dcc]. The ASCA National Model (2012), which stands as the national framework for conducting and implementing a professional school counseling program, repeatedly refers to the use of technology to support a comprehensive school counseling program. Particularly, programs driven in data-based decision-making will incorporate one, if not several integrated technologies, to support the program and appropriate job roles.

Model Framework

Romrell, Kidder, and Wood (2014) created the Substitution Augmentation Modification Redefinition (SAMR) Model framework for the evaluation of mLearning. Similar to e-learning (electronic learning), mobile learning is learning through different mediums, allowing social and content interactions to form through the use of electronic devices. According to Romrell, Kidder, and Wood (2014), the SAMR Model stands for the following:

> S (Substitution)—the technology provides a substitute for other learning activities without functional change, A (Augmentation)—the technology provides a substitute for other learning activities but with functional improvement, M (Modification)—the technology allows the learning activity to be redesigned, R (Redefinition)—the technology allows for the creation of tasks that could not have been done without the use of technology (271).

Another way to view mLearning is by learning across multiple contexts, such as handheld computers, portable or stationary technologies, mobile devices, or anything defined as conveniently accessible from mass locations (2014). This type of framework can aid a school counselor in technology selection, learning activities, program tracking, and decisions on how/when to update currently used integrated technology. School counselors can use the following acronym to assess current or dated integrated technologies (see Table 10.1). Integrated technology models such as this can assist in leadership's decision-making associated with integrated technology and what best serves the counselors, school, or district.

Format for Technology

Now that we have examined models for decision-making surrounding selection of technology integrations and previous technology history and use, let us move to understanding different delivery formats. While we know technology is extremely important in the evolution of education, there are always

Table 10.1 SAMR Model Examples

SAMR Acronym	Ideas for Integration of Model
S (Substitution)	Locating digital resources and information Taking notes on a digital document and digital textbooks
A (Augmentation)	Using/embedding digital graphics Using internet resources to improve writing (thesaurus, spell check, grammar check)
M (Modification)	Collaborative assignments are created using software like Google docs and PowerPoints. Work tasks can be accessed digitally in and outside of the classroom.
R (Redefinition)	Classrooms collaborate with others using Skype or Facetime. Virtual classrooms and multimedia are used to strengthen curriculum.

considerations for best practice. What is the best delivery format for my particular program/school? What are legal and ethical policies surrounding different types of delivery format in my school/district? Do these align with the integrity of my school/district?

Upon reflection on these questions, one can then move forward with technologies and their delivery format. At present, schools may be using a variety of integrated technologies, including websites and software, which are also gaining enormous popularity. These software platforms may include blogs, video conferencing, and editing programs, just to mention a few. The use of mobile devices/iPads/tablets to access apps, chatrooms, and social media/internet for teaching points has also exploded in popularity, as well as interactive whiteboards. Although this scratches the surface of technologies that are at the fingertips of school counselors, effective technology integration can tremendously aid in academic curriculum, access to up-to-date materials, advanced methods for collecting data, international collaboration, relevant learning, and enriched technology understanding. Table 10.2 defines types of integrated technology formats to consider. These types of formats can be described as technological forms of delivery into the educational setting or basic means of delivery before moving into the specific types.

Table 10.2 Types of Technology Format

Types of Technology Format	Defined
Web-based Format	Educational portals used for learning and teaching. Using resources located on the World Wide Web. Can be used as supplemental learning or live learning engagement.
Recording Software Format	Media used for voice or live STEM learning and teaching. Can be used during activities or previously recorded.
Video Format	Telecommunication that provides simultaneous communication using audio and video streaming. This enables the ability to bring someone or something into a classroom live from anywhere in the world.
Text Format	Text format allows multiple forms of communication and learning. Live polling, data collection, or Q & A format.

Types of Technology Format	Defined
Voice Format	Spoken word put into voiceovers or dictation. This might include text-to-speech, narration, or podcasts.
Interactive Smart Classroom Format	Screen or devices that add visual and interactive components to the classroom.
Software Program Format	Software that can be free or purchased as a part of integrated learning. These types of software may house many of the formats listed here.

How Technology Empowers the Professional School Counselor

The ASCA National Model is a collaborative framework designed to benefit students, teachers, parents, administrators, and community stakeholders (ASCA, 2012). The collaborative model is divided into four components and four themes. Foundation, management, delivery, and accountability encompass the major components while the themes are leadership, advocacy, collaboration, and systematic change (2012). The ASCA National Model effectively outlines the essential goals and functions to support a comprehensive school counseling program (Maras, Coleman, Gysbers, Herman, & Stanley, 2013), and these components can be independently or collectively supported through the use of integrated technology. As we move forward and discuss each part and various technology support systems, it is important to discuss that many states have adopted and implemented their own school counseling model. States such as Texas and Missouri have established independent comprehensive state models specific to their state needs. Make sure to know specific state policies and models used to support your program. In this chapter, we will use the ASCA National Model as an example for integrated technology throughout each comprehensive part. These same technologies explored can be applied to other state models.

Foundation of the ASCA National Model and Technology

At the core of the ASCA National Model is a focus on comprehensive school counseling program development (ASCA, 2012). The foundational components of the model focus on student outcomes and support for professional competencies. One of the first steps in adopting the model is to create a strategic plan for achieving the school counseling program's overall mission.

Under the ASCA National Model, school counselors create mission statements that capture the essence of a school counseling program's purpose and aspirational goals. The aspirational goals are then individually developed in measurable terms. Development and implementation of these measurable terms can be simplified with the correct integrated technology. These technologies can save valuable time on lesson design and data analysis that can be better used to conduct direct counseling services. Initially, school counselors might feel lost. Technology can help in all major aspects of the foundation. Let us discuss how these technologies can save counselors valuable time and confusion.

Program Development With Technology

The program focus of the foundation component of the ASCA National Model is data driven for direction and future goal planning. Establishing a clear picture of where the comprehensive program needs to go for best practice and implementation is vital. So how can technologies help? Consider where you would like the program to focus effort initially. The ASCA National Model has a brainstorming activity that can aid in jump-starting your program. Moving forward, you will want to involve many stakeholders from the community and school to mold the program's vision and mission statements. The following are ideas for collecting such information:

- Web-based survey devices—these can give you the opportunity to collect data from multiple sources on what others would like in the professional school counseling program. Administration, teachers, parents, and so forth can give opinions before any program is even implemented. This data is valuable because it shows community and school collaboration.
- Digital polling—creating a feedback poll that collects qualitative or quantitative data on specific proposed program ideas.

Student Outcomes and Technology Assistance

The primary goal of a comprehensive professional school counseling program is to establish a progressive impact on academic, career, and personal/social development for students. School counselors do this through a variety of assessment activities. However, these activities must be measured to establish achievement and program improvement. Technology used for tracking student outcomes can be used by implementing some of the following:

- Excel formulas/program—used to map out specific assessment activities for academic, career, and personal/social

- SMART (Specific, Measurable, Attainable, Result, Time) goal-tracking systems—self-created forms or software that organize student outcome goals through the SMART goals planning

Student and Professional Competencies Via Technology

Professional school counselors place an emphasis on the academic, career, and personal/social development of students within their school system. "The ASCA school counselor competencies outline the knowledge, attitude, and skills that ensure school counselors are equipped to meet the rigorous demands of the profession" (ASCA, 2012, p. 15). Professional school counselors must comprehend a range of professional and student competencies that ensure effective program delivery within a school system. The ASCA student and professional competencies help the school counselor to set goals aimed toward enhancing the learning process of all students (ASCA, 2012).

Before beginning this process, review the ASCA School Counselor Competencies and ASCA National Standards for Students, grasping the concept that the ASCA School Competencies specifically define detailed knowledge, attitudes, abilities, and skills for model success, whereas the ASCA National Standards for Students cover acquired skills, awareness, and knowledge to support each specific student in their academic, career, and personal/social advancement. Both standards and competencies are extremely useful in guiding the data driven program. Technology can tract these standards and competencies in the forms of baseline data, performance indicators, quantity addressed, and guidance for future program improvement. Specifically, ASCA School Counselor Competencies strongly emphasize the use of emerging technologies and information management systems. Use of data-tracking technology with student and professional competencies can map changes in the following:

- Skill Development—these can be direct service involving specific behavior change that impact academic, career, and personal/social.
- Transition Data—student tracking on how successfully students move into post-secondary, grade levels, or alternative setting changes
- College Fairs—career awareness and college advance planning in forms of college application and acceptances
- Career Readiness—tracking readiness in seeking employment, identifying the changing workplace for student
- Self-Knowledge—defining and pushing students towards personal goal setting, acquiring pro-social behaviors that support personalized success

- Self-Evaluations—supporting students to move forward in problem solving and critical decision-making while understanding personal boundaries, strengths, and areas of improvement
- Academic Development—establishing supportive school that link the importance of academic performance to career and personal/social advances
- Skill Improvement—tracking data on skills students need for success in both academic and interpersonal selves, aiding in improved critical thinking and self-directed learning
- School Counselor Knowledge—designing a program that is data driven and supported, knowledge of what isworking and what needs to be revisited

Management Technology in the ASCA National Model

The second component of the ASCA National Model is management. Although delivery is 80% of the primary duty of school counselors, they also must be able to effectively manage the school counseling program. Without a solid foundation and well-developed management, the delivery part of the ASCA National Model is almost impossible. Planning and data collection are key. Under the ASCA National Model, professional school counselors use organizational assessments and tools to manage school counseling duties effectively. School counselors can use the following forms of technology to organize the annual development and improvement of the management plan (see Table 10.3).

Delivery Through Technology and the ASCA National Model

The delivery component of the ASCA National Model is direct services for students, parents, teachers, administration, and the community. It is designed to support interaction and services, and has two main areas consisting of direct and indirect student services (ASCA, 2012). Direct services cover school counseling core curriculum, individual student planning, and response services (ASCA, 2012). Indirect student services result in referrals, consultation, collaboration, community organizations, resource collecting, as well as parent and teacher outreach (ASCA, 2012). The delivery system is the action component for collaboration of direct and indirect services. The delivery of the model encompasses 80% of all program services. Most models require this as the main focus of any comprehensive school counseling program. The delivery component is saturated in data, and data

Table 10.3 Types of Interactive Technology

Technology Type	Description	Examples
Calendar software	Organize daily, weekly, monthly, and yearly calendars that can be quickly updated or changed	Outlook, Calendarwiz, Efficient Calendar, Desktop Calendar, VueMinder, Fantastical 2, Google Calendar, Timepage, Solcalendar, Jorte Calendar
School Counselor Activities Developer/Tracking	Develop activities for future use in direct services	Drop-IN Data, SCARS (School Counseling Activity Rating Scale), Notability, Pinterest, Scribble Press
Response to Intervention (RTI) Planning	Develop screeners and guidance planning	Therapy Report Center, RTI-PMT App, Intervention Central
School Counseling Lesson Plan Developer	Design, align and modify specific guidance lesson plans	Lesson Planet for School Counselors, ASCA National Model Templates, LiveBinder, School Corporation, Missouri School Counselor Performance Assessment Lesson Plan, Pinterest, ASCA National Model
Needs Assessment Development	Create needs assessment that can be sent electronically or delivered via technology devices	Poll Everywhere, QUIZworks, Assess, Survey Monkey, Grapevine Surveys

programs immersed in technologies can save time and provide disaggregated data for program support and improvement. The following is integrated technology that can support direct classroom, group, and individual services:

- Mimio Boards—allow school counselors to maneuver website and incorporate dual technology
- Classroom PCs—students can directly access lessons, surveys, and web information for technology-based activities
- Interactive Whiteboard—allows for visual content interaction
- Document Camera—displays real-time visuals, can take still pictures or videos for later discussion
- Classroom Websites—class announcements, goals, classroom guidance, parent involvement and awareness of class activities

- Classroom/Counselor Blogs—easy to manage and access data information, encourages student involvement, embedded surveys and questionnaires

Accountability Driven Through Technology and the ASCA National Model

The accountability component of the ASCA National Model focuses on the analysis and interpretation of data. This focal point encourages school counselors to establish measurable goals that can assist in positive student change (ASCA, 2012). Collecting evidence from a variety of sources demonstrates the relationship between the CSCP and student achievement. Information on attendance, successes, failures, responsibilities, behaviors, or other measurable outcomes can provide insight into necessary areas for program improvement. The accountability component of this model can be aided in the following technologies to reduce time spend on paperwork and data analysis:

- Note Counselor—secure database that provides management for data collection in the k–12 area
- Penelope—internet-based case management software, develops smart forms and reports
- Hallways 5 for School Counselors—includes time tracking, data analysis, and accountability features for school counselors
- Rediker—integrated school software, manages more data for school administration and includes parent portals, not specific to school counselors
- School Counseling Central—entire program approach to accountability and data collect, designed specifically for school counselors and their specific needs, can also be purchased for districts or individual use

Whole Model Technology Support

Technology that supports an entire school program might work best for your school and should be considered. It is important to remember that many separate integrated technologies can be used to assist in specific activities within a comprehensive program, but many school counselors choose to use integrated software that incorporates an entire system technology-driven format. Accountability and data-driven comprehensive school counseling programs are vital to program success and integration with other school services. These might include services such as speech and hearing, occupational therapy, physical therapy, special education, inclusion, or pull-out services. Adopting a software program that links the school counselors to data on student performance in multiple areas can most definitely aid in best collaborative care for students receiving services or those who may be at-risk students.

Technology in the form of computer software designed to support the entire data-driven school can drastically increase data collection and data-driven efforts. School counselors might find themselves having to advocate for such technologies and software program's because of price or training time. With this to consider, make sure you do your homework before suggesting whole system integrated technologies. Reinforcing school districts' data to evaluate the use of technology and its benefits on data-driven programs will strategically set up programs that are continuously improving and meeting specific needs of students. The following are school-wide programs to consider (see Table 10.4).

ASCA Themes Supported Through Technology

It is important to discuss the ASCA National Model themes and how integrated technology truly supports such a model. As stated previously, the ASCA National Model consists of four themes that are concurrent for effective foundation, delivery, management, and accountability systems delivery. These four themes are leadership, advocacy, collaboration, and systematic change (ASCA, 2012).

ASCA defines school counseling leadership as academic/student support, advances in the comprehensive school counseling program, and professional identity promotion. Advocacy is a combination of the leadership role that ideally advocates for high academic, career, and personal/social standards and support. Collaboration is an essential theme within the National Model. School counselors are encouraged to implement effective team-building approaches that encourage collaboration of students, teachers, and all other staff in support of school and individual student success. Systematic change is encompassed in all of the model, ensuring that everything executed has a purpose to impact the school and students positively, promoting increased successes in academic, career, and personal/social success. Technology supports and promotes these themes while promoting follow-through and system implementation. Think of how technology can support all parts discussed previously, and now imagine how technology both software and web-based designed can promote leadership of the school counselor, advocacy of the

Table 10.4 Types of School Data Systems

System	MMS	GradeLink SIS	SchoolFront	Alma	Schoology	RenWeb	Skyward	School Counseling Central
Web	www.cri-mms.com/	https://gradelink.com/	www.schoolfrcnt.com/	www.getalma.com/	www.schoology.com/	www.renweb.com/	www.skyward.com/	http://schoolcounselorcentral.com/
$	$$$	$	$	$$	$$	$$$	$$	$$
K–12	*	*	*	*	*	*	*	*
Attendance Tracking	*	*	*	*	*	*	*	*
Individualized Assessments		*	*	*	*		*	*
Lesson Planning		*	*	*	*	*	*	*
Teacher Individual Dashboard	*		*	*				*
Progress Reports	*	*	*	*		*		*
Live Trainings	*	*	*	*	*	*	*	*
Free Trial	*			*	*	*	*	*

comprehensive school counseling program and services provided, collaboration of counselors all over the world, and system change from data-driven decisions.

Whether a school adopts the ASCA National Model or their state model, integrated technology supports comprehensive programs in ways that schools without it are unable to do so. Our schools and world are quickly changing because technology is giving people in the work force access to data and knowledge faster than ever before. It is our job as Professional School Counselors to ensure that we are modeling and adequately preparing our students for the quickly changing workforce. When executing the model effectively, the components of foundation, management, delivery, and accountability are executed through using model themes of leadership, advocacy, collaboration, and systematic change. All of these parts that make up a comprehensive school counseling program are vastly better supported with integrated technology.

Application of Technology

The application of technology and its appropriate use is vital in the work of the school counselor. In today's time, technology, for the most part, enhances how information is acquired, managed, stored, and distributed. Technology for school counselors reduces the amount of time spent on a task, allowing the inner workings of a school counseling program to run more efficiently. Notwithstanding the positive effect it can have on the work of each individual school counselor, there can be negative outcomes if technology is not handled or used appropriately. This section provides various suggestions and approaches on how school counselors can use technology on the job, while simultaneously highlighting cautions for use and a school counselor's professional responsibility and integrity. Some of these technological opportunities can appear cutting edge simply because the ideas presented here may be borrowed from practices utilized by and currently appropriate for licensed professional counselors.

Professional Website or Webpage

Professional websites or webpages are great approaches when describing, conveying, or advertising the programs and services offered within the school counseling program. Many districts have a standard template or shell for all professionals to use within the school building. These platforms usually already have school logos, school colors, and a general outline for specific information that needs to be placed on the website.

More often than not, school districts may not have user-ready websites for their employees, leaving school counselors with an opportunity to design and highlight their school counseling program online. Following that are many decisions needing to be made regarding whether or not the website or webpage will be professionally developed and paid for through allocated district or campus funds or alternatively purchased by the school counselor (www.wix.com or www.yola.com). There is also an online website program (www.weebly.com or www.wordpress.com) that allows for the creation of a basic webpage. Following is a recommended list of information to include on your website (This list is not exhaustive and can be adapted to meet the needs and priorities of your comprehensive school counseling program):

- Personal Biography and Photo
- ASCA National Model Standards
- State and District Standards
- Alignment of Curricular and Counseling Standards
- School Counseling Program Mission/Vision
- Definition of Comprehensive Counseling Program
- Counselor Role and Philosophy Statement
- Relevant Statistics or Trends
- Department Dates or Online Calendar
- Resource Links to ASCA or State Resources
- Resource Links to Career and College Readiness or Graduation Requirements
- Resource Links for Parents or Teachers
- Information for Special Programs/504/IDEA
- Guidance Curriculum or Responsive Services
- Resource Link to Anonymous Reporting Website or Hotline

Lambie and Williamson (2004) suggested that school counselors "need to be advocates of their profession and not submissive bystanders to be able to verbalize their professional role and educate others about what a PSC [professional school counselor] is and is not" (p. 129). This type of comment can be interpreted as a charge for school counselors to express who they are from a professional standpoint and the types of services offered through the program. It is an opportunity for technological innovation and creativity on the part of the school counselor.

Technological Applications (Apps)

There are many applications (apps) that can be used to enhance the work of a school counselor. One app is called VoiceNote, and it can be used to document SOAP, SOAPIE, or SOAPIER notes. This app is a convenient tool to immediately document individual counseling sessions, daily tasks or projects that need to be accomplished, or outlining points of reference prior to or during meetings and parent conferences. Another app is Docusign or SignEasy. These apps can be used for behavioral contracts needing to be signed by students or to float other documents to parents where electronic signatures are acceptable forms of consent. Once accounts are established, documents are stored electronically, making it easy to retrieve them at a later time.

Other apps, making the work for school counselors more effective, are the use of e-books, Netflix, YouTube, or TED Talks. The purpose of these apps are multifaceted, but largely they can be used to support individual or small group sessions. For example, you may have students participate in book studies, watch movies, or listen to TED Talks to enhance their understanding of concepts presented within the counseling session. These same apps can be used for hosted professional workshops and taught guidance lessons. Additional apps for possible use are Head Space, Calm, or Soothing Lite. These apps are used for relaxation, meditation, or for mindfulness practices. If used in your school counseling practice, listening to these sounds can be calming and restorative, helping others to cope, manage stress, and reduce anxiety. Finally, SCUTA (http://counselorapp.com/scuta-introduction/) allows school counselors to log their work and activities, to use calendars, to align with ASCA domains and competencies, to generate reports, and to maintain descriptive notes regarding activities.

Simple Practice, Therapy Notes, or Therapy Appointments

Currently, some school districts have technology available for school counselors to electronically document the students they have seen on a daily basis. Some may agree that long gone are the days for maintaining three-ring binders in counseling offices or using filing cabinets to store student files or records. This assumption is not true, as there are many campuses that maintain site-based records. Simple Practice (www.simplepractice.com), Therapy Notes (www.therapynotes.com), and Therapy Appointments (www.therapyappointments.com) are cloud-based management software programs, typically for therapists' use, for record-keeping that school counselors can use on a daily basis. Each software program has its features, and convenient comparison charts are made available online for potential users. A school counselor using any program should know there are associated costs for access online, but basically these platforms allow for academic or behavioral planning (also known as treatment planning), maintaining demographic information, scheduling, specialty notes, document storing, and appointment reminders. There are features that school counselors may not utilize, such as billing, but with these inherent limitations, school counselors may find these tools convenient.

Google Voice and Google Docs

Most people enjoy the tools Google has to offer its potential users. Google Voice is an app that creates an online telephone number linked directly to your cell phone. Calls can be both made and received. Districts and campuses usually have policies preventing counselors from sharing their personal telephone numbers, so in lieu of using a personal telephone number, school counselors may find Google Voice to be a more private, appropriate medium to use that allows parents and students to contact them, specifically in crisis, emergencies, or follow-up situations. "Google Voice gives you voice mail and online transcribing of voicemail, including the ability to listen to messages that are being left to block/unwanted callers or to make inexpensive international calls" (personal communication, Google Voice App, 2017).

Google Docs is a collaborative tool that can be used to either work on or edit documents, presentations, or spreadsheets with teachers, students, and administrators. Using Google Docs reduces the amount of time spent in *think tanks* or in committee meetings, and allows for members of your advisory council or other stakeholders to have input on the creation or revision of documents. It is a great way to give voice, delegate work to other individuals, and to track the contributions made from colleagues. Keep in mind this collaborative software allows multiple people to work on the same Microsoft Word document, Excel spreadsheet, PowerPoints, and a variety of templates.

Social Media Platforms

Using social media platforms for your classroom, school, or district does not have to be intimidating or overwhelming. In fact, the benefits could drastically increase visibility of counseling for students, staff, and parents. The social media platforms could include Twitter, Facebook, Pinterest, Instagram, LinkedIn, Flickr, Reddit, Snapchat, Tumbler, Google+, or Vimeo. Keep in mind there are currently over 52 social media platforms used today, and more are being developed daily, so find what fits the need. When considering a platform, it is also important to consider how you want to market or tell a story. This is how you can establish the greatest impact with maximum efficiency. Also consider that many/most social media platforms currently integrate with one another, allowing for one post to hit multiple sites and increase discernibility. It is also important that social media platforms are vetted through the school's media policies and ethical codes (ACA, 2014; ASCA, 2016) to protect minors and private information. Social media platforms can be a value to any program's identity and information sharing.

File Sharing

File sharing is a convenient way to store documents in the cloud and completely remove the need for device memory space. It is appropriate to make documents and forms available to stakeholders such as parents, students, or teachers. Long gone are the days of sending email attachments back and forth. File sharing enables quick and modern file distributing, editing, and developing all in one location. As file sharing grows in popularity, it is important to know how information is protected and do your research. Make sure you consider compatibility, spyware, user-friendly interface, file corruption dictation, download speed, and virus protection. When considering application use, remember file sharing saves money, increases performance, and simplifies administration tasks. A few popular file-sharing applications to consider are Dropbox, ShareFile, Google Drive, OneDrive, iCloud, Egnyte, LimeWire, Zapya, and many others.

Interactive Video Conferencing (IVC) Programs

Face-to-face communication has always been the best way to build teams and collaborate. Video conferencing unlocks face-to-face communication to anyone at any time. Video conferencing entirely changes management and administrative tasks with access to unlimited resources. IVC can be used in a variety of ways, including conferencing, telepresence systems, video streaming, and desktop applications. A few big video conferencing platforms are Skype, Facetime, Google Hangout, GoToMeeting, ClickMeeting, Cisco Webex, ZOHO, eVoice, join.me, Amazon Chime, Adobe Connect, and Zoom. All of these platforms could be used for collaboration, guest speakers, or student projects. The options are vast. Also, when considering IVC, professional school counselors might consider online counseling services. Consider for a moment if students had the ability to use IVC to review or watch lessons for reasons like students who are suspended and homebound—basically unable to come to campus—after-school or weekend programs, or online workshops for parents and guardians who are unable to come to campus. The ability to support students and families could dramatically increase through IVC-supported school counseling programs.

Talk Fusion is another platform software that could service programs in multiple facets. Have you ever just wanted to reach out to a parent, community member, student, or employee, but an email just did not convey the intended message? Talk Fusion is a video email messaging system that allows an added personal touch. Like many software programs, it is both synchronous and asynchronous: synchronous in terms of online/distance counseling or conducting live meetings or workshops and asynchronous in the form of electronic newsletters, birthday wishes, thank-you notes, and website prerecorded videos. This technology inherently offers a tracking system that conveys how many individuals received the technology—for instance, a program overview or welcome message—and how often they viewed your video. Technologies like Talk Fusion are the future of email communication when it is not IVC.

Ethical Considerations When Using Technology in a School Counseling Program

Technology can be a wonderful tool for advanced learning and knowledge assessments, but it does not come without caution. The ASCA Ethical Standards for School Counseling (2016) dedicated A.14 and A.15 to technical and digital citizenship and virtual and distance counseling. Reviewing each of these standards will help counselors successfully decide on best practice for integrated technology in a specific school. Sections stipulate that the school counselor should promote the benefits and provide clarity in the use and how to use with students (A.14.a., A.14.c., A.14.d). This means that the school counselor should advocate for technology, but also prepare others on the technology and correct use. A.14.f conveys that school counselors should always advocate and promote technology for all students, but particularly those who are underserved. As leaders and advocates in the school setting, making it a priority to advance and level the education platform for underserved students is of the highest priority. All students deserve equal opportunity to succeed, and advocating for technology will disseminate such equality.

A.14.b translated into student information protection. This includes any form of technology such as voicemail, computers, files, progress notes, or student files. As a rule of thumb, using at least two forms of coded protection can best protect student information (e.g., establishing one password to open a computer system and an additional passcode to open a student file). Protecting student information is imperative. A.12.a covers FERPA and protection of student information with the use of electronic records. It is best practice and ethical for a school counselor to lead and reinforce these efforts to protect electronic student information. It is important to make sure the school, staff, and administration receive training on student information privacy.

Last, but not least, of the ethical policies discussed under technology, A.11 explains how technology can interfere with internet bullying. Schools need to be aware and cautious of how technology can be used positively and negatively in the school setting. Technology can be a tremendous asset in any school setting as long as preparation and training are at the helm.

Appropriate Use of Technology

There are many considerations when using technology in the work of school counselors. For school districts that are technologically less progressive, school counselors may need to create a proposal for district and campus administrators requesting use of these various programs, with the following suggestions in this section included—stipulating your plan to protect the confidential information of students. This gives district leadership an opportunity to legally and ethically vet your proposal. It may be relevant to include within your proposal or published materials, policies that assist student users similar to the following:

> Services provided through Interactive Video Programs are not recorded by the school counselor and should not be recorded by the student. It is important to make sure when receiving online counseling services, you are alone and that a third party is not observing or present by while the school counselor is in session with you. It is recommended you use a personal computer instead of a public computer. When you are first accessing your account, you should login at least 30 minutes prior, just in case you need to download any form of flash media player. Students will receive a direct link through their confirmed email that will allow you to access the video chat. Please store this link in a confidential area. If for some reason you believe the link is compromised, contact the school counseling office so we may provide you a new link.

Equally important here is to make certain that prior approval and consent forms have been obtained from parents; these are critical in the use of these technologies with students. Information, such as this, may need to be published at the beginning of the school year and revisited as reminders to parents, perhaps issued through the campus or counseling department newsletter.

As with any technology, you must protect the integrity of student information and reduce the risk of compromising electronic information.

Therefore, consider using an internal coding system or aliases so that if information is breached, hackers are less likely to decode used pseudonyms. For example, instead of using student first and last name, school counselors may code the last name by using the initial and the month and day of the date of birth (W0226). The first name may be coded with the first initial and four-digit birth year (R1967). Oftentimes, districts have student ID numbers, which can be used as a part of the coding system. School counselors may choose to use the first or last four digits of a student's ID number. Use of social security numbers has to be avoided at all times.

Other ways information can be compromised is a school counselor's failure to log out of different applications being utilized in their office or on their personal devices. School counselors must make it a habit to log out, because if not, the next person using that device or accessing the website or app can easily load that information. Clearing your cookies and search history on all devices is another way to help maintain confidential information. Screen protectors for cell phones and desktop computers are recommended, along with minimizing screens for the brief time when you are away from your desk or device.

Organizational systems are critical when school counselors use technology. Passwords, file names, and internal coding systems all warrant organization for easy use and recall on the part of the school counselor. School counselors should reset passwords every 90 days regardless of the system prompting users to do so, and they should never share their login or password information with other persons.

One final consideration is whether or not to establish accounts at the district or departmental level. It is not best practice to use personal accounts, but if the school counselor is personally funding the use of that technology, then the school counselor should be clear on their ethical responsibilities to record-keeping and the privileges that districts or parents may have to those personal files.

Conclusion

Throughout this chapter, multiple integrated technologies were discussed. This information brings clarity to the broad spectrum of integrated technologies that can successfully and ethically support a data-driven comprehensive school counseling program. The use of integrated technologies to streamline accountability with evidence-based practice can save time for more direct service implementation, prepare students for a technology-driven workforce, increase access to knowledge, and support diverse learning. Figure 10.1 is a chart that can reflect on how to approach and support technology-driven school counseling programs.

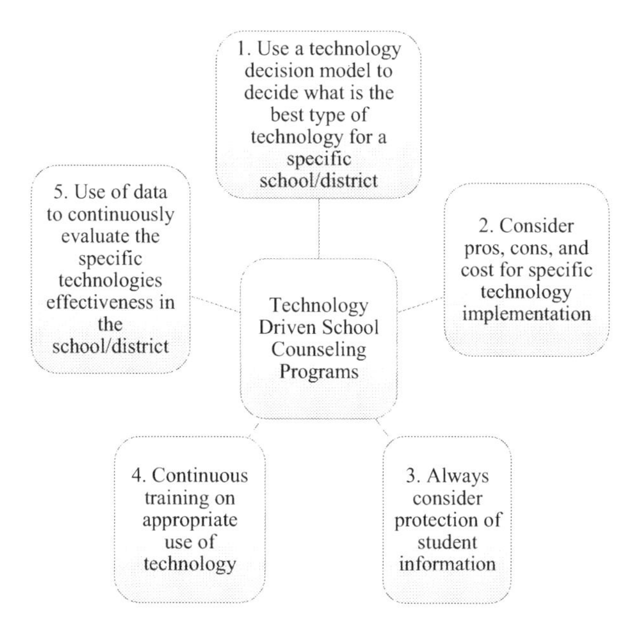

Figure 10.1 Continuous Technology Assessment for Best Practice

The process for continuous technology assessment for best practices is to use a technology decision model that would help determine the best forms of technology that are needed. Considering the pros and cons of each technology, along with monthly and annual cost, would be proactive in determining the needs of the comprehensive school counseling program. The protection of student information is not only outlined as critical in the ASCA ethical standards for school counselors, but districts across the nation deem protection of student information as a high priority. Training your faculty and administration on the technology program use in the school counseling program and different tools to support interventions with students is a great way to emphasize appropriate use. Finally, using data to support the outcome effectiveness in the use of specific technologies is recommended for school counselors to provide this information to stakeholders and school personnel who are directly involved with the comprehensive school counseling program.

Activities

1. Take a look at the process for continuous assessment. Go through each step and make technology decisions, along with garnering permission.

2. Create an action plan of technology implementation. Decide that selected technologies help reach your SMART goals as outlined in the comprehensive school counseling program.
3. Create a log book of all students assigned to you as a counselor. Then create confidential passwords to assign each student in your building.
4. Create a policy for technology use in your department and seek approval from your advisory council, administrators, or other stakeholders.

Resources

File-Sharing:

www.dropbox.com/
www.sharefile.com/
www.google.com/drive/
https://onedrive.live.com/about/en-us/
www.icloud.com/
www.egnyte.com/
https://limewire.en.softonic.com
https://zapya.en.softonic.com/

Google Voice:

www.google.com/voice

Interactive Video Conferencing Programs:

https://1877776.talkfusion.com/
www.skype.com/en/
https://facetime.en.softonic.com
https://hangouts.google.com/
www.gotomeeting.com/
https://clickmeeting.com/
www.webex.com/
www.zoho.com/
www.evoice.com/
www.join.me/
https://aws.amazon.com/chime/
www.adobe.com/products/adobeconnect.html
https://zoom.us/

Electronic Databases for Record-Keeping:
www.simplepractice.com
www.therapyappointments.com
www.therapynotes.com

School Data Systems:
www.cri-mms.com/
https://gradelink.com/
www.schoolfront.com/
www.getalma.com/
www.schoology.com/
www.renweb.com/
www.skyward.com/
http://schoolcounselorcentral.com/

Social Media Platforms:
https://twitter.com/
www.facebook.com/
www.pinterest.com/
www.instagram.com/
www.linkedin.com/
www.flickr.com/
https://itunes.apple.com/us/app/reddit-official-trending-news/id1064216828?mt=8
www.snapchat.com/
www.tumblr.com/
https://plus.google.com/
https://vimeo.com/

Technology and the School Counselor:
www.edweek.org/ew/articles/1998/10/28/09hart.h18.html

Technology Apps for Electronic Devices:
https://itunes.apple.com/us/app/voice-notes-voice-recorder/id593087833?mt=8
www.docusign.com/
https://app.getsigneasy.com/
www.ebooks.com/
www.netflix.com/
http://counselorapp.com/scuta-introduction/

www.youtube.com/
www.ted.com/
www.headspace.com/headspace-meditation-app
www.calm.com/
https://play.google.com/store/apps/details?id=com.lostego.SoothingSoundsLite&hl=en

Technology Enhances the Human Touch:
https://thejournal.com/articles/2012/06/07/for-school-counselors-technology-enhances-the-human-touch.aspx

Websites for Creating School Counselor Web Pages:
www.weebly.com
www.wix.com
www.yola.com
www.wordpress.com

References

American Counseling Association. (2014). *Code of ethics*. Alexandria, VA: Authors. Retrieved from www.counseling.org/docs/default-source/ethics/2014-aca-code-of-ethics.pdf?sfvrsn=fde89426_5

American School Counselor Association. (2012). *ASCA national model: A framework for school counseling programs* (3rd ed.). Alexandria, VA: Author.

American School Counselor Association. (2016). *Ethical standards for school counselors*. Retrieved from www.schoolcounselor.org/content.asp?contentid=173

Center for Credentialing in Education. (2014). *Distance credentialed counselor*. Retrieved January 12, 2017, from www.cce-global.org/dcc

Hallström, J., & Gyberg, P. (2011). Technology in the rear-view mirror: How to better incorporate the history of technology into technology education. *International Journal of Technology and Design Education*, *21*(1), 3–17. doi:10.1007/s10798-009-9109-5

Lambie, G. W., & Williamson, L. L. (2004). The challenge to change from guidance counseling to professional school counseling: A historical proposition. *Professional School Counseling*, *8*(2), 124–131.

Maras, M. A., Coleman, S. L., Gysbers, N. C., Herman, K. C., & Stanley, B. (2013). Measuring evaluation competency among school counselors. *Counseling Outcome Research and Evaluation*, *4*(2), 99–111.

Romrell, D., Kidder, L. C., & Wood, E. (2014). The SAMR model as a framework for evaluating mLearning. *Journal of Asynchronous Learning Networks, 18*(2), 1–16.

Steele, T. M., Jacokes, D. E., & Stone, C. B. (2014). An examination of the role of the online technology in school counseling. *Professional School Counseling, 18*(1), 125–135.

11

Data and Assessment in School Counseling

Dr. Tiffany Simon, Dr. Jana McLain, Letitia Powell, and Dr. Ernest Cox Jr.

ASCA NATIONAL MODEL THEMES

Advocacy

Collaboration

Systemic Change

ASCA NATIONAL MODEL SCHOOL COUNSELOR PROFESSIONAL COMPETENCIES

III-B-1a. Conducts a school counseling program assessment

III-B-2d. Reviews school data, school counseling program assessment and school counseling program goals with the advisory council

III-B-3g. Knows and understands theoretical and historical basis for assessment techniques

IV-B-2d. Understands career opportunities, labor market trends and global economics and uses various career assessment techniques to help students understand their abilities and career interests

V-A-4. School counseling program assessments and results reports

V-B-1b. Analyzes results from school counseling program assessment

V-B-2a. Analyzes self-assessment related to school counseling skills and performance

V-B-3b. Shares the results of the program assessment with administrators, the advisory council and other appropriate stakeholders

CACREP 2016

Section 5-G, Entry-Level Specialty Areas, School Counseling

Foundations
1.a assessments specific to P-12

Contextual Dimensions
2.a school counselor roles as leaders, advocates, and systems change agents in P-12 schools

2.b school counselor roles in consultation with families, P-12 and postsecondary school personnel, and community agencies

Practice
3.b design and evaluation of school counseling programs

3.d interventions to promote academic development

3.e use of developmentally appropriate career counseling interventions and assessments

3.k strategies to promote equity in student achievement and college access

ASCA ETHICAL STANDARDS FOR SCHOOL COUNSELORS (2016)

A.3.a. Collaborate with administration, teachers, staff and decision makers around school-improvement goals.

A.3.b. Provide students with a comprehensive school counseling program that ensures equitable academic, career and social/emotional development opportunities for all students.

A.3.c. Review school and student data to assess needs including, but not limited to, data on disparities that may exist related to gender, race, ethnicity, socio-economic status and/or other relevant classifications.

A.3.d. Use data to determine needed interventions, which are then delivered to help close the information, attainment, achievement and opportunity gaps.

A.13.a. Use only valid and reliable tests and assessments with concern for bias and cultural sensitivity.

A.13.b. Adhere to all professional standards when selecting, administering and interpreting assessment measures and only utilize assessment measures that are within the scope of practice for school counselors and for which they are licensed, certified and competent.

A.13.c. Are mindful of confidentiality guidelines when utilizing paper or electronic evaluative or assessment instruments and programs.

A.13.d. Consider the student's developmental age, language skills and level of competence when determining the appropriateness of an assessment.

A.13.e. Use multiple data points when possible to provide students and families with accurate, objective and concise information to promote students' well-being.

A.13.f. Provide interpretation of the nature, purposes, results and potential impact of assessment/evaluation measures in language the students and parents/guardians can understand.

A.13.g. Monitor the use of assessment results and interpretations and take reasonable steps to prevent others from misusing the information.

A.13. h. Use caution when utilizing assessment techniques, making evaluations and interpreting the performance of populations not represented in the norm group on which an instrument is standardized.

ASCA POSITION STATEMENTS

The School Counselor and Comprehensive School Counseling Programs (2012)

The School Counselor and Equity for All Students (2012)

The School Counselor and Gifted and Talented Student Programs (2013)

The School Counselor and Annual Performance Evaluation (2015)

The School Counselor and College Access Professionals (2016)

Data-Driven Programming

School counseling programs are integral components within the systemic structure of each school campus. To best serve students, school counseling programs should be student centered and guided by the needs of the students, campus, and district (Gysbers & Henderson, 2012). In alignment with the ASCA 21st-century vision of comprehensive school counseling programs (ASCA, 2012), school counselors are called to use data to drive programming goals. Data-driven comprehensive school counseling programs (CSCPs) make strong contributions to academic, personal-social, and career development

(Gysbers & Henderson, 2012; Schmidt, 2014). Additionally, a CSCP is designed to address district, state, and federal mandates. Effective program planning will assist school counselors in being active participants in implementing change in areas such as:

- Reducing dropout rates
- Increasing graduation rates
- Increasing college and career readiness
- Increasing student participation in advance coursework and/or coursework leading to industry licenses/certifications
- Improving scores on high-stakes testing
- Reducing discipline referrals, increasing participation in service learning and community participation
- Improving awareness/acceptance of diversity

According to Gysbers and Henderson (2012), stakeholders value local data that is reflective of the needs of their students. Although school counselors may be apprehensive to dive into data, data collection does not have to be an overwhelming task. Some of the fears that exist in data collection and analysis are due to school counselors' concerns about being able to find time to complete the necessary tasks. They may feel that they are not properly trained in data collection and analysis or that data collection is not a role of a school counselor (Dollarhide & Saginak, 2017; Schmidt, 2014; Stone & Dahir, 2011). School counselor leaders emphasize that a strong background in statistical analysis is not a necessary component for the types of data collection and analysis that are performed by the school counselor (ASCA, 2012; Dollarhide & Saginak, 2017; Erford, 2011; Gysbers & Henderson, 2012; Schmidt, 2014; Stone & Dahir, 2011).

It is important to remember that we can keep data collection and analysis simple and start with data that already exists (Dollarhide & Saginak, 2017; Gysbers & Henderson, 2012). School counselors can collect data from various reports that campus and districts collect annually. In collaboration with school administration, school counselors may have access to data available in their student learning management systems, campus/district report cards, individual student reports, and annual surveys conducted by the school district. Creating campus surveys, campus questionnaires, monitoring trends that affect students, and reviewing surveys conducted by outside agencies. For example, the Youth Risk Behavior Surveillance System (YRBSS) conducted by the Centers for Disease Control and Prevention (CDC) may also be used to gather data.

The CDC conducts the YRBSS, a biannual report that assesses six categories of behaviors that contribute to unintentional injuries and violence: (1) sexual behaviors related to unintended pregnancy and sexually transmitted diseases; (2) alcohol and other drug use; (3) tobacco use; (4) unhealthy dietary behaviors; (5) inadequate physical activity; and (6) other important health issues that affect youth. Information gathered from the YRBSS may assist school counselors in program planning for guidance lessons, small groups, and awareness campaigns (Centers for Disease Control and Prevention, 2015).

Evaluation Models

Data is helpful when trying to answer questions regarding the effectiveness of a school counseling program, the current trends, and needs of the students and school. Additionally, data can explain how the school counseling program is affecting individual students, as well as the system-wide impact (Stone & Dahir, 2011). The school counseling program should remain relevant, and use current and practical data to guide the decision-making process when program planning is reviewed. To begin the data collection and analysis process, school counselors must first establish the procedure that they will be using. The following example is an excellent process for a data collection and analysis protocol for school counselors.

The IDEAS! Model, developed by Lapan (Gysbers & Lapan, 2009), can be used as a guide for school counselors. The model begins by requiring school counselors to identify a problem area by completing a thorough review of the campus improvement plan or based on concerns brought forth by stakeholders. Lapan encourages a detailed description of the problem in the second step, including addressing the following questions: Who are the targeted students? Are the interventions aligned with the problem? Are the appropriate measurements being used? and What is the setting of the intervention?

School districts have existing data that may be available to address areas of concern, and the data may be readily available using an Excel spreadsheet software. Once again, a strong background in statistics is not required. School counselors may use the information available from the school district to analyze data by interpreting averages, percentages, and correlations in constructs. After the counselor interprets the day, the next step is to summarize the data so that the results are available to drive programming. The following acronym is helpful in remembering the process:

IDEAS!

I: Identify the problem
D: Describe the problem
E: Existing school data is collected
A: Analyze data
S: Summarize data

Data Collection: Types of Data

Data collection is gathered to aid school counselors in meeting the academic, behavioral, and social needs of students. To help better understand the role of school counselors and data collection, it is important to understand the meaning and purpose of several forms of relevant data terms. We can begin by examining the terms school counselors will see when they use the templates provided by ASCA (2012). In the ASCA National Model (third edition), the Template for Developing a School Counseling Program Goal in SMART Goal Format breaks data down into use-of-time data, perception data, outcome data, process data, and formative/summative data (www.schoolcounselor.org/school-counselors-members/asca-national-model/asca-national-model-templates) [ASCA, 2012].

Use-of-Time Data

Use-of-time data are compiled from tracking the amount of time school counselors spend planning and completing duties that are part of the CSCP. Some of the areas in which school counselors can track their use-of-time include duties related to individual planning, testing, guidance lessons, and collaboration with other personnel. Information documented on the use-of-time template is used to show how school counselors spend their time, how the caseload size affects the expenditure of time completing specific services, and how non-counseling-related duties affect the ability to participate/implement counseling-related services.

Perception Data

School counselors gather perception data from the results of surveys and needs assessments that have been completed by stakeholders (e.g., students, teachers, administrators, parents, school counselors, etc.). Perception data is used to gauge the attitudes, beliefs, and opinions of stakeholders. For example, if one of the goals of the school counseling department is to increase the awareness of the college financial aid process, a survey may be administered to gain baseline data on how informed parents and students are on the process. Statements such as: "I am comfortable completing FAFSA", "I understand what documents I need to complete the FAFSA", and "I am aware of the FAFSA deadline" are rated using likert scales. After the financial aid awareness activities, a follow-up survey can be administered to assess if there have been any changes on the level of awareness of the financial aid process. This data may be used to determine if additional awareness activities need to be modified to meet the targeted goal.

Outcome Data

Outcome data also confirms the impact of interventions, but differs from perception data due to how the data is collected. Outcome data provides data on whole groups and can be gathered from achievement results, attendance reports, behavior reports, or other data the school counselor may obtain from the student management system or school profile/report card. An example of outcome data is "the percentage of 3rd-grade students required to attend summer remediation for math decreased from 18% to 11% after students attended group counseling that focused on study skills."

Process Data

Process data are derived from collecting evidence about specific events or activities and offer evidence that services were provided. This form of data documents who was impacted, the number impacted, number of activities, and duration of activities. For example, 200 parents received an invitation to participate in a parent night targeting advanced placement course registration, and 117 parents attended the parent night meeting. Another example is all parents in the school were invited to attend a six-week parenting series, and 25 parents attended all six weeks of classes.

Formative and Summative Data

Formative and summative data are another way to describe information. Formative data are accumulated during the event to decipher the effectiveness of the intervention, perception of stakeholders, and allow for modifications to improve effectiveness. School counselors can use surveys, questionnaires, or interview stakeholders during the intervention activity to check for understanding and effectiveness of material (Dollarhide & Saginak, 2017). However, summative data are collected at the conclusion of the intervention as the outcome of the intervention is measured. Examples of summative data reports include curriculum, small-group, and closing the gap results reports (ASCA, 2012).

Disaggregation of Data

When analyzing data, understanding subpopulations can lead to effective program design. During the data analysis phase, data disaggregation can yield important trends that will help identify specific areas of need. Common fields of disaggregation include (ASCA, 2012; Gysbers & Henderson, 2012; Stone & Dahir, 2011):

- Gender
- Ethnicity
- Socioeconomic status (free and reduced lunch)
- Career and technology
- Participation in specialized programs (ESL/bilingual education, gifted/talented, special education, at-risk, etc.)
- Grade level
- Teacher(s)

Program Planning

After data has been collected and disaggregated, school counselors then have the responsibility to develop goals to address the determined needs. Schmidt (2014) stated that "gathering data from the consumers of school counseling services, counselors and their supervisors are in a stronger position to make purposeful and meaningful decisions about future directions for the program. It demonstrates a counselor's intentionality regarding evaluation" (p. 280). The following scenarios illustrate how data can be used to impact student, campus, and district goals.

Academic

Data gathered from standardized tests, academic reports (report cards or transcripts), and achievement tests are indicators that the counselor may use to determine college/career readiness. School counselors may use the data from these reports to determine what type of intervention programs the school counseling program can facilitate. In the following scenario, one of the campus goals was to increase the number of students who participate in college readiness exams.

Scenario: Ms. Woods, high school counselor, is analyzing the number of 11th-grade students who have signed up to take the ACT exam. Ms. Woods is concerned about her low-income students and their low participation in the ACT exam. Last school year, she had 125 11th-grade students who were eligible for a fee-waiver, and only 25 of those students registered to take the ACT exam. Although Ms. Woods has posted on the school website that students are eligible for a fee-waiver, only 10 of the 125 eligible students requested a fee waiver. Ms. Woods may use this data to demonstrate a need for increased awareness efforts for informing students of ACT fee-waivers. Ms. Woods puts together a plan on methods to better inform parents, students, and school staff on the eligibility requirements for ACT fee-waivers. After the increased efforts, Ms. Woods sees an increase in registration from students eligible for a fee-waiver. She reports this to the administration to highlight the effectiveness of the CSCP.

Behavior

Although the role of disciplinarian should never be an expectation or delivered by the school counselor, school counselors need to have knowledge of behavior reports to help structure and plan the comprehensive counseling program. Disaggregating behavior data will assist school counselors in designing small groups, individual planning, system support, and responsive services. The following scenario illustrates how school counselors effectively address behavior based on data analysis.

Scenario: In August, Mr. Terrell, 5th-grade counselor, is planning the small-group topics he would like to run this year. Mr. Terrell is aware that best practice suggests he refer to the data to help plan his counseling program. Mr. Terrell meets with Ms. Jones, the 5th-grade principal, and Ms. Smith, the school principal. The three review discipline records for the students who will be incoming fifth graders and identify trends in behavior referrals. The top two reasons for discipline referrals were related to interpersonal conflict and classroom disruptions. Based on the discipline report data, Mr. Terrell decides to create a conflict resolution small group. When reviewing the students who had discipline referrals based on classroom disruptions, Mr. Terrell and Ms. Smith are able to recognize that several of the students with multiple referrals have been identified as students with Attention Deficit Hyperactivity Disorder (ADHD). Mr. Terrell and Ms. Smith see a need to help provide teachers with strategies and tips for working with students with ADHD. Throughout the school year, Mr. Terrell monitors the behaviors of the students he is working with who he identified as having multiple referrals. He is able to see a decrease in behavior referrals for some of the students as a result of his work with the students. He re-evaluates his intervention for the students who have not exhibited a decrease in behavior referrals.

Social

School counselors are charged with the duty to meet the social and emotional needs of the students they serve. Implementing a CSCP, school counselors must determine what the social needs are of the student population, make program decisions that meet the mission, vision, and district/state mandates.

Scenario: During the spring staff development, Reagan Junior High school counselors review the mission statement of their campus. Included within the mission statement is a statement regarding "molding students to be stewards of global citizenship." Mrs. Poole, the lead counselor, would like to know which type of event students are most likely willing to demonstrate global citizenship. The school counselors work with the student council and create three possible campus projects that would convey that Reagan students are growing as global citizens. The counseling department creates a web-based short survey and asks all first-period teachers to have their students vote on a school-wide project. Students choose to sponsor a library for an elementary school in a low-income area. During the next three months, the counseling department and the student council promote the project, explain how students can contribute, and give updates on the progress of the project. At the conclusion of the project, the counseling department creates another web-based survey to gather feedback on the effectiveness of the project. After receiving feedback, the counseling department evaluates the identified strengths and weaknesses and uses the feedback to make adjustments to the counseling program.

The Counselor's Role in Assessment

Different types of assessments are given in a school setting: achievement tests, interest inventories, personality tests, and aptitude tests (Schmidt, 2003). Typically, school psychologists and diagnosticians administer intelligence tests and psychological tests (Davis, 2015). Although school counselors may administer interest inventories and achievement tests (Ekstrom, Elmore, Schafer, Trotter, & Webster, 2004), they may also administer needs assessments to campus staff, students, and parents (Ekstrom et al., 2004). School counselors' involvement with assessments and testing may vary based on the state, district, and school needs. Some school counselors may assist with organizing and administering standardized tests, while other school counselors may not be heavily involved with testing. Regardless of their involvement with testing, school counselors are ethically responsible for understanding the purpose and results of assessments. School counselors are able to interpret the results of test and relay the information to students and parents (Standard A.13.f).

Students and parents look to school counselors to clearly explain assessment results and how the results affect the students (Davis, 2015). The ASCA Ethical Standards (2016) require that school counselors use a language that is developmentally appropriate for the students to understand (A.13.f). Once parents receive a copy of the assessment results, school counselors should use a variety of methods to assist parents in understanding assessment results (Davis, 2015). For example, if the results of the assessments are mailed home, school counselors may include a detailed explanation of the results, which would include a breakdown of each measure or tested objective. Additionally, school counselors can collaborate with teachers to host an evening event for parents and students to explain the results of the assessments and provide guidance for additional support, discussion options, interventions, and answer any other questions or needs that may arise. Teachers will be available to discuss their gifted and talented curriculum, their intervention plan, and their tutoring availability. Coordinators over special populations such as students receiving special education, English Language Learners, Response to Intervention, and 504 plans, just to name a few, can also be available to discuss their plans to help their targeted group of students. Parents can receive additional resources that will assist them in supporting their student at home. If parents' schedules will not allow them to attend an evening event, school counselors can also host a lunch and learn opportunity for parents to receive the same information. All announcements should be posted on the school's website and sent home in the form of a memo.

In addition to assisting the parents and students with understanding the results, school counselors also explain how the results can affect the students' decisions with future educational plans, curriculum choices, career plans, and interests. Once parents and students have a clear understanding of their options, they are able to make informed decisions based on the students' best interests. For example, if parents learn that their child performed exceptionally well on the standardized tests, they may encourage their student to take a more demanding curriculum based on their areas of strengths. On the other hand, if parents learn that their child struggled on some parts of the test, they may seek additional tutoring or interventions for their student.

School counselors not only assist parents and students with understanding assessment results, but they also assist teachers and other key educators in understanding assessment results (Ekstrom et al., 2004). When teachers understand the assessment results, it can improve their instruction and approach with students. Using the assessment results, school counselors can assist teachers in identifying the students' strengths and weaknesses based on objectives or measured outcomes. Teachers have an opportunity to explore the achievement gaps of their students and create individualized instructions based on the students' needs. They can also work collaboratively with other teachers within the same department or across disciplines to meet the students' needs. Teachers' understanding of assessment results can also assist them in ensuring there is equitable learning for all groups.

Unlike teachers, school counselors are typically assigned to the same students for several years. This affords them the opportunity to continually monitor and document the students' performance on assessments. The counselor becomes aware of the students' areas of growth and their areas of non-proficiency. School counselors are then an asset to teachers, who only have students for one year. They can be instrumental in educating the teachers on the students' academic abilities, historical performances, and areas of strength and weakness. Having this prior knowledge will assist students and teachers with creating an effective plan that addresses student achievement.

Using Assessment Results for Programming

School counselors can use test results to create programs and activities based on students' needs. They may create guidance lessons or provide group and individual counseling to address the students' needs. School counselors can give students, staff, and parents the needs assessment to determine what topics to cover. Some of the test-related topics that can be covered include, but are not limited to: stress management, coping skills, test anxiety, test-taking strategies, and study skills.

Guidance Lessons, Group Counseling, and Individual Support

If the results from the needs assessment suggest that a high number of students would benefit from study skills, an interactive guidance lesson can be created to address study skills. Depending on the school's master schedule, school counselors can present lessons during a study hall, homeroom, or intervention class. They can also train subject area teachers (i.e., all English teachers) on the lesson, and ask that they present the lesson to all of their English classes. If the assessment indicates that a small number of students has test anxiety, the counselor can create groups of four to six students who are interested in learning how to manage their test anxiety. Furthermore, if the assessment indicates some students will benefit from more individualized attention on stress management, the counselor can schedule individual counseling sessions with those particular students.

Programs That Address Post-Secondary Options

Assessment results can also be used to promote and educate students on post-secondary options. Based on the results, school counselors may organize field experiences to colleges and businesses for students to explore their interests. They may also arrange college and career days, which allows college representatives, military recruiters, and business partners to present information to students about their organizations and programs. Once the students have been educated on their post-secondary options, they can take additional needs assessments. The results from the needs assessments will give the counselor a clearer picture of the student's individual post-secondary needs. For example, if middle school students indicate they would like to learn more about the different types of career options, then school counselors can work with the high school career and technology education teachers to organize a career fair using the high school students to present to the middle school students. If it is determined that students would benefit from individualized attention in applying for college, then school counselors can organize an application week. During this week, all counselors will assist small groups of students with their college applications.

Assessments and the Law

School counselors understand the history of assessments and how assessments are used to determine a student's performance across standards (ASCA, 2017). The No Child Left Behind (NCLB) Act included the use of assessments to determine graduation, retention, promotion, and academic placement (NCLB, 2002). On the other hand, the Every Student Succeeds Act (ESSA, 2015) supports educators using multiple measures to determine student success (White House, 2015). A school counselor's role with this act is to advocate for a reasonable number of measures that determine achievement and needs for local and state improvement (ASCA, 2017). School counselors also understand that with the change came a shift in school personnel's resources, time, and instruction (ASCA, 2017). The shift affected how information is presented to students, school counseling programs, and how school programs are evaluated.

Assessments and Accountability

Payne wrote:

> What method do we have of checking the results of our guidance? For particular groups was it guidance, misguidance or merely contributing experience? We simply must work out some definite method of testing and checking the results of our work. If we do not, some other group will, with possibly disastrous results for our work.
>
> (p. 63)

This statement from 1924 indicates that being accountable and using data to drive school counseling programs are not a new phenomenon to the counseling field. The focal point in the 1920s was to establish a set of standards that would assess the completeness of the counseling programs (Gysbers, 2010).

Accountability of school counseling programs will continue to be a topic of concern for school counseling programs (Gysbers, 2010). It is school counselors' professional responsibility to continue to show the need, the importance, and the effectiveness of their programs to students' success. The ASCA National Model (2012) can be instrumental in evaluating and assessing the effectiveness of counselor programs. The data gathered from the assessments will assist counselors in developing a comprehensive program that can meet the individual needs of the students and holistic needs of the school.

The methods for collecting data has expanded, and our rationale and the need for data has grown, but the foundational need has always been the same: to meet students' needs. If school counselors are to meet these needs, they must have a true understanding of those needs and must have multiple ways to assess those needs. Gone are the days of school counseling programs that simply exist because of repetition and tradition. It is important that the programs reflect students' needs. The 2016 ethical standards clearly identified the need for a data-driven school counseling program, and the term *data* is mentioned throughout various sections of the standards and in the newly created section A.3. Comprehensive Data-Informed Program.

Data, Assessment, and Technology

School counselors have been charged to be agents of change to support student needs (ASCA, 2012; Ratliff, Ebbs, & Isom, 2012). As such, they should be aware of the vast technological advances in society that can be used with regard to data collection (ASCA, 2012; Ratliff et al., 2012). Technology-driven data collection, as part of a comprehensive counseling program, can enable school counselors to meet students' needs on their academic and social/emotional level. There are many ways to meet the technological demand in the current educational settings. For instance, school counselors can integrate their technological knowledge into guidance lessons, small group activities, and school-wide climate initiatives (ASCA, 2012; Ratliff et al., 2012).

School counselors can use technology to collect and monitor data relating to their counseling program. Many school districts maintain a system to house all data relating to student success. Through these systems, school counselors can access information to address students who are at risk. For example, data warehouse systems such as eSchool (ESchool Media, Inc, n.d.) and Eduphoria (Eduphoria!, n.d.) can be used to create small group lists and to monitor students who are at risk of dropping out. Furthermore, school counselors and directors of school counseling programs can use programs such as these to report the work done by school counselors.

School counselor program directors must provide data to substantiate the work done by school counselors. These directors often spend a substantial amount of time collecting data to ensure school counselors' time is being used effectively. Websites such as Toggl are used to report how school counselors use their time (Toggl, 2017). This information can be taken to school district leadership to advocate for appropriate roles. Additionally, program directors can use data warehouses to show how school counselors are most effective when providing direct intervention with students.

Another avenue to incorporate technology into data collection is the use of interest inventories and other web-based assessment tools. A simple website search can lead school counselors to sites that provide access to data collection tools. The resources section of this chapter includes examples of websites that can be used to collect data relating to student interest and achievement. This information can drive the interventions implemented by school counselors.

The uses of an Excel data sheet can allow school counselors to collect, compile, and disaggregate data. Many data warehouse programs and online tools can export data into an Excel document. Once the data is imported into an Excel document, school counselors can disaggregate it to fit their specific needs. Excel documents are useful when there is a large amount of data to be examined. Finally, school counselors can use Excel to create graphs, charts, and tables to display the results of their data analysis.

Data is an integral component of a comprehensive counseling program. Typically, the most effective way to show parents, administrators, and the community the value of your work is through data collection. As an example, school counselors can use attendance records, discipline entries, number of small group and individual sessions, standardized testing scores, and high school credits to identify students who are at risk for dropping out of school. They can then meet with these students in individual and small-group settings to provide direct intervention and ongoing support.

Data, Assessment, and the Calendar

The use of calendars, as part of a comprehensive counseling program, allows school counselors an opportunity to advocate for appropriate roles and delineate where their time is best spent (ASCA, 2012). When examining assessment and data collection, school counselors can use a management agreement and calendar to plan opportunities to collect data. A management agreement is a tool used by school counselors to organize their school year to ensure the needs of students are met (ASCA, 2012). This data can be used to support the need for school counselors to engage in more counseling activities versus non-counseling activities (Gysbers & Henderson, 2012; McLain, 2014).

When composing a calendar of counseling-related activities, school counselors should include items such as individual and small-group counseling, school-wide climate initiatives, non-counseling tasks, and data collection/analysis (Gysbers & Henderson, 2012). Taking the time to provide a detailed plan of calendar events will create opportunities to collect data. For example, school counselors can collect data during small-group sessions by administering pre- and post-tests to participants. This information can help guide the lessons taught and create further groups. Pre- and post-test data can also be used to evaluate school-wide climate initiatives. Finally, school counselors can collect data related to how their time is spent regarding counseling versus non-counseling duties. Simple methods such as maintaining an Excel spreadsheet with time allocation listed helps foster positive conversations between school counselors and administrators (Dahir & Stone, 2011).

Data, Assessment, and Advocacy

Advocacy is an action response to areas of inequalities. School counselors can use data to lead their advocacy efforts. As social justice advocates, school counselors can use disaggregated data to focus on diverse populations and identify if any areas of inequity exist. If the data highlights a gap in services, school counselors are called to advocate for changes in inequitable policies, procedures, or instructional conditions that may negatively impact the development of students (Dollarhide & Saginak, 2017). Stone and Dahir (2011) explained that data brings attention to opportunities and demonstrates a commitment from school counselors to be active members in the change process. By providing data on how certain programming is affecting subpopulations or marginalized students to school administrators and school board committees, school counselors can be the voice of the underserved and lead the charge in ensuring better educational opportunities for all students.

Advocating for their role involves using data to support the need for their positions and how impactful their positions are on student success. The data can also be used to minimize being assigned non-counseling-related duties. The data can be collected from various platforms, including district improvement plans, campus improvement plans, student and staff needs assessments, and parent needs assessments. Because of the various platforms, school counselors should take advantage of opportunities to collect data using different methods. They should be prepared to use formal and informal assessments.

School counselors may request the district data from their Director of Guidance and Counseling or other district leaders. Counselors on each level—elementary, middle, and high school—can meet to discuss how each group can address the needs. Additionally, each campus counseling team can meet to discuss what measures they would like to implement to address the needs. Using the data, the counseling department can tweak their school counseling program to create preventative programs, intervention programs, guidance lessons, group counseling sessions, and individual counseling sessions that focus on the needs of the district. School counselors should collect data from each event or activity they organize. This data should be used to advocate for the school counselor position. The results of the data should be shared with all stakeholders: communities, principals, assistant principals, teachers, students, and parents. This effort will help educate stakeholders on the importance and impact of the counselor's role. In the following scenarios, school counselors show the importance of their roles by using data to meet the needs of the students, parents, and staff.

Scenario One

Data from the district improvement plan indicates there has been an increase in the number of students who have been disciplined for gang involvement. School counselors use the data to create guidance lessons that educate students, parents, and faculty on signs of gang involvement, the effects of gang involvement, how to address gang involvement, and alternative solutions to joining a gang.

School counselors work with community leaders and faculty to create a male and female mentor program for students who are at risk for joining a gang. They also work with older students to create a mentoring program for younger students who are at risk for joining a gang. School counselors work with the local police department and the district police department to organize events throughout the year to continue to address gang activity. Additionally, school counselors work with their administrators on ways to handle gang involvement in the school.

Feedback from students and parents, data intervention programs and preventative programs, and discipline referrals will be analyzed to determine the effectiveness of the programs. Counselors' roles in each activity will be assessed to determine effectiveness. Adjustments will be made based on the results of the data.

Scenario Two

During the senior parent night, school counselors review the senior timeline and present senior-related information to educate them on senior student responsibilities. Former students share their senior year experiences with parents and students, and parents and students are given an opportunity to meet with different teachers to discuss the curriculum and academic expectations. At the end of the night, the school counselors poll the audience to determine who would benefit from assistance with completing the financial aid paperwork. More than half of the parents in the room raise their hands expressing an interest in receiving help.

At the end of the event, parents are given an evaluation form to provide feedback on the parent night. The information from the evaluations will be used to revise upcoming parent events and make adjustments to the future senior nights. They are also given an index card that asks for their contact information, preferred language, availability, interest in a financial aid workshop, and preferred group size. The counselors will use the information from the index cards to organize a financial aid workshop. Depending on the data collected from the index cards, the school counselors will collaborate with local college financial aid representatives to create a day and evening workshop for both students and parents.

School counselors will access the Free Application for Federal Student Aid (FAFSA) completion data to determine which students have not submitted their financial aid application. The school counselors will compare the students who have not turned in their application with the students who indicated they have different post-secondary plans. School counselors will meet individually with students who once expressed an interest in attending college, but who had not completed their financial aid application to determine if their interests were still the same. If so, they would assist them with the financial aid application. They will also meet with students who expressed a different post-secondary interest to determine their progress toward their post-secondary goals and offer assistance as needed.

School counselors must also use data to advocate for marginalized students. To advocate for their students, they must be knowledgeable of their students and their educational, social, and cultural influences. They must be familiar with the societal issues and educational issues that plague their students and assist them with addressing those issues (Lee, 2007). Using data to advocate for student needs is not a foreign concept. ASCA Ethical Standards require that school counselors advocate for students' needs (A.1.k). School counselors are unable to advocate if they do not have the data to educate others on the needs of the students or the counseling program. School counselors can start obtaining this data by the students' self-report.

Scenario Three

Middle school counselors plan to teach a guidance lesson on students' career options. Prior to the lesson, they give the students an informal pre-test to assess their current knowledge. Using an icebreaker, they poll the class, asking questions that will assist them in determining the students' knowledge base. The guidance lesson and activities are interactive, which allows the counselors to foster engagement while continuing to collect data. During the lesson, the counselors will collect data by making note of the student responses to the activities. They will also make note of the questions and answers that may arise during the lesson. After the lesson is complete, another informal post-test will be given to assess what the students learned and what they would be interested in learning about in the future. The data collected throughout the guidance lesson is useful because it will assist the school counselors in determining the next steps to addressing the students' career needs.

Scenario Four

High school counselors noticed that the number of parents who attended school-related events had decreased over the years. Less than 10% of parents attended the open house night. Even fewer parents attended the yearly college and career night. Student achievement and award recognition also had a small number of parents present. The school counselors met with the campus leaders to discuss the change and to review the school data. The school counseling department decided to take the lead on this issue, assess the situation, and propose a solution.

School counselors gathered data by several means. They reviewed the available data to determine what had changed. Analyzing demographic data for the area, talking with parents with whom they had a relationship, and talking with students, school counselors discovered several differences. They noticed there was an increase in the number of students who qualified for free and reduced lunch, an increase in the number of students who lived in single-parent homes, an increase in the number of students who were considered first-generation immigrants, and an increase in the number of students whose home language survey indicated their home language was not English. Other changes included more students met at least one of the at-risk indicators, and the overall passing standard for students was lower. School counselors realized several groups of students were underserved.

School counselors advocated for change for the marginalized groups of students. They presented their findings to the building principal, assistant principals, and teachers with plausible solutions. They invited the principals and teachers to get involved with making the changes. A group was formed that included individuals who had expressed an interest in helping to make an impact. This group then made personal phone calls to solicit help from parents with whom they had a relationship. They asked parents to become volunteers who could serve as liaisons between the school and the parents in the community.

School counselors shared the data with the group of parents and provided plausible solutions that involved the help of the parent volunteers. School counselors asked parents to share the information with parents who were unable to attend a school function and provided additional copies of information for parent liaisons to post in the churches, community centers, clubhouses, apartment manager offices, stores, and other frequently visited community establishments.

Because the home language surveys indicated students spoke Spanish, Mandarin, and Vietnamese in their homes, the school counselors created forms that the district office translated in the top three languages identified on the survey. The forms were made available on the school's website and in the front office of the school. School counselors requested a translation option be added to the website so that parents could have the content of the website translated to their preferred language. Parent/teacher conferences were scheduled based on a time that was feasible for parents, which allowed for more parental involvement. Additionally, school counselors assured parents that a district translator would be present to convey the pertinent information to parents.

School counselors provided information during a lunch and in the evening to accommodate parents' schedules. The counselors deemed it necessary to get the students involved with the change and promote student involvement and volunteerism. They met with the culinary sponsors in the district to request that they have their students provide small dinner or snack options for some parent night events. The school counselors also asked for student volunteers to babysit for parents who attended parent night. Students who were interested in being a teacher were encouraged to use this opportunity to create engaging activities for kids. Students who were interested in careers as photographers had a booth set up to take family portraits that were printed the same day. Finally, school counselors worked with the district offices to have presentations translated in the top three languages. The information was presented for each of the top three languages identified on the language survey.

School counselors collected evaluations after each event to determine the effectiveness and areas of improvement prior to the next scheduled event. Additionally, they met with their committees after the events to debrief and discuss successes and failures. Additional meetings with the committees were held quarterly to review progress toward set goals. Changes were implemented as needed. School counselors started to see some improvement in parent involvement, which improved marginalized students' overall academic achievement.

A Case Study: One District's Journey to Change the Role of the School Counselor

This is a case study of how one school district explored and learned how to use data to re culture the district's CSCP. Historically in this district, school counselors were called upon to provide responsive services. Additionally, the focus was on individual counseling and crisis counseling services on an *as-needed* basis. There was an uneven emphasis on services for individual students instead of focusing on the trends and needs of all students. School counselors were quasi-administrators and were largely involved in administrative duties, such as state assessment coordination, discipline, section 504, language proficiency coordination, and of course, other duties as assigned. The CSCP was non-existent for most and unstructured for all. School counselors needed guidance, structure, and support. The department included many advocates for students, but lacked direction for the program and a way to measure and track effectiveness, and the department lacked a program leader.

Program in Development

Over the past seven years, the district's school counseling program has gone through a re-culturing phase. The district created and hired a director of school counseling. Since the hiring, the district and program have taken active steps moving away from a program that lacked direction to a program with focus; the counseling program now provides equitable services for all students delivered with intentionality; the school counseling program is planned, developed, implemented, analyzed, and evaluated on an ongoing basis; the school counseling program is comprehensive in scope, preventative in design, and developmental in nature. The program is designed to ensure that every student receives access to the CSCP and the services provided by school counselors. The school counseling program is data driven, results oriented, and involves all stakeholders (students, staff, and parents). Over a four-year period, the school counselors decreased non-counseling-related activities from 45% to 11% and increased direct services to students.

Step 1: Types of Data

Several steps were required to reshape the counseling program. The initial step was to evaluate the program and communicate with campus and district leadership. Determining the effectiveness of service delivery is a pressing concern of education practitioners in charge of program evaluation (Murray, Levitov, Castenell, & Joubert, 1987). Therefore, the first step was to focus on data to document how students are impacted because of the school counseling program.

Student outcome and perception data is imperative in a CSCP, but process data would be the data source used to identify what was being done, when it was happening, and what needed to change. Therefore, the first step was to focus on the third type of data, process data. Process data provides evidence of where school counselors are allocating time within the four service components and non-school-counseling duties. Process data describes the activities conducted and the number of students participating in an activity. The department elected to focus on developing a method where school counselors could identify where time was being allocated and if there was a disproportionate amount of time being allocated to non-school-counseling duties.

Step 2: Developing a Tool and Buy-In: Standardizing, Calibrating, Building Trust

There are several data templates available for free, at cost, for subscription, or on the Internet. The key was to find a tool that was easy to use, tracked what we wanted, and could be modified over time. Using an Excel spreadsheet, The Professional School Counselor: Guidance and Counseling Program

Tracking and Data Analysis Report was created. This provided a method to help the school counselors and director of counseling develop, monitor, and organize the school counseling program. This data report provided a tool that the school counselors could use to identify how time was being allocated. Based on process data (weekly, monthly, and annually), the counselors can initiate a plan of action to reallocate time to the service components requiring attention. If school counselors identify that there is a disproportionate amount of time being allocated to non-school-counseling duties and/or indirect services, they may modify the data analysis template to more intentionally focus on the areas requiring change.

Prior to implementing the data tool, it was imperative to stress the importance of the use of the tool. The process data-tracking tool was (and continues to be) an "I got your back" rather than an "I got you." Data was gathered and calibrated for two years prior to publishing the findings for others to see. Initially, some of the members of the department were ambivalent and fearful of data. Some people did not see the point and felt that they were being questioned unnecessarily. Over time the department came to trust the data once they observed how the results were being used.

Step 3: Using the Data

Gysbers and Henderson (2006) reported that guidance and counseling departments often provide support for regular educational programs as well as other programs, such as testing, discipline, and management. They found that 30% to 40% of the school counselors' time was consumed by non-counseling-related activities, thus decreasing the amount of time allocated for the delivery of the CSCP (Gysbers & Henderson, 2012). Non-counseling duties impede the implementation of the CSCP (ASCA, 2012). Therefore, a greater awareness to counselor responsibilities is required to define, communicate, and clarify the difference between counseling and non-counseling services.

The first step in gathering process data was to specifically identify where time and services were being allocated. Prior to collecting data, school counselors spoke in feeling words—"I feel that . . . " They communicated that they were performing certain clerical/non-counseling-related tasks, but lacked evidence. Things changed once the counselors had data! Year one findings were not surprising. The department data indicated that over 45% of a school counselor's time was spent in non-counseling-related functions such as state assessments, clerical duties, or serving in a number of coordinator-type capacities (e.g., Section 504, ARD, LPAC, or RTI). The data provided an opportunity to move from "I can feel" to "I can show."

Step 4: Spreading the Word Using Data and Advocating for Change

The next step was to meet with campus and district leaders and share the data. Data allocations were presented in a side-by-side format with school counselors' codified roles. Supportive documentation and expansion was provided in alignment with state and national definitions. The school counselors' roles and responsibilities were discussed in relation to non-counseling-related or duties not related to the development, implementation, or evaluation of the CSCP. The presentation of data and literature was met with an immediate response to change historical practice. Program leaders immediately supported the district counseling department by taking steps to remove clerical and administrative (non- counseling-related) responsibilities such as testing and other coordinator duties. These responsibilities were reassigned to administrators, and the role of the school counselor began to shift. Structures were put in place to begin to implement a CSCP that serviced all students, meeting their academic, personal, social, and career development needs.

Step 5: Continuous Evaluation Using Data

The district's CSCP is continuously developing. School counselors continue to submit monthly data, allowing for reports to be compiled, published, and reviewed by campus principals, district leadership, the board of trustees, and district constituents. The program's focus has expanded to utilize and incorporate process, perception, and student outcome data into practice. School counselors use data to identify school counseling program goals; monitor student progress; assess and evaluate programs; and demonstrate school counseling program effectiveness (Kaffenberg & Young, 2014). This is evident in the school counseling program process of developing needs assessments; assessing stakeholders (students, staff, and parents); gathering and disaggregating the data; identifying priorities; creating calendars (based on priority needs); implementing guidance lessons, small groups, and individual counseling services; conducting pre-/post-tests; gathering student outcome data; reviewing the data; publishing the results; and identifying next steps.

School counselors manage the school counseling program and use data to aid the growth and development of the students and the counseling program. Data has created an opportunity for the CSCP to develop and sustain direct counseling services for all students. District school counselors inspire change and have a reinvigorated outlook on the innovative school counseling services they provide. What is your next step?

Conclusion

School counselors are leaders on school campuses who must advocate for their students and for the counseling field. When advocating with administrators and policy makers, school counselors must be armed with data to support their claims, justify their roles, and demonstrate their impact. Without the data to support their position, school counselors are at risk of being ineffective, which leads to students' needs not being met.

Schmidt (2014) reminded school counselors to collect and analyze data that will aid in creating meaningful goals and objectives for school counseling programming. The process should not be overwhelming and should not be too time consuming. We do not want the data process to overshadow the school counselors' role in working with students. When analyzing the data, we want to focus on areas that will strengthen the comprehensive counseling curriculum. Stone and Dahir (2011) encouraged school counselors to disaggregate data, identify inequities, and make systemic changes that create a climate of equity in practice and policy. We agree wholeheartedly!

Activities

1. Using data for your elementary or secondary school and the CSCP, decide which type of instruments you would use to find out where you spend your time; what your students need based on grades, discipline reports, and attendance logs; and what teachers, parents, and other stakeholders think the school counselor could do to help with student success. Map out the assessments you would use to collect this data. Who would provide the data you need? When would you collect this data? How would you use the data?
2. After you have collected the data in item #1, how would you use the data to be a systemic change agent? Who would need this information, and how would you present it? Create a PowerPoint or some other presentation format to alert administrators and teachers to what the data shows. Be sure to show how your CSCP could improve.
3. This chapter described several types of data. For each type, explain how you could use it in either an elementary or secondary school setting.

4. Discuss the scenarios in this chapter. In each scenario, the school counselor is pro-active and uses data to inform decisions regarding the needs of students. Describe another scenario of your own and explain how data could inform the decisions of a school counselor.
5. The last section of this chapter describes how one school district collected data and implemented systemic changes that enhanced the CSCP and the students in the district. In a small group, discuss how you could use data to benefit any school environment in which you may work.

Resources

Student Interest Survey for Career Clusters:

https://careertech.org/student-interest-survey

Career Test for Students and Adults:

http://yourfreecareertest.com/

References

American School Counselor Association. (2017). *ASCA position statement on high-stakes testing*. Retrieved from http://assessmentresources.pbworks.com/f/High+Stakes.pdf

American School Counselor Association. (2016). *Ethical Standards for School Counselors*. Retrieved from https://www.schoolcounselor.org/asca/media/asca/Ethics/EthicalStandards2016.pdf

American School Counselor Association. (2012). *The ASCA national model: A framework for school counseling programs* (3rd ed.). Alexandria, VA: Author.

Centers for Disease Control and Prevention. (2015). *Youth risk behavior survey data*. Retrieved from www.cdc.gov/yrbs

Dahir, C., & Stone, B. (2011). *School counselor accountability* (3rd ed.). [Bookshelf Online]. Retrieved from https://bookshelf.vitalsource.com/#/books/9780133000450/

Davis, T. E. (2015). *Exploring school counseling: Professional practices and perspectives* (2nd ed.). Stanford, CT: Cengage Learning.

Dollarhide, C. T., & Saginak, K. A. (2017). *Comprehensive school counseling programs: K-12 delivery systems in action* (3rd ed.). Upper Saddle River, NJ: Pearson.

Eduphoria! (n.d.). Retrieved from www.eduphoria.net/

Ekstrom, R. B., Elmore, P. B., Schafer, W. D., Trotter, T. V., & Webster, B. (2004). A survey of assessment and evaluation activities of school counselors. *Professional School Counseling, 8*(1), 24–30.

Erford, T. E. (2011). *Transforming the school counseling profession* (3rd ed.). Upper Saddle River, NJ: Pearson.

ESchool Media, Inc. (n.d.). Retrieved July 11, 2017, from https://eschoolmedia.com

Every Student Succeeds Act (ESSA) s1177 (114th). (2015).

Gysbers, N. C. (2010). *School counseling principles: Remembering the past, shaping the future*. Alexandria, VA: American School Counselor Association.

Gysbers, N. C., & Henderson, P. (2006). *Developing & managing your school guidance and counseling program* (4th ed.). Alexandria, VA: American Counseling Association.

Gysbers, N. C., & Henderson, P. (2012). *Developing and managing your school guidance and counseling program* (5th ed.). Alexandria, VA: American Counseling Association.

Gysbers, N. C., & Lapan, R. T. (2009). *Strengths-based career development for school guidance and counseling programs*. Ann Arbor, MI: Counseling Outfitters.

Kaffenberg, C., & Young, A. (2014). *Making data work*. Alexandria, VA: American Counseling Association.

Lee, C. C. (2007). *Counseling for social justice*. Alexandria, VA: American Counseling Association.

McLain, J. M. (2014). *Aligning Hispanic school counselor roles with administrator perceptions* (Order No. 3581906). ProQuest Dissertations & Theses Global (1635277084). Retrieved from https://ezproxy.shsu.edu/login?url=http://search.proquest.com/docview/1635277084?accountid=7065

Murray, P. V., Levitov, J. E., Castenell, L., & Joubert, J. H. (1987). Qualitative evaluation methods applied to a high school counseling center. *Journal of Counseling and Development, 65*(5), 259–261.

No Child Left Behind Act of 2001, Pub. L. No. 107-110, 20 U.S.C. 6301 et seq. (2002).

Schmidt, J. (2003). *Counseling in Schools: Essential services and comprehensive programs* (4th ed.). Boston, MA: Allyn & Bacon.

Payne, A. F. (1924). Problems in vocational guidance. *National Vocational Guidance Association Bulletin, 2*, 61–63.

Ratliff, K., Ebbs, S., & Isom, M. (2012). *Influence of technology in school counseling*. Retrieved June 5, 2017, from http://edutrendsonline.com/2012/12/18/influence-of-technology-in-school-counseling/

Schmidt, J. J. (2014). *Counseling in schools: Comprehensive programs of responsive services for all students* (6th ed.). Upper Saddle River, NJ: Pearson.

Stone, C. B., & Dahir, C. A. (2011). *School counselor accountability: A MEASURE of student success* (3rd ed.). Upper Saddle River, NJ: Pearson.

Toggl—Free Time Tracking Software. (n.d.). Retrieved July 11, 2017, from https://toggl.com/

White House. (2015, December 2). *FACT SHEET: Congress acts to fix no child left behind*. Retrieved from www.whitehouse.gov/the-press-office/2015/12/03/fact-sheet- 123 congress-acts-fix-no-child-left-behind.

Section IV

Leadership, Professional Ethics, and Supervision

12

School Counselor Leadership

Dr. Lisa A. Wines, Dr. Carol Hightower-Parker, Dr. Lia Rosales, and Sharon D. Bey

ASCA NATIONAL MODEL

Leadership

Advocacy

ASCA SCHOOL COUNSELOR COMPETENCIES

I-B-2. Serves as a leader in the school and community to promote and support student success

I-B-3. Advocates for student success

ASCA PRINCIPLES

Principle 7: School counselors can help other adults enhance their work with students' academic/educational, career, and personal-social development and for the purpose of removing barriers to individual student success.

Principle 20: Leadership for the school counseling programs is a shared responsibility between school counselors and school principals.

ASCA ETHICAL STANDARDS FOR SCHOOL COUNSELORS (2016)

A.1.g. Are knowledgeable of laws, regulations and policies affecting students and families and strive to protect and inform students and families regarding their rights.

A.3.a. Collaborate with administration, teachers, staff and decision makers around school-improvement goals.

A.10.c. Identify resources needed to optimize education.

B.1.c. Adhere to laws, local guidelines and ethical practice when assisting parents/guardians experiencing family difficulties interfering with the student's welfare.

B.1.e. Inform parents of the mission of the school counseling program and program standards in academic, career and social/emotional domains that promote and enhance the learning process for all students.

B.2.b. Design and deliver comprehensive school counseling programs that are integral to the school's academic mission; driven by student data; based on standards for academic, career and social/emotional development; and promote and enhance the learning process for all students.

B.2.d. Provide leadership to create systemic change to enhance the school.

B.2.f. Provide support, consultation, and mentoring to professionals in need of assistance when in the scope of the school counselor's role.

B.2.g. Inform appropriate officials, in accordance with school board policy, of conditions that may be potentially disruptive or damaging to the school's mission, personnel and property while honoring the confidentiality between the student and the school counselor to the extent feasible, consistent with applicable law and policy.

CACREP STANDARDS 2016

Section 5-G, Entry-Level Specialty Areas, School Counseling

Contextual Dimensions

2.a. School counselor roles as leaders, advocates, and systems change agents in P-12 schools

2.d. School counselor roles in school leadership and multidisciplinary teams

2.j. Qualities and styles of effective leadership in schools

Practice

3.b. Design and evaluation of school counseling programs

3.l. Techniques to foster collaboration and teamwork within schools

3.n. Use of accountability data to inform decision making

3.o. Use of data to advocate for programs and students

Introduction

Leadership in the school counseling literature has been described as a school counselor having the ability to enact and effect change, within students and the program (Studer, 2015; Wright, 2012). Another prominent author in the field of school counseling has linked leadership and advocacy as a part of the transformation movement (Erford, 2015). On the American School Counselor Association (ASCA) website, leadership is described as an attitude and state of mind, not necessarily an innate ability. For the authors of this chapter, leadership for the school counselor is not *just doing*; it is the *process to becoming* catapulted into a *way of being*. In other words, leadership is usually a series of actions, often embellished with identified titles, subsequently becoming one's true professional essence. Inherent identities or alternative/graduating titles often given to school counseling professionals are as follows: lead counselor, counselor liaison, coordinator of counseling, district counseling director, and guidance director—just to mention a few. These titles are often viewed in the light of leadership and considered as a promotion from simply serving in the role of a school counselor.

Across the nation, the field of counseling has experienced initiatives that supported the shifts in making school counselors equal partners in the academic success of students. Several professional development initiatives for school counselors are on the forefront of the continued transformation of the profession. There are no one-size-fits-all school initiatives. Each school district, as well as the schools in the districts, have unique characteristics and needs; therefore, incorporating interventions and initiatives can enhance counseling-related services for students in need, along with those on the cusp of reaching remarkable goals.

State Initiatives, Federal Mandates, Training Initiatives

State initiatives for school counselors as leaders can be inherent within the laws of the residing state, whereas federal mandates are imposed on the states and their local governments. Both state and federal directives should serve as excellent opportunities to begin to understand the calls being placed on school counselors for the students served in public and private educational establishments. Figure 12.1 will aid in understanding the intersection of federal, state, and local mandates, along with integration of standards and competencies for both the school counselor and the student—serving as a basis to strategically plan and work through elements of designing and refining a comprehensive school counseling program.

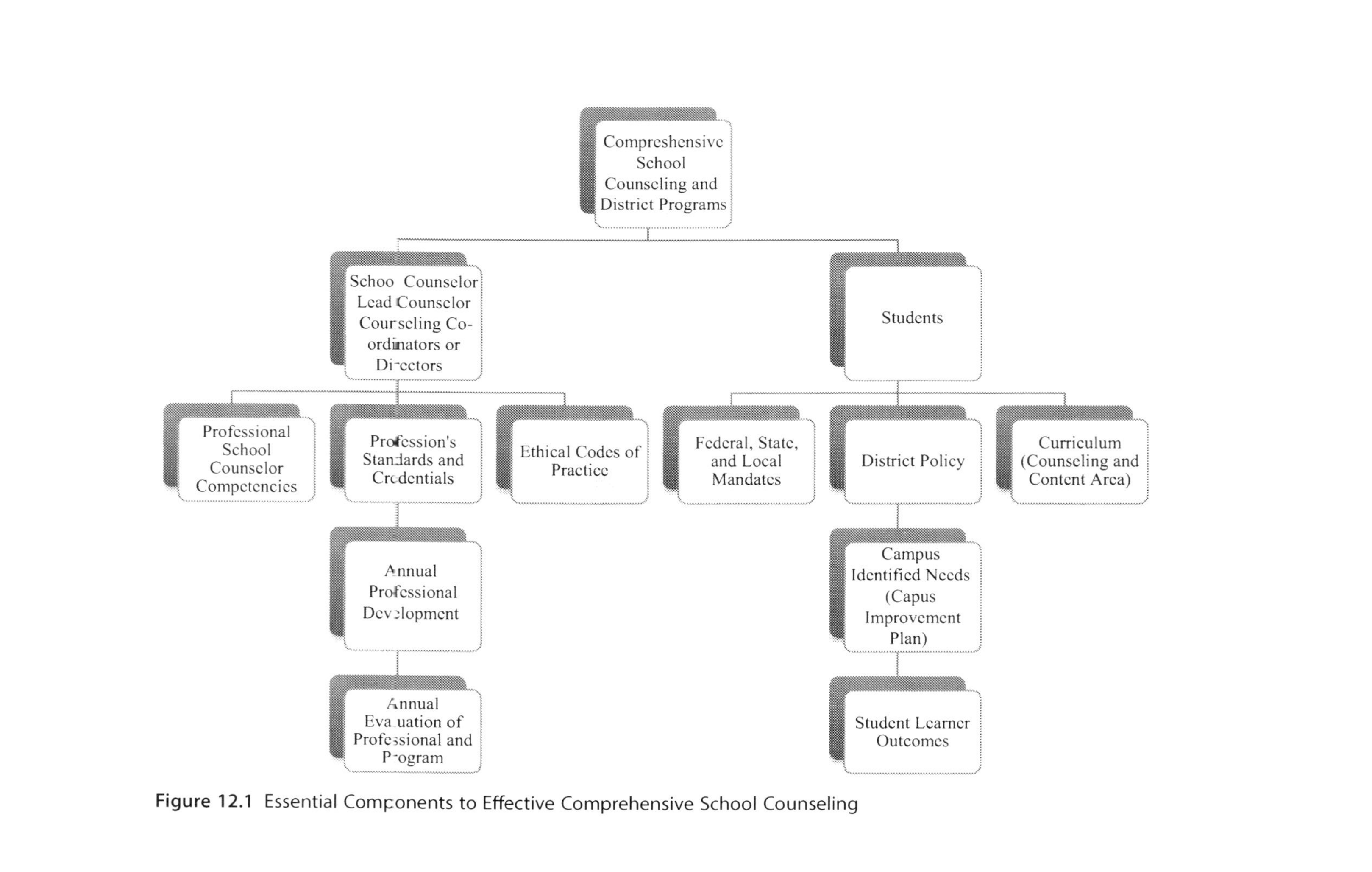

Figure 12.1 Essential Components to Effective Comprehensive School Counseling

Figure 12.1 details the essential components relevant to building a comprehensive school counseling program. These components, relative to the school counselor leader, should be infused within and throughout the comprehensive school counseling program. The ASCA Professional School Counselor Competencies, CACREP 2016 Standards, Credentials (earned or in-progress), ASCA Ethical Codes of Practice, and the professional development and annual evaluation are essential components. For students, considering and then combining driving forces of mandates, policy, and curriculum are essential when establishing the needs of the campus drives student learning outcomes.

ASCA Leadership Specialist Training

To ensure a competent leadership school counseling program, the American School Counselor Association (ASCA) offers a new leadership program, The School Counseling Leadership Specialist Program. This 50-contact-hour program is focused on developing and using leadership qualities in various school settings. Participants complete reading assignments and exams to earn this special designation, which is good for five years.

The training developed for school counseling leadership outlines learning objectives that contribute to understanding the nature and attributes of school counselor leadership, highlight various leadership theories and principles, demonstrate effective leadership in traditionally non-leadership roles, identify the sources of power and authority in the school environment, develop personal leadership attributes, assist in development of greater self-awareness, describe how leaders affect systemic change organizationally, and encourage collaboration with individuals at higher levels of authority. Essentially, these are all ways to effectively collaborate with all stakeholders, provide an overview of inherent challenges of leadership in educational settings, highlight policy governance, and monitor, evaluate, and manage your comprehensive program. Details regarding the leadership specialist training can be found on the ASCA website, www.schoolcounselor.org.

In addition to the leadership training, ASCA has developed several specialist trainings that would optimize the practices of school counselors and expand their leadership abilities. These trainings consist of school counselors having the option to specialize in anxiety and stress problems, bullying prevention, closing the achievement gap, cultural competency, grief and loss, legal and ethical issues, mental health specialist issues, school counseling data, school counseling leadership, students with special needs, and trauma and crisis (www.schoolcounselor.org/school-counselors-members/professional-development/asca-u). Becoming a specialist in any of these areas can provide critical information and assistance to students, families, and teachers and enhance the role of the professional school counselor. Expertise is an important part of being a school leader, along with establishment of a known professional identity. In general, the school counselor has unique expertise in mental health issues, communication and collaboration skills, and consultation abilities, making no other school personnel known to have had the extensive training in these areas.

Indiana Gold Star School Counselor Initiative

The Indiana Gold Star School Counseling Initiative provides a model for exemplary counseling programing and resources available to support success in any school counseling program. Since 1989, the state of Indiana, through the Indiana Student Achievement Institute, provides a four-part workshop series for schools wishing to upgrade their school counseling program. The workshops are presented to school teams that are made up of two to six members of parents, teachers, community members, and students. The results of many years of effort are influenced by materials that can be adopted and used by other states and schools, such as meeting agendas, PowerPoint presentations, facilitator notes, and document template and related consensus-building tools. These resources are available at www.asainstitute.org/schoolcounseling.

Colorado Department of Education Grant Program

The state of Colorado's Department of Education offers a School Counseling Corps Grant Program in order to support effective school-based counseling. This program began in 2008, allowing for increased effectiveness and availability of programs and services. An article published by Arredondo, Jesse, Billig, and Weston-Sementelli (2016) provided a report creatively highlighting a justification and need for the grant, a description of program requirements, a student exemplar, grant cycle, method of program delivery and implementation cycle, along with expectations of goal setting and establishment of interventions. The report is finalized with provided resources for those considering applying to the request for proposal.

Texas Model for Comprehensive School Counseling Programs

Texas Education Agency has a comprehensive school counseling model for school counselors called The Texas Model for Comprehensive School Counseling Programs (2017). Not only has the model been revised and is currently in its fifth edition, but the state board of education adopted it into administrative code beginning in 2019. The model has an introduction and five subsequent sections. The introduction provides the history, purpose, and rationale. Section one outlines the responsibilities of school counselors and other staff in a comprehensive school counseling program. Section two highlights the implementation cycle of a program. Section three conveys the foundational components to a comprehensive program. Section four thoroughly defines the four service delivery components of guidance curriculum, responsive services, individual student planning, and system support. Section five presents a scope and sequence in four content areas, such as interpersonal effectiveness, intrapersonal effectiveness, personal health and safety, and post-secondary education and career readiness (The Texas Model for Comprehensive School Counseling Programs, 2017).

Tennessee Model for Comprehensive School Counseling Programs

The state of Tennessee has a model for comprehensive school counseling programs, established in 1997. It has an introduction and appendix with five sections articulated as preconditions, foundation, management systems, delivery systems, and accountability. Preconditions are structural components that incorporate technology, materials, and budget. Foundation covers mission statements, program definition, laws, and policy. Management systems are indicative of data use, action plans, and use of calendars. Delivery systems are identical to those highlighted in the Texas Model Guide. Accountability measures includes report use, audits, and evaluations.

School District Policy

School district policies provide a clear distinction between management responsibilities and governors. Hence, policies related to school counseling programs and changes in federal or state law and local options satisfy current needs at the local level. School counselors have a long record of policies governing education preparations, but few consistent policies and procedures for school-based counseling programs that address student needs are evident. Broadly, school district policy can address ethics, confidentiality, crisis intervention and prevention, and teen pregnancy. As a school leader, it is essential to know policy and have resources available when interpretation of the policies are needed.

This section provides many state and federal initiatives to consider in leading comprehensive school counseling programs. Our suggestion is to research your district policy regarding school counseling, and then visit your state agency's website and see what information is available to school counselors that helps identify or provide structure to your work ahead. Then, from a national or federal perspective, you may wish to locate resources that help the school counselors in your building to gain perspective on essential components necessary for your program. Finally, adopt a state model, regardless if it is your own state's or borrowed from another state model. Your program must have an underpinning framework that helps outline and justify the work of the school counselor leader and the necessity of such an operation, relative to your campus or district needs.

Generalizations of the School Counselor Role, Job Description, and Responsibilities

The role of the school counselor varies dependent upon the district and the campus in which the counselor works. Most of the time, the role is predicated upon what predecessors have done before or on school culture. It is our belief that the role of the school counselor is to help others understand what school counseling is, in terms of skills and training, to advocate for students' needs and the delivery of services, to create a comprehensive school counseling program that is data-driven with evaluative components, and to communicate how individuals in the school can access services.

As a school counselor, the role is described as a professional individual, highly qualified to administer counseling services, to students in a K–12 grade setting. School counselors, prior to the new school year beginning, are often responsible for a particular group of students (e.g., either delineated by grade and/or alphabet assignment). Today's school counselors are vital members of the education team. They help all students in the areas of academic achievement, personal/social development, and career development, ensuring that today's students become the productive, well-adjusted adults of tomorrow. The school counselor's daily tasks vary based on whether the work setting is an elementary school, middle school/junior high school, or high school. However, at all levels the counselor's job is to make sure students receive the support they need to succeed academically.

At all levels, the school counselor is a resource for parents to help them understand how to help their children at home with academic, social, and emotional problems. Counselors assist parents in finding resources or agencies for their children with mental health needs that require outside-of-school counseling or therapy. They also assist teachers in helping students with behavior problems and academic problems. Counselors observe children in the classroom or within a small group to assess their strengths, weaknesses, and special needs and provide counseling individually, in small groups, or in classroom settings. Classroom lessons on topics such as bullying, abuse, character development, time management, study habits, anger, self- harm, conflict resolution, and drug and alcohol awareness may be presented during classroom guidance. The selected topics will be based on the needs of your school and the age of your students.

At the high school level, for example, more individual crisis counseling to help students Figure out what they are going to do after high school may be in order. Helping students to select courses that outline a four-year plan in preparation for graduation, then college, and hopefully a career is necessary. Students and parents will need to understand the steps necessary to prepare for and apply to colleges, inclusive of how to apply for financial aid, fill out the Free Application for Federal Student Aid (FAFSA), search for colleges and careers that best fit their needs, complete college applications, prepare for SAT and/or ACT tests, write resumes, and even how to develop good interview skills.

Working with the principal and other building administrators helps ensure that the school counseling curriculum meets the academic needs of your students. In doing the aforementioned, school counselors should set goals for the upcoming year that are reflective in nature (i.e., what went well last year or what would I like to implement that time was not available to do so), and idealistic, in the sense that you hope to see every student assigned to your load benefit from this process.

Program Plan and School Improvement Plan

First and foremost, as the leader and manager of the counseling program, school counselors need to develop program goals that are in alignment with the campus improvement plan (CIP). The CIP (see Appendix 12.1) is the campus' fiscal and instructional blueprint for how identified areas of concerns will be addressed. Within that, goals are created and define how the vision and mission statements of both the counseling program and the school will be carried out (https://tea.texas.gov/Finance_and_Grants/Grants/Federal_Flexibility_Initiative/Schoolwide_Programs/Schoolwide_Programs__Campus_Improvement_Plan/). Additionally, the CIP is a document that the school should understand, have access to, and utilize in establishing the comprehensive school counseling program. The focus should be on the data collected, including the information regarding administrator, student, faculty, and staff needs. Once the school counselor has set three to five SMART (**S**pecific, **M**easurable, **A**ttainable, **R**elevant, and **T**imely) goals, the counselor and the Advisory Council (see Chapter 7 for more information on the Advisory Council) can plan activities to meet those goals, decide on resources needed and who will carry out which tasks, and delineate how the activities will be evaluated. It is our recommendation that the Advisory Council meet at least three times throughout the school year: (1) at the beginning of the year to set up goals and activities for the year, (2) mid-year to review and revise activities, if necessary, for the second semester; and (3) at the end of the year to evaluate the effectiveness of the counseling program and discuss pertinent needs for the next school year.

Use of Data in Planning the Year

The school year can begin at various times dependent upon many factors. The summertime can be convenient for planning to develop the comprehensive school counseling program for the school year. By this time, state and district mandates will be finalized, results from needs assessments and surveys sent out in the spring will be returned and calculated, data from state-mandated tests or other assessments will be available, and the principal will have determined his or her school goals and vision for the upcoming year. The rationale behind the use of data is to understand areas of deficiency or potential growth, along with having a purpose for providing certain services or delivering particular programs (action plans, setting priorities, reporting results, and crafting interventions) [Hatch, 2014].

The first step for the school counselor leader is to collect data from all of these sources, as well as from attendance and discipline records (see Chapter 11 on Data and Assessment). Then, plan an Advisory Council meeting with key people who might include some of these: the principal, assistant principals, curriculum directors, behavior specialists, department chairs, teachers from each subject area, parents, students, community members, feeder school personnel, and other counselors in the building, if there are any. The lead counselor will generally schedule this meeting, but all counselors have a role to play in this important meeting:

- At this meeting, belief statements are developed, making sure everyone understands (a) the counselor's role as an advocate for all students; (b) how the data collected will be used to make program decisions; and (c) what is involved in planning, managing, delivering, and evaluating counseling program activities. All Advisory Council members need to understand that they are valuable and contributing members in developing statements they believe are accurate for the students at your school. Some sample belief statements are:
  - All students are important.
  - All students have the right to participate in the school counseling program.
  - All students deserve the opportunity to achieve their fullest potential.
  - All students' ethnic, cultural, and sexual differences, and special needs are considered in planning and implementing the school counseling program.

Meeting Etiquette and Efficiency

People who work in schools are busy! It is important for the school counselor, who will probably lead many meetings, to be respectful of everyone's time.

Generally, teachers will need to meet during their conference time, before, or after school, so time efficiency is most important. Administrators and staff have many responsibilities; therefore, in the case of any school personnel, meetings should be scheduled in advance. To conduct an efficient meeting, follow these simple steps:

- Create an agenda (see Appendix 12.2) with a time frame in mind. In other words, if there are several items to discuss, provide the number of minutes that will be dedicated to each item.
- When the meeting convenes, ask someone to be a timekeeper who will advise the group when the time is about to run its course for each of the items.
- Start the meeting by asking everyone to introduce themselves and focus on the agenda items in order to accomplish as much as possible in the allotted time.
- Do not let the group members get sidetracked. You can let them know that you are willing to discuss other items not on the agenda later.
- At the end of the discussion of each agenda item, ask the participants to volunteer for the specific tasks that need to be completed, and write these in the notes of the meeting.
- When the meeting is over, review the tasks of each item and who will complete them.
- If possible, on the same day the meeting was held, send an email to the participants to thank them for their attendance and input, provide some brief minutes of the meeting, remind them again of their tasks, and, if necessary, set the date for the next meeting.

Standard Counseling Department Procedures

School counselors must understand and put into place several department procedures as leaders of their schools. A department procedure is best described as a structured process that specifies the operations or activities for the school counseling program, including the responsibilities of the school counselors. Examples of procedures include how to refer students for counseling services or modify graduation plans. As primary members of the counseling department, school counselors should take time to develop department procedures and policies that are continuously implemented and revised on an annual basis. Having department procedures conveys that school counselors who are in leadership positions may wish to outline these procedures for stakeholders on their campus, such as students, administrators, teachers, parents, and staff. It is up to school counselors as to whether these procedures are published to the faculty or staff, or if it serves only as an internal document that administration and school counselors agree upon and can access. Information on what the comprehensive school counseling program is and how to maximize its use are items to include and will be discussed later in this chapter.

In designing the departmental procedures, it is important to pinpoint your audience as students, parents, administrators, teachers, and staff. For students, the department procedures highlight ways in which students can see a school counselor, discuss various timelines that are relevant to student and counselor schedules, and emphasize the importance of returning documents back to the counseling office by the requested deadline and what to do if they are not. It is also recommended to highlight how students actually arrive at the counseling office, what to do if they or a friend are in crisis, and other information that reveals the role of the school counselor while these students are at school throughout the day. Also relevant to students is which counselor they can or should access based on grade level or alphabet assignment or who to contact for specific campus programs. On secondary campuses, there are generally multiple counselors; thus, students need to know who their specific counselor is and what to do if that person is not available.

Department procedures for parents can be fluid because parents need to see school counselors on an as-needed basis. Parents need to be made aware of what the school counseling program offers in terms of services or events provided for students (see Appendix 12.3). They should know a counselor's availability, contact information, and the anticipated time expected to return phone calls and emails. Parents need clarity on how to make requests of the school counselor to see their child for counseling services, and an electronic and site-based location to access all forms and documents relevant to the school counseling department. Parents should be provided website information and know how to access resources available to support their needs.

Department procedures outlined for administrators could consist of describing the purpose of the counseling program, appropriate ways administrators refer students to the counselor, the department approach for other duties as assigned, calendars and schedules and how these different periods of time in the school year affect the school counselor's availability, confidentiality and the counselor's limitations, or perhaps it might address the working and collaborative assistant principal and counselor relationship. Educating administrators about the appropriate role of the school counselor is one of the most important tasks facing school counselors. Working collaboratively on the aforementioned issues helps administrators understand what school counselors should be doing and assures them that there is an organized program for which the school counselor is responsible.

Department procedures for teachers are not dissimilar to what has already been suggested. It is relevant for teachers to understand their roles and responsibilities in a comprehensive school counseling program. Staff development is an essential function when training teachers on these roles. There should be a description of the program in the areas that are addressed for students and how the counseling office can be of assistance to the teachers in the building. The four components of any comprehensive school counseling program should be highlighted for teachers, with emphasis on the areas that they can contribute to or influence. For example, teachers might participate in school counseling core curriculum by conducting lessons that the school counselor has developed. Teachers may also attend individual student planning meetings to help develop four-year plans or other plans for the student's future. Participation in the collection of data is an area that should be highlighted for teachers. For example, their participation in a perception survey that would help to improve the counseling department is an option to highlight. Teachers often want to know how they refer students and then what they need to do in their classrooms to support the student. A section on collaboration, such as team meetings or parent meetings and the process/procedures for those meetings, should be addressed with teachers.

Finally, department procedures for staff are a critical component to training all school personnel. The staff needs to know how important they are to the counselors in the comprehensive school counseling program. Staff includes, but is not limited to, cafeteria employees, custodians, paraprofessionals, secretaries or administrative assistants, translators or interpreters, and other district support personnel such as the school psychologist, speech therapist, Community Youth Services (CYS) workers, and mental health or special education counselors. These important persons need to be aware of their observations of students' behaviors or statements that students might make while in their presence. Counselors are always able and should be willing to train any of these individuals regarding what signs to look for that may signal a need to see the counselor. These types of trainings are critical to effectively managing the comprehensive school counseling program. Additionally, if training is not an option due to time restrictions, counselors can address in the policy and safe schools plan how staff can access the school counselor to use their experience and expertise to make sure those students are safe and secure (see Appendix 12.1).

Professional Development for Staff and Faculty

It is ideal to remember that the school counselor is a leader and the developmental expert on the campus, and therefore, a provider of important information to the school faculty and staff. School counselors as leaders prepare to train faculty and staff at multiple points during the year. Usually, they consider information that is helpful for teachers and administrators to use regarding students who are in vulnerable and volatile situations (i.e., suicide threat, pregnancy outcry, suspected abuse, cutting or other self-harming behaviors). Additionally, administrators and teachers need to be updated on changes in state laws or statutes regarding the role of the school counselor and students enrolled in K–12 schools. Each year, school counselors decide on the topics to cover during staff development or in-service days and narrow them down to what information is needed to help students during times of crisis or what information is required to be disseminated to the school faculty and staff.

Topics include, but are not limited to, how to report child abuse or neglect, the procedures of the counseling office, threat assessment, or how to recognize specific characteristics in students that help identify areas in need of support. School counselors can spend time training on different issues students may have that could affect their learning. These trainings create an understanding of how teachers and staff can recognize these characteristics in students and provide them with strategies that are most helpful in their response.

Initially, school counselors might plan staff development to create a schedule indicative of trainings that are offered. This schedule should be produced for all stakeholders to review as a part of the comprehensive school counseling program. Next, school counselors schedule time with the building principal or the person responsible for putting together the training schedule. The needs of the campus and understanding the areas that teachers have felt less competent in are relevant in deciding the topics to focus on during that training. Keep in mind that often, because of other important topics needing to be conveyed to teachers, it is difficult for various individuals to get placed on the schedule and granted the period of time needed to present these topics. Table 12.1 is a chart of topics available for these in-service or staff development trainings.

Once the school counselor's calendar of training is complete, then the programs must be planned and implemented. School counselors must organize a training agenda that considers the amount of time needed to accomplish the training. A sign-in sheet should be created and maintained so that there is a record of attendance and an easy identification for those who need to make up the training. Most participants appreciate a handout and something to view during a presentation (e.g., PowerPoint, Prezi, video). Handouts and visual aids will help the counselor organize the presentation and maximize time. Remember that time will probably be limited, so it is best to be organized, brief, and to the point. Staff development may occur in the

Table 12.1 Suggested Topics for In-Service or Staff Development

Assessment Information	Confidentiality	Program or Service Update
Accommodations for Students	Elements or Updates to the Comprehensive School Counseling Program	Referral Process for Teachers and Students
Behavioral Modification	Emergency Procedures for Counseling	Reporting Procedures for Abuse or Neglect
Characteristics of Specific Mental Health Concerns	Individual Educational Plans	Role of the Professional School Counselor
Classroom Management Techniques	Next Year Registration and Transition Procedures	State Law or Statute Update

mornings before school begins, after school adjourns, or on specially designated staff development days.

Role of the Lead Counselor

The role of a lead counselor is to serve as the "head" of the school counseling department and as a liaison between the counselors and administrators of the school building. The principal will often convey messages through the lead counselor to deliver to the team, and in a similar fashion, the lead counselor shares the needs and desires as requested by his or her counselor counterparts to the principal. Consider the lead counselor a spokesperson or representative of the department, who should be aware of the programs and services taking place at each grade level. The lead counselor serves as the primary consultant to crisis situations, thus liaising between the campus and the district coordinator or director of school counseling. Following is a general job description of the roles and responsibilities of a lead counselor:

- Know all facets and elements of your comprehensive school counseling program, including the data that drives the program
- Oversee the operations of a school counseling program
- Delegate other coordinated programs and services for homeless and homebound students, before- and after-school clubs, and tutoring
- Conduct evaluations of secretary and department counselors
- Manage department budget or allocate funding for programs
- Develop and/or revise the comprehensive school counseling program

- Conduct weekly or monthly department meetings
- Serve as a consultant in crisis or critical incidents
- Act as liaison between campus and district administrators
- Help colleagues coordinate student transition efforts between elementary and secondary counselors
- Share professional development/workshop information received with the team
- Mediate parent concerns regarding the work of their child's assigned school counselor
- Ensure that counselors have all pertinent information needed to be effective in their job roles
- Establish or revise the counseling department phone tree
- Attend and report on information obtained in administrative, district, and school board meetings
- Share data obtained from administrators and databases with team members
- Understand district policy and monitor its implementation department-wide
- Assist the Principal with the hiring of qualified school counselors

Specifically, here are some programs the first author coordinated or delivered in her 10 years of experience. Although inappropriate counselor activities exist, the truth of the first author's experience entailed serving as testing coordinator (state and AP testing), dance team director, peer mediation coordinator, district trainer, peer assistance & leadership (PALS) program coordinator, professional learning community (PLC) facilitator, new arrival center (NAC) coordinator, student assistance liaison, homeless liaison (EASE counselor), gear-up coordinator, counselor's corner, and communication liaison.

A Counselor's Exemplar

The fourth author was a school counselor and lead counselor for over 30 years in a large, fast-growing suburban/urban school district. During this time, she served as a school counselor at the elementary, middle/junior high, and high school levels. The duties assigned differed over the years, partly due to state legislative changes and partly due to the needs of the administration. The position was unique in the structure of the school, and everyone had a different idea of what counselors do. Their ideas were based on their own experiences and not on a true knowledge of the role. The responsibility to teach the leadership role to her staff and administration was her priority, therefore being done purposefully and with transparency.

I discovered, first hand, that when I advertised to all stakeholders my goals and the activities planned for the school year, solicited their input, and used data to show the needs and outcome of my activities, I gained their support, which enabled me to spend more time on counseling-type activities with direct contact with students, and I was assigned fewer non-counseling duties. Through leadership, advocacy, and collaboration, I understood that school counselors promote equity and access to rigorous educational experiences for all students. Equally, school counselors support a safe learning environment and work to safeguard the human rights of all members of the school community (Sandhu, 2000) and address the needs of all students through culturally relevant prevention and intervention programs that are a part of a comprehensive school counseling program (Lee, 2001). Inevitably, the school counselor is an important leader in a school's education team.

As the leader and chief facilitator of the comprehensive school counseling program, my work was directly tied to the academic success of the students; therefore, it was my job to provide counseling services to all students in the areas of academic achievement, personal and social development, and career development. There were resources available to help organize, plan, design, implement, and evaluate the school counseling program. The ASCA National Model (2012) and the Texas State Model for Comprehensive School Counseling Programs were resources that provided a framework to guide counselors through the process of planning and implementing a balanced counseling program. These same resources will help manage your time, so all students benefit from the school counseling program. Without a program, counselors will most likely provide only direct services to SOME students as opposed to ALL students.

We offer a few closing thoughts related to being in a leadership role. It is highly collaborative—less directive or top-down. School counselors feel supported by this individual and often times, when time crunches are evident, the lead counselor is the most reliable resource available. Depending on life's happenings, they are often the first to arrive and last to leave, and usually the one to take up the slack when necessary. They often partner with other colleagues on extreme student cases, and will sit in on counseling sessions to ensure that district policy and procedures are followed. These individuals tend to be fair, reasonable, recognize the strengths in their counselors, and are a positive asset to a campus and program.

Role of the District Guidance and Counseling Director

The responsibility of the district leader of guidance and counseling is complex and calls for delivery services that impact the entire school system. This leader must engage in: (1) a meticulous study and understanding of national, state, and school mandates; (2) understanding of district and school data and school improvement plans that impact comprehensive counseling programs that meet the expressed and implied needs of all students; and (3) leading school counselors to be change agents while working with students, families, faculty, the community, and with the cooperation of district administrators and campus principals. District guidance and counseling directors' access district and school data and collect campus improvement plan information. Additionally, these district leaders must study and understand national, state, and school district mandates, which often can be accomplished by actively participating in state professional counseling organizations. The descriptions that follow detail the role and responsibilities of the director or coordinator of counseling and includes the school district central administration expectations, the American School Counselor Association (ASCA) National Model: A Framework for School Counseling Programs (ASCA, 2012), as well as the expectations of the campus principal.

Supervisor and District Administrator

Directors or coordinators of guidance and counseling serve as the supervisor and/or administrator responsible for coordinating the delivery of comprehensive guidance and counseling services for K–12 students in the school district. The person in this position often has broad areas of responsibility, such as working to promote student academic success with counselors, staff, parents, and community citizens, obtaining and developing personnel in the district, maintaining effective relationships with the community, and managing budget(s) and facilities use. General district supervision involves leadership, teaming and collaborating, advocacy, assessment, and the use of data within the framework of technological and multicultural competencies for academic achievement and to demonstrate accountability.

A primary responsibility for the director or coordinator of guidance and counseling is also to organize, supervise, and evaluate the work of counselors at all levels, as well as to supervise and coordinate the district organizational unit, implementation and evaluation of career guidance, college readiness, and admissions initiatives in the schools. As schools become accountable for removing barriers to student academic access, the director or coordinator is likely to provide consultation or related services to address special academic needs. In addition, the following may also be provided: career planning and testing services, educational and occupational services, school counseling core curriculum, impact of counseling services, and follow-up information that may be provided to administrators and other stakeholders. To continue the synergistic process, the director or coordinator may guide department meetings that serve to generate new ideas and provide a platform for participation in continuous improvement to remain a strategic partner in data-driven school improvement. Following is a general job description found at the El Paso Independent School District website:

Instructional and Program Management

- Assists school counselors to develop, implement and evaluate comprehensive school guidance and counseling program.
- Assists with individual and group monitoring/mentoring of school counselors and at-risk coordinators.
- Assists with the monitoring/mentoring of school counselor interns.
- Represents the district as a liaison with school and community agencies.
- Assists with the supervision of student records and transcripts to ensure compliance as per state and federal regulations.
- Assists with post-secondary planning and implementation.
- Assists with post-secondary education funding options and financial aid.
- Assists with planning and implementation of transitioning plans from elementary to middle, middle to high, and high school to a post-secondary institution.
- Assists in planning and implementation of college/career awareness and exploration program.
- Assists in the identification and implementation of interventions to enhance student success and reduce the dropout rates.

Monitor Programs

Assists with monitoring PEIMS data collection to ensure appropriate data submission to the Texas Education Agency.

Student Management

Collaborates with other departments which provide counseling services to ensure cohesive implementation and delivery of services.

Personnel Management

Assists with the training, supervision and monitoring of new counselors and at-risk coordinators.

Policy, Reports and Law

- Supports the goals and objectives of the District.
- Adheres to state and district standards, policies, regulations, and procedures.
- Commits to current professional standards of competence and practice.
- Promotes and follows ethical standards for school counselors, including confidentiality.
- Commits to professional development.

Communication and Community Relations

- Serves as a district representative to a variety of District and community committees.
- Demonstrates professional and responsible work habits.
- Uses professional written and oral communication and interpersonal skills.

Maintaining High-Quality School Counselors

To keep high-quality school counselors, district guidance and counseling leaders play a significant role in interviewing candidates, making hiring recommendations, and mentoring successful school counselors. The director or coordinator is frequently expected to offer ongoing professional development workshops and activities for the school counselors in the district. Also, the district leader is the chief advocate for the school counselors in the district. In this role, the director or coordinator presents information to district personnel regarding the appropriate roles of school counselors and the value that school counselors bring to their schools and the students who attend them. Generally, this information is well-received if accompanied by data.

School counselors deal with life-threatening situations, heartbreaking family issues, rules, regulations, district policies, and all manner of complex situations. School counselors often need consultation on any number of issues, and the district leader must be available to provide this to those who seek it. Consultation requires a special set of skills and vast knowledge of the many issues that school counselors shoulder. See Chapter 14 on Supervision for more information on the skills needed to provide ample support to school counselors.

Budget

School counselors are often allocated an annual budget. This budget is sometimes given by the building principal or allocated at the district level.

Depending on the amount of resources available, budgeted funds are available to assist counselors in the design of the comprehensive program and in the delivery of necessary services to students (see Appendix 12.4). When school counselors receive their annual budget, it is important to have a projected use for budget and expenditures at the end of the year. This includes the use of donated money or resources. Likewise, the use of the budget should directly align with program goals or campus initiatives. Never should available resources be utilized for a school counselor's personal gain.

Too Many Non-Counseling-Related Duties: Case Examples

In one district, at all three levels, the counselors did not have school counseling programs, and they were conducting many non-counseling duties such as testing coordination for state-mandated tests, gifted and talented screening, 504 coordination, response to intervention (RTI) coordination, fundraising, performing morning duty, attending bus duty and lunch duty, and conducting other duties as assigned by their principals (others were listed in the role of the lead counselor section). In small districts where staff is limited and everyone has extra duties, it is not uncommon to find counselors involved in many non-counseling tasks; however, when the non-counseling duties clearly outweigh counseling duties, red flags should be raised. The problem in this district was that these counselors were not doing enough counseling because they just could not fit it in. Their other duties took up too much of their time, and they had to squeeze in time to have direct contact with students.

After speaking with one elementary school counselor who was extremely frustrated about her lack of time with her students, the fourth author went to talk to her principal to see if she was aware of the frustration level of her school counselor. The fourth author found out that the principal had no evidence that the counselor was doing any counseling lessons and activities and had not been introduced to the idea of a comprehensive school counseling program; thus, she felt her counselor wanted to do these extra duties and had the time to do them. This speaks volumes to the importance of planning, advertising, and involving administrators in developing the counseling program. A calendar of planned activities is necessary to publish each semester, and an evaluation of the impact that your counseling activities has on the success of your students is critical.

Advocacy in School Counselor Leadership

It is important that school counselor leaders are knowledgeable about their roles as school counselors and utilize their training as a tool to educate and advocate for their profession and their counselor colleagues. In 1998, Chi Sigma Iota, the honor organization of professional counselors, suggested that "without advocacy for both counselors and their clients, neither is meaningful. The school counseling profession has put leadership and advocacy in the central place for all school counselors as part of the National Center for Transforming School Counseling's (NCTSC) new vision for school counseling" (Erford, 2015).

Advocacy can be a group effort or an individual endeavor. Either way, school counselor leaders should take the helm when it comes to advocacy. School counselors are expected to assist every student to reach his or her academic, career, and college dreams beginning in kindergarten (Erford, 2015). How can counselors be expected to do this without first advocating for their profession?

Training graduate students and school counselors to advocate and set up an advocacy plan will assist future and current counselors as they grow in their professional positions. All too often, school counselors are asked to do tasks that are out of their job description and scope. Counselors need to remember that most administrators have never taken school counseling courses and are not familiar with the parts of the professional school counseling role. In many situations, an administrator's realities of the school counseling role differ from the ideals offered by trained counselor leaders. In a time when school districts are graded by standardized assessment scores, school counselors are being asked to do non-guidance activities such as tutoring, administering tests, registering new students, and changing schedules. In hopes of raising scores, there is a need to inform other school professionals on the role of the school counselor.

The ASCA National Model: A Framework for School Counseling (2012) reveals the academic, personal/social, and career development component for all students. Counselors often do not have time to address the personal/social component, and educators do not realize the importance of this component. Working and stressing the personal/social aspect of improving student achievement only comes from advocating for the school counseling profession. Everything school counselors do should be done with the intention of improving student achievement. That is the role of the school counselor; therefore, it is imperative that advocacy training for school counselors take place. School counselors do this in a variety of ways. Counselor leaders need to realize that advocacy is a must, as our students are depending on us. School counselor leaders are critical players in ensuring that all school counselors are advocating for their profession. They cannot afford not to. The future of our students and our profession are at stake. Counselor leaders are in an optimal position to be change agents.

Baggerly and Osborn (2006) found that school counselors who more frequently implemented the ASCA National Model (2012) roles and duties were more likely to be satisfied and committed to their career than were those who performed such duties less frequently. With increasing the counselor job satisfaction, there is a relational benefit to the effectiveness of improving student achievement. Those responsible in the development of the ASCA National Model (2012) seem to advocate for the Certified School Counselor (CSC), allowing a focus on academic, personal/social, and career well-being of all the students through the delivery system that includes guidance curriculum, individual student planning, responsive services, and system support. Delivery of an effective ASCA National Model is essential in order to improve student academic performance and address behaviors that are barriers to academic performance and achievement. School counselor leaders address the elements of the counseling program relevant to the numerous student needs associated with the achievement gap. If the comprehensive school counseling program is created, implemented, and managed correctly, student achievement will take place, and this only comes with advocacy of the profession.

District directors and lead counselors should lead by example in order to gain the respect of their fellow counselor colleagues by being engaged and offering continued support to all school stakeholders. As a matter of fact, in the February 2010 *Professional School Counseling Journal* revealed seven overarching strategies that participants used as social justice advocates enacting change in their communities. One strategy stressed the importance of educating others about the school counseling role as an advocate. That is the only way change will come about is through advocacy, and it begins with the leaders. One counselor shared in her own words that she has to help not only the principals, but teachers too. She helps them see the connections between academic performance and developmental issues, social issues, emotional issues, and realizing that you cannot just attend to one of these areas without the others. When counselors were asked to do tasks that deterred them from their advocacy work, they had to clarify the nature of their role.

Another counselor mentioned that non-guidance tasks were hindering her advocacy. She had to say to her administrators, "I'm not really able to do these things. I'm really here to do my area of expertise." Counselors had to clarify their role, and this can be problematic for them. This can be difficult as school counselors feel the pressure of being liked and also because most counselors want to avoid conflict. School counselors need the support of their fellow counselor colleague leaders more than ever in order to feel comfortable and confident to say this to their administrators. It all starts at the top. Participants in this study perceived their identity as an advocate as central to their advocacy work, and training programs should support trainees in the assessment and development of this identity throughout the training process (ASCA, 2010). If we are to lead and advocate, change must come from the inside out. If you can change the heart, then and only then can you inspire others to change. After all, that's what drives us to do our jobs.

School Counselor Leadership Academy

The development and implementation of a leadership academy is ideal for school counseling districts and departments. In description, the leadership academy is a program designed to cultivate school counselor leaders through curriculum, collaboration, mentorship, and activity design. The purpose of a leadership academy is to groom future school counselors into leadership roles in which competence is the basis of the program, a systemic form of continuous recruitment efforts. There are five considerations described in the following sections.

Establishment of a Selection Committee

Each leadership academy should have a selection committee identified, with diverse representation consisting of differences in gender, years of experience, ethnic and racial make-up, and various experiences at elementary or secondary levels with similarities in a commitment and desire to serve on the committee. The district organizer or chair of this committee should remember to outline the roles of the committee members (e.g., to create a formal rubric for selection, to select a certain number of cohort members, to develop the program requirements, and to make recommendations to building principals for hiring purposes, to send out notification of acceptance, and the amount of time committed to this particular work). Committee members should have the opportunity if they have demonstrated a job well done to serve a certain number of years keeping the option open to recruit new members over time.

Recruitment of Cohort Members

Typically, recruitment efforts begin in late spring for the following year and are spear-headed and structured by the district guidance and counseling department. These recruitment efforts can be for current teachers who are pursuing school counseling as a profession or for current school counselors who desire to become lead counselors or school district counseling directors. A cohort model is recommended so that participants formulate networks and relationships district-wide. An email invitation is sent to all lead counselors and counselors who are the only one assigned on their campus (see Appendix 12.5).

Criteria for Applying

The criteria established for eligibility begins with the interested individual writing a letter of intent. Depending on whether the individual is a teacher or counselor, three years' counseling and/or teaching experience is required. The following requirements must be met: the individual must (a) write his or her own letter of interest; (b) have an advocate, a lead counselor, and principal identified who will write recommendation letters; and (c) already be employed in the district. The letter written by a lead counselor should convey demographic information such as name and years of experience and should highlight the strengths of the individual and rationale for recommending this applicant. Finally, a letter from the principal should be submitted with similar information that the lead or head counselor provided. These letters allow the selection committee to see the applicant from a panoramic perspective. The individual that designs the program has the autonomy to stipulate what needs to be included in the letters from the applicant, the lead counselor, and principal and whether a survey is included for these individuals to complete.

Cohort Selection Process

The selection process of cohort members is non-biased and should take approximately two weeks depending on the number of applicants. A rubric (quantitative portion) is what committee members use in their reviews of the applicants' information packets, along with an interview process (qualitative portion). After calculating total scores, applicant packets should be ordered from the highest scores obtained to the lowest scores obtained, and decision letters should be either emailed or mailed to the interested applicants only. Members selected for the cohort are individuals who come highly recommended from the school district and are the first to be considered for school counseling leadership positions (e.g., lead counselor, district directors or coordinators, vertical leads, or district crisis team membership).

Program Requirements

The trainer should stipulate that all requirements must be fulfilled for the applicants to remain in the leadership program. These requirements are suggested and can be modified or changed based on the recommendations of so the selection committee. Schools are normally in session for approximately nine to ten months. Although the leadership academy has requirements, it should not be impossible for participants to complete the program. Consider having participants meet five to six times throughout the year. Each meeting can be two to three hours long, with the following activities designed to increase one's leadership skills:

- Book study
- Training by former cohort members, facilitators, or district leaders
- Theme-based teaching (leadership skills, communication, effective documentation, mentorship)
- District policy and procedures in counseling
- Development or change of school culture

In understanding a district's need to groom future school counselors, a leadership academy such as the one outlined here is a timely process available to maintain highly qualified, trained school counselors. These professionals, often just graduating from university programs, fail to have this sort of insight provided to them prior to being hired on a campus.

Activities

1. Select a comprehensive school counseling model that will serve as the foundation for your school's program. Outline and then document the process of selection, which includes the voice of many stakeholders.
2. Access your school district policies to understand how the work of a school counselor is governed within the district. Then begin to develop your campus department policy and procedures for the school counseling program.
3. Using suggested topics, plan the professional development training schedule for faculty and staff.
4. Plan the annual budget for the counseling department by making this request to the campus principal far in advance. A proposal may need to be created, prior to the budget line items, to indicate purpose, need, goals to accomplish, and services to be provided.
5. Help to create a leadership academy in your school district. Make an effort to include specialty training components, which will help to diversity cohort members.

Resources

American School Counselor Association Websites
www.schoolcounselor.org/
www.schoolcounselor.org/asca/media/asca/Ethics/EthicalStandards2016.pdf
www.schoolcounselor.org/asca/media/asca/home/SCCompetencies.pdf
American Student Achievement Institute
www.asainstitute.org/schoolcounseling
Colorado Department of Education Website
www.cde.state.co.us/postsecondary/schoolcounselorcorps
Colorado Department of Education Website
www.cde.state.co.us/postsecondary/colorado-school-counselor-corps-grant-program-early-experiences-and-lessons-learned
Council for Accreditation of Counseling & Related Educational Programs Website
www.cacrep.org/wp-content/uploads/2017/07/2016-Standards-with-Glossary-7.2017.pdf
El Paso Independent School District Website
https://tools.episd.org/tools/inline/file_manager/hr/jobdesc/MTYsNDYsMTYk1E5vMW4e6S4JeOiTKFTcVL9NsSy01Eb-ZMh4BNk488FNOYE7_eCfpCxWidavW4Npq8lUzwfxfkVQ0XXKCYpb0Z7dPIGqP6Zw0E_oh5Ij
Tennessee State Government
https://tn.gov/
Texas Counseling Association
www.txca.org

References

American School Counselor Association. (2010, February). *Professional school counseling*. Alexandria, VA: American School Counselor Association.

American School Counselor Association. (2012). *ASCA national model: A framework for school counseling programs*. Alexandria, VA: American School Counselor Association.

Arredondo, S., Jesse, D., Billig, S. H., & Weston-Sementelli, J. (2016). *Colorado school counselor corps grant program: Early experiences and lessons learned*. San Francisco, CA: WestEd. Retrieved from www.cde.state.co.us/postsecondary/colorado-school-counselor-corps-grant-program-early-experiences-and-lessons-learned

Baggerly, J. & Osborn, D. (2006). School counselors' career satisfaction and commitment: Correlates and predictors. *Professional School Counseling, 9*(3), 197–205.

Erford, B. T. (2015). *Transforming the school counseling profession*. Upper Saddle River, NJ: Pearson Education, Inc.

Hatch, T. (2014). *The use of data in school counseling*. Thousand Oaks, CA: Corwin, a SAGE Company Sandhu (2000).

Studer, J. R. (2015). *The essential school counselor in a changing society*. Thousand Oaks, CA: SAGE Publications.

Texas Education Agency. (2017). *The Texas model for comprehensive school counseling programs* (5th ed.). Austin, TX: Texas Education Agency.

Wright, R. J. (2012). *Introduction to school counseling*. Thousand Oaks, CA: SAGE Publications.

Appendix 12.1

Safe School Plan

(School Year) Committee Members

CHAIRMAN/COUNSELOR
ADMINISTRATOR/PRINCIPAL
PK MEMBER
K MEMBER
1ST MEMBER
2ND MEMBER
3RD MEMBER
4TH MEMBER
SPECIAL EDUCATION
BLOCK
CONTENT
CIS

(School Name)

Safe School Plan (School Year)

SAFE SCHOOLS MISSION STATEMENT
(School Name) in collaboration with parents, community, and staff will:
***increase self-esteem in a positive safe environment**
***promote risk-taking and encourage life-long learning**
***create successful and productive citizens of an ever-changing global society**

Personal Characteristics of Students and Staff

Goal 1: Promote cultural acceptance and an appreciation for diversity amongst everyone.**

Goal 2: Implement a counseling program that provides sound mental health amongst faculty and students.*,**

The School's Physical Environment

Goal 1: Increase the safety of faculty, staff, and students by consistent implementation of our visitor's monitoring system.*

Goal 2: Increase the knowledge of crisis prevention and intervention plans through repetitious practice and training for faculty, staff, and students.*,**

The School's Social Environment

Goal 1: Increase parental involvement at home and in school to achieve goals set forth by (School District) and (Campus Name to increase student success.*

Goal 2: Increase the quality of students' life skills and leadership through Character Education.**

Goal 3: Promote a safe, drug and violence free school.*

The School's Culture

Goal 1: Decrease the acts of disorderly conduct inside and outside the classroom by promoting close bonds between administration, teachers, parents, and students.**

Goal 2: Provide a least restrictive environment for all students.*

***Short Term Goals ~ Goals that are set to be accomplished within the school year. These goals demonstrate immediate improvement in related areas amongst administration, faculty, students, and parents and are expected to increase by roughly 10%.**

****Long Term Goals ~ Goals that are set to be accomplished over an extended period of time. These goals demonstrate gradual improvement in related areas amongst administration, faculty, students, and parents and are expected to increase by roughly 30%.**

Personal Characteristics of Students and Staff

GOAL 1: Promote cultural acceptance and an appreciation for diversity amongst everyone.**

NEEDS ASSESSMENT: Cultural acceptance and appreciation of diversity are generally not things that are embedded in us. It takes exposure, experience, and education to discover these commonalities that exist across our culturally diverse world in which (Campus Name) intends to provide for our students.

Research Based Strategies

*Promote close bonds—Provide opportunities for students to connect to each other, teachers, parents, and the community.

*Change the Norm—Change the misperception that "everyone's doing it."

ACTIVITY	PERSON(S) INVOLVED	TIMELINE	BUDGET IMPACT
Hispanic Heritage	Counselor/Entire Staff	Month and Year	None
Asian American Heritage	Counselor/Entire Staff	Month and Year	None
Cinco de Mayo	Counselor/Entire Staff	Month and Year	None
Black History Month	Counselor/Entire Staff	Month and Year	None

Evaluation

1. Increase an understanding of various cultures by surveying attitudes of our faculty and students.
2. All teachers will take a poll on how these activities promoted cultural awareness.

GOAL 2: Implement a counseling program that provides sound mental health amongst faculty and students.*,**

NEEDS ASSESSMENT: A Counseling Program that delivers a message of sound mental health is important. Faculty and students need to be provided counseling services that prevent, intervene, or remediate all factors that obstruct sound mental health.

Research Based Strategies

*Provide opportunities for service and leadership.

*Provide a caring environment.

*Attend conferences & continue professional development.

ACTIVITY	PERSON(S) INVOLVED	TIMELINE	BUDGET IMPACT
Apple Arena	Counselor/Entire Staff	Month and Year	None
Student **A**ssistance **P**rogram	Counselor/Chen/Wells	Month and Year	$ 200.00
Mentor/Mentee Program	Counselor	Month and Year	None
K.E.E.P.	Counselor/CIS	Month and Year	None

Evaluation

1. Pre and Post survey will be given to establish anticipated effectiveness.
2. Questionnaires will be issued to determine program benefits.

The School's Physical Environment

GOAL 1: Increase the safety of faculty, staff, and students by consistent implementation of our visitors' monitoring system.*

NEEDS ASSESSMENT: Safety is an important factor in a learning environment. Implementation of a school wide monitoring system is critical to reduce and/or eliminate the number of strangers being found present without the proper identification.

Research Based Strategies

*Provide safe environment.

*Actively involve the family and the community so that prevention strategies are reinforced across settings.

*Training staff.

ACTIVITY	PERSON(S) INVOLVED	TIMELINE	BUDGET IMPACT
Preparing Name Tags	Administration/Staff	Month and Year	None
Check-In Procedures for the front office	Administration/Faculty/Staff	Month and Year	None
Duty for Administration, Faculty, and Staff	Administration/Faculty/Staff	Month and Year	None

Evaluation

1. A survey will be issued to students to assess their level of safety and security while at school.
2. Teachers will complete a questionnaire on effectiveness of (Campus Name) monitoring system.

GOAL 2: Increase the knowledge of crisis prevention and intervention plans through repetitious practice and training for faculty, staff, and students. *,**

NEEDS ASSESSMENT: With our ever-changing world, effective communication regarding crisis prevention and intervention plans are a necessity. Making certain that all individuals know what to do in the event of a crisis and strategies to prevent such occurrences are needed.

Research Based Strategies

*Integrate prevention into curriculum using lessons with interactive teaching techniques such as role-rehearsals, discussions, brainstorming, and cooperative learning.
*Actively involve the family and the community so that prevention strategies are reinforced across settings.
*Set clear boundaries with high expectations.
*Training of staff.

ACTIVITY	PERSON(S)INVOLVED	TIMELINE BUDGET	IMPACT
Drills and training for natural disasters, fire, evacuation, shelter in place, suicide, abduction and hostage attempts.	Entire Staff Staff/Parents/ Students	Month and Year	None
Guest Speakers	Counselor/CIS/Law Enforcement Agencies	Month and Year	None
Available literature and brochures	District/Counselor	Month and Year	None

Evaluation

1. Pre and Post survey will be given to establish anticipated effectiveness.

The School's Social Environment

GOAL 1: Increase parental involvement at home and in school to achieve goals set forth by (District Name and Campus Name) to increase student success.*

NEEDS ASSESSMENT: Increasing parental involvement is an ongoing initiative. Parents need to be aware of goals set forth by the district and the school to assist in their child's mental, physical, emotional, and educational development.

Research Based Strategies

*Provide opportunities for service and leadership.
*Provide caring environment where they feel like school cares for them.
*Model appropriate behavior.

ACTIVITY	PERSON(S) INVOLVED	TIMELINE	BUDGET IMPACT
Creation of Community Resource Center	Counselor	Month and Year	None
Self-Help and Parenting Seminars	Counselor	Month and Year	None
Calendar of Events for Parents	Entire Staff	Month and Year	None

Evaluation

1. Parental surveys given at the end of the year.
2. Staff surveys on effectiveness of activities.

GOAL 2: Increase the quality of students' life skills and leadership through character education.**

NEEDS ASSESSMENT: In an effort to educate the "whole child," emphasis on life skills and leadership (Campus Name) has taken an active approach in making certain our students receive this message and apply it inside and outside of the school environment.

Research Based Strategies

*Teach character education.
*Provide healthy role models.
*Set clear boundaries with high expectations.

ACTIVITY	PERSON(S) INVOLVED	TIMELINE BUDGET	IMPACT
Classroom Guidance Lessons	Counselor	Month and Year	None
Character Education	Counselor	Month and Year	None
Student **A**ssistance **P**rogram	Counselor/Person 1/Person 2	Month and Year	None
CIS	Counselor/Person 1/Person 2	Month and Year	None

Evaluation

1. Parent of the students who have received character education will give feedback pertaining to the development of their child's life skills.
2. Students will complete a survey on whether or not their leadership skills have been enhanced.

GOAL 3: Promote a Safe, Drug, and Violence free school.*

NEEDS ASSESSMENT: In a world in which we live, ways and strategies to protect ourselves are always changing. In addition to this, drugs and violence are prevalent and real. It is important to inform all students at (Campus Name) on ways to prevent or handle unforeseen occurrences related to drugs and violence.

Research Based Strategies

*Raise their level of perceived harm—educate.
*Promote close bonds—Provide opportunities for students to connect to each other, teachers, parents, and the community.
*Use lessons with interactive teaching techniques such as role—plays, discussions, brainstorming, and cooperative learning.
*Teach media literacy—Help students recognize external pressures like advertising that influence to them to use alcohol, tobacco, and drugs.
*Provide a safe environment and actively involve the family and the community so that prevention strategies are reinforced across settings.

ACTIVITY	PERSON(S) INVOLVED	TIMELINE BUDGET	IMPACT
Red Ribbon Week	Counselor/Entire Staff	Month and Year	None
Guest Speakers	Counselor	Month and Year	None
Safe & Drug Free Conference	Counselor	Month and Year	None
Classroom Guidance Lessons	Counselor	Month and Year	None

Evaluation

1. Feedback from guest speakers and presenters.
2. Application of new techniques/approaches learned at conference.
3. Teacher feedback/evaluation.

The School's Culture

GOAL 1: Decrease the acts of disorderly conduct inside and outside the classroom by promoting close bonds between administration, teachers, parents, and students.**

NEEDS ASSESSMENT: Promoting close bonds with parents, teachers, and students will decrease the acts of disorderly conduct. Teachers will continue to communicate with parents by keeping them informed on their

child's progress as well as activities and guidance lessons promoting bonds between students and teachers.

Research Based Strategies

*Promote close bonds—Provide opportunities for students to connect to each other, teachers, parents, and the community.
*Teach social skills and life skills—anger management, communication, and empathy.
*Provide caring environment where they feel like school cares for them.

ACTIVITY	PERSON(S) INVOLVED	TIMELINE	BUDGET IMPACT
Character Education	Counselor	Month and Year	None
Social Skills	Counselor	Month and Year	None

Evaluation

1. Pre and Post survey will be given to establish anticipated effectiveness and effectiveness.
2. Questionnaires will be issued to determine program benefits.

GOAL 2: Provide a least restrictive environment for all students.*

NEEDS ASSESSMENT: The educational system has special populations that need to be serviced. Offering a least restrictive environment at (Campus Name) entitles all students equal opportunities to receive not only an academic education, but a social and interpersonal education as well.

Research Based Strategies

*Change the norm—Change the misperception that "everyone's doing it."
*Teach social skills and life skills—anger management, communication, and empathy.
*Staff training.

ACTIVITY	PERSON(S) INVOLVED	TIMELINE	BUDGET IMPACT
Target Success	Assistant Principle	Month and Year	None
504 Committee	Counselor	Month and Year	None
Field Trips	Entire Staff	Month and Year	None
Dyslexia Representative	Counselor	Month and Year	None

Evaluation

1. Number of recommendations for these committees.
2. Survey staff members to assess whether or not these committees provided a least restrictive environment.

(School Name)

Safe School Plan (School Year)
Campus Budget
Year

OBJECT/BUDGET CODE	DESCRIPTION OF ACTIVITIES	AMOUNT
	Substitute Teachers ($85/day or $42.50 per ½)	
	Extra Duty Pay—Teachers ($20/hour)	
	Extra Duty Pay—Paraprofessionals ($10.50/ hour if different from their regular duties	
	Consultants/Out-of-District Presenters	
	Printshop	
	Books	
	Food (snacks for students)	
	Software	
	Warehouse	
	Supplies/Videos	
	Travel	
	Registration	
	Student Transportation	
	TOTAL	

Appendix 12.2

Counselor Department Meeting Agenda

(Title/Meeting Focus)

Date

Time

Campus or Department Mission Statement:

At (Name of Campus) we envision an environment in which all individuals demonstrate mutual ***respect***, are ***accountable*** for their behavior, and ***prepare*** for the future. By maintaining ***positive*** interactions, ***consistent*** expectations, and a ***proactive*** approach to problem-solving, we ***work*** for the success of all.

Agenda Overview

District Business:

Old Department Business:

New Department Business

Action Items and Person Responsible

Miscellaneous Information

Appendix 12.3

Counseling Department Academic and Career Planning Events Schedule

(School Year)

Date

(Greeting),

As we approach the end of the (school year), the Guidance and Counseling Department at (School Name) would like to prepare you and our students for their exciting future! Our intent is to provide information that is needed and helpful in academic and career planning. Below is a chart that explains upcoming events and their purpose.

Name of Event	Date/Location of Event	Time of Event	Description
Electives Fair	Date Location in School	Beginning and Ending Time	Information and presentations regarding elective options for ____ school year
Electives Fair ***Gear Up Presentation***	Date Location in School	Beginning and Ending Time	Information on Financial Aid and Resources for students interested in attending college
Graduation Plan	Date Location in School	Beginning and Ending Time	State requirements for minimum, recommended, and distinguished achievement graduation plans along with earning high school credit in middle school
Registration During Science Classes	Date Location in School	Beginning and Ending Time	Selection of electives for (school year)
Registration During Science Classes	Date Location in School	Beginning and Ending Time	Selection of electives for (school year)

All information is extremely important to your child's future! Parents and/or guardians are welcome and invited to attend the above events. We

want your child's transition to be as smooth and successful as possible. If you have any questions, please call (department or school number). We look forward to seeing you and your middle school student.

Sincerely,
Counselor Name
Grade Level or Alphabet Assignment

Appendix 12.4

Counseling Department (Year) Campus Budget

Please complete the following and attach to Safe School Plan.

Campus: ____________________

Fund ______________________________

Object/ Budget Code	Description	Amount
	Substitute Teachers ($85/day or $42.50/per ½ day)	
	Extra Duty Pay—Teachers ($20/hour)	
	Extra Duty Pay—Paraprofessionals ($10.50/hour if different from their regular duties)	
	Consultants/Out-of-District Presenters	
	Printshop	
	Books	
	Food (snacks for students)	
	Software or Technology	
	Warehouse	
	Supplies/Videos/Planners/Game Room Supplies	
	Travel	
	Registration	
	Student Transportation (Buses)	
TOTAL		

If you have any questions, please feel free to contact (Persons Name) at extension (1234).

Appendix 12.5

Invitation to School Counselors

Date

Dear School Counselors,

The *(Name of District Department)* is pleased to announce the (*number of years since inception*) School Counselor Leadership Academy, which will start in the fall. This is an exciting opportunity to network with other counselors as we build the leadership capacity of counselors across the district.

The School Counselor Leadership Academy will be an interactive community of counselors who examine their own beliefs about leading others, discover their own unique personality and leadership style, and identify characteristics of effective leaders.

If you are interested in participating in this growth-producing opportunity, submit a letter of intent and request a letter of recommendation from your principal, cluster leader, or coordinating counselor by (date). There are a limited number of spots available and accepted applications.

Please note the *School Counselor Leadership Academy* in the subject line of your email and scan your letter and supporting recommendation to (name of contact person).

In closing, the Guidance & Counseling department is committed to empowering and equipping each counselor to maximize their full potential as leaders.

13

Professional Issues in School Counseling

Dr. Lisa A. Wines, Dr. Kathy Ybañez-Llorente, Dr. Joydel Snook, and Dr. Judy A. Nelson

ASCA NATIONAL MODEL THEME

Advocacy and Social Justice

ASCA SCHOOL COUNSELOR PROFESSIONAL COMPETENCIES

II-B-4f. Resolves ethical dilemmas by employing an ethical decision-making model appropriate to work in schools

II-B-4g. Models ethical behavior

II-B-4h. Continuously engages in professional development and uses resources to inform and guide ethical and legal work

II-B-4i. Practices within the ethical and statutory limits of confidentiality

II-B-4j. Continually seeks consultation and supervision to guide legal and ethical decision making and to recognize and resolve ethical dilemmas

II-B-4k. Understands and applies an ethical and legal obligation not only to students but to parents, administration and teachers as well

ASCA PRINCIPLES

Principle 4: School counselors are qualified to make contributions to all students development in the areas of academic (educational), career and personal/social development

ASCA ETHICAL STANDARDS FOR SCHOOL COUNSELORS (2016)

E.1.f. Enhance personal self-awareness, professional effectiveness and ethical practice by regularly attending presentations on ethical decision-making. Effective school counselors will seek supervision when ethical or professional questions arise in their practice.

F.1.e. Adhere to ethical standards of the profession, other official policy statements, such as ASCA's position statements, role statement and the ASCA National Model and relevant statutes established by federal, state and local governments, and when these are in conflict work responsibly for change.

F.3.a. Provide support for appropriate experiences in academic, career, college access and personal/social counseling for school counseling interns.

G.3. When faced with any ethical dilemma school counselors, school counseling program directors/supervisors and school counselor educators use an ethical decision-making model such as Solutions to Ethical Problems in Schools (STEPS) [Stone, 2001].

CACREP STANDARDS 2016

Section 5-G, Entry-Level Specialty Areas, School Counseling

Contextual Dimensions

2.l. professional organizations, preparation standards, and credentials relevant to the practice of school counseling

2.n. legal and ethical considerations specific to school counseling

Ethical Issues in School Counseling

School counselors face ethical dilemmas due to several factors that are unique to a profession that works mainly with minor children in a school setting. First, there may be conflicts among the ASCA Ethical Standards for School Counselors (2016), school district policy, and state or federal laws on decisions regarding student welfare. The school counselor is expected to adhere to these rules, regulations, and codes, and yet, it may not be possible to do that. Sometimes judgments must be made regarding the best outcome for a student and his or her family. While counselors adhere to the *do no harm* ethical concept, sometimes there is conflict between the law and the impact of a decision on student safety. In cases where the counselor must break confidentiality because of the law, it is imperative that students and parents understand, before counseling begins, what the limits of confidentiality are and what rights parents have regarding a student's school records. Additionally, school counselors often find that they may be involved in unavoidable dual relationships. For example, a parent may come to the counselor for help with an acting-out teenager, and that parent is also on a school committee with the counselor or employed as a teacher in the building. The school counselor does not want to deny services to this parent, but it may be awkward to see this parent on a regular basis in a different setting. It might also confuse the parent as to what the appropriate boundaries are in their relationship. Clearly, school counselors need to be vigilant regarding the decisions they make, and ASCA and other entities provide assistance to school counselors in the decision-making process.

Help Is on the Way!

Mullen, Lambie, Griffith, and Sherrell (2016) studied a group of school counselors ($N = 287$) to determine "the relationship between practicing school counselors' levels of ethical and legal self-efficacy, ethical and legal knowledge, and general self-efficacy" (p. 418). The researchers found that there was "no relationship between general self-efficacy and ethical and legal knowledge" (p. 424). However, the results showed a positive relationship between school counselors' general self-efficacy and ethical and legal self-efficacy. This may indicate that when counselors have higher optimistic self-beliefs, they may believe that they are able to manage ethical and legal issues. The researchers cautioned that this finding should be interpreted carefully due to a small effect size. Additionally, Mullen et al. (2016) found that school counselors' ethical and legal knowledge correlated with their ethical and legal self-efficacy. Again, the effect sizes were small; therefore, caution must be used in interpreting these data. However, these data may indicate that school counselors' ethical and legal knowledge may have a relationship to their belief about their ability to manage ethical dilemmas.

To best serve students and the school community, experts suggest the use of a decision-making model (Corey, Corey, & Callanan, 2011) and encourage school counselors to seek supervision (Remley & Herlihy, 2010). Most importantly, the ASCA Ethical Standards for School Counselors (2016) is the standard of the profession on the appropriate behaviors for school counselors in which to engage and should be consulted. You can find the link to the ASCA Ethical Standards for School Counselors under resources at the end of this chapter. Additionally, ASCA offers Legal and Ethical FAQs addressing topics such as case notes, subpoenas, confidentiality and the concept of *need to know*, reporting child abuse or neglect, pregnancy, suicide and self-harm, dual relationships, and social media (ASCA, n.d.). The ASCA website also includes ethical and legal tips for school counselors. Links to the FAQs and the tips can be found in the resources section at the end of the chapter.

Examples of Ethical Dilemmas

Some examples of the types of difficult decisions with which school counselors must contend include limits of confidentiality, child abuse reporting, drug use and abuse, pregnancy, dangerous relationships, and violence. For example, each state has laws regarding the reporting of child abuse. The question is not about reporting the suspected abuse because that is the law. The dilemma is that school counselors are supposed to provide a safe place for students to discuss their issues and promise that the information shared will be confidential. That is, unless the information falls under the limits of confidentiality, which generally states that abuse of a child, elder, or person with disabilities must be reported. It is important, therefore, that school counselors alert all parties to these exceptions. This can be done by putting a statement in the school handbook or on the school website. Students can be informed during an introduction to the counselor during classroom guidance sessions. In addition, school counselors should post the limits to confidentiality in their offices where students, teachers, and the school counselor can view it before beginning a session with any student. The language of such a posting should be relevant to the age and grade of the children with whom the counselor works.

Drug use and abuse, pregnancy, and dangerous relationships can be health dangers to students' developing bodies and brains. Most often, students do not want to reveal these situations to their parents for fear of being in trouble or disappointing their parents. Most parents want to know if their child's health and well-being are in jeopardy. Parents have the right to information regarding their children according to the Family Educational Rights and Privacy Act (FERPA) [1974]. Conversations that school counselors have with students who are engaged in risky behaviors should include a great deal of empathy, yet a firm acknowledgement that the student is breaking the law and/or endangering his or her health and well-being. Collaborating with the school nurse can be helpful, and she/he may have resources available that will support the student and his or her family. Depending on school district policy, it may be required that the school counselor reveal these behaviors to the parent immediately. The school counselor could suggest to the student that the parent(s) are called to the counselor's office for the counselor and the student to convey the student's current truth. The student would have a safe and supportive place to talk to the parents about the problem, and the counselor would be the student's advocate, helping the parents to understand the seriousness of the behavior or situation and the steps that need to be taken to help the teen recover from effects of the problem. The FERPA law gives parents the right to review their child's school records, the right to ask the school to amend educational records, the right to consent in writing that the educational records be shared, and the right to file a complaint with the Family Policy Compliance Office regarding an alleged violation of FERPA; therefore, keeping the information from the parent could be a legal issue for the counselor. School counselors should be knowledgeable about FERPA and their states' statutes having to do with parental rights. See the link to the law in the Resources section.

Educational and Training Standards

The Council for Accreditation of Counseling and Related Educational Programs (CACREP) outlines current 2016 standards for training and preparation for seven entry-level specialty areas, of which school counseling and clinical mental health counseling are two. Many similarities exist across the educational standards of the two specialties, beginning with contextual dimensions. The specific standards in the school counseling specialty that overlap with those of clinical mental health counseling begin with CACREP standard G.2.d., school counselors serving on the leadership team heading the school. As such, school counselors are responsible for addressing the students' academic/educational, career, and personal/social development through the implementation of guidance lessons, individual responsive services, and character education—often in the form of classroom guidance lessons. Counselors also share the responsibility of helping to remove obstacles to individual student success with school principals and other administrators (Zalaquett & Chatters, 2012). Subsequent standards of G.2.e. addresses the school counselor role in emergency crises, disasters, and traumas, and standard G.2.g. focuses on the school counselor's ability and knowledge regarding detection of mental health and behavioral disorders affecting children in schools. These two standards are paramount given the fact that youth spend a majority of their day in a school setting (Huffman, 2013), and this is often where the negative impact of mental health issues may be seen. Due to a multitude of reasons, the front-line interventions by school counselors may sometimes be the only mental health treatment some students will receive. As more children are diagnosed and receiving treatment of mental health and behavioral issues with psychotropic interventions, Standard G.2.h. addresses the increasing importance of school counselors holding knowledge of psychopharmacological effects of medication on youth. Standard G.2.i. addresses knowledge of substance abuse signs and symptoms, not only of children and adolescents' use, but also impact on the youth in which this is a household concern. Of equal importance, Standard G.2.n. requires training in legal and ethical concerns specific to school counseling, many of which overlap with clinical mental health concerns, such as confidentiality and maintaining professional boundaries.

Practice standards across the two specialty areas also hold areas of overlap, with many counselor education programs intentionally training all students across specialty areas the same clinically, ensuring standardization of practice, independent of setting. CACREP Standard G.3.d. and G.3.e. address appropriate interventions to address academic development and career counseling, both areas that a clinical counselor may pursue with school-aged clients. Standard G.3.f. notes the importance of training counselors in techniques of personal/social counseling, in addition to having skills to connect social, familial, emotional, and behavioral problems' impact on academic achievement (Standard G.3.h.). Again, these skills are those that counselors in clinical practice would be addressing with youth, as they work to consider the systemic influences on the presenting problem or issue.

Brown (2006) cautioned that "counselors must carefully scrutinize the match between their training and experience combined. Moving from a school counseling practice to providing mental health services may involve relatively little change from the counselor's current level of knowledge and skills" (p. 190). The real dilemma might be that school district administrators and state education agencies may not recognize that school counselors possess the necessary skills to be considered mental health professionals (Lockhart & Keys, 1998). We have seen this in a few states. For example, one state considers school counselors to be educators rather than mental health professionals. This implies that school counselors deal with academic and career issues, but not emotional or social issues. As has been stated previously, school counselor training includes training in the clinical skills that other mental health professionals receive. In another state in a university setting, the administrators hesitated to approve a clinic site because they did not think that school counselors would need a training site for practicing clinical skills. Clearly, there is a great deal of advocacy work to be done for school counselors!

An emphasis on clinical skills development to address mental health concerns for all professional counselors-in-training does not negate the importance of counselors understanding the influence of setting on the provision of services. There are legal and ethical implications specific to each setting. Standardization of clinical training models may continue to be encouraged given the stance of the American Counseling Association and most of its divisions that we are all first professional counselors who practice in a variety of settings (Kaplan, Tarvydas, & Gladding, 2014). This acceptance of various professionals working toward the same goal and definition of counseling does not include the differences within the scope of practice for each specialty. This also leads to questions of professional identity, and how the roles of professional school counseling (Mau, Li, & Hoetmer, 2016) and mental health counseling can be best intertwined.

Mental Health Counseling by School Counselors

School counselors are often expected to address mental health concerns throughout the day, even though some school districts do not consider school counselors as mental health professionals, in addition to the multitude of additional responsibilities. Through transformation of school counseling programs, it is suggested that the mental health counseling services also improved (Gruman, Marston, & Koon, 2013; Kaffenberger & O'Rorke-Trigiani, 2013). When students present crisis situations during the school day, school counselors are generally the first to respond. DeKruyf, Auger, and Trice-Black (2013) explored issues of professional identity after proposing "a conjoint school counselor identity that include the roles of both educational leader and mental health professional positions school counselors to better respond to all students, including those with mental health needs" (p. 271). The researchers went on to enumerate the specific reasons why mental health should be included in the role of the school counselor:

> the large number of students who have unmet mental health needs, the unreliability of referrals, the displacement of school counselors by other mental health providers in schools, the potential loss of the uniqueness of the role of the school counselor, and the link between the mental health professional role and person-social variable that influence student achievement.
>
> (p. 274)

The possible shift in the role of school counselors can be directly impacted by issues of professional identity, administrator expectations, and a school counselor's own perception of their role regarding mental health.

Administrator Expectations

Paisley and Borders (1995) were some of the first researchers to review the development of school counseling as an evolving specialty area. At that time, they questioned what control over the profession would look like as a future issue, and the impact lack of control school counselors may have over their daily work.

> School counselors are directly accountable to school principals and directors of school counseling. . . . [M]any times these individuals do not have a counseling background. . . . [T]hese administrators (sometimes unknowingly) may make requests that school counselors consider unethical, such as request for program evaluation reports that include lists of clients' names and their reasons for seeing the counselor.
>
> (p. 151)

A little over twenty years later, these same concerns still exist for many of today's school counselors (Beale & McCay, 2001), from the person they are accountable to, who they are supervised by, and the kinds of things they are asked to do throughout the day.

School Counselor Perception

Carlson and Kees (2013) noted that "school counselors make up the greatest number of school-based mental health providers by providing brief counseling interventions with individuals, families, and groups and prevention activities through classroom guidance" (p. 213). Given their idea of the school counselors' role within the schools, Carlson and Kees surveyed 120 school counselors and found that a majority felt most comfortable addressing student issues such as academic concerns, relationship concerns, and stress management, while least comfortable addressing immigration concerns, addiction and substance abuse, and spirituality. Also of concern was working with more severe *Diagnostic and Statistical Manual* (DSM) diagnoses, using the DSM to diagnose students, doing treatment planning, and doing family therapy. Survey results indicated that "school counselors feel they are qualified to provide mental health counseling to students, but that the nature of their job precludes them from doing so on a large scale" (p. 217).

Credentialing

The mental health of students in public school settings is becoming more widely recognized by researchers and practitioners (Porter, Epp, & Bryan, 2000). Recently, it is more challenging to separate the work of the school counselor and that of a clinical mental health counselor. The question becomes why is it more challenging to separate the work and practice of these professionals? The answer is simple. Although these settings are quite different, the fact remains that a student's mental health concerns tend to be relevant to the student's capacity to focus and learn throughout the school day. In fact, we argue that these mental health concerns may be exacerbated due to the length of time spent in school daily, the various expectations placed upon students to succeed in a school setting, the social aspects that inevitably happen among peers and adult relationships, and the challenges some students face developmentally, in their home environments, and biologically, which all directly affect their day-to-day experiences at school. Additionally, without excellent health care insurance or low-cost community resources, many families simply do not have the resources to access the services their children may need. The school counselor may be the only mental health professional that some students can access.

School counselors are taking it upon themselves to seek out ways to obtain dual or multiple credentials and various specializations in the realm of counseling in general. The motivation to obtain a terminal degree, an additional license and/or certification, may be the result of the limitations school counselors have in school districts to be recognized as mental health professionals. They also may be motivated to earn additional money by having their own private practice or being able to work within a hospital setting on weekends, or it simply could be that counselors have a desire to expand their knowledge base about the field of counseling. They only want to be able to best serve those individuals with whom they are currently working. However, there is a lack of information available to these professionals who have dual or multiple credentials and how to operate within the scope of practice of their professional setting and their area of expertise.

Licensure and Certification

As with all relatively new professions, the counseling profession is "an organic process" (Bergman, 2013, p. 61) that experiences growing pains. While counseling professionals have established many of the important properties of a profession, including ethics, standards, and organizations (Ponton & Duba, 2009; Spurgeon, 2012), the profession continues to struggle with issues of a collective identity. For school counselors, the collective identity is further muddled because some states license school counselors whereas other states certify them. Additionally, licensing and certification requirements are not consistent among the various states, which is not conducive to a unified identity among professional counselors. Furthermore, as mentioned earlier, some professionals and community members do not necessarily view school counselors as mental health professionals who can provide mental health services. School counselors themselves are cautious about not providing *therapy* to their clients as this implies long-term assistance that is impractical for counselors with such large caseloads.

Counselor education programs that are training school counselors follow standards set forth by CACREP, the National Council for the Accreditation of Teacher Education (NCATE), state departments of education, and university graduate schools. The focus of each of these bodies can vary, but ultimately the school counselor-in-training must achieve school counselor certification to practice within the schools. In 2012, the American Counseling Association's Office of Public Policy published a report regarding states' laws and regulations on professional school counseling (American Counseling Association Office of Public Policy and Legislation, 2012). State education agencies were surveyed in 2011, and findings were reported according to certification/licensure requirements, state mandates, and student-to-counselor ratios. One of the most interesting, and confusing, findings is that different terms are used for credentials across states:

> Professional school counselors are required by law and/or regulation in every state, the District of Columbia, Guam, Puerto Rico, and the Virgin Islands to obtain a state-issued credential in order to be employed in public schools. In some states, this credential is called "Certification" while in others it is termed "Licensure" or "Endorsement."
>
> (p. 2)

This fact makes the discussion of certified school counselors pursuing licensure a little more confusing, as licensure in one state can refer to both school counseling and mental health counseling. Additionally, national certifications in both school counseling and just counseling confuse the issue even more.

National Certifications

In 1992, the National Certified School Counselor (NCSC) credential went into effect, through a joint effort by the American School Counselor Association, American Counseling Association, and the National Board of Certified Counselors (NBCC), the group that manages the certificate. "Applicants to the NCSC credential must first meet requirements for the generic National Certified Counselor (NCC) credential and then complete specialized coursework and additional experience specific to school counseling" (Paisley & Borders, 1995, p. 151). Requirements for the NCC credential include successful completion of a master's degree covering nine specific content areas (CACREP core), including counseling experience in the field (Internship), obtaining a passing score on the National Counselor Exam (NCE) or National Clinical Mental Health Counseling Examination (NCMHCE), completing 3,000 hours of counseling experience, and documenting a minimum of

100 hours of post-graduate counseling supervision. Prior to 2017, the NCC credential was one that most counseling graduates could qualify for post-graduation. Beginning January 1, 2022, in order to apply for the NCC credential, NBCC will require a master's degree or higher from a CACREP-accredited counseling program. What was once available to most school counseling graduates, national certification will now begin to be limited to those graduating from programs that are national accredited by CACREP.

Closing Thoughts on Credentials

While the American Counseling Association continues to work towards a unified profession, school counselors might find themselves in a quandary about who they are exactly. Again, as we stated earlier, many school counselors work toward licensure as a Licensed Professional Counselor (LPC) or Licensed Marital and Family Therapist (LMFT) to gain status, to be able to provide services in a setting other than schools, or to obtain further knowledge and skills to assist them in their current school setting. A national committee was created that included representatives from every ACA division to respond to the current needs of the profession. In 2011, the outcomes for Phase I of *20/20: A Vision for the Future of Counseling* (2010) were presented, including "strengthening identity" and "presenting ourselves as one profession" (Kaplan & Gladding, 2011, p. 371). Therefore, despite the many specialty areas in the counseling field, professional counselors continue to work towards a unified identity to set themselves apart from other mental health professionals.

Supervision in School Counseling

Supervision for school counselors is a necessary aspect for the vitality of the profession (Cook, Trepal, & Somody, 2012). Per the 2016 CACREP standards, professional school counseling practice, which includes practicum and internship, provides for the application of theory and the development of counseling skills under supervision. These experiences will provide opportunities for students to counsel clients who represent the ethnic and demographic diversity of their community.

Broadly, supervision has been known as a process to monitor individuals, whereby "the work of the counselor is reviewed" (Remley & Herlihy, 2016) during their fieldwork or clinical experience, also known as practicum and internship (Studer, 2006). Supervision as a practice is designed to maintain the safety and protection of those served, to provide structure and understand one's intent behind interventions used, to gauge professional fit and development, to ascertain ethical and multicultural competence, and to orient the individual into an unwritten culture that exists in a school setting or the profession at-large. The gravity of supervision, as a process, is relevant to field experience (Hamlet, 2017), to grow potential membership in the profession of school counseling, to use when uncertain of a direction to take or how to intervene on the behalf of the student, and necessary in "demonstrating an awareness of your developing professional skills" (Hamlet, 2017, p. 6).

Supervision for school counselors-in-training is essential (during graduate school), and the necessity for this process to continue, once hired as a professional (after graduation), is equally relevant (Christman-Dunn, 1998; Moyer, 2011). Societal issues, critical incidents, and the influx of social media all are critical components affecting the need for available, ongoing school counselor supervision. While supervision can have an inherent negative connotation, viewing it as an opportunity to share accountability, to consult with other professionals, to receive support, and to reduce ineffective delivery of services is recommended (Moyer, 2011). Because serving the public requires school counselors to do no harm, our profession is quite relevant in working with the mental health, emotional, and behavioral aspects of our students and their families.

Who Is Supervising the School Counselor?

All counselors need supervision, and typically supervision is a teaching and learning relationship between a novice counselor and a more experienced professional counselor (Bernard & Goodyear, 2014). The purpose of a supervisory relationship is to induct new counselors into the profession and to improve performance and provide professional growth and development. However, in the profession of school counseling, school counselors often ask, "Who is supervising me?" It is a complex question. In the school setting, ultimately supervision is up to the principal, an administrator leader, or possibly an administrator at the central office who is not a professional counselor. Therefore, school counselors only can obtain administrative supervision from one of those professionals. To gain clinical supervision, school counselors must rely on lead counselors, guidance directors who are counselors, current and past professors, counselor colleagues, and licensed professional counselors who have the special designation of supervisor.

Supervision During Graduate School

During the master's degree training period, school counselors-in-training are primarily supervised by the professors that teach them throughout the program. Professors provide learning opportunities and feedback during didactic and clinical courses. Once a trainee is ready to embark on the practicum or internship phase of the program, the school counselor-in-training reports primarily to two supervisors: the professor of record of the class and the site supervisor who oversees the work of the trainee in the school setting. These two supervisors consult regularly on the student's progress to determine the preparedness of the trainee for graduation and a career as a school counselor. Dependent upon the program, there may be field supervisors in place who have various responsibilities for supervision components. If a counselor education program includes a doctoral program in counselor education, it is possible that a doctoral student will be the supervisor for master's-level students during the supervised practicum.

The supervisors of graduate students becoming school counselors may be called a site supervisor, site mentor, or lead counselor. These titles can vary, but the role of all of them is to oversee the work of a school counselor intern, provide feedback, track the hours of work conducted on the campus, gate-keep, and basically induct the student into the profession of school counseling. Serving as a site supervisor is a major responsibility in addition to continuing in the current role of the school counselor. Because most districts do not recognize school counselors as supervisor eligible or qualified, the university or institution the graduate student belongs to is usually responsible to train the site supervisor on their role and expectations of serving in this capacity. The primary role of the site supervisor is to ensure the protection and safety of the students and families served. The site supervisor is an individual who has interest in gaining supervisory experience and wants to stay connected to cutting-edge school counseling.

Supervision After Graduate School

Once the graduate is in the field functioning as a school counselor, the principal or assistant principal will probably provide administrative supervision in terms of expectations of job performance and relationships with staff. This type of supervision may not align with the role that the novice school counselor expects to play, and it does not address the need for clinical supervision. However, it is important for the inductee to become a trusted and loyal member of the school staff in order to begin to implement and manage the school counseling program and to be in a position to advocate for appropriate roles (see Chapter 9). Thus, administrative supervision is important; it is just not enough!

A number of options are available for clinical supervision after graduate school depending on the size of the school district and the organization or assignment of individuals or teams of school counselors, the availability of licensed or certified persons for supervision of new counselors, the logistics of time and location of those involved, and the exact purpose of the supervision. Some examples of a variety of situations are as follows:

- A new school counselor in a rural setting with no other school counselors on staff and no director of counseling
- A new school counselor working in a large high school with a team of eight other counselors
- A school counselor who has completed coursework to become an LPC or LMFT or other licensed professional and needs to accrue clinical counseling hours and receive weekly supervision from a supervisor who is licensed (the rules about being a licensed supervisor vary among states)

Novice school counselors who work in isolation need clinical supervision to cope with the daily crises and difficult decisions that present themselves in the complex environment of the school setting. The assumption has been that "school counselors are expected to act as seasoned professionals upon graduation and their basic learned skills can be applied in complex situations" (Christman-Dunn, 1998, p. 7). While face-to-face supervision is ideal, it may be necessary for counselors in remote areas to engage in Internet-based supervision from another school counselor, a former professor, or another licensed professional. It may be necessary for the school counselor to pay for this type of service if it occurs outside of school hours. An occasional face-to-face meeting would enhance the supervisory process. Fees for supervision typically mirror fees for therapy for one hour of contact per week and may be less for Internet supervision.

For school counselors who work in large school districts with a substantial counseling department that includes school counselors at all levels of experience, the task of finding supervision should be relatively easy. Often another counselor in the district or in the school is assigned as a mentor to a new school counselor, or the new person may request that type of mentorship from a seasoned professional. The challenge of this type of informal relationship is that regular weekly meetings do not always occur, and the new counselor relies on the mentor for crisis intervention rather than professional growth. This type of informal supervision is not ideal, as it does not address the countertransference issues, the theoretical perspectives, and the fears of the new school counselor. Informal supervision may not be viewed as an ongoing vehicle for professional growth. It may be that the novice school counselors will need to shop around for an appropriate supervisor, keeping in mind the role of the supervisors during their graduate programs. Fees may be waived in this type of supervisory relationship as it may seem more like mentorship than supervision. In other words, a mentor does not face the same professional responsibility and liability that a supervisor faces.

For new counselors who are also working toward state licensure as professional counselors, supervised hours are required and must be documented by both the supervisee and the supervisor. These contact hours are obtained outside of the regular school day, and fees are generally charged. Again, it is likely that fees for supervision will be like fees for therapy; however, sometimes an LPC who works as a school counselor will be amenable to providing supervision for a reduced fee or for no fee at all.

What to Look for in a Supervisor

In the University Setting

During the training experience, graduate students usually have little to say about which professors will supervise them during the practicum or internship. Per the CACREP (2016) standards, counselor education program faculty members serving as individual/triadic or group practicum/internship supervisors for students in entry-level programs must have (1) relevant experience, (2) professional credentials, and (3) counseling supervision training and experience.

In Practice Sites

Students might be expected to find their own site supervisors, in which case they would have considerable leeway in this choice as long as the supervisor meets minimum standards as set forth by programs and professional organizations. CACREP (2016) standards for site supervisors include (1) a minimum of a master's degree, preferably in counseling, or a related profession; (2) relevant certifications and/or licenses; (3) a minimum of two years of pertinent professional experience in the specialty area in which the student is enrolled; (4) knowledge of the program's expectations, requirements, and evaluation procedures for students; and (5) relevant training in counseling supervision. At the beginning of each term prior to engaging in the supervision process, orientation, consultation, and professional development opportunities must be provided by the counselor education program faculty to the site supervisors. Additionally, written supervision agreements define the roles and responsibilities of the faculty supervisor, site supervisor, and student during practicum and internship. Upon signing an agreement that details the format and frequency of consultation to monitor student learning, individual/triadic practicum supervision is conducted by a site supervisor in consultation with counselor education program faculty.

Choosing a Site Supervisor

Choosing a site supervisor should be done with as much thought and care as possible. In some instances, such as in small or rural school districts, the choices might be limited. The qualities of a supervisor are much like those of a practicing counselor. The supervisor should be therapeutic in nature and utilize him or herself as the primary tool of impact, development, and change in the supervisory relationship. Corey (2017) encouraged the supervisory mindset by recommending counselors to "examine their own ideas about what kind of person can make a difference in the lives of others" (p. 19). Supervisors should have a strong identity with a strong appreciation and respect for self. They are flexible and live life authentically. Supervisors have a sense of humor and are willing to admit when they are wrong. They appreciate culture and diversity among an ever-changing pluralistic society and do not seek to have power and control over others. They sincerely wish for the success and well-being of clients and colleagues alike. They tend to be passionate, be effective communicators, and maintain appropriate boundaries (Corey, 2017). These qualities may not be apparent immediately to those who are new to the field. Therefore, some questions to ask a potential supervisor might be as follows:

- What was it that enticed you to become a school counselor?
- In what professional organizations are you involved and what is your involvement?
- How do you envision your relationship with me as a supervisor?
- What will your goals be for me as an inductee into the profession? How will you help me reach these goals?
- How will you address the differences in our (age/race/ethnicity/abilities/gender/sexual orientation, etc.)?
- When and where will we meet? What should I do if there is an emergency that I need to discuss with you outside of our supervisory sessions?

Choosing a site supervisor can have a lasting effect on how students view their professional identity and responsibilities. Everyone benefits from excellent supervisory practices in the field of professional school counseling.

What to Expect in Supervision

Counselor development can occur in many ways. Typically, supervisors employ the use of a supervision model or framework, which can be developmental, integrated, or orientation-specific in nature to aid in the process of supervision. Regardless of the chosen type, models attend universally to the development of a safe supervisory relationship, a task-directed structure, and methods that complement a variety of learning styles, supervisory roles, and communication skills (Leddick, 1994). Thus, the supervision process can be structured in an infinite number of ways. For example, upon initiating supervision, a supervisor may engage in informed consent practices where he or she states clear parameters for weekly meetings. It is crucial to one's success as a practicum and internship student that the supervisor and supervisee establish a working alliance. It is important that they work together and co-develop, as well as regularly evaluate, goals that enhance the supervisee-client alliance. Consistent feedback about work with clients as well as the status of supervisory goals is another essential component of the supervision process. Supervisors offer multiple sources of feedback in a regular, ongoing fashion and encourage ongoing supervisee self-evaluation as well.

Methods of Supervision

There are various methods of supervision beyond traditional one-on-one or face-to-face approaches. These methods consist of group supervision, peer supervision, and online supervision. They are all plausible with inherent limitations and are discussed in detail within this section.

Group Supervision

Group supervision is a time-efficient way to supervise many school counselors simultaneously and reduce the number of needed supervisors (Christman-Dunn, 1998). On some campuses, many school counselors are employed, particularly at the secondary levels. Group supervision can be organized in a number of ways. For example, the director of the counselors in a large, suburban district can meet with groups of counselors once a month to provide this type of supervision. The groups might include all elementary counselors at one meeting, all secondary counselors at another meeting, or counselors from a particular school cluster, such as a middle school and the elementary feeder schools. These are just examples, and the groups will be determined by the make-up of the school district. Group supervision can be divided into several sections: one that provides new learning for counselors, one that allows counselors to bring forward their tough cases and get feedback on those, and one that provides counselors with the opportunity to share guidance lessons and interventions that have been effective.

Peer Supervision

Peer supervision models offer another opportunity for clinical supervision in interns (Agnew, Vaught, Getz, & Fortune, 2000). Agnew et al. (2000) found that peer clinical supervision enhanced confidence and promoted professional growth. Peer supervision can easily continue after the internship experience if novice school counselors are motivated to grow professionally and protect their clients. In addition, Thomas (2005) described a model in which university alumni from school counseling programs met as a group at their former university campus every other month to garner support, solve problems, network, and discuss clinical issues. A school counseling faculty member facilitated the group, provided direction to the new school counselors, and acted as a safety net for solving tough problems.

Online or Distance Supervision

Clinical supervision began decades ago with live meetings and has progressed over time, "with education embracing technological developments, we are now able to conduct supervision at a distance" (Leggett, Strickland, & Krzewskik, 2016, p. 256). More recently, to meet the demands of today's society and promote the accessibility of higher education, computer-based technology has been utilized to assist in the delivery of classroom instruction and counseling supervision, thus eliminating the need for face-to-face contact (Ellis, Ginns, & Piggott, 2009).

There are multiple advantages to engaging in online supervision, including but not limited to, flexibility (Nelson, Nichter, & Henriksen, 2010), convenience, as well as the elimination of transportation and money concerns. Furthermore, the elimination of time and space constraints promotes access to peer and expert feedback during supervision, provides an opportunity for supervisees to observe interactions between the supervisor and other supervisees, and grants immediate access to information supplied by the supervisor and/or other supervisees (Butler & Constantine, 2006).

School counselors can use various technologies in order to conduct online supervision. Technology applications, such as Talk Fusion, Adobe Connect, GoToMeeting, and Zoom are all conducive for use. Many of these connections are free for limited usage. With the school environment being so high-paced, this approach may be most convenient or allow you to work with other school counselors at different campuses.

On the other hand, face-to-face supervision allows for the observation of both verbal and non-verbal cues rather than relying on the written word. Additionally, technical problems, as well as a lack of technological competence, can hinder the supervision process and slow it down considerably (Ellis, Ginns, & Piggott, 2009). Finally, engaging in the supervision process from home or work may prove to be distracting and threaten confidentiality as family members, friends, co-workers, and even household pets may be unaware of your engagement in the supervision process and seek your attention.

Regardless of personal preference, as counselor education continues to advance within the 21st century, so too must our willingness to remain flexible and open-minded to the infusion of technology within the counseling supervision process. It is important to keep in mind that technology is utilized to facilitate clinical supervision and is not the process itself. Put another way, whatever the medium, the process for clinical supervision, whether in an academic or professional setting, will remain largely unchanged.

Process of Supervision

In order to engage in the process of supervision, there are many relevant components to consider. The process for supervision has five steps: (1) creating the mindset of both supervisor and supervisee, (2) selecting a supervision model, (3) establishing an operational contract, (4) choosing topics, and (5) conducting observations, remediation, and evaluation.

Mindset

School counselors should have a mindset conducive to engaging in the supervision experience. Preparing ourselves to serve as a supervisor of the school counselor mentally enables a mindset of success to take shape. The supervisor desires experiences beyond traditional roles inherent in being a school counselor. Going into the role of a supervisor feeling as if it is too daunting or with negative thinking is not an optimal mindset to have, thereby directly affecting how you approach this role and the outcomes of this experience. In this way, having a positive mindset allows one to serve as a leader when the individual is in training, and then changing into a mentor when the intern becomes a colleague. The mindset of the supervisee or school counselor-in-training should entail recognizing a need for supervision, in that knowing mistakes will be made, and that supervision along with consultation are appropriate strategies for prevention and intervention (Cochrane & Salyers, 2006). Gaining an understanding and acceptance of where you are personally and professionally allows for growth in areas of weakness. Demonstrating an appreciation for the supervisor who was willing to assist you in this process conveys a spirit of willingness and professionalism. Perhaps most important, understanding the risks involved with no available supervision processes could be detrimental to the maintenance of your license or certification, could risk the protection of students, could increase stress and burnout, and could reduce shared accountability and modeling consultative practices (Christman-Dunn, 1998).

Model of Supervision

The next consideration within the process of supervision would be to make certain a model of supervision is being utilized by the site supervisor. It is helpful for the site supervisor to share this information, including a review of the stages or phases inherent within each model. The broad categories of supervision models are characterized under the psychotherapy, developmental, and social-role models. The five psychotherapy models are as follows: (1) Psychodynamic, (2) Person-Centered, (3) Cognitive Behavioral, (4) Systemic, and (5) Constructivist Narrative/Solution-Focused. The three developmental models are as follows: (1) Integrative Developmental Model (Stoltenberg, McNeil, and Delworth), (2) Conceptual Model (Loganbill, Hardy, and Delworth), and (3) Skovolt and Ronnestad's model. The three social-role models are as follows: (1) Discrimination model, (2) Hawkins and Shohet's model, and (3) a Systems Approach to Supervision (SAS). Brief descriptions of these models are found at www.marquette.edu/education/grad/documents/Brief-Summary-of-Supervision-Models.pdf.

Supervision Contracts

According to Bernard and Goodyear (2014), the supervision relationship is evaluative, extends over time, and has the simultaneous purposes of enhancing the professional functioning of the more junior person(s), monitoring the quality of professional services offered to clients (p. 8). The role of a qualified supervisor is twofold: (1) to provide learning opportunities surrounding the school environment (Perera-Diltz & Mason, 2012), and (2) to serve as a gatekeeper for the counseling profession (Lazovsky & Shimoni, 2005). It is critical to the success of the supervision process that supervisors make their expectations clear to their supervisees before entering a supervisory relationship, and to diversify the learning experiences to reflect the totality of the school counselor role. To accomplish this, a supervisor will develop a supervision contract (see Appendices 13.1 and 13.2) with his or her supervisee in which supervisory roles, expectations, and evaluation methods are clearly defined

(Lazovsky & Shimoni, 2005; Osborn & Kelly, 2010). Items to include in a supervision contract are as follows (Bernard & Goodyear, 2014):

- Purpose, goals, and objectives
- Context of services
- Method of evaluation
- Duties and responsibilities of supervisor and supervisee
- Procedural considerations
- Supervisor's scope of practice

The supervision contract is an amendable document that can be revised and revisited throughout the supervision process. Once the contract is in place, it is the basis for the discussion of topics to come during supervision.

Topics

The establishment of topics should be based on supervisor recommendation, program considerations, and supervisee needs and desired exposure. Topics should be a part of the agenda (Appendix 13.3) created by the supervisee for use during the weekly supervision meeting. Table 13.1 is a list of proposed topics that can be discussed during the supervision.

Table 13.1 Topics for Supervision

Annual Evaluation Measures	Departmental and School Culture	Indirect Services	Job Interviewing (Applicant or Committee Member)	Professional Development Opportunities
Building Comprehensive School Counseling Program	Direct Counseling Services (Guidance, Individual, or Groups)	Informal and Formal Assessments and Data	Student Cases or Concerns	Various Risk/Threat Assessments
Counseling or Supervision Model	District Policy and Procedures	Identity in Profession	Supervision Expectations	Working with Counselors on Other Campuses
Departmental Operations	Documentation of Counseling Services	Funding/ Fundraising	Supervisee Development, Impact, Counter-Transference, and Experiences	Working with Other Mental Health Professionals

These topics can be addressed over time. Priority of these are to be agreed upon between supervisor and supervisee, and can be modified based upon whether or not the supervisee is a student or actual school counselor.

Observation, Remediation, and Evaluation

Once the process of supervision is underway, it is important that the supervisor observe the supervisee. Observations of the supervisees' work with students help supervisors to ascertain strengths and identify areas for growth in the area of competence or skill level. Observations are conducted when the supervisor is present during a live counseling session with the student. Observations can also be made when supervisor and supervisee co-facilitate a counseling session. Observations are also appropriate when observing the supervisee in classroom guidance, hosting counselor-lead team-based meetings, when conducting parent conferences, or when providing training or a workshop to the faculty and staff in order to observe the supervisee's work with clients to assess their competence and skill development. Use of the school counselor observation form is one way to formally document what was witnessed during the 45-minute session (Appendix 13.4).

Occasionally, when the supervisee's skill level, competence, or behavior (Appendix 13.5) is lacking, it may be necessary to develop a remediation plan (Appendix 13.6) that targets these deficiencies and set a plan of action to correct and address the areas of concern. Similar to other contractual agreements in counseling (i.e., supervision contract, informed consent, consultation contracts), the supervisor and supervisee should discuss these deficiencies and agree upon the components to specify within the document. Remediation plans can be considered as a form of due process erring on the side of the supervisee's growth, and in very rare cases, continuation in the field.

The evaluation component for school counselors is necessary to provide feedback, usually on an annual basis. School counselors are often evaluated by school administrators, and sometimes those evaluations are not necessarily appropriate for school counselors. With respect to the supervision process, school counselors should be evaluated on their work with students and receive documentation of that evaluation to support their continued development. One strategy used during the evaluation process is to first discuss the evaluation tool utilized to provide feedback. Next, have the supervisee complete the evaluation on their own time so that the supervisor allows the input from the supervisee on each component of the evaluation from his or her perspective. Essentially, this helps determine the supervisee's ability to be reflective and to have insight on his or her work in the field. It also reveals alignment in the perceptions carried by both the supervisor and supervisee.

Special Issues in Supervision

When it comes to supervision, special issues must be taken into consideration. It is true that because supervision is not an inherent practice in school counseling departments across the nation, initiating this as a practice and attempting to alter the mindset and culture systemically among administrators may require much effort, planning, and advocacy on the part of the school counselor.

Choosing a Supervisor After Graduation

As mentioned in earlier sections, school counselors often do not receive adequate or any clinical supervision. It might be up to the new inductee to obtain supervision on a regular basis. When school counselors work to become LPCs in addition to their school counseling credentialing, they will have the benefit of several years of weekly supervision. Choosing a supervisor for licensure will depend on the state regulations, laws, or mandates relating to licensure in a particular state. Most states require that the supervisor is licensed in that state and has some type of supervisory training approved by the state. Following those regulations carefully is essential to making sure that the accrued hours count toward the licensing process. The best scenario for new school counselors for choosing a supervisor is to find someone who has both the school counseling and clinical experiences, and yet, the rules must be followed, which narrows the field of choices. The information provided regarding choosing a site supervisor is relevant to choosing a supervisor after graduation.

Advocating for Supervision

For novice school counselors who are not receiving supervision for state licensure, finding someone to provide clinical supervision may be challenging. Although it may be outside of one's comfort zone to ask for help, a lack of clinical supervision during a school counselor's induction into the profession can be frustrating for the counselor and possibly dangerous for clients. It is our recommendation that new school counselors advocate for their supervisory needs. Asking former professors for ideas about clinical supervision is one way to begin to find a supervisor. Generally, professors who teach school counseling courses are in contact with school districts, school counselors, and directors of counseling services. If a counselor works in a district that is large enough to have a director of counseling, advocating to that person is another way to investigate supervision possibilities.

Activities

1. Create a poster that explains the limits of confidentiality to students, parents, and teachers who want a session with the counselor. Remember to use language that fits the age group with whom you might work. When the posters are completed, share them with the entire class.
2. Imagine that you are a school counselor in a high school, and your client is a 16-year-old female student. She has revealed to you that she is pregnant, and you explain that her parents must be informed due to her own health and safety as well as that of the unborn child. Role-play with a peer with one of you as the school counselor and one as the student. Help the student practice what she will say when her parents come to school for the conference with the counselor and the student.
3. With your peers, role-play a graduate counseling student interviewing a potential site supervisor using the suggested questions in this chapter.
4. Interview a school counselor about the ethical dilemmas that he/she has faced in professional practice. Report back to the class about what you heard.

Resources

American School Counselor Association
www.schoolcounselor.org/asca/media/asca/Ethics/EthicalStandards2016.pdf
www.schoolcounselor.org/school-counselors-members/legal-ethical/legal-ethical-faq
www.schoolcounselor.org/school-counselors-members/legal-ethical/ethical-tips-for-school-counselors
United States Department of Education
https://www2.ed.gov/policy/gen/guid/fpco/ferpa/index.html

References

Agnew, T., Vaught, C. C., Getz, H. G., & Fortune, J. (2000). Peer group clinical supervision programs fosters confidence and professionalism. *Professional School Counseling, 4*(1), 6–12.

American Counseling Association. (2014). *ACA code of ethics*. Alexandria, VA: Author.

American Counseling Association Office of Public Policy and Legislation. (2012). *A guide to state laws and regulations on professional school counseling*. Alexandria, VA: Author.

American School Counseling Association. (2012). *ASCA national model: A framework for school counseling programs*. Alexandria, VA: ASCA.

Beale, A. V., & McCay, E. (2001). Selecting school counselors: What administrators should look for in prospective counselors. *Clearing House, 74*(5), 257–260. doi:10.1080/00098650109599203

Bergman, D. M. (2013). The role of government and lobbying in the creation of a health profession: The legal foundations of counseling. *Journal of Counseling & Development, 91*, 61–67.

Bernard, J. M., & Goodyear, R. K. (2014). *Fundamentals of clinical supervision* (5th ed.). Boston, MA. Pearson, Inc.

Brown, M. B. (2006). School-based health centers: Implications for counselors. *Journal of Counseling & Development, 84*, 187–191.

Carlson, L., & Kees, N. L. (2013). Mental health services in public schools: A preliminary study of school counselor perceptions. *Professional School Counseling, 16*(4), 211–221.

Christman-Dunn, R. (1998). The necessity of providing clinical supervision for school counselors. *Information Analyses, 70*, 1–12. Retrieved from http://files.eric.ed.gov/fulltext/ED426320.pdf

Cochrane, W., & Salyers, K. (2006). Collaborative consultation training: The missing link to the enhancement of collaborative relationships among education and mental health professionals. *Improving Schools, 9*(2), 131–140. doi:10.1177/1365480206064737

Cook, T., Trepal, H. & Somody, C. (2012). Supervision of school counselors: The SAAFT model. *Journal of School Counseling, 10*(21), 1–22. Retrieved from https://files.eric.ed.gov/fulltext/EJ981202.pdf

Corey, G. (2017). *Theory and practice of counseling and psychotherapy*. Boston, MA: Cengage Learning.

Corey, G., Corey, M. S., & Callanan, P. (2011). *Issues and ethics in the helping professions*. Belmont, CA: Brooks/Cole.

Council for Accreditation of Counseling and Related Educational Programs. (2016). *2016 CACREP standards.* Retrieved from www.cacrep.org/for-programs/2016-cacrep-standards/.

DeKruyf, L., Auger, R. W., & Trice-Black, S. (2013). The role of school counselors in meeting students' mental health needs: Examining issues of professional identity. *Professional School Counseling, 16*(5), 271–282.

Ellis, R. A., Ginns, P. & Piggott, L. (2009). E-learning in higher education: Some key aspects and their relationship to approaches to study. *Higher Education Research & Development, 28*(3), 303–318.

Family Educational Rights and Privacy Act of 1974, 20 U.S.C. § 1232g (1974).

Gruman, D. H., Marston, T., & Koon, H. (2013). Brining mental health needs into focus through school counseling program transformation. *Professional School Counseling, 16*(5), 333–341.

Huffman, A. M. (2013). Students at risk due to a lack of family cohesiveness: A rising need for social workers in schools. *The Clearing House, 86*(1), 37–42. doi:10.1080/00098655.2012.731022

Kaffenberger, C. J., & O'Rorke-Trigiani, J. (2013). Addressing student mental health needs by providing direct and indirect services and building alliances in the community. *Professional School Counseling, 16*(5), 323–332.

Kaplan, D. M., & Gladding, S. T. (2011). A vision for the future of counseling: The 20/20 Principles for unifying and strengthening the profession. *Journal of Counseling & Development, 89*, 367–372. doi:10.1002/j.1556-6678.2011.tb00101.x

Kaplan, D. M., Tarvydas, V. M., & Gladding, S. T. (2014). 20/20: A vision for the future of counseling: The new consensus definition of counseling. *Journal of Counseling & Development, 92*, 366–372. doi:10.1002/j.1556-6676.2014.00164.x

Lazovsky, R., & Shimoni, A. (2005). The working contract between the on-site mentor and school counseling students during internship: Contents and processes. *Mentoring & Tutoring: Partnership in Learning*, 13, 367–382. doi:10.1080/13611260500105857

Leddick, G. R. (1994). Models of clinical supervision. ERIC Digest. Retrieved from https://www.counseling.org/resources/library/ERIC%20Digests/94-08.pdf

Lockhart, E., & Keys, S. G. (1998). The mental health counseling role of school counselors. *Professional School Counseling, 1*(4), 3–6.

Mau, W. J., Li, J., & Hoetmer, K. (2016). Transforming high school counseling: Counselors' roles, practices, and expectations for students' success.

Administrative Issues Journal: Connecting Education, Practice, and Research, 6(2), 83–95. doi:10.5929/2016.6.2.5

Moyer, M. (2011). Effects of non-guidance activities, supervision, and student-to-counselor ratios on school counselor burnout. *Journal of School Counseling, 9*(5), 1–31.

Mullen, P. R., Lambie, G. W., Griffith, C., & Sherrell, R. (2016). School counselors' general self-efficacy, ethical and legal self-efficacy, and ethical and legal knowledge. *Ethics & Behavior, 26*, 415–430. doi:10.1080/10508422.2015.1033627

Nelson, J.A., Nichter, M. & Henriksen, R. (2010). On-line supervision and face-to-face supervision in the counseling internship: An exploratory study of similarities and differences. Retrieved from http://counselingoutfitters.com/ vistas/vistas10/Article_46.pdf.

Osborn, C. J., & Kelly, B. L. (2010). No surprises: Practices for conducting supervisee evaluations. In J. R. Culbreth & L. L. Brown (Eds.), *State of the art in clinical supervision* (pp. 19–44). New York: Routledge.

Paisley, P. O., & Borders, L. D. (1995). School counseling: An evolving specialty. *Journal of Counseling & Development, 74*, 150–153.

Perera-Diltz, D. M., & Mason, K. L. (2012). A national survey of school counselor supervision practices: Administrative, clinical, peer, and technology mediated supervision. *Journal of School Counseling, 10*(4).

Ponton, R. F., & Duba, J. D. (2009). The ACA code of ethics: Articulating counseling's professional covenant. *Journal of Counseling & Development, 87*, 117–121. doi:10.1002/j.1556-6678.2009.tb00557.x

Porter, G., Epp, L., & Bryant, S. (2000). Collaboration among school mental health professionals: A necessity, not a luxury. *Professional School Counseling, 3*(5), 315–322.

Remley, T. P., & Herlihy, B. (2010). *Ethical, legal, and professional issues in counseling*. Boston, MA: Merrill.

Spurgeon, S. L. (2012). Counselor identity: A national imperative. *Journal of Professional Counseling: Practice, Theory, & Research, 39*, 3–16.

Stone, C. (2001). *STEPS: Solutions to ethical problems in schools*. Alexandria, VA: American School Counseling Association.

Studer, J. (2006). *Supervising the school counselor trainee: Guidelines for practice*. Alexandria, VA: American School Counseling Association.

Thomas, C. (2005) *What's in a name? Strengths-based supervision: reality or rhetoric, an analysis*. Palmerston North: Massey University MSW Thesis.

Zalaquett, C. P., & Chatters, S. J. (2012). Middle school principals' perceptions of middle school counselors' roles and functions. *American Secondary Education, 40*(2), 89–103.

Appendix 13.1

Supervision Contract (Example 1)

The supervisory relationship is an experiential learning process that the site supervisor assists the supervisee (candidate) in developing therapeutic and professional competence. This contract is designed to assist the supervisor and supervisee in establishing clear expectations about the supervisory process (Bernard & Goodyear, 2014).

PURPOSE: The purpose of a supervision contract is to outline and agree upon the supervisory process. Supervisors and supervisees can expand past the number of items allowed by using multiple copies of this form.

NATURE OF THE SUPERVISORY RELATIONSHIP: A site supervisor, who is also certified/licensed to be a school counselor, has received specific training that can facilitate professional growth of the supervisee through: monitoring client (student) welfare; encouraging compliance with legal, ethical, and professional standards; teaching/modeling therapeutic skills; providing regular feedback and evaluation; and providing professional experiences and opportunities.

PLEASE STATE IN LISTED FORMAT THE NATURE OF THE SUPERVISORY RELATIONSHIP:

1.
2.
3.
4.

EXPECTATIONS OF THE INITIAL SUPERVISORY SESSION: The supervisee has the right to be informed of the supervisor's expectations of the supervisory relationship. The supervisor shall clearly state expectations of the supervisory relationship that may include: supervisee identification of supervision goals for oneself; supervisee preparedness for supervisory meetings; supervisee determination of areas of non-professional growth and development; supervisor's expectations regarding formal and informal evaluations; supervisor's expectations of the supervisee's need to provide formal and informal self-evaluations; supervisor's expectations regarding the structure and/or the nature of the supervisory sessions; weekly review of case notes until supervisee demonstrates competency in case conceptualization. The supervisee shall provide input to the supervisor regarding the supervisee's expectations of the relationship.

PLEASE STATE IN LISTED FORMAT THE ITEMS DISCUSSED IN THE INITIAL SUPERVISORY SESSION:

1.
2.
3.
4.

EXPECTATIONS OF THE SUPERVISORY RELATIONSHIP: A supervisor is a professional counselor with appropriate credentials. The supervisee can expect the supervisor to serve as a mentor and a positive role model who assists the supervisee in developing a professional identity. The supervisee has the right to work with a supervisor who is culturally sensitive and is able to openly discuss the influence of race, ethnicity, gender, sexual orientation, religion, and class on the counseling and the supervision process. The supervisor is aware of personal cultural assumptions and constructs and is able to assist the supervisee in developing additional knowledge and skills in working with clients from diverse cultures. Since a positive rapport between the supervisor and supervisee is critical for successful supervision to occur, the relationship is a priority for both the supervisor and supervisee. In the event that relationship concerns exist, the supervisor or supervisee will discuss concerns with one another and work towards resolving differences. Therapeutic interventions initiated by the supervisor or solicited by the supervisee shall be implemented only in the service of helping the supervisee increase effectiveness with clients. A proper referral for counseling shall be made if appropriate. The supervisor shall inform the supervisee of an alternative supervisor who will be available in case of crisis situations or known absences.

PLEASE STATE IN LISTED FORMAT THE ITEMS OUTLINED REGARDING THE EXPECTATIONS OF THE SUPERVISORY RELATIONSHIP:

1.
2.
3.
4. Several forms of evaluation will take place- informal observations; midterm evaluation; final evaluation.

LIST THREE THERAPEUTIC SKILLS YOU WOULD LIKE TO DEVELOP

1.
2.
3.

LIST THREE GENERAL GOALS YOU WOULD LIKE TO ATTAIN DURING THE SUPERVISION PROCESS

4.
5.
6.

_________________	_________________	__________
Site Supervisor Signature	Candidate Signature	Date

Appendix 13.2

Supervision Contract (Example 2)

Memo:
From the desk of ____________

Campus Information and School Motto/Logo

Supervision Contract

This contract provides an understanding of clinical supervision within school settings. Clinical supervision for school counselor trainees infers that the inexperienced individual is seeking licensure/certification and/or is fulfilling university course requirements for their practicum or internship courses at the masters or doctoral level. School counselor trainees are willing to engage in a process of documented observation and evaluation, either individually, small group, or triadically, under agreement with their supervisor, to ensure professional competence, ethical practices, and the welfare of the future students in which they are to serve.

I have _____ of experience in public school systems, with _____ of those years served as a school counselor. I am a certified school counselor, qualified in the state of ______, to serve as a supervisor for school counselor trainees. My certification is scheduled to expire in the year _____. I have been trained as a supervisor in my doctoral studies, and have worked for institutions where my primary role was to supervise counseling trainees.

The models of supervision I subscribe to are the integrated developmental model (IDM) and the discrimination model. The combination of these two models is advantageous to both the supervisor and supervisee, as the following are accomplished through implementation:

1. The IDM allows the supervisor to clearly see trainee behavior at different levels, and the gradual development or regression in the context of each level.
2. The discrimination model allows the supervisor to possess several roles with the trainee, such as teacher, counselor, consultant, and evaluator.

There are multiple areas that will be addressed in the context of supervision. Implementation of the ASCA Model and Texas Model for Comprehensive School Counseling Programs (5th ed.) will be promoted and monitored. Additionally, the supervisor will understand the theoretical framework and

techniques the school counselor trainee subscribes to when working with students. Trainees must be willing to address multiculturalism, their use of technology, ethical/legal considerations, and the relativeness each has for specific students. Further, trainees must be willing to address their countertransference/personal limitations, and how these interrupt therapeutic alignment or processes with students.

Each supervision meeting or interactive session entails one or more of the following actions:

1. Supervision contract and insurance must be in place
2. Bring an agenda to each supervision session
3. Bring audio/video tapes of your counseling sessions with students and families
4. Discuss cases of students and families
5. Discuss techniques or strategies utilized (research-based/school district policy)
6. Discuss personal strengths and areas of concerns
7. Meet weekly for one hour and a half
8. Conduct three 45-minute state-mandated observations for Texas Education Agency (live supervision), as appropriate

Trainees must be aware that there are other inherent difficulties that may occur during the supervision process as it relates to their development process. These issues may be related but not limited to collaboration, motivation, reluctance/resistance, problematic /unprofessional dress or behaviors, egocentrism, limited or too much disclosure, and site-based issues. As a supervisor, I will take such issues and use them as potential insight for identifying deeper, perhaps more serious issues. In such cases, measures for remediation will be taken, with the commitment toward effective gatekeeping practices.

In closing, this contract remains fluid and can be revised and resigned at any time our scope of practice changes. Our signatures represent that we have read, reviewed, and discussed this contract in its entirety, and that all parties are in agreement to the specifications outlined herein.

Please initial all that apply:

_____ University Internship Course
_____ University Practicum Course
_____ Doctoral Student
_____ Masters Student
_____ Practicing School Counselor Trainee

____________________ School Name/District
____________________ Name of University or Institution

______________________________ ______________________
School Counselor Trainee Printed Name Date or Revised Date

____
School Counselor Trainee Signature

______________________________ ______________________
Supervisor or Site Supervisor Printed Name Date or Revised Date

____
Supervisor or Site-Supervisor Signature

Appendix 13.3

Supervision Agenda

Supervision Session #___

Day of Week

Date

Beginning Time to Ending Time

Example Items Prepared by Intern:

- Adding an additional site
- What is considered direct/indirect hours
- State practicum/internship documentation form (601.80 Total/396.35 Direct)
- Discuss hours and supervision log
- Discuss hour accumulation on school breaks and holidays
- Discuss student cases/issues

Items Discussed by Supervisor:

- University course expectations
- Working together to accomplish comprehensive
- Service delivery models (individual/group)
- Preparing short video clips or observations of counseling sessions

Appendix 13.4

Observation Form

Student Name:	Date of Observation:
Formal Observation Start Time:	Formal Observation End Time:
Interactive Conference Start Time:	Interactive Conference End Time:
Start/End Date of the Assignment:	Practicum I Practicum II Internship I Internship II
Observation I_____ Observation II________ Observation III________	

The rating scale used for this formal observation is as follows:

5 = Clearly Outstanding, **4** = Exceeds Standard, **3** = Meets Standard, **2** = Below Expectation
1 = Unsatisfactory, **0** = Not Observable/Applicable

Standard I. Learner-Centered Knowledge: The certified school counselor has a broad knowledge base. The certified school counselor must know and understand:						
the history of school counseling; **(CACREP 5.G.1.a)**	5	4	3	2	1	0
counseling and consultation theories and practices; **(CACREP 5.G.1.d)**	5	4	3	2	1	0
career development theories and practices; **(CACREP 5.G.1.c)**	5	4	3	2	1	0
assessment principles and procedures, including the appropriate use of tests and test results; **(CACREP 5.G.1.e)**	5	4	3	2	1	0
changing societal trends, including demographic, economic, and technological tendencies, and their relevance to school counseling; **(CACREP 5.G.2.a)**	5	4	3	2	1	0
environmental, social, and cultural factors that affect learners' development and the relevance of those factors to guidance and counseling programs; **(ASCA A.4)**	5	4	3	2	1	0
learners' developmental characteristics and needs and their relevance to educational and career choices;	5	4	3	2	1	0

legal and ethical standards, practices, and issues; **(ASCA F; CACREP 5.G.2.n)**	5	4	3	2	1	0
the characteristics and educational needs of special populations;	5	4	3	2	1	0
theories and techniques in pedagogy and classroom management;	5	4	3	2	1	0
the integration of the guidance and academic curricula;	5	4	3	2	1	0
the roles and responsibilities of the counselor in a developmental guidance counseling program that is responsive to all students; and **(ASCA A.1)**	5	4	3	2	1	0
counseling-related research techniques and practices.	5	4	3	2	1	0
Standard II. Learner-Centered Skills: The certified school counselor applies the knowledge base to promote the educational, personal, social, and career development of the learner. The certified school counselor must:						
develop processes and participates in the design procedures for planning, designing, implementing, managing, and evaluating a developmental guidance and counseling program; **(CACREP 5.G.3.b)**	5	4	3	2	1	0
provide a proactive, developmental guidance program based on the needs of students;	5	4	3	2	1	0
counsel individuals and small groups using appropriate counseling theories and techniques in response to students' needs; promotes and advocates for the academic, career, personal, and social development of students;	5	4	3	2	1	0
consult with parents/guardians, teachers, administrators, and other individuals as appropriate to enhance their work with students, and to promote the academic, career, personal/social development of students; **(ASCA B.1, C; CACREP 5.G.2.b)**	5	4	3	2	1	0
coordinate resources for students within the school and community; **(ASCA B.2)**	5	4	3	2	1	0

demonstrate proficiency in teaching small and large groups by actively engaging students in the learning process;	5	4	3	2	1	0
participate in the selection, use, and interpretation of assessments and assessment results; **(CACREP 5.G.1.e)**	5	4	3	2	1	0
use varied sources of information about students for assessment purposes;	5	4	3	2	1	0
use counseling-related research techniques and practices to address student needs;	5	4	3	2	1	0
advocate for a developmental guidance and counseling program that is responsive to all students, including an ability to assess and manage suicide risk;	5	4	3	2	1	0
*design and implements prevention and intervention plans related to the effects of (a) atypical growth and development, (b) health and wellness, (c) language, (d) ability level, (e) multicultural issues, and (f) factors of resiliency on student learning and development; and **(CACREP 5.G.3.m)**	5	4	3	2	1	0
*conduct programs designed to enhance student academic development **(CACREP 5.G.3.d)**	5	4	3	2	1	0
Standard III. Learner-Centered Process: The certified school counselor participates in the development, monitoring, and evaluation of a developmental school guidance and counseling program that promotes learners' knowledge, skills, motivation, and personal growth. The certified school counselor must:						
collaborate with others in the school and community to implement a guidance curriculum that promotes learners' development in all domains, including cognitive, social, and emotional areas;	5	4	3	2	1	0
facilitate learners' ability to achieve their potential by helping them set and attain challenging educational, career, and personal/social goals based on various types of information;	5	4	3	2	1	0

use both preventive and intervening strategies to address the concerns of learners and to help them clarify problems and situations, set goals, explore options, and implement change;	5	4	3	2	1	0
implement effective referral procedures to facilitate the use of special programs and services, and to secure assistance for students and their families;	5	4	3	2	1	0
act as a consultant and/or coordinator to help learners achieve success inside and outside of school; and assesses barriers that impeded students' academic, career, and personal/social development; **(CACREP 5.G.3.k)**	5	4	3	2	1	0
*selects the appropriate assessment strategies used to evaluate and analyzes assessment information in a manner that produces valid inferences when evaluating the needs of individual students, such as academic, career, and personal/social development **(CACREP 5.G.3.e)**	5	4	3	2	1	0
*assess the effectiveness of educational programs and develop measurable outcomes for the school counseling programs, activities, interventions, and experiences; **(CACREP 5.G.3.b)**	5	4	3	2	1	0
*analyze and uses data to enhance the school counseling program; and **(CACREP 5.G.3.o)**	5	4	3	2	1	0
*use peer helping strategies in the school counseling program. **(CACREP 5.G.3.m)**	5	4	3	2	1	0

Standard IV. Learner-Centered Equity and Excellence for All Learners: The certified school counselor promotes academic success for all learners by acknowledging, respecting, and responding to diversity while building on similarities that bond all people. The certified school counselor must:						
understand learner differences, including those related to cultural background, gender, ethnicity, and learning styles, and know ways to create and maintain a positive school environment that is responsive to all learners; **(ASCA B.3)**	5	4	3	2	1	0
demonstrate multicultural competencies in relation to diversity, equity, and opportunity in student learning and development and advocates for a school environment in which diversity is acknowledged and respected, resulting in positive interactions across cultures; (**ASCA B.3)**	5	4	3	2	1	0
facilitate learning and achievement for all students, including special populations, by promoting a cooperative, inclusive, and purposeful learning environment. **(ASCA A.10)**	5	4	3	2	1	0
*assess and interprets students; strengths and needs, recognizing, uniqueness in cultures, languages, values, backgrounds, abilities **(ASCA B.3)**	5	4	3	2	1	0
*implement differentiated instructional activities that draw on subject matter and pedagogical content knowledge and skills to promote student achievement; and	5	4	3	2	1	0
*implement strategies and activities to prepare students for a full range of postsecondary options an opportunities **(CACREP 5.G.3.f)**	5	4	3	2	1	0
Standard V. Learner-Centered Communications: The certified school counselor, an advocate for all students and the school, demonstrates effective professional and interpersonal communication skills. The certified school counselor must:						
demonstrate effective communication through oral, written, and nonverbal expression;	5	4	3	2	1	0
use knowledge of group dynamics and productive group interaction;	5	4	3	2	1	0

support responsive interventions by effectively communicating with parents/guardians, teachers, administrators, and community members; **(ASCA B.1)**	5	4	3	2	1	0
facilitate learners' access to community resources and locates resources in the community that can be used in the school to improve student achievement and success;	5	4	3	2	1	0
develop and implement strategies for effective internal and external communications;	5	4	3	2	1	0
facilitate parent/guardian/families involvement in their children's education and to act on the behalf of their children to address problems that affect student success in school; **(ASCA B.1; CACREP 5.G.3.h)**	5	4	3	2	1	0
develop partnerships with parents/guardians, businesses, and other groups in the community to facilitate learning; **(ASCA B.1)**	5	4	3	2	1	0
work effectively as a team member to promote positive change for individuals, groups, and the school community and consults with teachers, staff, and community-based organizations to promote student academic, career, and personal/social development; **(ASCA B.2)**	5	4	3	2	1	0
*advocate for school policies, programs, and services that enhance a positive school climate and are equitable and responsive to multicultural students populations; **(ASCA B.3; CACREP 5.G.3.k)**	5	4	3	2	1	0
*plan and present school counseling-related educational programs for use with parents and teachers (e.g. parent education programs, materials used in classroom guidance, and advisor/advisee programs for teachers); **(ASCA B.1)**	5	4	3	2	1	0

Standard VI. Learner-Centered Professional Development: The certified school counselor continues professional development, demonstrating a commitment to learn, to improve the profession, and to model professional ethics and personal integrity. The certified school counselor must:						
use reflection, self-assessment, and interactions with colleagues to promote personal professional development; **(ASCA A.13)**	5	4	3	2	1	0
use counseling-related research techniques and practices as well as technology and other resources to facilitate continued professional growth;	5	4	3	2	1	0
strive toward the highest level of professionalism by adhering to and modeling professional, ethical, and legal standards;	5	4	3	2	1	0
apply research-based practice and relevant research findings to improve the school guidance and counseling program; **(CACREP 5.G.3.n)**	5	4	3	2	1	0
continue professional development to improve the school guidance and counseling program.	5	4	3	2	1	0
*demonstrate the ability to articulate, model, and advocate for an appropriate school counselor identity and program; **(CACREP 5.G.2.f)**	5	4	3	2	1	0
*demonstrate self-awareness, sensitivity to others, and the skills needed to related to diverse individuals, groups, and classrooms; and **(ASCA B.3)**	5	4	3	2	1	0
*demonstrate the ability to recognize his or her limitations as a school counselor and to seek supervision or refer clients when appropriate; **(ASCA B.3)**	5	4	3	2	1	0

Observable Counseling-Related Duties

_ Academic Planning/Six- or Four-Year Planning
_ Assessment/Test Interpretation
_ ARD Meeting/RTI Referral Process/504 Meeting
_ Behavioral Observations/Behavior Planning
_ Career and College Readiness/Post-Secondary Opportunities
_ Classroom Guidance Lessons

_ Consultation/Collaborative Meeting
_ District Counselor Meetings
_ Faculty/Staff Training
_ Family Counseling
_ Group Counseling
_ Individual Counseling
_ Parent Conferences
_ Parent Workshop or Training
_ Peer Mediation/Advisory/Advising Programs
_ Program Coordination
_ Record Keeping
_ Referral Services
_ Responsive Services
_ Scheduling/Student Placement
_ Student Success Initiatives/Grade Placement Committee (SSI)
_ Testing Coordination
_ Transition Program/Meetings

Observable Non-Related Counseling Duties

_ Discipline or OCS
_ Duties (Bus, Lunch, Hallway)
_ Clerical Activities
______Other__________________
______Other__________________

Documentation of Additional Support or Informal Feedback

Required Signatures as Evidence of Completion	**Date**
______________________________ University Supervisor or Field Supervisor	
______________________________ School Counselor Intern or Candidate	
______________________________ Building Principal or Principal Representative	

Appendix 13.5

Professional Issues and Behavior Rating Scale

In addition to counseling skills, professional counselors should demonstrate appropriate professional behavior as well as the ability to manage themselves effectively and appropriately. Items below are representative of the kinds of behavior practicum and internship instructors and supervisors will consider as part of their overall evaluation of students in practicum/internship. Faculty members may indicate other specific items as needed.

Depending on severity, number of issues, and response to faculty/supervisor feedback, results on this evaluation may impact grade in the course, ability to proceed to the next course in the practicum/internship sequence, and/or the departmental remediation process.

-2	-1	0	+1	+2
Poor: Consistently or usually performs in a way that is unacceptable or inconsistent with professional behavior	Unsatisfactory: Often behaves in a way that is unacceptable or inconsistent with professional behavior; however, there is some evidence of growth	Adequate: Evidence of professional behavior at a level consistent with the counselor-in-training's development; however, there is inconsistency	Good: Professional behavior generally demonstrated	Excellent: Professional behavior consistently demonstrated to a high degree

Is open and receptive to supervision	-2	-1	0	+1	+2	N/O*
Is prepared for supervision	-2	-1	0	+1	+2	N/O
Willingly makes changes in response to supervision	-2	-1	0	+1	+2	N/O
Actively solicits feedback about their work	-2	-1	0	+1	+2	N/O
Receptive to feedback from peers	-2	-1	0	+1	+2	N/O
Is actively attentive when peers present their work	-2	-1	0	+1	+2	N/O
Provides appropriate and useful feedback to peers	-2	-1	0	+1	+2	N/O
Demonstrates ability to be self-reflective about work with clients	-2	-1	0	+1	+2	N/O
Demonstrates ability to be self-reflective about personal attitudes, behaviors, and beliefs	-2	-1	0	+1	+2	N/O
Demonstrates good interpersonal skills with peers	-2	-1	0	+1	+2	N/O

-2	-1	0	+1	+2		
Demonstrates a collaborative stance with peers	-2	-1	0	+1	+2	N/O
Adheres to general standards of professional ethics and practice (e.g., ACA, IAMFC)	-2	-1	0	+1	+2	N/O
Demonstrates knowledge of and adheres to state regulatory rules and regulations (e.g., TSBEPC, TSBEMFT, TEA)	-2	-1	0	+1	+2	N/O
Demonstrates sound judgment in matters related to the profession and practice of counseling	-2	-1	0	+1	+2	N/O
Demonstrates commitment to personal growth and professional development	-2	-1	0	+1	+2	N/O
Demonstrates openness to new ideas	-2	-1	0	+1	+2	N/O
Demonstrates ability to accept personal responsibility	-2	-1	0	+1	+2	N/O
Demonstrates ability to regulate and express emotions effectively and appropriately	-2	-1	0	+1	+2	N/O
Demonstrates awareness of own impact on others	-2	-1	0	+1	+2	N/O
Demonstrates openness to issues of multiculturalism and diversity, including willingness to enhance skills and competence in these areas	-2	-1	0	+1	+2	N/O
Faculty Member Signature	**Date of Completion/Review**					
Student Signature	**Date**					

*N/O denotes Not Observed.

Appendix 13.6

School Counselor Remediation Form and Growth Plan

Counselors, school counselors, or counselor educators—in training—are required to be supervised during their practicum and internship experiences (CACREP, 2016). Both practicing and certified school counselors [or supervisors of school counselors] have an ethical obligation to train, mentor, supervise, professionally develop, instruct, and protect the welfare of clients/students (ACA, 2014; ASCA, 2005; Studer, 2006). If the trainees experience difficulty during this process, it is the supervisor's responsibility to remediate and grow these professionals-in-training. The supervisor should document his/her concerns and collaborate with other faculty supervisors, administrators, and site supervisors to corroborate the sentiment needed for remediation. All areas of concern should be written to reflect the supervisor's substantiated effort to implement the ACA, ACES, and ASCA ethical codes, along with having a discussion with the trainee regarding the problematic areas in order to provide an adequate amount of time to respond.

Problem Areas or Behaviors: Following are the areas of concern presented by the individuals responsible for gatekeeping the profession and protecting the welfare of clients or students.

The trainee, ____________________, should:

1. (example) know the school culture and/or adhere to school district policy, as evidenced by not allowing a male stranger onto the campus without garnering permission from the campus administrator and ensuring this individual had received the district-required background check.
2. (example) facilitate a working relationship and foster appropriate communication with the current campus administrator.

Application of Appropriate Ethical Codes: Following are the ethical codes that are suggested for your review. This should keep you aware of the expectations set forth by our governing professional organizations and supervisor who will professionally endorse you as a school counselor.

American Counseling Association

C.1. Knowledge of Standards
C.2.d Monitor Effectiveness
C.2.e Consultation on Ethical Obligations

D.1.g Employer Policies
F.8.a Standards for Students

American School Counselor Association

A.1.d Is knowledgeable of laws, regulations, and policies relating to students
B.1.a Establishes a collaborative relationship with parents/guardians to facilitate the student's maximum development
C.1.a Establishes and maintains professional relationships with faculty, staff, and administration to facilitate an optimum counseling program
E.1.a Accepts responsibility for the consequences of his/her actions
E.1.b Monitors personal well-being and effectiveness

Growth and Remediation Plan: The trainee will review the following information and document how these areas have been addressed by __________ ____.

The trainee, ________________, should:

1. (example) obtain, read, and know the school culture, district and campus policy relevant to her role as school counselor trainee. It is also incumbent upon the trainee to disclose who the guitarist was she invited to the ECDC without the permission of the district and campus administrator.
2. (example) set an appointment with the campus administrator to rectify and clear up any miscommunications or misunderstandings. The purpose of this meeting is to demonstrate your willingness to collaborate and work together for the benefit of your professional growth and development.
3. (example) (A.) seek input from the teachers and campus administrator to find out their perceived needs for the students in your building (needs assessment).

   (B.) have a structured guidance lesson that lacks chaos and elevated noise levels. Objectives will be written on the board, students will be engaged in the lesson, and the retention of material will be evident in the students at the end of the lesson.
   (C.) arrive to work on your scheduled days, on-time, at the beginning of the school day.

(D.) work to address the needs of the parents and attempt to positively influence their perceptions of your commitment to their child's personal issues or academic

______________________________ ______________________________

Supervisee Signature Date

______________________________ ______________________________

Supervisor Signature Date

14

Common-Sense Counseling

Franklin D. Sampson

ASCA NATIONAL MODEL THEME

Leadership

Advocacy and Social Justice

ASCA SCHOOL COUNSELOR PROFESSIONAL COMPETENCIES

I-B-2. Serves as a leader in the school and community to promote and support student success

I-B-2c. Identifies and demonstrates professional and personal qualities and skills of effective leaders

I-B-5. Acts as a system change agent to create an environment promoting and supporting students' success

II-B-4. Applies for ethical standards and principles of the school counseling profession and it hears to the legal aspect of the role of the school counselor

II-B-4g. Models ethical behavior

IV-B-1g. Uses personal reflection, consultation and supervision to promote professional growth and development

IV-B-2a. use of leadership skills to facilitate vision and positive change for the comprehensive school counseling program

ASCA PRINCIPLES

Principle 7 School counselors can help other adults enhance their work with students' academic/ educational, career and personal-social development removing barriers to individual students' success

Principle 18 There are organizational procedures school counselors can use to manage implementation of their programs for effectiveness, efficiency and relevancy to the school

ASCA ETHICAL STANDARDS FOR SCHOOL COUNSELORS (2016)

B.2.a. Develop and maintain professional relationships and systems of communication with faculty, staff and administrators to support students.

B.2.r. Work responsibly to remedy work environments that do not reflect the profession's ethics.

B.3.g. Monitor personal behaviors and recognize the high standard of care a professional in this critical position of trust must maintain on and off the job. School counselors are cognizant of and refrain from activity that may diminish their effectiveness within the school community.

B.3.l. Make clear distinctions between actions and statements (both verbal and written) made as a private individual and those made as a representative of the school counseling profession and of the school district.

E.a. School counselors consult with professional colleagues to discuss the potentially unethical behavior and to see if the professional colleague views the situation as an ethical violation. School counselors understand mandatory reporting in their respective district and states.

F.d. Consider the setting, parental rights and minors' rights

F.e. Apply the ethical principles of beneficence, autonomy, nonmaleficence, loyalty and justice

F.f. Determine potential courses of action and their consequences

CACREP STANDARDS 2016

Section 5-G, Entry-Level Specialty Areas, School Counseling

Contextual Dimensions

2.a. School counselor roles as leaders, advocates, and systems change agents in P-12 school

2.d. School counselor roles in school leadership and multidisciplinary teams

2.j. Qualities and styles of effective leadership in schools

Practice
3.1. Techniques to foster collaboration and teamwork within schools

What Is Common Sense?

One of the most underrated terms in counseling is *common sense*. For some school counselors, using common sense in their work has never crossed their mind. Just think, you can save a person's life using common sense, or can influence them to reach higher heights. Similar to this textbook, common sense is being level-headed—one's ability to use good sense and make sound decisions in practical situations. Common sense is understanding how the majority would choose to react or respond in various situations. A critique published on ethics, wisdom, and common sense was made available to the field of counseling in 2007 (Abeles, 2007). Prior to that, an ethics and counseling decision article was made available in 1970 (Daubner & Daubner, 1970). In the field of school counseling, one article was discovered about an uncommon common-sense solution (Williams, 1994). Essentially, there is a dearth in the literature related to common sense; it has been said that not everyone is blessed with the gift of common sense, but I beg to differ. It is a skill that is developed over time and consistently exercised.

Our brain is a very complex part of our body, and it holds many different answers to our questions relative to school counseling or private practice. Common sense has to do with the school counselor reaching deep within their minds seeking out solutions. Lives are too valuable for us to make mistakes. The reality is that common sense is used daily. The question becomes how do I utilize common sense in my daily practice? How do I make sure that I used common sense when speaking to a student? The answer is very simple: first, think; next, think more; and finally, think more deeply. Yes, it is that simple. We simply have to learn how to think critically at deeper levels.

Critical and Deep Thinking in School Counseling: Moving Beyond the Surface

Within the idea of common sense comes that of critical thinking. In the field of counseling, the counselor helps students recognize their potential success or failure throughout the process. Paul and Elder (2014) stated: "[that] much of our [thought], left to itself, is biased, distorted, partial, uniformed, or down-right prejudice . . . yet the quality of life . . . depends precisely on the quality of our thought" (p. 2). With access to multiple therapies and different areas of specialization, many have a *within reach option* to help students make the right decision. Along with these inherent resources in the school counselor, we sometimes find ourselves needing to go back to old faithful. Unfortunately, I am not referencing the World Wide Web, but I am referring to what has been used since scribes—the end of a piece of wood grounded in black ink on a scroll. You guessed it, many of the answers are found in a book. Specifically, "critical thinking is the art of analyzing and evaluating thinking with a view to improve it" (Paul & Elder, 2014, p. 2). When you think critically, you take what is on the surface, horizontal in nature, and generate questions and answers (internally and externally with student) that spirit deeper levels of understanding—a way to move vertically on all issues. Figure 14.1 helps explain this process.

The integrative and panoramic process of critical thinking depicts ways to move more deeply on a topic of concern. The process begins with the student issue and perspective, which is relevant, but isolated in nature, and usually unilateral or horizontal in context. As you go deeper, moving vertically, you allow the integrative process to take place. The left side of the arrow are the multiple perspectives (stakeholders, family, and research) that should be taken into consideration when working with a student. The right side of the arrow are the many variables that exist to help explain the issue juxtaposed in social, emotional, behavioral, and cultural aspects. Giving consideration to a student's environment and his or her mental health and health-related issues may help the process of reasoning and rationale for understanding what is going on with the student. School counselors, in their

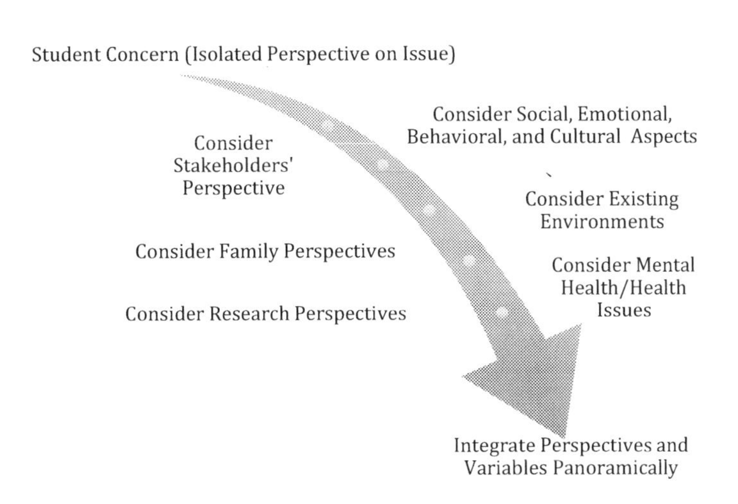

Figure 14.1 Integrative and Panoramic Process to Critical Thinking in School Counseling

effort to think critically, must take a panoramic (or wrap-around) approach to understanding situations and the gravity around these circumstances.

Common-Sense Practices

The three great essentials to achieve anything worth while are: Hard work, Stick-to-itiveness, and Common Sense.

Thomas A. Edison

Practicing common sense has been noted as an uncommon ability within individuals (Williams, 1994). The problem may be that our instincts fail to mix with wisdom, a conflict among our impulses and emotions (Berkun, 2012). In school counseling, the following common-sense practices will help bring a shared common-sense factor as we work with colleagues, students, and their families.

Mentorship: The Need to Groom the Future

Mentorship in an educational setting is often under-utilized. However, many school counselor predecessors have been able to achieve their goals because of the assistance of a mentor. More often than not, in the field of school counseling, we find ourselves guilty of not practicing what we preach. We talk to students consistently and encourage them to look for positive people in their lives, and we teach them to think critically. Honestly, some counselors will not allow a student to leave their offices without their helping to identify at least one person who has been a positive influence in their lives.

It was once interpretively said by a wise philosopher, Aristotle, that every great leader was once a great follower. In other words, as school counselors, we must learn how to follow greatness. We must know how to seek those who are where we want to be. Common sense tells us that if we want to be like someone else, then we must figure out what they do and how they do it. We must ask ourselves: can I become like someone who is great if I have not studied their patterns? Can I replicate their success if I have not become a student under their teaching?

It amazes me to see the huge differences among professions. When a young athlete wants to become a great professional athlete, common sense tells them to look at the television or YouTube to find a professional athlete in their arena that is doing great things and performing with excellence. When a young musician is aspiring to be the best that they can be and improve their performance capabilities, they seek out an accomplished musician. When was the last time a school counselor studied the actions and the advanced techniques of another—listening so close as to not miss any of the actions of this counselor?

I am not saying to watch videos of a successful school counselor; I am asking you to find someone closer than that—someone within your reach. Once you have found this individual, you may want to sit down with your new mentor. You may offer to buy them lunch every now and then. But optimally, you would want to Figure out what makes their clock tick. You want to watch their approach towards certain things or to ask them questions about multiple scenarios that they have had to encounter during their careers. Sometimes, you may desire to gather with colleagues because people usually gravitate towards people who are like-minded and on the same level that they are on. Common sense tells us, if I want to go higher, then I must start looking up. When you look up, you will find a mentor who has traveled a similar pathway. The only difference is that they have been where you are trying to go.

There is one saying that was shared with me by my father many years ago. He also shared it with many people who grew up with me. I have used it at different times in my life. It will help you with your students and give you a quick reminder to look up towards your mentor. There is one saying that reigns true, and that is, "KEEP YOUR CHIN UP!" When your chin is up, inadvertently so will your head be. When your head is up, you will be focused on the road ahead. When you focus on the road ahead, you will not be afraid to ask someone to help you "ease on down the road."

Practicing Professionalism: Perception Is Everything

The dignity of our profession must be upheld. We have fought for the respect of the counseling profession in the schools and private sectors, and we should set a certain *air of excellence* in the professional arena. Professionalism must be on the mind of every school counselor at all times. I would argue that the majority of individuals in our society actually judge a book by its cover. You may ask, is this fair or right? Well, maybe not, but it is a reality. We live in a world where others know your name, address, phone number, and likes and dislikes before they meet you face to face. I am not saying that I agree with this, but common sense tells us to observe, analyze, and to accept reality as we are constantly being evaluated. Many students these days will look at a picture on a website, search your social media page, look for any reviews or comments about you before they ever meet or see you. Many students in the school setting will talk to their friends, older siblings, or other teachers about you before they divulge any of their inner secrets to you.

Professional Appearance

We must face these facts that people tend to judge based on the way we present ourselves. We must look *the part* as we go about during the day. We should have a sense of pride about the way we dress, the way we carry ourselves, and the way we respond and comment to certain situations. "Dress to impress!" Many say that this is a thing of the past. They say that you should not have to dress up anymore because that is what the old people did. Common sense tells me that if I want to make a lasting impression on someone, then I must make sure that our first encounter is a good one. Furthermore, you never know what opportunities are in the making for you—so being prepared in your presentation of self is optimal.

I am reminded of a story that I once heard. A young lady named Hope was scheduled to meet a man for the first time for a blind date. She went to the store and tried on many different dresses. After a couple of hours, Hope finally found the perfect dress. She walked through the mall in search for new shoes that would match her newly purchased dress. She tried on a shoe here and another shoe there, and found the pair that went perfectly with her dress. She texted her stylist and made an appointment for that afternoon and went home to put on her best made-up face. Hope had everything that she needed. Then she remembered that she wanted to make a lasting impression on this young man for their blind date, so she sprayed her most expensive perfume. She waited for her 7:00 p.m. date to show up, but the clock said 7:15 p.m. More time passed by, and finally it was 7:50 p.m. She checked her phone, and she looked to see if she had any missed calls or new text messages. She did not.

At 8:15 p.m. her blind date knocks on the door, even though she had a doorbell. She asked, who is it? He responded, your blind date! She slightly opened the door, unsure if she should, only because she recognized his voice from the previous phone calls. He helped to fully open the door, and to her surprise, he had on tennis shoes, blue jean shorts, an unbuttoned shirt, and a baseball cap. His nails were not clean, and shall we say, he was not smelling the best. On one side you have someone who was ready for the encounter, and on the other side you have someone who seemed apathetic and unprepared. He did not communicate well, was late, looked disheveled, appeared unconcerned about what she may think—the list could go on. He simply was not dressed for the occasion. We should never want to be the counselor who is tying his neck-tie and adjusting his belt while putting on his coat as he walks into a session. We should never be the therapist who has one high heel shoe on and one flat shoe on transitioning from driving to a counseling session. We should not become the therapist who has mascara in her hand or is brushing her hair as she is walking into the office.

Words to Live By

What goes on in my house stays in my house. Well, not really when you are a professional of a community.

Living a Dichotomous Life

Living life authentically is one way to approach professionalism. Being one person at work and then another at home lacks authenticity and presents as disingenuous once others learn of the truth. But even more than that, as reflective practitioners, it should feel unsettling to you to live a misaligned and incongruent life. As a school counselor, your personhood matters. If you live your life accepting mistreatment of yourself or others, not practicing forgiveness, or failing to make yourself the best version of you possible, how are you best equipped to assist students in this way? Have you heard the saying repeatedly: what happens in Vegas stays in Vegas? Well, this is far from the truth, simply because we are humans and have the ability to communicate our observations and experiences. Therefore, common sense tells us that one is bound to report what happened on a trip to a state that is filled with the desert and skyscrapers suspended in the middle of it. If one really cannot conceal what happened on a trip, what makes school counselors think they can conceal their own lack of professionalism?

Professional Agreement

School counselors ought to know how important it is to talk to one another and gain as much information as possible from the experiences of others. It is a misnomer to think that one cannot talk to a fellow colleague with similar credentials and qualifications in regards to an issue that is transpiring in the midst of a counseling session. The reason why we know how to take aspirin when we have a severe headache is because, at some point, this option was shared or talked about. Word of mouth or the act of sharing experience can be one quick way to discover answers to our questions. By no means am I saying that we must talk about every situation that happens, but there are times when we scratch our heads attempting to Figure out what to do when the answer is simply in the mind of another school counselor. However, it is important to remember, through our use of common sense, not to reveal the name of the student or demographic information identifying the student you are discussing. It may be a diagnosis you have not dealt with before; it may be some mental disorder that you have not ever addressed previously; or it just may be a conglomeration of different small issues, and you really have no experience or insight to pull from. We must know when to talk and when to remain quiet.

Understand that confidentiality is central, but by the same token, we can exercise our choice to consult with someone else. Can the person guess who I'm talking about? Am I thinking before I speak so that my colleague is clueless and cannot guess who we are discussing? Am I protecting the student's identity, ensuring there was anonymity? When the FBI or other authority agencies are on the lookout for someone, they post many different descriptions about a person. They will mention the individual's race, gender, height, weight, and where they were last seen. Of course, school counselors will not be that obvious when discussing the matter with a fellow professional, but they must remember the importance of leaving certain details out of their descriptions with other professionals. We are to avoid breaching confidentiality when conversing with another professional, and through this process, it is best to attain agreement among yourself and those you are in consultation with, and should never feel afraid to consult or to communicate with others.

People with good intentions make promises. People with good character keep them. Follow through on promises made.

Your Word Is Your Bond

Promises made in our lives, and in our profession, can make us or break us if not kept. In the field of counseling, there are times when we should promise, and there are other times when we should not make such guarantees. If one decides that he or she will promise a student something, it is imperative that there is follow-through. It is not wise for a school counselor to continue to make unfulfilled promises. Doing so, in light of common sense, detracts from the authenticity of the school counselor. If counselors decide to extend a promise, they must make sure that they are physically, financially, and spiritually capable of upholding their end of the bargain. We must not harbor feelings of guilt by not fulfilling our verbal obligations. It is important to make sure that we maintain our integrity by truth-telling and carrying out what was promised to those we serve.

It is better to be an hour early than a minute too late.

District Contracted Time

It comes as no surprise that some school counselors are hyper-aware of their contracted time. Some believe that their commitment to the job begins only when they are supposed to be at work and ends when their contracted time is up. Common sense might reveal that the job we are to perform will require more of our time than is contracted. This is applicable in the field of counseling because some will wonder if we are in it for the money or if we are in it because we seriously want to help people. It is rare to see a doctor or dentist run back into their office when we show up for our appointment. Granted, you will have to wait on them, but ultimately in our profession, we do not have the luxury of having someone to assess the student before we work with them. Usually, we are the first one students encounter, which means that we should make ourselves available for the student prior to them arriving and be willing to stay late when necessary.

Synergizing Work-Life Balance

There has to be a time that school counselors just stop and take a breath before beginning a new day. You may begin to think about starting your day by simply meditating, praying, or just thinking about a few goals that you have set for the day. It could be sort of your pregame warm-up. Similar to stretching before an athletic event or your pep-talk before you work out, there must be a time to pause before going from one session to the next. When counselors book clients for a 50-minute session, it is because of the unwritten rule that you will leave available 10 minutes in-between to get ready for the next session, chart notes, or to take a break. In a school setting, activities often change every 15 to 30 minutes, so it is essential to learn how you best are able to transition from one task to another. Furthermore, eating healthy in a school setting is often negated. Considerate colleagues who love preparing treats, vending machines, office refrigerators stuffed with our favorite snacks, and cafeteria food are sometimes inhibitors to healthy eating. Because school counselors are often rushing to get something on their stomachs, we fail to allow time to eat properly.

There must be purpose and passion that co-exist in your work. Purpose and passion mixed allows for the day to be outlined properly. I do know that things happen throughout the day, and various needs and situations pop up suddenly. But when we come early, let us be committed to why we are coming early and have meaning (purpose) along with relentless desire (passion) to serve each day. Yes, time for yourself, time for meditation, and time for prayer is important. At the end of the day, it may be best to recap the events, set things for tomorrow, organize your desk, or utilize that time to check your inbox of the day's emails. Common sense here echoes *Have purpose*! *Have passion*! *Be productive*! *Promote healthy living*!

Educated professionals should act accordingly.

In the minds of many, being educated is one thing, and responding or acting educated is another. We know right from wrong, in most cases, so allowing our training and education to take precedence regardless of the variables presented is a necessity. Educators are reminded that professionalism is a priority and should be maintained in difficult situations.

Off-Record Conversations

Can we ever have a conversation off-the-record? Can we have a conversation that will never be brought up again? Can we trust someone when we say, "let's have an off-the-record conversation"? I do believe it can happen, but by the same token, you do not want to have that conversation with just anybody and everybody. There are things, as a school counselor, that are bothersome, and we have nowhere else to turn to besides someone available for that off-the-record talk. These plaguing issues may be related to students, teachers, or administrators. You may wonder if having this conversation is the right thing to do. You must really get to know someone—not just on the surface, but deep down within. I am not saying that if you have an off-the-record conversation that you will need to sign a contract, some type of oath, or agreement, but I am suggesting that if you do have a conversation off-the-record, common sense tells you to discern the trustworthiness of the person. Treading lightly in this area is suggested because all people you work with may not have your best interest at heart, and they can take what is shared out of context—making it something unintended or misconstrued in the delivery or to the receiver of this information.

Disposition, Attitude, or Behavior

The disposition, attitude, and behavior of a school counselor must be rooted in that which they want their students to exemplify. Similar to the apple not falling far from the tree, what we teach and model for our own children at home can be carbon-copied throughout their day. The last thing anyone would want on a team is for it to operate with dysfunction or a team that is a team by name only, and does not practice the general philosophy of what it means to be a team. Gossip, negativity, jealousy, and envy are four conduits tied to unprofessional behavior, and they can quickly destroy workplace relationships. We must strive as counselors in this profession to remember what type of behavior we want to see in those we help and model that behavior consistently.

Gossip can never find itself in or on a counseling team because the more gossip we spread, the more negativity we create. If we build one another up in our practice as counselors, we create a culture of positive support. We should be asking ourselves how we are treating others. During a self-evaluation, this should be a top priority. How are others on the team being treated? Are we building each other up, or do we harbor jealousy and envy for the talents others exhibit? When teams work together, there is the strong possibility of greater things happening in the counseling field. If we believe in our goals, we can make them happen. Common sense conveys that positive energy is particularly useful when working on strategic planning, creating and implementing the comprehensive school counseling program.

Low Morale and Keeping Company With Negativity

In a school setting, it is very easy to sometimes partner with individuals who are negative by nature. Every building principal's dream is to have high morale on a campus. But with human dynamics at its finest, it is often difficult to maintain morale with so many expectations, obligations, and requirements of stakeholders daily. Some school counselors may want to fit in with a faculty or staff member, even if it means keeping company with those who have a negative spirit. A negative spirit is defined as a person who does not see the good in anything happening on campus. This individual will constantly highlight what is wrong, and often spends excessive amounts of time focusing on that which feels counter-productive. The term *guilty by association* is so relevant in a school setting. If you spend time at work with people who are critical, biased, opinionated, inflexible, and even cantankerous, common sense reveals it likely they will have an impact on you and maybe even your performance. Remaining positive is essential for a school counselor, and self-care is the way to combat negativity. Additionally, school counselors are adept at listening, no matter what the complaint. Using active listening skills and providing empathy to those who complain open the door for potential collaboration.

Reporting Considerations

There are many considerations around reporting child abuse or neglect, including making a decision to report the safety and well-being of a student. Likewise, reporting in terms of providing updates to administrators and teachers who have concerns with the students they have referred to the counselor is an issue. Let us begin with the discussion of making a report to Child Protective Services. In my years of serving as a school counselor and lead counselor, the question always arises as to if a call should be made to Child Protective Services.

The decision to report should be based on the report made by the child, physical or emotional indications, or interviews with siblings or witnesses such as friends. Additionally, allowing the school nurse to visit with the child should also be a part of the process. Never should a school counselor forget or take for granted that a family under investigation for child abuse is a very serious matter, nor should your morals regarding corporal punishment be used as the litmus or measuring stick to making these reports. You should not want a family to endure being investigated if there is uncertainty around your report. For example, as a school counselor, your moral system may be that you do not believe in spanking children for discipline purposes. However, with this family, the belief is if you spare the rod, you spoil the child. From a common sense and multicultural perspective, it is critical to consider if this is a part of the family's culture. Certainly, a report to Child Protective Services should not be made solely based on the child being physically disciplined by the parent or guardian. However, all states have laws regarding what constitutes abuse, and all counselors must know and understand these laws. In some states, the person to whom the child first reveals the abuse is the one who files the report. This person is often a teacher; therefore, the counselor can be helpful in leading the teacher through the reporting process.

Another opportunity to report is when administrators and teachers are awaiting the outcome of your interventions and services with the students they have referred. Often, this is conversational and could be an instance of conveying too much information or oversharing. Specifically, when a school counselor provides updates to various stakeholders, parents included, it is best practice to garner the student's permission first, to have an action plan that is agreed upon, to share without details, and to make stakeholders feel comfortable that their concerns for the student have been addressed. It might be appropriate to allow the child to hear the conversation or to tell the student what information you plan to provide. According to ethical codes, counselors provide information when there is an educational *need to know*. Certainly, teachers can be advocates for students when they know that a home situation has deteriorated or when a child is experiencing mental illness.

Interaction With Other Professionals: The Formality of It

There are many opportunities to work with other professionals in a school building, such as a youth service specialist, Community Youth Services (CYS) worker, school psychologist, licensed professional counselor, school nurse, and assistant principal—just to mention a few. In the field of counseling, our common sense says to us that we must be willing to allow others to help, as well as to assist others when dealing with students and families. Many times, social workers who have a base or foundation in counseling generally just have a heart to help. There will be times where you will not be the lead professional when helping someone who has a mental, physical, or social need. However, by the same token, if you offer assistance to them and are willing to serve as a strong helper, the one who is in need of help will get exactly what they need. Social workers, CYS workers, or youth service specialists are—and should be—a great resource to all school counselors.

Now, the services that the local county office offers sometimes are available to those in the school setting or in a private setting. But many times, counselors are unaware of what is available. You should try to always establish, maintain, or re-establish a good relationship with social workers simply because they usually attend multiple sessions where they gain information relevant to the situation with which you have to deal. The county, city, state, and nation are becoming more and more aware of mental health issues; therefore, there has been legislative movement to assist and help those who suffer from all types of disorders or challenges as it pertains to the field of counseling. The counselor in the school setting is usually engulfed with multiple schedule changes, several classroom guidance lessons, and many testing requirements needing fulfillment to assist their students, so they might be less available to attend seminars or conferences. The next best thing is to use another mental health professional as a resource to bring materials back to you.

School nurses are also an important group of professionals to have a tight-knit relationship with. You might be saying to yourself that a school nurse is usually someone who just takes temperatures and checks the accuracy of vision. The truth is that the role of a school nurse entails more than we think. They are needed in multiple settings and capacities. It is good to have a school nurse who understands what you do, and by the same token, we understand their role. One reason a counselor may go into the school clinic is if a child has been a victim of child abuse. It is always good to have established that relationship prior to bringing in a student who is either emotionally distraught or has been physically abused. Non-verbal communication is important because students could feel uncomfortable with both a nurse and school counselor present. Like counselors, the nurses I have worked with were compassionate and had a medical perspective that helped bring understanding to a student's physical health.

Use of Research and Resources in School Counseling as a Tool

The process of counseling in the schools should be supplemented via use of research and various resources. School counselors should have access to online libraries where searching various topics encountered while working with students will be helpful in understanding what researchers suggest as appropriate interventions. This information can be evidence-based and best-practice recommended.

Complacent Counseling

School counselors must stay current with the research and resources in their profession. What's your new challenge? What's your new ambition? What is your new desire? What good things will you do today when you step into the office? These questions we must ask ourselves daily upon walking into the school counseling office. This is essential because it helps us to avoid complacency in the field of counseling. Many times, I have seen those counselors who go through a routine over and over again, and for some reason, they do not understand why their careers feel stale and void of passion. Common sense requires us to stay fresh and abreast of current practices of counseling. We have to make sure that we gather research and attend professional development sessions in order to make ourselves better practitioners. I believe that a counselor is and should be a life-long learner. I would like to share with those who have graduated from four-year institutions with a bachelor's degree that they now possess the foundation of being an educated person. Then, a master's degree in counseling lays the foundation for the profession in counseling.

Next begins the life-long learning that can be obtained through workshops, conferences, seminars, special trainings, and even the pursuit of a terminal degree. As I attend conferences and workshops, I notice that some counselors are engaged and actively taking notes. On the contrary, I see others who are falling asleep. As I reflect upon those experiences, I cannot help but think that they might exist as complacent counselors. Avoid this kind of apathy and complacency. It can start with you, and you can be the encourager on your team to help others see the benefits of being a life-long learner. Right now, I would like to deputize you as one who will serve as an advocate for the field of counseling. If you know a complacent counselor in your office, I challenge you to invite that person to the next conference with you. I challenge you to share a meaningful article and have an open discussion about it. I challenge you to speak with that counselor about why we are in the field of counseling.

Counseling or Consoling: Getting on the Right Side of the Fence

Some counselors believe they are counseling because the students leave feeling good or better. I am sorry to be the bearer of bad news, but there will be times when a student leaves your office not feeling great. Counseling does have to do with people feeling better, but it does not always make people happier, because sometimes counseling requires you to challenge your student. The best way to know if your student is better is to track their progress with hard data or evidence. Sometimes, a counselor must show tough love, even though it is not that popular in our profession. There will be times that you will have to be frank with a client or a student, but I believe that honesty is important when dealing with those in our field. Tough love and common sense reminds us that we still care about the student, but are we willing to say what it takes to make sure we are helping them? It is not always easy, but common sense reminds us of this necessity.

Feeling Sorry for Those With Disadvantages

You have to always remember that there will be some who will need extra assistance in our field. With limited resources available to meet their needs, we try as counselors to help them out as much as possible. Some will differ with me on this philosophy, but I strongly believe we must teach those who are at an economic disadvantage how to advocate for themselves, their children, and their families. Common sense reminds us we did not all start on the same playing field; therefore, allowing one's privilege to reign is something that needs immediate regulation.

It is normal for parents who are struggling to turn to the one whom they believe they can talk to, the school counselor. They are going to seek out someone who should have resources available to help them. We may not have the answer immediately, but I believe that a counselor should be resourceful enough to assist those in need. By that I mean, we can teach students and parents how to problem-solve, how to access resources, and how to identify the resources they already have.

It Is Not Always Appropriate: The Use of Judgment

School counselors can never think of a student as a friend. We must remember that our relationship with students is professional. Appropriate relationships in the field of education are of paramount importance for the benefit of both the students and the counselors. Those who do not have appropriate boundaries with their students almost always end up in trouble. Should you give your cell phone number out? My answer is absolutely not. I am under the strong conviction that if a student is in crisis, they need to call 911. No student should have your personal information that was given to them by you because it jeopardizes their perspective on who you really are. Common sense mandates that no student should be texting or calling a school counselor on his or her private line or cell phone. Many times, inappropriate relationships begin with a simple text message. I do not think that any of us have our medical doctor's cell phone number. I do not recall ever obtaining my dentist's cell phone number. I never had my attorney's cell phone number. So why would our profession be any different than others? Providing our students and their families with our private phone numbers implies that they need a lifeline to us at all times. This implication is inappropriate, is not true, and certainly is not healthy. We teach our clients to be advocates for themselves, not to depend on us for going about their daily lives.

Feeling Like You Are the Child's Parent

I believe if you lived in this world for a few years that you would have heard the phrases *deadbeat dad* and *latchkey children*. I mention these two phrases because if you study them both, the common fact is that one or more of the children's parents are not present consistently in their lives. Common sense calls for school counselors to show sensitivity toward those students who do not have parents or guardians who are available and present in their daily lives. Some absences in parents are unavoidable: death, illness, divorce, and incarceration—to name a few. While we may not be in a position to be surrogate parents to all of our students who need that kind of support, we do have an obligation to find the resources and support that they need. This may involve reaching out to the parents or finding other family members who can help or perhaps looking for community resources that are geared toward children with basic needs.

Taking Sides

Let's face it, we have been choosing sides since we were little children. Very young children have to select which side of the chalk line they would stand on. As we grow older, we must decide who we would have as a friend and who wouldn't be someone we would want to have as a close friend. Even when one grows into adulthood, we are asked to determine our politics, our religious preferences, and so forth. In counseling and dealing with sensitive subjects and delicate situations, we have to avoid taking sides over one parent or the other. It is normal for counselors to have personal preferences, opinions, and beliefs; however, our ethical responsibility is to leave those outside of the counseling office when we are working with families. Sometimes parents who are involved in contentious conflict will try to gain our position as one that favors their point of view. We are not in the business of deciding which parent is more fit. We are neutral unless there is a report of abuse. Promising allegiance to one parent over another will generally result in catastrophe for the counselor. While remaining neutral may be difficult because you like one parent more than another, common sense reminds us of our ethical responsibility to do so. Even when we are called to testify in court regarding custody issues, we do not hold ourselves up as forensic experts. We simply make it clear that we do not recommend one parent over the other.

Final Thoughts

My intent in these pages was to outline some of the day-to-day issues that confront counselors that may not be discussed in the textbooks or even in classrooms. Everyday school counselors deal with difficult people and tough situations. I am reminding you that you are prepared to deal with these issues. You have the language, the knowledge, and the skills to deal with these situations, and you have the common sense. As I stated at the beginning of this chapter, many conflicts or conundrums simply require that we think, think again, and then think some more. Keep thinking, counselors!

Activities

1. Create a checklist of the areas addressed in this chapter that you have historically struggled with. After doing so, maintain a journal that is reflective and highlights the ways in which you are mediating, rectifying, changing, or releasing certain habits or beliefs that are counterproductive to working with your students, colleagues, and parents.
2. Many school counselors have aspirational goals they set for themselves. Utilizing the information in this chapter, set aspirational goals, and timelines in accomplishing them, that would help to remain objective as a school counselor practitioner.
3. If you are a school counselor in a department of other counselors, read this chapter as a form of a book study, and have open dialogue in a safe environment with your colleagues related to the topics herein. Establish, set, and evaluate these departmental goals in an effort to resist engaging in some of these possible dysfunctional patterns among team members.

Resources

The Foundation for Critical Thinking:
www.criticalthinking.org

References

Abeles, N. (2007). Ethics, wisdom, and common sense. [Review of the book *Ethics in psychotherapy and counseling: A practical guide*, by K. S. Pope & M. J. T. Vasquez]. *PsycCRITIQUES*, *52*(38). doi:10.1037/a0008883.

Berkun, S. (2012, 2014). *Why common sense is not a common practice*. Retrieved from http://scottberkun.com/2012/why-common-sense-is-not-common-practice/

Daubner, E. V., & Daubner, E. S. (1970). Ethic and counseling decision. *Personnel & Guidance Journal*, *48*(6), 433–442.

Paul, R., & Elder, L. (2014). *Miniature guide to critical thinking- concepts and tools*. Tomales, CA: Foundation for Critical Thinking.

Williams, G. R. (1994). An uncommon common sense solution: Family systems counseling in the schools. *The Family Journal: Counseling and Therapy for Couples and Families*, *2*, 360–367. doi:10.1177/1066480794024012

Index

Note: Page numbers in **bold** indicate tables; *italics* indicate figures.

Printed in the United States
by Baker & Taylor Publisher Services